Teach Yourself
VISUAL J++™
in 21 days

Patrick Winters
David Olhasso
Laura Lemay
Charles Perkins

201 West 103rd Street
Indianapolis, Indiana 46290

International Standard Book Number: 1-57521-158-0

Library of Congress Catalog Card Number: 96-68939

99 98 97 96   4 3 2 1

Interpretation of the printing code: the rightmost double-digit number is the year of the book's printing; the rightmost single-digit, the number of the book's printing. For example, a printing code of 96-1 shows that the first printing of the book occurred in 1996.

Composed in AGaramond and MCPdigital by Macmillan Computer Publishing

Printed in the United States of America

Trademarks

Visual J++ is a trademark of Microsoft Corporation.

All terms mentioned in this book that are known to be trademarks or service marks have been appropriately capitalized. Sams.net Publishing cannot attest to the accuracy of this information. Use of a term in this book should not be regarded as affecting the validity of any trademark or service mark.

President, Sams Publishing   Richard K. Swadley
Publishing Team Leader   Dean Miller
Managing Editor   Cindy Morrow
Director of Marketing   John Pierce
Assistant Marketing Managers   Kristina Perry
Rachel Wolfe

Acquisitions Editor
Kim Spilker

Development Editor
Dean Miller

Software Development Specialist
Cari Skaggs
Patty Brooks

Production Editor
Brice P. Gosnell

Copy Editors
Heather Butler
Kris Simmons
Mary Inderstrodt
Brice P. Gosnell

Indexers
Erika Millen
Christine Nelsen
Benjamin Slen

Technical Reviewer
Greg Perry

Editorial Coordinator
Katie Wise

Technical Edit Coordinator
Lynette Quinn

Editorial Assistants
Carol Ackerman
Andi Richter
Rhonda Tinch-Mize

Cover Designer
Tim Amrhein

Book Designer
Gary Adair

Copy Writer
Peter Fuller

Production Team Supervisor
Brad Chinn

Production
Carol Bowers
Georgiana Briggs
Chris Livengood
Timothy Osborn
Andrew Stone

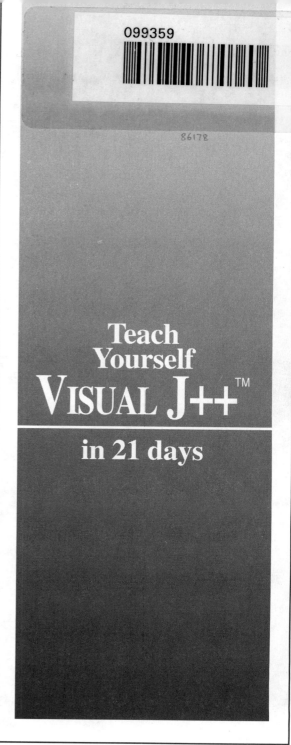

Teach
Yourself
VISUAL J++™

in 21 days

Overview

Contents

Acknowledgments

From Laura Lemay:

To Sun's Java Team, for all their hard work on Java the language and on the browser, and particularly to Jim Graham, who demonstrated Java and HotJava to me on very short notice in May and planted the idea for this book.

From David Olhasso:

To my wife, Alizabeth, who is not only my inspiration for all that I do, but who also accepts and supports the long hours I spend on my projects.

From Charles L. Perkins:

To Patrick Naughton, who first showed me the power and the promise of OAK (Java) in early 1993.

From Patrick J Winters:

I know acknowledgments should be kept short, but because this is my first book, I have to thank those who have helped make this work possible. The thanks I give is not only sincere, but also shows, in a small way, who I am.

To my wife, Colleen Watson, who not only helped me when I couldn't find the proper words, but stayed awake with me on many nights to eke out the last bit of what she knew I had in me.

To my sons Dustin and Zachary, who endured the weekends of seeing my back and hearing the clickety-clack of my keyboard instead of going to movies, playing video games, or simply spending time together.

To my fellow Merrill co-workers (Frank "The Big Cheese," David, Charles, and Jennifer), who picked up the slack while I was dragging myself about the office on two hours of sleep.

To Jane Graver Sandlar, for taking a chance and giving me my first technical writing assignment.

To Big Brothers/Big Sisters of America, who very early in my career allowed a boy to do a man's job.

To Miss Whiteside, my sixth grade Language Arts teacher, who managed to show me so much about literature and writing that, 20 some odd years later, the spark alit in me and I realized I wanted to be a writer.

And finally, to all the people at Sams and Sams.net, who persevered despite all the obstacles I placed in their path.

About the Authors

Laura Lemay is a technical writer and a nerd. After spending six years writing software documentation for various computer companies in Silicon Valley, she decided writing books would be much more fun (but has still not yet made up her mind). In her spare time she collects computers, e-mail addresses, interesting hair colors, and nonrunning motorcycles. She is also the perpetrator of *Teach Yourself Web Publishing with HTML in 14 Days*.

You can reach her by e-mail at `lemay@lne.com`, or visit her home page at `http://www.lne.com/lemay/`.

David Olhasso's first experience in the PC industry was with the original IBM PC back in 1982. Back then he was writing property management and accounting software using dBase. Since then he has spent his time absorbing and working with all of the latest and greatest technologies (especially since there seems to be only a six month life cycle these days) as well as collecting quite a few more computers.

David has worked with a wide variety of technologies including wireless packet protocols, world-wide PC networks, custom distributed installation systems, and enterprise-wide intranet/Internet systems. David works as an independent consultant specializing in enterprise Windows NT solutions.

Charles L. Perkins is the founder of Virtual Rendezvous, a company building a Java-based service that will foster socially focused, computer-mediated, real-time filtered interactions between people's personas in the virtual environments of the near future. In previous lives, he has evangelized NeXTSTEP, Smalltalk, and UNIX, and has degrees in both physics and computer science. Before attempting this book, he was an amateur columnist and author. He's done research in speech recognition, neural nets, gestural user interfaces, computer graphics, and language theory, but had the most fun working at Thinking Machines and Xerox PARC's Smalltalk group. In his spare time, he reads textbooks for fun.

You can reach him via e-mail at `virtual@rendezvous.com`, or visit his Java page at `http://rendevous.com/java`.

Patrick J Winters' entry into the realm of technical writing took a circuitous route. While working in the restaurant business, his chosen and educated profession, his boss decided to cut costs by automating. Patrick tackled the job of investigating the options, and upon looking at some very expensive inventory control programs that ran on Apple][computers, decided that MBASIC was an easy way to make a living...yeah, right!

After receiving his first computers in 1979 (like rabbits they quickly multiplied), Patrick started programming for some small, but immensely rewarding, companies. But after many sleepless nights and endless rewrites, he realized he needed to go back to school. As his college days drew to a close, he gathered with his fellow students at the local watering hole to discuss where they'd be working. After a myriad of corporate names were tossed out, Patrick said, "I want to be a consultant," to which they all laughed and simultaneously agreed that nobody becomes a consultant first.

Not being one to heed the advice of those with so little experience, for the next five years Patrick *made* his living as a consultant, selling himself and his dBASE programs to whomever wanted them. But along came kids, and paid benefits and steady hours started looking good. Big Brothers/Big Sisters of America provided Patrick with one of the toughest, yet rewarding, educational, and enjoyable work experiences an MIS Director could hope for.

But, all good things had to come to an end; he felt the lure of the consulting road again, but this time as a writer—a technical writer and online help specialist. After many great assignments at some terrific Fortune 1000 corporations, Merrill Lynch turned him once again into a full time employee. From there, who knows, but New Mexico is beckoning.

Tell Us What You Think!

As a reader, you are the most important critic and commentator of our books. We value your opinion and want to know what we're doing right, what we could do better, what areas you'd like to see us publish in, and any other words of wisdom you're willing to pass our way. You can help us make strong books that meet your needs and give you the computer guidance you require.

Do you have access to CompuServe or the World Wide Web? Then check out our CompuServe forum by typing GO SAMS at any prompt. If you prefer the World Wide Web, check out our site at `http://www.mcp.com`.

Note: If you have a technical question about this book, call the technical support line at (800) 571-5840, ext. 3668.

As the team leader of the group that created this book, I welcome your comments. You can fax, e-mail, or write me directly to let me know what you did or didn't like about this book— as well as what we can do to make our books stronger. Here's the information:

FAX: 317/581-4669

E-mail: `opsys_mgr@sams.mcp.com`

Mail: Dean Miller
            Sams.net Publishing
            201 W. 103rd Street
            Indianapolis, IN 46290

Introduction

How This Book Is Structured

This book is intended to be read and absorbed over the course of three weeks. During each week, you'll read seven chapters that present concepts related to Visual J++.

 NOTE

A Note box presents interesting pieces of information related to the surrounding discussion.

 TECHNICAL NOTE

A Technical Note presents specific technical information related to the surrounding discussion.

 TIP

A Tip box offers advice or teaches an easier way to do something.

A Warning box advises you about potential problems and helps steer you clear of disaster.

WARNING

 NEW TERM *New Terms* are introduced in New Term boxes, with the term in italics.

 TYPE A Type icon identifies some new HTML code that you can type in yourself.

 OUTPUT An Output icon highlights what the same HTML code looks like when viewed in either Netscape or Mosaic.

 ANALYSIS An Analysis icon alerts you to the author's line-by-line analysis.

Day 1

An Introduction to Java Programming

Welcome to *Teach Yourself Visual J++ in 21 Days*! For the next three weeks you'll learn all about the Java language, Java applets, and Java applications. Not only will you learn these important and transportable fundamentals, but also how to use Microsoft's Visual J++ development tool to quickly and efficiently create reusable Java programs using the standard Java language. You'll also get a taste of how to extend your Java programs using the Microsoft Component Object Model (COM) platform including ActiveX.

As you might know, all of the preceding browsers listed are World Wide Web browsers used to view Web pages, follow links, and submit forms. They are also capable of downloading and playing Java applets on the user's system.

Today you'll learn about the following:

- [ ] What exactly Java and Visual J++ are
- [ ] Why you should learn Java—its various features and advantages over other programming languages
- [ ] Getting started programming in Java and touring Microsoft Developer Studio for Visual J++

What Is Java?

Java is an object-oriented programming language developed by Sun Microsystems, a company best known for its high-end UNIX workstations. Modeled after C++, the Java language was designed to be small, simple, and portable across platforms and operating systems, both at the source and at the binary level (more about this throughout the book).

What makes Java different from most other programming languages is that, in addition to being a full featured language capable of creating stand-alone applications, it can create Java applets. Java applets have the same basic functions as Java applications, but their *raison d'être* is the ability to run inside a Java-capable browser. Applets appear in a Web page much in the same way as images do, but unlike images, applets are dynamic and interactive. Applets can be used to create animation, figures, or areas that can respond to input from the user, games, or other interactive effects on the same Web pages among the text and graphics. As a Java developer you need only create the applet once; the Java-capable browsers perform the interpretation specific to their own platform.

Although HotJava (Sun's browser) was the first World Wide Web browser to be able to play Java applets, Java support is available in other browsers. Microsoft Internet Explorer 3.0 and Netscape version 2.0x and greater provide support for Java applets. Other browser developers have also announced support for Java in forthcoming products.

To create an applet, you write it in the Java language, compile it using a Java compiler, and refer to that applet in your HTML Web pages. You put the resulting HTML and Java files on a Web site much in the same way that you make ordinary HTML and image files available. Then, when someone using a Java-capable browser views your page with the embedded applet, that browser downloads the applet to the local system and executes it. The user can then view and interact with your applet in all its glory (users using non-Java–enabled browsers might see text, a static graphic, or nothing). You'll learn more about how applets, browsers, and the World Wide Web work together further on in this book.

The important thing to understand about Java is that you can do so much more with it besides create applets. Java was written as a full-fledged programming language in which you can accomplish the same sorts of tasks and solve the same sorts of problems that you can in other programming languages, such as C or C++. To give you an idea of the power of Java, HotJava itself, including all the networking, display, and user interface elements, was written in Java.

What Is Visual J++

NOTE

> Throughout the remainder of this book, Visual J++ will be referred to as VJ++.

VJ++ is Microsoft's Integrated Development Environment (IDE) for developing, compiling, testing, and debugging your Java applets and applications. It's based upon Microsoft Developer Studio (See Figure 1.1.) If you've used Visual C++ or Visual Test, you'll be quite familiar with the workings of the VJ++ IDE. For those of you who haven't used Microsoft Developer Studio, VJ++ delivers what you would expect from a Java development tool, and, additionally, has robust features for ease-of-use, re-use of common libraries, and maintenance of your Java code. VJ++ also has the built-in capability to combine Microsoft's new technology, Component Object Model (COM), with your Java applets and applications. You'll learn all about the Microsoft Developer Studio starting tomorrow.

Figure 1.1.

Microsoft Developer Studio.

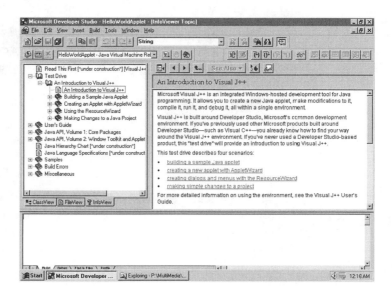

Embedding a Java Applet on an HTML Page

Up to this point, we've discussed Java, Java applets, Java applications, development tools, and Web browsers. To put it all in a basic context, Listing 1.1 is a simple example demonstrating how your Java applets are viewed by the world. The first step-by-step hands-on exercise you'll do in this book will be to re-create this example.

To include an applet in a Web page, you refer to that applet in the HTML code for that Web page. Here is a very simple HTML file (See Listing 1.1.) Notice the line beginning with `<APPLET CODE=`. This line in the HTML file causes a Java-capable Web browser to load and play the applet contained in the quotes (`"HelloWorldApplet.class"`). Notice also the `.class` file extension, which all compiled Java applets have.

TYPE   **Listing 1.1. The HTML with the applet in it.**

```
1: <HTML>
2: <HEAD>
3: <TITLE>Hello to Everyone!</TITLE>
4: </HEAD><BODY>
5: <P>My Java applet says: </P>
6: <APPLET CODE="HelloWorldApplet.class" WIDTH=150 HEIGHT=25><APPLET>
7: </BODY>
8: </HTML>
```

You refer to an applet in your HTML files with the <APPLET> tag. You'll learn more about the <APPLET> tag later on, but here are three things to note:

☐ As mentioned before, only Java-enabled Web browsers can display applets. Other browsers will display different results instead of the applet; some will display nothing at all.

☐ Using the CODE attribute indicates to a Java-enabled Web browser the name of the class that contains your applet.

☐ Using the WIDTH and HEIGHT attributes tells the browser the size of the applet. The browser uses these values to know how big a chunk of space to leave for the applet on the page. Here, a box 150 pixels wide and 25 pixels high is created.

Once an applet has been included as a reference in an HTML page, all you need is a Java-enabled Web browser to view it. If you don't have a proper browser, the appletviewer application, which is part of the Java Development Kit, will work. Although the appletviewer is not a Web browser and won't enable you to see the entire Web page, it's an acceptable alternative to test how an applet will look and behave.

NOTE

If you're using HotJava to view your applets, make sure it's not the alpha version. Applets developed with VJ++ cannot be viewed with the alpha version.

Because you'll probably be using Microsoft Internet Explorer 3.0 to view an applet file (see Figure 1.2), you can use File | Open and type in the name of the HTML file, or use Browse to navigate to the HTML file containing the applet. Also, because you're viewing a local copy of the applet file, you don't need to connect to a Web site.

Figure 1.2.

Microsoft Internet Explorer 3.0.

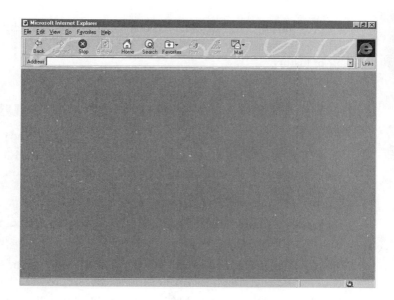

Depending upon your point of view, creating applets that are available to everyone who has a Java-capable browser might be the most important thing that Java can do. Or, the fact that Java is a full-featured, object-oriented development language, capable of producing the same kind of applications as C++ could be the reason you want to learn Java development.

Understanding Applets and Applications

Java programs fall into two main groups: applets and applications.

Applets, as you know, are Java programs that are downloaded over the World Wide Web and executed by a Web browser on the user's machine. This makes applets dependent upon a Java-capable browser. Applets do not have the necessary code to run independently of a browser. Applets are therefore smaller than applications because each browser, not applet, contains the Java virtual machine to do all the work to run the applet.

Java applications are more general use programs written in the Java language. Java applications don't require a browser to run, and in fact, Java can be used to create the same applications that you would normally use another programming language to create. As mentioned before, Sun's HotJava browser is a Java application. It, as well as other Java applications, have all the necessary code to run independently of a browser; they need only the Java virtual machine to run.

Other than the preceding basic browser or non-browser distinction, there is really very little difference between an applet and an application. A single Java program can be an applet, an application, or both, depending upon how you write that program and the capabilities that the program uses. Throughout this book you'll be creating both applets and applications. But wait, before we go on about the exciting development projects you'll be involved in, a little bit of history.

Java's Past, Present, and Future

The Java language was developed at Sun Microsystems in 1991 as part of a research project to develop software for consumer electronics devices—television sets, VCRs, toasters, and the other sorts of machines you can buy at any department store. Java's goal at that time was to be small, fast, efficient, and easily portable to a wide range of hardware devices. It is that same goal that made Java a general purpose programming language for developing programs that are easily usable and portable across different platforms, as well as an ideal language for distributing executable programs via the World Wide Web.

The Java language was used in several projects within Sun, but did not get very much commercial attention until it was paired with HotJava. HotJava was written in 1994 in a matter of months, both as a vehicle for downloading and running applets and also as an example of the sort of complex application that can be written in Java.

Shortly thereafter, Sun released to the public the Java Developer's Kit (JDK). Version 1.0 of the JDK includes tools for developing Java applets and applications on Sun systems running Solaris 2.3 or greater and for Windows NT, Windows 95, and the Macintosh. However, the JDK is a command line based Java development environment. And, as the word kit implies, you have to put the separate tools together yourself—making it not the easiest tool to use for development efforts.

NOTE   All the examples and code in this book are written to support the Java 1.0 language specification released with the JDK.

Today, Java has taken the world by storm. There are a flood of tutorial and reference books on the market. The latest Netscape and Microsoft browsers are Java-enabled. New Java-specific magazines and conferences abound. Each time you revisit a Web page, more things dance, jump, sing, and want to interact with you. Web pages that are not Java-enabled are sliding off the Hot List. In short, if you ask a group of people "What's Java," very few will say it's coffee, and even fewer still will say, "It's a densely populated Indonesian island republic whose chief agricultural crop is actually rice and not coffee."

What's in store for Java's future? Sun is still committed to Java. They are preparing a new release of the JDK, and they've also released Java Workshop, a Java development tool using a GUI environment to facilitate the creation of Java applets. Other major companies like

Microsoft, IBM, Novell, Netscape, Borland, and Symantec have licensed the Java technology from Sun. This indicates that these industry leaders have confidence in the viability of Java as a serious development language. From some of these companies, end-user tools incorporating Java-enabled technology are available, for example, the Microsoft Internet Explorer and Netscape browsers. Development tools such as Microsoft's VJ++, and Symantec's Café have been released. Borland has been working on their Java-based visual development tool, Latte, which is scheduled for release later this year. Java platform extensions, such as COM from Microsoft as well as application development tool extensions for Microsoft's VC++ and Borland's C++ 5.0, are also available.

As of this writing, both Microsoft and Netscape are developing just-in-time compilers for Java applets and incorporating support for the compilers into their browser products. These compilers will decrease the amount of time it requires for an applet to run in a Web browser. The browser and compiler work in conjunction to download, compile, and display the applet. Microsoft's plans for Java go even further. By the end of the year, Java support will be incorporated at the operating system level in Windows 95 and support capabilities will be extended in Windows NT.

In addition to this three-prong acceptance—end-user tools, development tools, and platform extensions—major corporations are coming up with other ways to promote Java. Recently, a venture capital firm and ten leading high-technology corporations put together a 100 million dollar venture fund to support small companies in the development of new applications for the Java programming language. The Java Fund, managed by the venture firm of Kleiner Perkins Caufield & Byers, includes as its investors, Sun Microsystems Inc., IBM, and Netscape Communications Corp. Many of these corporations believe that Java's real value will come in the form of more sophisticated applications that will help companies do business over the Internet. That was the impetus behind the development of the Java Fund.

So you see, the interest is truly there. With all of this support and development activity, Java is sure to have a bright future.

Why Learn Java?

Java has a lot of things going for it. Not only is it a major topic of discussion, but it also has the following:

- ☐ Has significant support from a major vendor
- ☐ Is based upon a common development platform
- ☐ Is portable across operating platforms
- ☐ Is easy to integrate applets into the Web and a corporate intranet
- ☐ Replaces learning the intricacies of multiple tools like HTML, CGI, and C++

Of all of these benefits, arguably the most important is that Java is used to create Java applets. Because applets run inside a Web browser, applets have superior independence to many other executable programs or scripting languages. Applets, by their inherent nature of platform-independent, object-oriented technology and Web browser execution and presentation, will extend the reach of corporate information storage, retrieval, and presentation in ways that are limited only by your imagination. The following section describes some of these advantages.

Java Is Platform-Independent

Platform independence is one of the most significant advantages that Java has over other programming languages. Unlike some other platform-independent languages, such as ANSI C, Java is platform-independent at both the source and the binary level.

NEW TERM *Platform independence* is a program's capability of moving from one computer system to another.

At the source level, Java's primitive data types have consistent sizes across all development platforms. Java's foundation class libraries make it easy to write code that can be moved from platform to platform without the need to rewrite it to work with that platform.

Platform independence doesn't stop at the source level, however. Java binary files are also platform-independent and can run on multiple platforms without the need to recompile the source. How does this work? Java binary files are actually in a form called bytecodes.

NEW TERM *Bytecodes* are a set of instructions that look a lot like machine code, but are not specific to any one processor.

Normally, when you compile a program written in C++, or most other programming languages, the compiler translates your program into machine codes or processor instructions. Those instructions are specific to the processor your computer is running; so, for example, if you compile your code to run on a 32-bit, Intel-based 80x86 system, the resulting program will run only on other 80x86 systems. If you want to use the same program on another system, you have to go back to your original source, get a compiler for that system, and recompile your code. This additional compile step is required even though the source code might require little or no changes to run on a different system. This is because the executable program created by the compiler has specific instructions for the computer system the compiler was designed for. Figure 1.3 shows the result of this system: multiple executable programs for multiple systems.

Things are different when you write code in Java. The Java development environment has two parts: a Java compiler and a Java interpreter. The Java compiler takes your Java program and, instead of generating machine codes from your source files, it generates bytecodes.

Figure 1.3.

Multiple executable programs for multiple systems.

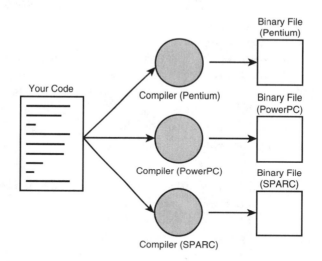

To run a Java program, you run a program called a bytecode interpreter, which in turn executes your Java program. (See Figure 1.4.) You can either run the interpreter by itself, or—for applets—a bytecode interpreter (called the Java virtual machine), built into Java-capable browsers, can run the applet for you.

Figure 1.4.

Java programs.

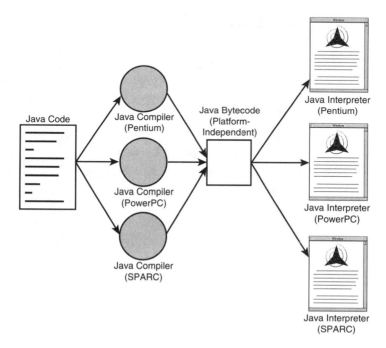

Why go through all the trouble of adding this extra layer of the bytecode interpreter? Having your Java programs in bytecode form means that instead of being specific to any one system, your programs can be run on any platform and any operating or window system, as long as the Java interpreter is available. This capability of a single binary file to be executable across platforms is crucial to what enables applets to work, because the World Wide Web itself is also platform-independent. Just as HTML files can be read on any platform, so applets can be executed on any platform that is a Java-capable browser. Ponder this power for a moment…amazing isn't it? Okay, read on.

The disadvantage of using bytecodes is in execution speed. Because system-specific programs run directly on the hardware for which they are compiled, they run significantly faster than Java bytecodes, which must be processed by the interpreter. For many Java programs, the speed might not be an issue. If you write programs that require more execution speed than the Java interpreter can provide, you have several solutions available to you, including being able to link native code into your Java program or using tools to convert your Java bytecodes into native code, which both are beyond the scope of this book. Note that by using any of these solutions, you lose the portability that Java bytecodes provide. Also, remember the future: With the deployment of just-in-time compilers, the speed issues might become less significant.

Java Is Object-Oriented

To some, object-oriented programming (OOP) technique is merely a way of organizing programs that can be accomplished using any language. Working with a real object-oriented language and programming environment, however, enables you to take full advantage of object-oriented methodology and its capabilities for creating flexible, modular programs and reusing code.

Many of Java's object-oriented concepts are inherited from C++, the language on which it is based, but it borrows many concepts from other object-oriented languages as well. Like most object-oriented programming languages, Java includes a set of class libraries that provide basic data types, system input and output capabilities, and other utility functions. These basic classes are part of the Java Developer's Kit, which also has classes to support accessing network data, common Internet protocols, and user interface toolkit functions. Because the JDK class libraries are written in Java, they are as portable across platforms as all Java applications.

You'll learn more about object-oriented programming and Java on Day 3, "Object-Oriented Programming and Java."

Java Is Easy to Learn

In addition to its portability and object orientation, one of Java's initial design goals was to be small and simple, and therefore, easy to write, compile, and debug. Keeping the language small also makes it more robust because there are fewer chances for programmers to make difficult-to-find mistakes. Despite its size and simple design, however, Java still has a great deal of power and flexibility.

Java is modeled after C and C++, and much of the syntax and object-oriented structure is borrowed from the latter. If you are familiar with C++, learning Java will be particularly easy for you, because you have most of the foundation already.

Although Java looks similar to C and C++, most of the more complex parts of those languages have been excluded from Java, making the language simpler without sacrificing much of its power. There are no pointers in Java, nor is there pointer arithmetic. Strings and arrays are real objects in Java. Memory management is automatic. To an experienced programmer, these omissions might be difficult to get used to, but to beginners or programmers who have worked in other languages, they make the Java language far easier to learn.

Java Is Easier to Learn Using Visual J++

If you're used to using IDEs, using the Java Development Kit and you're own programming editor to create Java applets and applications might seem quite antiquated. Even with the JDK's very simple beginnings, Java still gained amazing popularity. So popular and so similar to Visual C++, in fact, that Microsoft created VJ++ as the IDE for Java program development. If you're already familiar with Microsoft Developer Studio, the development platform VJ++ is based upon, using the VJ++ IDE will be quite simple for you. Even if you're not familiar with Microsoft Developer Studio, it will still be easy to develop Java applications using VJ++. Although this book will teach you Java, it will concentrate more on creating Java applets and applications using VJ++. So, you'll get the benefit of knowing both the language and, specifically, the tool.

The Visual J++ IDE

What is an IDE? An IDE is a self-contained application development environment that contains all the tools you need to write, compile, test, and debug your application. VJ++ also includes InfoView (an expanded online help system, including links to code examples and classes), object viewers, access to source control packages, and wizards—helper applications that walk you through creating certain objects.

A Picture Tour of Visual J++

Microsoft Developer Studio for VJ++ is a very powerful tool for developing Java programs. It maintains consistency across Microsoft's other development platforms (like VC++), making it easy to learn and use. It is also a full-featured IDE with many extras that the Microsoft tool developers added based on input from the scores of VC++ developers. Figure 1.5 depicts a common work area and some of the key components in VJ++. Notice how the work area is divided into three sections. The pane on the left is the Project Workspace. It is an index view of the currently selected tab from the bottom of the workspace (currently selected is InfoView). The pane on the right shows the detail pertaining to the selected index item from the left (an Introduction to Visual J++). The bottom pane is the Output window. It has four tabs: Build, Debug, Find Files, and Profiles. As its name implies, output is placed here by VJ++.

Figure 1.5.

Common work area.

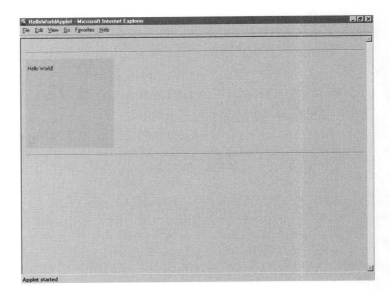

Even if you've never used a Microsoft Developer Studio tool before, by the end of this book you'll be quite a wizard of the desktop, as well as a top-flight Java developer.

Brewing Java in Visual J++

NOTE Pardon the poetic license of the title. When VJ++ was in development, its code name was Jakarta. The title (Brewing Java in Jakarta) then steeped of alliterative value and island fantasies. We kept it as a fanciful reminder of chicory coffee and sunny beaches.

VJ++ adheres to the tenants of the original JDK—none of the original class libraries have been changed. However, VJ++ goes a lot further. Microsoft Developer Studio itself makes developing and deploying your Java programs easier. The development environment also includes tools to inspect classes and OLE objects. Microsoft has also added wizards to make creating baseline applets and applications quite easy. The COM extensions and Microsoft Java classes will add OLE automation, ActiveX, and Java ODBC to your applications. VJ++ will allow you to easily create industry standard portable Java programs, as well as add the new Microsoft extensions.

Getting the Software

In order to write VJ++ programs, you will, of course, need Microsoft Visual J++. In order to run VJ++, your development system must be Windows NT 4.0 or Windows 95.

☐ At the time this book is being written, the beta copy is available from Microsoft's Web site at `http://207.68.137.34/visualj/`.

☐ The CD-ROM that comes with this book also contains a full copy of the VJ++ beta (although it might not be the most recent copy). The CD-ROM also contains the JDK 1.0 release. See the CD information for installation instructions.

☐ The latest JDK can be downloaded from Sun's Java FTP site at `ftp://java.sun.com/pub/` or from a mirror site (`ftp://www.blackdown.org/pub/Java/pub/` is one).

Summary

Today, you got a basic introduction to the goals and features of the Java language, and to Microsoft Visual J++. Java is a programming language, similar to C or C++, in which you can develop a wide range of programs. The most common use of Java at the moment is in creating applets for Java-capable Web browsers such as Microsoft Internet Explorer 3.0 and Netscape 2.0x or greater. Applets are Java programs that are downloaded and run as part of a Web page. Applets can create animation, games, interactive programs, and other multimedia effects on Web pages.

Java's strengths lie in its portability—both at the source and at the binary level—in its object-oriented design, and in its simplicity. Each of these features help make applets possible, but they also make Java an excellent language for writing more general-purpose programs that do not require Java-capable browsers to run. These general-purpose Java programs are called applications. HotJava itself is a Java application.

You viewed a sample applet and learned the differences and benefits of applets and applications. You also had an initial view of the Microsoft Developer Studio for VJ++. From here, you now have the foundation necessary to proceed with the creation of applications and applets.

Q&A

Q What Web browser should I use to view my Java applets?

A VJ++ includes the Microsoft Internet Explorer 3.0 browser. It is part of Microsoft Developer Studio for VJ++ and is the tool used to test your applets in a sample Web page.

Q I know a lot about HTML, but not much about computer programming. Can I still write Java programs?

A If you have no programming experience whatsoever, you most likely will find programming Java significantly more difficult. However, Java is an excellent language to learn programming with, and if you patiently work through the examples and the exercises in this book, you should be able to learn enough to get started with Java.

Q According to today's lesson, Java applets are downloaded via a Java-enabled browser such as Internet Explorer 3.0 and run on the user's system. Isn't that an enormous security hole? What stops someone from writing an applet that compromises the security of my system—or worse, that damages my system?

A Sun's Java team has thought a great deal about the security of applets within Java-capable browsers and has implemented several checks to make sure applets cannot do nasty things.

The checks obviously cannot stop every potential security hole (no system can promise that!), but they can significantly reduce the potential for hostile applets. You'll learn more about security on Day 16, "Connecting Java to a Network and Other Tidbits."

Q Why use Visual J++?

A VJ++ uses Microsoft Developer Studio, which is the common development platform for all Microsoft development products. It is designed to easily create reusable, object-oriented applets and applications in less time than the JDK by itself. VJ++ maintains the industry standard JDK 1.0 specification, while providing new technologies such as COM. The VJ++ InfoView provides a help system with code and class examples, which also integrates with the debugger for troubleshooting any errors your programs might encounter. By using VJ++ you will be able to produce amazing things in less time, with fewer errors.

Day 2

Introducing Visual J++

Today you'll learn how to Install Microsoft Visual J++ and use VJ++ to create a simple Java applet. In doing so, you will be introduced (albeit briefly) to Microsoft Developer Studio. Microsoft Developer Studio is the Integrated Development Environment (IDE) that Microsoft is using to standardize all of its development platforms.

Installing Visual J++

The first day dealt with an overview of Java and Visual J++. From here on out we're going to get to the meat of the matter. No more simple reading, it's hands-on time! Before you can begin using Visual J++, you have to install it (what a novel concept). This section will walk you through installing Visual J++. Even if you have Visual J++ already installed, please follow along; there are some issues presented that you should be aware of.

System Requirements

Microsoft Visual J++ is specifically designed to work on Windows 95 and Windows NT 4.0 workstations. The typical requirement is to run the preceding operating systems effectively is a 486DX processor with 8MB of RAM (16MB of RAM for NT). For optimal performance, we suggest you have at least a Pentium processor with 16MB of RAM (32MB of RAM for NT). Depending on the options installed, VJ++ takes between 12MB and 20MB of disk space.

Starting the Installation

☐ Insert the Microsoft Visual J++ CD into your CD-ROM Drive. The AutoPlay feature of Windows 95 or NT 4.0 will automatically start the Visual J+– Master Setup program. (See Figure 2.1.)

 NOTE

> If the Master Setup program doesn't start, it will be necessary for you to manually run Setup. This can be done from within Microsoft Explorer or File Manager.

Figure 2.1.

VJ++ Master Setup screen.

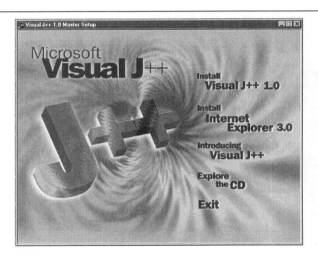

☐ Choose the Install Visual J++ option.

☐ On the Welcome screen, click Next to proceed with the Setup procedure.

☐ On the following screen, a fairly typical license agreement is displayed. As always, be sure that you read and understand the license agreement before clicking Yes to proceed.

☐ When the Registration screen appears, enter your Name, your Organization's Name, and the CD Key. Typically, the CD Key for a Microsoft product can be found on the back of the CD case. When the Next button is no longer grayed, you have entered all necessary information and may click Next to proceed.

Installation Options

☐ On the Installation Options screen, there are four types of installation for Visual J++ from which to choose: Typical, Minimum, CD-ROM, and Custom. (See Figure 2.2.) From this screen, you also are able to change the location that VJ++ will be installed.

Figure 2.2.

VJ++ Installation Options screen.

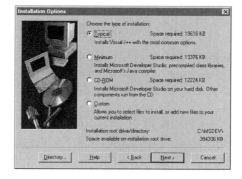

☐ The first three options (Typical, Minimum, and CD-ROM) are rather straightforward and do not particularly merit discussion. The fourth option, Custom, allows you to selectively pick which components of VJ++ you want to install. These options include: Database Options, Books Online, and Class Library source code.

☐ For our purposes, we will select the Custom option because we want to make sure that all of the database options are installed. When you have selected your Installation Options, click Next to continue the installation process.

☐ The next screen displays a list of options to install along with a corresponding check box for each option. Make sure that all options are checked to be installed. When you have completed this screen, click Next to continue.

☐ Setup will display one last confirmation window just to make sure that you have selected all the options that you want to install. When satisfied, click Finish to complete the installation.

NOTE

After the previous screen, various Setup messages might appear on your screen informing you of components that need to be or are being installed. These screens are Operating System Dependent as well as Visual J++ version dependent. If any screens do appear, the best advice that we can give you is to simply "follow your nose."

Reinstalling Visual J++

If for some reason you need to reinstall VJ++ (for example, one of the CLASS files becomes corrupted), simply insert the CD-ROM, and follow the same instructions in the preceding list. However, you should not have to re-enter any of the information (Name, Company, Directory, and so on) that you entered the first time you ran the installation.

Uninstalling Visual J++

As with any Windows 95 compliant application, VJ++ comes with its own Uninstall application. If for some reason you need to Uninstall VJ++ (and we wholeheartedly hope you don't!), just select the Uninstall Visual J++ item from the Start menu. You can also uninstall Visual J++ by using Control Panel's Add/Remove Program. The Uninstall application will start and you can simply follow the instructions presented to you to remove VJ++. This is the cleanest way to uninstall VJ++ (or any application with an Uninstall application) because it will clean up the Registry and remove *all* the files associated with VJ++, not just the ones in the MSDEV directory.

Microsoft Developer Studio

This section is designed to acquaint you with using Microsoft Developer Studio. Microsoft Developer Studio is the Integrated Development Environment for Visual J++. It is also the IDE for Microsoft Visual C++ 4.0 and greater, Visual Test, and FORTRAN PowerStation. When Visual Basic 5.0 is released, Microsoft Developer Studio will be the IDE for it as well. In the future (most likely), it will be the only IDE for all Microsoft Development Products.

NOTE

> If you are currently using Microsoft Developer Studio with another Microsoft development product, you might want to simply browse through this section and skip ahead to the next section: "Getting Started with Microsoft Visual J++."

If Microsoft Developer Studio is the first IDE that you have used, it is understandable that it might appear to be a bit intimidating. But do not fear: Once you have a basic understanding of what all the buttons, tabs, and windows mean, you will hardly believe that any sort of development actually occurred before developers had the benefit of Microsoft Developer Studio.

Microsoft Developer Studio gives you all the tools you need to write, compile, test, debug, and refine your VJ++ programs—all in one easy-to-use interface. It includes a text editor, resource editors, an integrated debugger, an integrated compiler, and online help. Microsoft Developer Studio also has a group of default toolbars that allow you to access nearly all of the VJ++ functionality just by clicking on a button. If you are not satisfied with the functionality provided on the default toolbars, you can easily build your own toolbar using simple drag and drop techniques. If you have a subscription to Microsoft Developer Network, Microsoft Developer Studio also provides an interface to the Microsoft Developer Library.

TIP

As you go through the rest of this chapter, do not hesitate to experiment within the IDE, especially with the right mouse button: It is so loaded with functionality that it would take forever (well almost) to describe it all.

Starting Microsoft Developer Studio

If you accepted the defaults when installing Microsoft Developer Studio (and have not since changed its location), perform the following instructions. If you've installed (or moved) Visual J++ to another location, you know much better than we do how to start Visual J++ on your system, so please start Microsoft Developer Studio yourself.

To start Microsoft Developer Studio, select the Start menu, Programs, Microsoft Visual J++, and Microsoft Developer Studio.

The Project Workspace Window

For people new to an IDE, the Project Workspace Window will be the most welcome enhancement of all. The Project Workspace Window is the window docked to the left side of your screen. At this time, there should be a single TAB at the bottom of the window that reads InfoView. (See Figure 2.3.)

A *docked* window is a window that is tied to a given side of Microsoft Developer Studio. If you resize Microsoft Developer Studio, all docked windows remain docked to their side.

Figure 2.3.

Microsoft Developer Studio main screen.

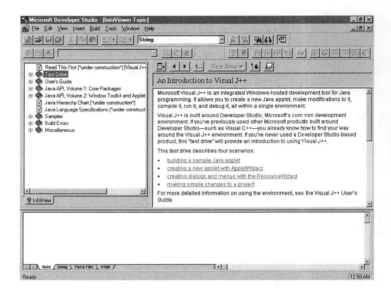

Navigating the Project Workspace Window

All items displayed in the Project Workspace Window are in the form of a hierarchical indexed list. If an item in the list window has any items beneath it (that is, its children) in the hierarchy, a + will be displayed to the left of its icon. Simply double-click the item, or click the +, to expand the item and see an item's children.

InfoView

When the InfoView tab is selected in the Project Workspace Window, a list of all available online materials is presented. This information includes the full VJ++ user's guide, API guide, Samples, and Build Errors. You are also able to search on a given subject by clicking anywhere in the InfoView window with the right mouse button and selecting Search.

Files

Once you create a Project Workspace, selecting the Files tab will display a list of all source files that are included in your project. This will include all *.java files on which your application is dependent. You can open any of these files by double-clicking on the file or by using your right mouse button to bring up the pop-up menu and select Open.

2

NOTE

The preceding paragraph might seem confusing because of the way Project Workspace is used. Here is some clarification. The Project Workspace Window is the window that we have been talking about that is, by default, docked to the left side of Microsoft Developer Studio. A Project Workspace, which is saved as a *.MDP file is a configuration for a given project. It specifies what the *.MAK file is, and what the current Microsoft Developer Studio screen configuration is. The .MAK file is carried over from C/C++ and specifies all files that are included in a project as well as how to compile them into their final form.

Classes

Classes are the heart of VJ++ and the Project Workspace Window displays them in the most logical of formats. (You will learn more about Classes on Day 4.) By selecting the Classes Tab, Microsoft Developer Studio will display all classes that are in your project. You can easily open the file that contains a method within one of your classes by simply double-clicking the item or by using the right mouse button to select Open.

Customizing the Workspace

One of the advantages of using an IDE is the ability to customize your workspace for the way that you work. Suppose you tend to always look to the left most side of your screen for the code that you are working on currently. At first glance, you might be annoyed that the Project Workspace Window is there. Not to worry. Microsoft has made it incredibly easy to not only move the Project Workspace Window to anywhere on the screen that you want, but they have given you the ability to customize nearly any aspect of Microsoft Developer Studio. Now, look at some of the ways you can customize your workspace.

Toolbars and Docking Windows

The two easiest and most useful things to modify in Microsoft Developer Studio are the Toolbars and the Docking window. Remember, these are just a couple of the numerous customizable parameters in Microsoft Developer Studio.

Toolbars

To modify (move, create, change) anything about a toolbar, select Tools | Customize from the Microsoft Developer Studio menu. The Customize window will appear. (See Figure 2.4.)

Once this window is displayed, you can change any of the currently displayed toolbars. Try some of the following to get a feel for how customizing toolbars works.

Figure 2.4.

Customize window.

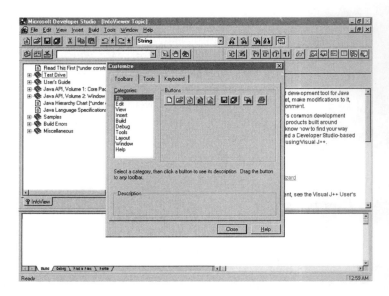

☐ Hold down your Ctrl key and drag an icon from one of the toolbars to another toolbar.

☐ Select a Category and then drag one of the Buttons from the Customize window to any of the toolbars.

☐ Select a Category and then drag one of the Buttons from the Customize window to a place on the screen where there is no toolbar.

☐ Select a drop-down listbox on an existing toolbar and change its size by using your mouse on the edge of the listbox.

Once you have played a bit, close the Customize window. Now try the following: Click and hold the mouse button down on a location in any of the toolbars. Now move your mouse into the center of the screen. The toolbar should follow and end up floating.

Docking Windows

Try the following: Resize Microsoft Developer Studio.

Assuming that the Project Workspace Window is still visible, notice how it travels with the outside edge of Microsoft Developer Studio. That informs us that the Project Workspace Window is docked. To change that docking feature, do the following: Select Tools | Options from the Microsoft Developer Studio menu. The Options Window appears. (See Figure

2.5.) Click on the Workspace tab. Experiment a bit and see what happens when you change the Docking characteristic for the Project Workspace window.

Figure 2.5.
Options window.

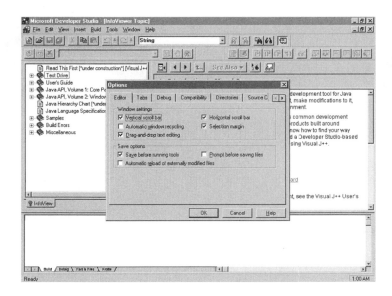

Saving the Workspace

To save the current configuration of the workspace (toolbars, Project Workspace window, and so on), exit Microsoft Visual J++ by selecting File | Exit from the menu.

Getting Started with Microsoft Visual J++

Enough introduction to VJ++! You'll complete today by creating a VJ++ application (and an applet!), compiling them, and finally testing them. Even though you are going to build the rather simple obligatory Hello World program, it will do a good job of demonstrating the basics of working with VJ++.

Creating a New Project Workspace

Select File | New from the Microsoft Developer Studio menu. A small dialog box will appear prompting you to select the type of file you wish to create. Select Project Workspace. The New Project Workspace Window appears. (See Figure 2.6.) At this point, do not change any of the defaults. Type in a name for your Hello World application in the Name field. Although it's not required, we suggest you use the name of the highest level class as the name for the project workspace, which for this example would be HelloWorld.

Figure 2.6.

*New Project Workspace
window.*

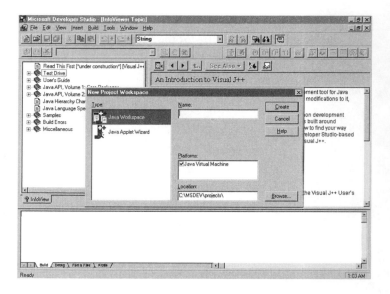

Creating a VJ++ Application

Open a new source file window in the Workspace. You can do this either by selecting
File | New | Text File from the Microsoft Developer Studio menu or by clicking the New
Source File button on the toolbar. Once the new source file window is open, type the program
in Listing 2.1. Be careful to include all the parentheses, braces, and quotes.

TYPE   Listing 2.1. Your first VJ++ application.

```
1: class HelloWorld
2: {
3:     public static void main (String args[])
4:     {
5:         System.out.println("Hello World!");
6:     }
7: }
```

WARNING

The numbers before each line are part of the listing and not part of the
program; they're there so we can refer to specific line numbers when we
explain what's going on in the program. Do not include them in your
own file.

This program has two main parts:

- ☐ All of the program is enclosed in a class definition—here, a class called HelloWorld.
- ☐ The body of the program (here, just the one line) is contained in a method (function) called main(). In Java applications, as in a C or C++ program, main() is the first method (function) that is run when the program is executed.

NOTE

> For those of you used to programming in other languages, remember that a method is almost identical to a function in other languages.

You'll learn more about both of these parts of a Java application as the book progresses.

Once you finish typing the program, you need to save the file. Java source files are typically named the same name as the class they define, with an extension of .java. This file should therefore be called HelloWorld.java.

In most cases the name of the .java file does not particularly matter. What does matter is that the name of your class and the name of your project match exactly, both in spelling and in case. If the names do not match exactly, the results can be somewhat unpredictable. To play it safe, we recommend that you always name your .java and .class files the same (same case too), as well as the name of your project.

To save the file, select File | Save from the Microsoft Developer Studio menu or click on the Save button (looks like a floppy disk) on the button bar.

If you look in the Project Workspace window and click on the Files tab, you will notice that there are still no files defined for your HelloWorld project. This is because you have not added your recently saved source file to the project. Add that file now. Select Insert | Files into Project from the Microsoft Developer Studio menu. In the dialog that appears, select the HelloWorld list and click Add. Now, if you look in the Project Workspace Window, you will notice that there is a file listed called HelloWorld.java.

To compile your Hello World application, select Build | Build HelloWorld from the menu. If you look at the bottom of the screen, you should see the status of the build process. If there are any errors, go back to the source code (using Project Workspace Window to get to the source file) and fix the problem. Repeat this process until a message displays with no errors and warnings, like the following:

```
HelloWorld - 0 errors(s), 0 warning(s)
```

Testing Your VJ++ Application with JVIEW

Once you build your program, you'll want to see it run and also test it. To execute your program, do the following:

Select Build | Execute. The Information for Running Class dialog box displays. In the Class file name text box, type in the name of your class (HelloWorld). In the Run project under group box, select Stand-alone interpreter, and click OK. A command window will open and your application will run (depending on how your system is configured, the window might close quite quickly or remain open until you close it yourself. You can change this behavior, using Windows 95 or NT, to suit your own preferences.)

NOTE The next time you select Build | Execute, the Execute command will have changed to read Execute *yourclassname*. You'll not have the option of specifying a class name or runtime environment. If you need to change any of this information, you can do so by selecting Build | Settings. In the Settings For list box, select the debug version of your program, then select the Debug tab—change the settings as need be.

Creating a VJ++ Applet

Creating applets is different from creating a simple application, because Java applets run and are displayed inside a Web page with other page elements and, as such, have special rules for how they behave. Because of these special rules for applets, in many cases (particularly the simple ones) creating an applet might be more complex than creating an application.

For example, to do a simple Hello World applet, instead of merely being able to print a message, you have to create an applet to make space for your message and then use graphics operations to paint the message to the screen.

NOTE If you were to run the Hello World application as an applet, the Hello World message would print to a special window or to a log file, depending upon how the browser has screen messages set up. It will not appear on the screen, as you might expect, unless you write your applet to put it there. Remember, applets depend upon a browser, so they need to include special instructions (code) to be able to interact with the browser.

2

In the next example, you create that simple HelloWorld applet, place it inside a Web page, and view the result.

Open a new source code window in Microsoft Developer Studio and enter the code from Listing 2.2.

TYPE **Listing 2.2. The Hello World applet.**

```
1: import java.awt.Graphics;
2:
3: public class HelloWorldApplet extends java.applet.Applet
4: {
5:     public void paint(Graphics g)
6:     {
7:         g.drawString("Hello world!", 5, 25);
8:     }
9:}
```

Save this file as HelloWorldApplet.java. Remember the case.

Are you wondering what features to note about applets? There are a couple we'd like to point out:

☐ The import line at the top of the file is somewhat analogous to a #include statement in C; it enables this applet to get access to the JDK classes (standard library) for creating applets and for drawing graphics on the screen.

☐ The paint() method displays the content of the applet onto the screen. Here, the string Hello World gets drawn. Applets use several standard methods to take the place of main(), which include init() to initialize the applet, start() to start it running, and paint() to display it to the screen. You'll learn about all of these in Week 2.

Now go over to the Project Workspace Window and select the File tab. Highlight the existing HelloWorld.java file and press Del to remove the file from your project. Now insert the new file into the HelloWorldApplet.java project. Compile the modified project using the same procedure as before.

Unlike VJ++ applications, applets are designed to be run from within a browser. For an applet to be run, it needs to be embedded within an HTML file. Create an HTML file for your Hello World applet now. Open a new code window in Microsoft Developer Studio and type in Listing 2.3. (Yep, same as Day 1.)

TYPE   **Listing 2.3. The HTML with the applet in it.**

```
1: <HTML>
2: <HEAD>
3: <TITLE>Hello to Everyone!</TITLE>
4: </HEAD><BODY>
5: <P>My Java applet says: </P>
6: <APPLET CODE="HelloWorldApplet.class" WIDTH=150 HEIGHT=25>
7: </APPLET>
8: </BODY>
9: </HTML>
```

Save the code window as an HTML file with a descriptive name. (We suggest: HelloWorld.html.)

To test your new VJ++ applet, you must first confirm some settings. Select Build | Options from the menu. The Project Settings window appears. (See Figure 2.7.) Select the Debug tab, making sure that the Category selected is General and that the Debug project under is set to Browser.

Figure 2.7.

Project Settings window.

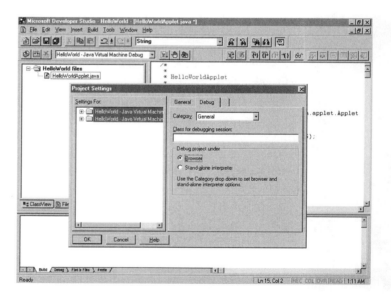

Set the Category to Browser and make sure that the HTML page selected is the HelloWorld.html that you created a few minutes ago. You can click OK to close this window now.

Now to test your new HelloWorld VJ++ applet! Select Build | Execute HelloWorldApplet from the Microsoft Developer Studio menu. This should start your default browser (probably Microsoft Internet Explorer or Netscape). At this point your Hello World applet should be displayed in the browser.

2

If your browser supports loading of HTML files from the local machine, then you could simply load your browser and load the `HelloWorld.html` that you created. The results should be the same.

It is important to note that you do NOT have to create your own `*.HTML` file in order to test your applets. By default, VJ++ will create one for you. VJ++ will create its own `*.HTML` when you select Execute and will name it `vjxxx` (where *xxx* is a VJ++ generated alpha-numeric sequence), for example, `vj934.html`. VJ++ does this each time you execute your applet, so making your own changes to the VJ++ created `.html` will be of no use. If you do create (or want to reuse) your own `.html` file, you must add it (Insert | Files into Project) to your project.

Summary

Today you were given a basic tour of Microsoft Developer Studio and of some of its features. Microsoft Developer Studio is an immensely powerful IDE that allows you, the developer, to customize your workspace however you see fit. It effectively encompasses all of the separate applications that a developer of just a few years ago would have had to use: editor, compiler, debugger, online help system, and online reference materials.

You also learned how to use VJ++ and Microsoft Developer Studio to create a simple applet and a simple application. The two programs that you created today form the basis for every VJ++ program that you will write in the future.

Q&A

Q I have been looking at Microsoft Developer Studio and I can't seem to make it look the way I want. Where can I go for more help?

A The best location to go for Microsoft Developer Studio help is the Books Online that are included with VJ++. If you did not install the Books Online, then you can do so by running the setup procedure again.

A second great reference for Microsoft Developer Studio is the Microsoft Developer Network CDs. This subscription (available from Microsoft) includes full documentation on all of their development tools and SDKs.

Q I have previously used the SUN JDK to create some Java applications/applets and I would like to know if I can use any of their tools with VJ++.

A To the best of our knowledge, the file `JAVA.EXE` that is part of Version 1.0 of the JDK works very well on VJ++ compiled applications.

Day 3

Object-Oriented Programming and Java

Object-oriented programming (OOP) is one of the biggest programming ideas of recent years, and you might worry that you must spend years learning all about object-oriented programming methodologies and how they can make your life easier than *the old way* of programming. It all comes down to organizing your programs in ways that echo how things are put together in the real world.

Today, you'll get an overview of object-oriented programming concepts in Java and how they relate to how you structure your own programs:

☐ What classes and objects are, and how they relate to each other

☐ The two primary parts of a class: its properties and its methods

☐ Inheritance and how inheritance affects the way you design your programs

☐ Some preliminary information about packages and interfaces

If you're already familiar with object-oriented programming, much of today's lesson will be familiar to you. You might want to kick back and skim it, but you might find some tidbits of new information here. Tomorrow, you'll get into more specific details.

Thinking in Objects: An Analogy

Consider, if you will, Legos. Legos, for those of you who don't spend much time with children, are small plastic building blocks in various colors and sizes. Each Lego has small round nibs (bumps) on one side that fit into the small round holes on the other side of another Lego. By the successive joining of the nibs to the holes, so that they fit together snugly, you create larger shapes. With different Lego bits (Lego wheels, Lego engines, Lego hinges, Lego pulleys), you can put together castles, automobiles, giant robots that swallow cities, or just about anything else you can imagine. Each Lego bit is a small object (ah, that word object) that fits together with other small objects in predefined ways to create other larger objects.

Here's another example. You can walk into a computer store, and with a little background information, assemble an entire PC computer system from various components: a motherboard, a CPU chip, a video card, a hard disk, a keyboard, and so on. Ideally, when you finish assembling all the various self-contained units, you have a system in which all the units work together to create a larger system that can solve the problems you bought the computer for in the first place.

Internally, each of those components might be vastly complicated and engineered by different companies with different methods of design. But you don't need to know how each component works, what every chip on the board does, or how, when you press the A key, an A gets sent to your screen. As the assembler of the overall system, each component you use is a self-contained unit, and all you're interested in is how each component interacts with one another. Will this video card fit into the slots on the motherboard and will this monitor work with this video card? Will each particular component speak the right commands to the other components it interacts with so that each part of the computer is understood by every other part? Once you know what the interactions are between the components and can match the interactions, putting together the overall system is easy.

What does this have to do with VJ++ programming? Everything. Object-oriented programming works in exactly this same way. When you use object-oriented programming, your overall program is made up of lots of different self-contained components (objects), each of which has a specific role in the program and all of which can communicate to one another in predefined ways.

Objects and Classes

Object-oriented programming is modeled on how, in the real world, large objects are often made up of many kinds of smaller objects. This capability of combining objects, however, is only one very general aspect of object-oriented programming. Object-oriented programming provides many other concepts and features to make creating and using objects easier and more flexible, and the most important of these features is that of classes.

New Term   A *class* is a template for multiple objects with similar features.

When you write a program in an object-oriented language, you don't define actual objects. You define classes of objects.

For example, you might have a Tree class that describes the features of all trees (has leaves and roots, grows, creates chlorophyll). The Tree class serves as an abstract model for the concept of a tree. In order to reach out and grab—or interact with or cut down a tree—you have to have a concrete instance of that tree. Of course, once you have a tree class, you can create lots of different instances of that tree, and each different tree instance can have different features (short, tall, bushy, drops leaves in Autumn) while still behaving like and being immediately recognizable as a tree. (See Figure 3.1.)

Figure 3.1.
The tree *class and* tree *instances.*

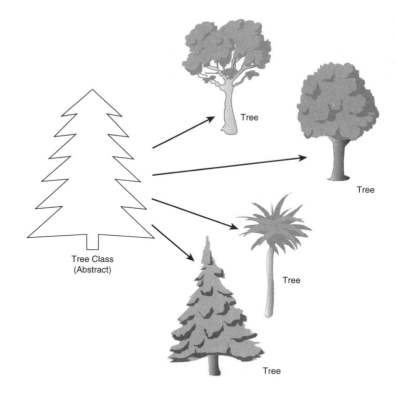

Tree

Tree

Tree Class
(Abstract)

Tree

Tree

New Term   An *instance* of a class is another word for an actual *object*. If class is the general (generic) representation of an object, an instance is its concrete representation.

So what, precisely, is the difference between an instance and an object? Nothing, really. Object is the more general term, but both instances and objects are the concrete representation of a class. In fact, the terms instance and object are often used interchangeably in OOP language. An instance of a tree and a tree object are both the same thing.

In an example closer to the sort of things you might want to do in Java programming, you might create a class for the user interface element called a button. The Button class defines the properties of a button (its label, its size, its appearance) and how it behaves. (Does it need a single-click or a double-click to activate it, does it change color when it's clicked, what does it do when it's activated?) Once you define the Button class, you can easily create instances of that button—that is, button objects—that all take on the basic features of the button as defined by the class, but might have different appearances and behavior based on what you want a particular button to do. By creating a Button class, you don't have to keep rewriting the code for each individual button you want to use in your program, and you can reuse the Button class to create different kinds of buttons as you need them in this program and in other programs.

 TIP

> If you're accustomed to programming in C, you can think of a class as sort of creating a new composite data type by using struct and typedef. Classes, however, can provide much more than just a collection of data, as you'll discover in the rest of today's lesson.

When you write a Java program, you design and construct one or more classes that your program will use. Then, when your program runs, instances of those classes are created and discarded as needed. Your task, as a Java programmer, is to create the right set of classes to accomplish what your program needs to accomplish.

Fortunately, you don't have to start from the very beginning: The Java environment comes with a library of classes that implement a lot of the basic behavior you need, not only for basic programming tasks (classes to provide basic math functions, arrays, strings, and so on), but also for graphics and networking behavior. In most cases, the Java class libraries are enough so that all you have to do in your Java program is create a single class that uses the standard class libraries. For complicated Java programs, however, you might have to create a whole set of classes with defined interactions between them.

NEW TERM   A *class library* is a set of classes.

Behavior and Attributes

Every class you write in Java is generally made up of two components: properties and methods. In this section, you'll learn about each one as it applies to a theoretical class called Motorcycle. To finish this section, you'll create the Java code to implement a representation of a motorcycle.

Properties

Properties are the individual things that differentiate one object from another and determine the appearance, state, or other qualities of that object. You'll now create a theoretical class called `Motorcycle`. The properties of a motorcycle might include the following:

- ☐ *Color:* red, green, silver, brown
- ☐ *Style:* cruiser, sport bike, standard
- ☐ *Make:* Harley Davidson, BMW, Indian

Properties of an object can also include information about its state; for example, you could have properties for engine condition (off or on) or current gear selected.

Properties are defined by variables; in fact, you can consider them analogous to global variables for the entire object. Because each instance of a class can have different values for its variables, each variable is called a data member.

NEW TERM   *Data Members* define the properties of an object. The class defines the type of the property, and each instance stores its own value for that property. (You will learn more about data members tomorrow.)

Each property, as the term is used here, has a single corresponding data member; changing the value of a variable changes the attribute of that object. Data members might be set when an object is created and stay constant throughout the life of the object, or they might be able to change at will as the program runs.

In addition to data members, there are also class variables, which apply to the class itself and to all its instances. Unlike data members, whose values are stored in the instance, a class variables' values are stored in the class itself. You'll learn about class variables later on this week; you'll learn more specifics about data members tomorrow.

Methods

A class' methods (behavior) determine how the instances of the class change their internal state or react when the instance is asked to do something by another class or object. Methods are the only way objects can do anything to themselves or have anything done to them. For example, to go back to the theoretical `Motorcycle` class, here are some methods that the `Motorcycle` class might have:

- ☐ Start the engine
- ☐ Stop the engine
- ☐ Speed up
- ☐ Change gear
- ☐ Stall

To define an object's behavior, you create methods, which look and behave just like functions in other languages but are defined inside a class. Java does not have functions defined outside classes (as C++ does).

NEW TERM   *Methods* are functions defined inside classes that operate on instances of those classes.

Methods don't always affect only a single object; objects communicate with each other using methods as well. A class or object can call methods in another class or object to communicate changes in the environment or to ask that object to change its state.

Just as there are instance and class variables, there are also instance and class methods. Instance methods (which are so common they're usually just called methods) apply and operate on an instance of a class; class methods apply and operate on the class itself. You'll learn more about class methods later on this week.

Putting Properties and Methods Together

At this point, you might be wondering "Why do I care about objects, classes, properties, methods, instances, and so on?" To that end, lets put some of the concepts that you have learned together. The easiest way to do this is to use some real-world examples.

> Liz is an object of class type Person. She is a woman (property) and she talks (method). Liz's truck is an object of class Vehicle. It is blue (property) and its engine starts and stops (method).
>
> Patrick's PC is an object of class Computer. It is an SMP-P90 (property) and it plays a music CD (method).
>
> Dave's PC is also an object of class Computer. It is a P5-66 (property), it plays a music CD (method), and it can print a document (method).

Think of a few other real-world objects (not related to programming or computers) and see if you can describe them as in the preceding examples.

Here's one to get you started. A tabby cat chases mice. Pick out the class, property, and method.

Creating a Class

Up to this point, today's lesson has been pretty theoretical. In this section, you'll create a working example of the Motorcycle class so that you can see how data members and methods are defined in a class. You'll also create a Java application that creates a new instance of the Motorcycle class and shows its data members.

NOTE

We're not going to go into a lot of detail about the actual syntax of this example here. Don't worry too much about it if you're not really sure what's going on; it will become clear to you later on this week. All you really need to worry about in this example is understanding the basic parts of this class definition.

Before you begin, open a New Project Workspace in Microsoft Developer Studio and open a new source window. Type the following:

```
class Motorcycle
{

}
```

Congratulations! You've now created a class. Of course, it doesn't do very much at the moment, but that's a Java class at its very simplest.

First, create some data members for this class—three of them, to be specific. Just below the second line, after the {, add the following three lines:

```
String m_Make;
String m_Color;
boolean m_EngineState;
```

Here, you've created three data members: two, `m_Make` and `m_Color`, can contain `String` objects. (`String` is part of that standard class library mentioned earlier.) The third, `m_EngineState`, is a Boolean that refers to whether the engine is off or on.

TECHNICAL NOTE

`boolean` in Java is a real data type that can have the value `true` or `false`. Unlike C, true and false data types do not equate to the numbers 0 and 1 (or 0 and non-zero for C++). You'll hear about this again tomorrow so you won't forget.

Now add some methods (behavior) to the class. There are all kinds of things a motorcycle can do, but to keep things short, add just one method—a method that starts the engine. Add the following lines below the data members in your class definition:

```
void startEngine()
  {
    if (m_EngineState == true)
        System.out.println("The engine is already on.");
    else
    {
        m_EngineState = true;
```

```
        System.out.println("The engine is now on.");
    }
}
```

The `startEngine` method tests to see whether the engine is already running (in the line `m_EngineState == true`) and, if it is, merely prints a message to that effect. If the engine isn't already running, it changes the state of the engine to `true` and then prints a message.

With your methods and properties in place, save the program to a file called `Motorcycle.java`. (Remember, we recommend that you name your Java files the same name as the class they define.) Here's what your program should look like so far:

```
class Motorcycle
{
String m_Make;
String m_Color;
boolean m_EngineState;

void startEngine()
    {
    if (m_EngineState == true)
        System.out.println("The engine is already on.");
    else
    {
        m_EngineState = true;
        System.out.println("The engine is now on.");
    }
    }
}
```

TIP

Notice that Microsoft Developer Studio indents your statements automatically. This makes it much easier to read and catch typing errors (like a missing }). Even though the indentation of each part of the class isn't important to the Java compiler, using some form of indentation makes your class definition easier for you and for other people to read. The indentation used here, with data members and methods indented from the class definition, is the style used throughout this book.

Before you compile this class, add one more method. The `showAtts` method prints the current values of the data members in an instance of your `Motorcycle` class. Here's what the function looks like:

```
void showAtts()
{
    System.out.println("This motorcycle is a "
        + color + " " + make);
    if (m_EngineState == true)
        System.out.println("The engine is on.");
```

```
    else System.out.println("The engine is off.");
}
```

NOTE

Be sure to add this function before the final } of the class definition.

The showAtts method prints two lines to the screen: the m_Make and m_Color of the motorcycle object, and whether or not the engine is on or off.

Save the file, insert it into your Project (select Insert | Files into Project from the menu), and compile the project (Build | Compile from the menu).

NOTE

After this point, the instructions will simply instruct you to build your projects, compile, and run your VJ++ application or applet.

What happens if you now use the JVIEW interpreter to run this compiled class? Try it. VJ++ assumes that this class is an application and looks for a main method. This is just a class, however, so it doesn't have a main method. The JVIEW interpreter (JVIEW) gives you an error like this one:

```
In class Motorcycle: void main(String argv[]) is not defined
```

To do something with the Motorcycle class—for example, to create instances of that class and play with them—you're going to need to create a VJ++ application that uses this class or add a main method to this one. For simplicity's sake, do the latter. Listing 3.1 shows the main() method you'll add to the Motorcycle class.

TYPE   **Listing 3.1. The main() method for Motorcycle.java.**

```
 1: public static void main (String args[])
 2:{
 3:    Motorcycle mMyCycle = new Motorcycle();
 4:    mMyCycle.m_Make = "Harley Davidson Sportster";
 5:    mMyCycle.m_Color = "yellow";
 6:    System.out.println("Calling showAtts...");
 7:    mMyCycle.showAtts();
 8:    System.out.println(" — — — —");
 9:    System.out.println("Starting engine...");
10:    mMyCycle.startEngine();
11:    System.out.println(" — — — —");
12:    System.out.println("Calling showAtts...");
13:    mMyCycle.showAtts();
14:    System.out.println(" — — — —");
15:    System.out.println("Starting engine...");
16:    mMyCycle.startEngine();
17:}
```

With the main() method, the Motorcycle class is now an application, and you can compile it again and this time it'll run. Here's how the output should look:

```
Calling showAtts...
This motorcycle is a yellow Harley Davidson Sportster
The engine is off.
— — — —
Starting engine...
The engine is now on.
— — — —
Calling showAtts...
This motorcycle is a yellow Harley Davidson Sportster
The engine is on.
— — — —
Starting engine...
The engine is already on.
```

The contents of the main() method are going to look very new to you, so go through it line by line so that you have at least have a basic idea of what it does. (You'll get details about the specifics of all of this tomorrow and the day after.)

ANALYSIS   The first line declares the main() method. The main() method always looks like this; you'll learn the specifics of each part later this week.

Line 2, Motorcycle mMyCycle = new Motorcycle(), creates a new instance of the Motorcycle class and stores a reference to it in the variable mMyCycle. Remember, you don't actually operate on classes in your Java programs; rather, you create an instance (objects) from those classes and then call the methods and the properties in those objects.

Lines 3 and 4 set the data members for this motorcycle object: The make is now a Harley Davidson Sportster (one of the greats), and the color is yellow.

Lines 5 and 6 call the showAtts() method, defined in your motorcycle object. (Actually, only 6 does; 5 just prints a message that you're about to call this method.) The new motorcycle object then prints out the values of its data members—the m_Make and m_Color as you set in the previous lines—and shows that the engine is off.

Line 7 prints a divider line to the screen; this is just for nicer looking output.

Line 9 calls the startEngine() method in the motorcycle object to start the engine. The engine should now be on.

Line 12 prints the values of the data members again. This time, the report should say the engine is now on.

Line 15 tries to start the engine again, just for fun. Because the engine is already on, this should print the error message.

Inheritance, Interfaces, and Packages

Now that you have a basic grasp of classes, objects, methods, variables, and how to put it all together in a Java program, it's time to add some more object terms to your knowledge-base. Inheritance, interfaces, and packages are all mechanisms for organizing classes and class behaviors. The Java class libraries use all these concepts, and the best class libraries you write for your own programs will also use these concepts.

Inheritance

Inheritance is one of the most powerful concepts in object-oriented programming, and it has a direct effect on how you design and write your Java classes. Inheritance is a very powerful mechanism. The concept of inheritance is that when you write a class, you only have to specify how that class is different from some other class; inheritance will give you automatic access to the information contained in the original class.

When using inheritance, all classes—those you write, those from other class libraries that you use, and those from the standard utility classes as well—are arranged in a strict hierarchy. (See Figure 3.2.)

Figure 3.2.

A class hierarchy.

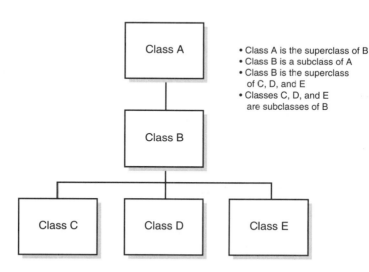

- Class A is the superclass of B
- Class B is a subclass of A
- Class B is the superclass of C, D, and E
- Classes C, D, and E are subclasses of B

Each class has a superclass (the class above it in the hierarchy), and each class can have one or more subclasses (classes below that class in the hierarchy). Classes further down in the hierarchy are said to inherit from classes further up in the hierarchy.

Subclasses inherit all the methods and variables from their superclasses—that is, in any particular class, if the superclass defines behavior that your class needs, you don't have to redefine it or copy that code from some other class. Your class automatically gets that behavior from its superclass, that superclass gets behavior from its superclass, and so on all the way up the hierarchy. Your class becomes a combination of all the methods and properties of the classes above it in the hierarchy.

At the top of the Java class hierarchy is the class Object; all classes inherit from this one superclass. Object is the most general class in the hierarchy; it defines behavior inherited by all the classes in the Java class hierarchy. Each class farther down in the hierarchy adds more information and becomes more tailored to a specific purpose. In this way, you can think of a class hierarchy as defining a very abstract concept at the top of the hierarchy and then having those ideas become more concrete the farther down the chain of superclasses the concept goes.

Most of the time when you write new Java classes, you'll want to create a class that has all the information some other class has, plus some extra information. For example, you might want a version of a Button with its own built-in label. To get all the Button information, all you have to do is define your class to inherit from Button. Your class will automatically get all the behavior defined in Button (which means the behavior specifically defined in Button, in Button's superclass, and so forth all the way up to Object), so all you have to worry about are the things that make your class different from Button itself. This mechanism for defining new classes as the differences between the new class and its superclasses is called subclassing.

NEW TERM   *Subclassing* involves creating a new class that inherits from some other class in the class hierarchy. Using subclassing, you only need to define the differences between your class and its parent; the core behavior (of the parent/superclass) is available to your class through inheritance.

What if your class defines entirely new behavior, and isn't really a subclass of another class? Your class can also inherit directly from Object, which still allows it to fit neatly into the Java class hierarchy. In fact, if you create a class definition that doesn't indicate its superclass in the first line, Java automatically assumes you're inheriting from Object. The Motorcycle class you created in the previous section automatically inherited from Object.

Creating a Class Hierarchy

If you're creating a larger set of classes, it makes sense for your classes not only to inherit from the existing class hierarchy, but also to make up a hierarchy themselves. This might take some planning beforehand when you're trying to figure out how to organize your Java code, but the advantages are significant once it's done:

☐ When you develop your classes in a hierarchy, you can factor out information common to multiple classes in superclasses and then reuse that superclass' information over and over again. Each subclass gets that common information from its superclass.

☐ Changing (or inserting) a class further up in the hierarchy automatically changes the behavior of the lower classes—no need to change or recompile any of the lower classes, because they get the new information through inheritance and not by copying any of the code.

For example, go back to that Motorcycle class and pretend you created a Java program to implement all the features of a motorcycle. It's done, it works, and everything is fine. Now, your next task is to create a Java class called Car.

Car and Motorcycle have many similar features; both are vehicles driven by engines. Both have transmissions, headlamps, and speedometers. So, your first impulse might be to open up your Motorcycle class file and copy over a lot of the information you already defined into the new class Car.

A far better plan is to factor out the common information for Car and Motorcycle into a more general class hierarchy. This might seem like a lot of additional effort for just the classes Motorcycle and Car, but once you add Bicycle, Scooter, Truck, and so on, having common behavior in a reuseable superclass significantly reduces the amount of work you have to do overall.

Now design a class hierarchy that might serve this purpose. Starting at the top is the class Object, which is the root of all Java classes. The most general class to which motorcycle and car both belong might be called Vehicle. A vehicle, generally, is defined as a thing that propels someone or something from one place to another. In the Vehicle class, you define only the behavior that enables propulsion from point a to point b, and nothing more.

Below Vehicle? How about two classes: PersonPoweredVehicle and EnginePoweredVehicle? EnginePoweredVehicle is different from Vehicle because it has an engine, and the methods might include stopping and starting the engine, having certain amounts of gasoline and oil, and perhaps the speed or gear in which the engine is running. Person-powered vehicles have some kind of mechanism for translating people motion into vehicle motion—pedals, for example. Figure 3.3 shows what you have so far.

Now, we'll get even more specific. With EnginePoweredVehicle, you might have several classes: Motorcycle, Car, Truck, and so on. Or you can factor out still more behavior and have intermediate classes for TwoWheeled and FourWheeled vehicles, with different behaviors for each. (See Figure 3.4.)

Finally, with a subclass for the two-wheeled engine-powered vehicles you can have a class for motorcycles. Alternatively, you could define scooters and mopeds, both of which are two-wheeled, engine-powered vehicles but have different qualities from motorcycles.

Where do properties such as make or color come in? Wherever you want them to go—or, more usually, where they fit most naturally in the class hierarchy. You can define the make and color on Vehicle, and all the subclasses will have those variables as well. The point to remember is that you have to define a feature or a behavior only once in the hierarchy then it's automatically reused by each subclass.

Figure 3.3.
*The basic vehicle
hierarchy.*

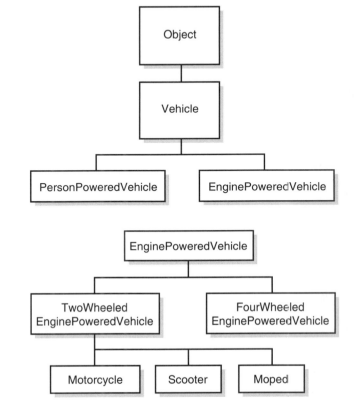

Figure 3.4.
*Two-wheeled and four-
wheeled vehicles.*

How Inheritance Works

How does inheritance work? How is it that instances of one class can automatically get variables and methods from the classes further up in the hierarchy?

For data members, when you create a new instance of a class, you get a "slot" for each variable defined in the current class and for each variable defined in all its superclasses. In this way, all the classes combine to form a template for the current object and then each object fills in the information appropriate to its situation.

Methods operate similarly: New objects have access to all the method names of its class and its superclasses, but method definitions are chosen dynamically when a method is called. That is, if you call a method on a particular object, Java first checks the object's class for the definition of that method. If it's not defined in the object's class, it looks in that class' superclass, and so on up the chain until the method definition is found. (See Figure 3.5.)

Figure 3.5.

How methods are located.

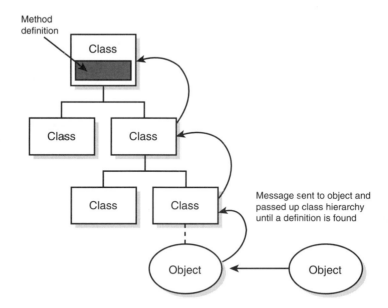

Method definition

Message sent to object and passed up class hierarchy until a definition is found

Things get complicated when a subclass defines a method that has the same signature (name, number, and type of arguments) as a method defined in a superclass. In this case, the method definition that is found first (starting at the bottom and working upward toward the top of the hierarchy) is the one that is actually executed. Because of this, you can purposefully define a method in a subclass that has the same signature as a method in a superclass, which then "hides" the superclass' method. This is called *overloading* a method. You'll learn more about methods on Day 7, "Creating Classses and Applications in Java."

Overloading a method is creating a method in a subclass that has the same signature (name, number, and type of arguments) as a method in a superclass. That new method then hides the superclass' method. (See Figure 3.6.)

Figure 3.6.
Overriding methods.

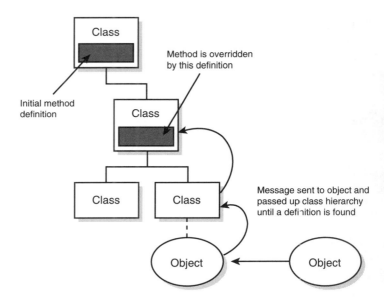

Single and Multiple Inheritance

Java's form of inheritance, as you learned in the previous sections, is called single inheritance. Single inheritance means that each Java class can have only one superclass (parent class). Remember, though, that any given superclass can have multiple subclasses.

In other object-oriented programming languages, such as C++, classes can have more than one superclass, and they inherit combined variables and methods from all those classes. This is called multiple inheritance. Multiple inheritance can provide enormous power in terms of being able to create classes that factor in just about any imaginable behavior, but it can also significantly complicate class definitions and the code to produce them. Java makes inheritance simpler by only allowing single inheritance.

NOTE

The lack of support for multiple inheritance does not necessarily mean less power for an object-oriented language. When multiple inheritance is used, it is easy for a developer to create a clouded and difficult to maintain class hierarchy. By only allowing single inheritance, Java forces a well-defined class structure that is easier to understand and most importantly, easy to maintain.

Interfaces and Packages

Java has two remaining concepts to discuss here: packages and interfaces. Both are advanced topics for implementing and designing groups of classes and class behavior. You'll learn about both interfaces and packages on Day 18, "Packages, Interfaces, and Exception Handling," but they are worth at least introducing here.

Recall that Java classes have only a single superclass, and they inherit variables and methods from that superclass and all its superclasses. Although single inheritance makes the relationship between classes and the functionality those classes implement easy to understand and to design, it can also be somewhat restricting—in particular, when you have similar behavior that needs to be duplicated across different "branches" of the class hierarchy. Java solves this problem of shared behavior by using the concept of interfaces.

 An *interface* is a collection of method names, without actual definitions, that indicate that a class has a set of behaviors in addition to the behaviors the class gets from its superclasses.

Although a single Java class can have only one superclass (due to single inheritance), that class can also implement any number of interfaces. By implementing an interface, a class provides method implementations (definitions) for the method names defined by the interface. If two very disparate classes implement the same interface, they can both respond to the same method calls (as defined by that interface), although what each class actually does in response to those method calls might be very different.

You don't need to know very much about interfaces right now. You'll learn more as the book progresses, so if all this is very confusing, don't panic!

The final new Java concept for today is that of packages.

 Packages in Java are a way of grouping together related classes and interfaces. Packages enable modular groups of classes to be available only if they are needed and eliminate potential conflicts between class names in different groups of classes.

You'll learn all about packages, including how to create and use them, in Week 3. For now, there are only a few things you need to know:

☐ The class libraries in the Java Developer's Kit are contained in a package called java. The classes in the java package are guaranteed to be available in any Java implementation, and are the *only* classes guaranteed to be available across different implementations. The java package itself contains other packages for classes that define the language itself, the input and output classes, some basic networking, and the window toolkit functions. Classes in other packages (for example, classes in the sun or netscape packages) will only run on specific platforms. For example, if you use a netscape specific class, it will only run within a netscape operating environment.

☐ By default, your Java classes have access to only the classes in java.lang (the base language package inside the java package). To use classes from any other package, you have to either refer to them explicitly by package name or import them in your source file.

☐ To refer to a class within a package, list all the packages that class is contained in and the class name, all separated by periods (.). For example, take the Color class, which is contained in the awt package (awt stands for Abstract Windowing Toolkit). The awt package, in turn, is inside the java package. To refer to the Color class in your program, you use the notation java.awt.Color.

Creating a Subclass

To finish up today, create a class that is a subclass of another class and override some methods. You'll also get a basic feel for how packages work in this example.

Probably the most typical instance of creating a subclass, at least when you first start programming in Java, is in creating an applet. All applets are subclasses of the class Applet (which is part of the java.applet package). By creating a subclass of Applet, you automatically get all the behavior from the window toolkit and the layout classes that enables your applet to be drawn in the right place on the Web page and to interact with system operations, such as keypresses and mouse clicks.

In this example, you'll create an applet similar to the HelloWorld applet from yesterday, but one that draws the Hello string in a larger font and a different color. To start this example, first construct the class definition itself. Remember the HTML and classes directories you created yesterday? Return to those and go back to Microsoft Developer Studio. Create a new Project Workspace and open a new source window. Enter the following class definition:

```
public class HelloAgainApplet extends java.applet.Applet
{

}
```

Here, you're creating a class called HelloAgainApplet. Note the part that says extends java.applet.Applet—that's the part that says your applet class is a subclass of the Applet class. Note also that because the Applet class is contained in the java.applet package (and not java.lang), you don't have automatic access to that class. So, you have to refer to it explicitly by package and class name.

The other part of this class definition is the public keyword. Public means that your class is available to the Java system at large once it is loaded. Most of the time you need to make a class public only if you want it to be visible to all the other classes in your Java program; but applets, in particular, must be declared to be public. (You'll learn more about public classes in Week 3.)

A class definition with nothing in it doesn't really have much of a point; without adding or overriding any of its superclasses' variables or methods, there's little point to creating a subclass at all. Add some information to this class to make it different from its superclass.

First, add a data member to contain a Font object (remember, the Font object will be an instance of class Font:

```
Font m_f = new Font("TimesRoman", Font.BOLD, 36);
```

The m_f data member now contains a new instance of the class Font, part of the java.awt package. This particular font object is a Times Roman font, boldface, 36 points high. In the previous Hello World applet, the font used for the text was the default font: 12 point Times Roman. Using a font object, you can change the font of the text you draw in your applet.

By creating a data member to hold this font object, you make it available to all the methods in your class. Now create a method that uses it.

When you write applets, there are several standard methods defined in the applet superclasses that you will commonly override in your applet class. These include methods to initialize the applet, to start it running, to handle operations such as mouse movements or mouse clicks, or to clean up when the applet stops running. One of those standard methods is the paint() method, which actually displays your applet on screen. The default definition of paint() doesn't do anything—it's an empty method. By overriding paint(), you tell the applet just what to draw on the screen. Here's a definition of paint():

```
public void paint(Graphics g)
{
    g.setFont(m_f);
    g.setColor(Color.red);
    g.drawString("Hello again!", 5, 25);
}
```

There are two things to know about the paint() method. First, note that this method is declared public, just as the applet itself was. The paint() method is actually public for a different reason—because the method it's overriding is also public. If a superclass' method is defined as public, your override method also has to be public or you'll get an error when you compile the class.

Secondly, note that the paint() method takes a single argument: an instance of the Graphics class. The Graphics class provides platform-independent behavior for rendering fonts, colors, and basic drawing operations. You'll learn a lot more about the Graphics class in Week 2, when you create more extensive applets.

Inside your paint() method, you've done three things:

☐ You've told the graphics object that the default drawing font will be the one contained in the data member m_f.

☐ You've told the graphics object that the default color is an instance of the `Color` class for the color red.

☐ Finally, you've drawn your `"Hello Again!"` string onto the screen itself, at the x and y positions of 5 and 25. The string will be rendered in the new font and color.

For an applet this simple, this is all you need to do. Here's what the applet looks like so far:

```
public class HelloAgainApplet extends java.applet.Applet
{

  Font f = new Font("TimesRoman",Font.BOLD,36);

  public void paint(Graphics g)
  {
    g.setFont(m_f);
    g.setColor(Color.red);
    g.drawString("Hello again!", 5, 50);
  }
}
```

If you've been paying attention, you'll notice something is wrong with this example up to this point. If you don't know what it is, try saving this file (remember, save it to the same name as the class: `HelloAgainApplet.java`) and compiling it using the VJ++ compiler. You should get a bunch of errors similar to this one:

```
HelloAgainApplet.java:7: Class Graphics not found in type declaration.
```

Why are you getting these errors? Because the classes you're referring to are part of a package. Remember that the only package you have access to automatically is `java.lang`. You referred to the `Applet` class in the first line of the class definition by referring to its full package name (`java.applet.Applet`). Further on in the program, however, you referred to all kinds of other classes as if they were already available.

There are two ways to solve this problem: refer to all external classes by full package name or import the appropriate class or package at the beginning of your class file. Which one you choose to do is mostly a matter of choice, although if you find yourself referring to a class in another package quite often, you might want to import it to cut down on the amount of typing.

In this example, you'll import the classes you need. There are three of them: `Graphics`, `Font`, and `Color`. All three are part of the `java.awt` package. Here are the lines to import these classes. These lines go at the top of your program, before the actual class definition:

```
import java.awt.Graphics;
import java.awt.Font;
import java.awt.Color;
```

TIP

> You also can import an entire package of (`public`) classes by using an asterisk (*) in place of a specific class name. For example, to import all the classes in the awt package, you can use this line:
>
> ```
> import java.awt.*;
> ```

Now, with the proper classes imported into your program, `HelloAgainApplet` should compile cleanly to a class file. To test it, use Microsoft Developer Studio (Build | Execute) to create a default HTML for you or type in the example below.

Here's an HTML file to use:

```
<HTML>
<HEAD>
<TITLE>Another Applet</TITLE>
</HEAD>
<BODY>
<P>My second Java applet says:
<APPLET CODE="HelloAgainApplet.class" WIDTH=200 HEIGHT=75>
</APPLET>
</BODY>
</HTML>
```

For this HTML example, your Java class file is in the same directory as this HTML file. Save the file as `HelloAgainApplet.html` and fire up your Java-capable browser. Figure 3.7 shows the result you should be getting. (The words `Hello Again` should display in red.)

Figure 3.7.
The
`HelloAgainApplet`.

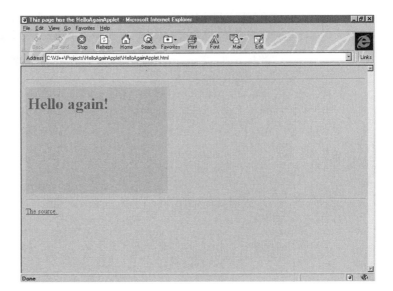

Summary

If this is your first encounter with object-oriented programming, a lot of the information in this chapter is going to seem really theoretical and overwhelming. Fear not; the further along in this book you get, and the more Java applications you create, the easier it is to understand. You might even want to read the beginning sections of this chapter again, now that you have some hands-on experience with objects.

One of the biggest hurdles of object-oriented programming is not necessarily the concepts, it's their names. OOP has lots of jargon surrounding it. To summarize today's material, here's a glossary of terms and concepts you learned today:

Class: A template for an object that contains properties and methods representing attributes and behavior. Via inheritance, classes can inherit properties and methods from other classes.

Object: A concrete instance of some class.

Instance: The same thing as an object; each object is an instance of some class.

Superclass: A class further up in the inheritance hierarchy than its child, the subclass.

Subclass: A class lower in the inheritance hierarchy than its parent, the superclass. When you create a new class based on some parent class, that is often called *subclassing.*

Instance method: A method defined in a class, which operates on an instance of that class. Instance methods are usually just called *methods.*

Class method: A method defined in a class, which operates on the class itself, and can be called via the class or any of its instances. (More on this tomorrow.)

Data member: A variable that is owned by an individual instance and whose value is stored in the instance. (More on this tomorrow.)

Class variable: A variable that is owned by the class and all its instances as a whole, and is stored in the class. (More on this tomorrow.)

Interface: A collection of abstract behavior specifications that individual classes can then implement.

Package: A collection of classes and interfaces. Classes from packages other than `java.lang` must be explicitly imported or referred to by full package name.

Q&A

Q **Methods are functions that are defined inside classes. If they look like functions and act like functions, why aren't they called functions?**

A Some object-oriented programming languages do call them functions (C++ calls them member functions). Other object-oriented languages differentiate between functions inside and outside a body of a class or object, where having separate terms is important to understanding how each works. Because the difference is relevant in other languages, and because the term method is now in such common use in object-oriented technology, Java uses the word as well.

Q **I understand data members and methods, but not class variables and class methods.**

A Most everything you do in a Java program will be with objects. Some behaviors and attributes, however, make more sense if they are stored in the class itself rather than in the object. For example, to create a new instance of a class, you need a method that is defined for the class itself, not for an object. (Otherwise, how can you create an instance of a class? You need an object to call the new method in, but you don't have an object yet.) Class variables, on the other hand, are often used when you have an attribute whose value you want to share with all the instances of a class.

Most of the time, you'll use data members and methods. You'll learn more about class variables and class methods later this week.

Day **4**

Java Basics

In the last three days you learned about Java programming in very broad terms—what a Java program and an executable look like, and how to create simple classes. You also learned (again in broad terms) Microsoft Developer Studio. For the remainder of this week, you're going to get down to details, and learn the specifics of what the Java language looks like by using Microsoft Developer Studio.

Today, you won't define any classes or objects or worry about how any of them communicate inside a Java program. Rather, you'll draw closer and examine simple Java statements—the basic things you can do in Java within a method definition such as main().

Today you'll learn about the following:

- ☐ Java statements and expressions
- ☐ Variables and data types
- ☐ Comments
- ☐ Literals
- ☐ Expressions and operators
- ☐ String arithmetic

TECHNICAL NOTE

Java looks a lot like C++, and—by extension—like C. Much cf the syntax will be very familiar to you if you are used to working in these languages. If you are an experienced C or C++ programmer, you might want to pay special attention to the Technical Notes (such as this one), because they will provide information about the specific differences between these and other traditional languages and Java.

Statements and Expressions

A statement is the simplest thing you can do in Java; a statement forms a single Java operation. All the following are simple Java statements:

```
int iTemp = 1;
import java.awt.Font;
System.out.println("This motorcycle is a "
    + color + " " + make);
m.engineState = true;
```

Statements sometimes return values—for example, when you add two numbers together or test to see whether one value is equal to another. These kinds of statements are called expressions. We'll discuss these later today.

The most important thing to remember about Java statements is that each one ends with a semicolon. If you forget a semicolon, errors will display and your Java program won't compile. Often, a single missed semicolon will generate an error on each line following the forgotten semicolon, so be careful: one missed semicolon can generate many errors.

Java also has compound statements called blocks. Wherever a single statement can be used, blocks can be used. Block statements are surrounded by braces ({ }). Microsoft Developer Studio automatically indents and matches { } to help make your code easier to read. You'll learn more about blocks on Day 6, "Arrays, Conditionals, and Loops."

Variables and Data Types

Variables are locations in memory where values can be stored. They have a name, a type, and a value. Before you can use a variable, you have to declare it. After it is declared, you can assign values to it. The following are a few examples of variables:

```
String sTemp = "Judith" \\set variable sTemp to hold the data "Judith"
int iTemp;
iTemp = 2 + 5;  \\set variable iTemp to hold the sum of 2 + 5
```

4

Java actually has three kinds of variables: data members, class variables, and local variables.

Data members, as you learned yesterday, are used to define attributes, or the state of a particular object. Class variables are similar to data members, except their values apply to all of that class' instances (and to the class itself) rather than having different values for each object.

For example, local variables are declared and used inside method definitions. They can be used for index counters in loops, as temporary variables, or to hold values that you need only inside the method definition itself. They can also be used inside blocks, which you'll learn about later this week. Once the method (or block) finishes executing, the variable definition and its value cease to exist. You'll use local variables to store information needed by a single method and data members to store information needed by multiple methods in the object.

Although all three kinds of variables are declared in much the same way, class variables and data members are accessed and assigned in slightly different ways from local variables. Today, you'll focus on variables as used within method definitions; tomorrow, you'll learn how to work with data members and class variables.

TECHNICAL NOTE

Unlike other languages, Java does not have global variables—that is, variables that are accessible to all parts of a program. Instead, data members and class variables can be used to communicate global information between and among objects. Remember, Java is an object-oriented language, so you should think in terms of objects and how they interact and communicate with one another, rather than in terms of a single program containing subroutines accessing public memory variables.

Declaring Variables

To use any variable in a Java program, you must first declare it. Variable declarations consist of a variable type and a variable name:

```
int iMyAge;
String sMyName;
boolean bIsTired;
```

Variable definitions can be placed anywhere in a method definition (that is, anywhere a regular Java statement can go). They are most commonly declared at the beginning of the definition in which they are being used:

```java
public static void main (String args[])
{
    int iCount;
    String sTitle;
    boolean bIsAsleep;
...
}
```

You can string together variable names with the same type:

```java
int iX, iY, iZ;
String sFirstName, sLastName;
```

You can also give each variable an initial value when you declare it:

```java
int iNumDollars, iNumCentury, iNumCranes = 100;
String sBigCityName = "New York";
boolean bIsTired = true;
int iA= 4, iB = 5, iC = 6;
```

If there are multiple variables on the same line with only one initializer (as in the first line of the previous example), the value (100) applies to only the last variable (iNumCranes) in the declaration. You can also group individual variables and initializers on the same line by using commas, so that each is initialized, as in the preceding example.

Local variables must be given values before they can be used; your Java program will not compile if you try to use an unassigned local variable. For this reason, it's a good idea to always give local variables initial values. Data member and class variable definitions do not have this restriction. (Their initial value depends on the variable type: null for instances of classes, 0 for numeric variables, '\0' for characters, and false for Booleans.)

Notes on Variable Names

Variable names in Java can start with a letter, an underscore (_), or a dollar sign ($). They cannot start with a number. After the first character, your variable names can include any letter or number. Symbols, such as %, *, @, and so on, are often reserved for operators in Java, so be careful when using symbols in variable names.

TECHNICAL NOTE

It is very important to understand that the preceding naming convention applies to all identifiers, which includes variables (int, String, and so on), and to method names (MyMethod(), YourMethod()).

4

In addition, the Java language uses the Unicode character set. Unicode is a character set definition that not only offers characters in the standard ASCII character set, but also several million other characters for representing most international alphabets. This means that you can use accented characters and other glyphs as legal characters in variable names, as long as they have a Unicode character number above 00C0, which is ASCII character 130.

WARNING

The Unicode specification is a two volume set that lists thousands of characters. If you don't understand Unicode, or don't think you have a use for it, it's safest just to use plain numbers and letters in your variable names. You'll learn a little more about Unicode later.

Finally, note that the Java language is case-sensitive, which means that uppercase letters are different from lowercase letters. This means that the variable X is different from the variable x, and a rose is not a Rose is not a ROSE. Keep this in mind as you write your own Java programs and as you read Java code other people have written.

By convention, Java variables have meaningful names, often made up of several words combined. The first word is lowercase, but all following words have an initial uppercase letter:

```
Button btnTheButton;
long lReallyBigNumber;
boolean bCurrentWeatherStateOfPlanetXShortVersion;
```

Variable Types

In addition to the variable name, each variable declaration must have a type, which defines what values that variable can hold. The variable type can be one of three things:

- ☐ One of the eight basic primitive data types
- ☐ The name of a class or interface
- ☐ An array

You'll learn about how to declare and use array variables on Day 6.

The eight primitive data types handle common types for integers, floating-point numbers, characters, and Boolean values (true or false). They're called primitive because they're built into the system and are not actual objects, which makes them more efficient to use. Note that these data types are machine-independent, which means that you can rely on their sizes and characteristics to be consistent, regardless of the computer on which your Java program is running.

There are four Java integer types, each with a different range of values. (See Table 4.1.) All are signed, which means they can hold either positive or negative numbers. Which type you choose for your variables depends on the range of values you expect that variable to hold. Be careful though when declaring integers: if a value becomes too big for the variable type, the value is truncated without warning, and more than likely producing runtime errors in your program. This doesn't mean though to declare all your integers as long!

Table 4.1. Integer types.

Type	Size	Range
byte	8 bits	−128 to 127
short	16 bits	−32,768 to 32,767
int	32 bits	−2,147,483,648 to 2,147,483,647
long	64 bits	−9,223,372,036,854,775,808 to 9,223,372,036,854,775,807

Floating-point numbers are used for numbers with a decimal part. Java floating-point numbers are compliant with IEEE 754 (an international standard for defining floating-point numbers and arithmetic). There are two floating-point types: float (32-bits, single-precision) and double (64-bits, double-precision).

The char type is used for individual characters. Because Java uses the Unicode character set, the char type has 16-bits of precision, unsigned.

Finally, the boolean type can have one of two values, true or false. Note that, unlike in other C-like languages, boolean is neither evaluated to the numbers 0 and 1, nor is it treated as one. All tests of Boolean variables should test for true or false.

NOTE

To anyone not familiar with object-oriented programming, this next little piece might seem quite confusing. After reading it, you might even turn back a page or two and say, "Hey, didn't I declare String sLastName as type String; how can String be a class too? How does Java know which is which?" On Day 5, "Working with Objects," we'll go deeply into objects and classes. You might want to re-read this little piece a few times and mark it, so after Day 5 you can refer to it.

4

In addition to the eight basic data types, variables in Java can also be declared to hold an instance of a particular class:

```
String sLastName;
Font fntBasicFont;
OvalShape ovlMyOval;
```

Each of these variables can then hold only instances of the given class. As you create new classes, you can declare variables to hold instances of those classes (and their subclasses) as well.

TECHNICAL NOTE

Java does not have a typedef statement (as in C and C++). To declare new types in Java, you declare a new class; then variables can be declared to be of that class' type.

Assigning Values to Variables

Once a variable has been declared, you can assign a value to that variable by using the assignment operator =:

```
iSize = 14;
bTooMuchCaffiene = true;
```

4

One Last Thing

As all good programmers know (or eventually find out), one of the most important aspects to writing good code is to use a naming convention for your variables. Naming your variables using some meaningful convention makes your code easier to read and, most importantly, easier to maintain.

There are many theories and concepts for defining a standard naming convention. One widely used naming convention is the Hungarian convention that is most often found in C or C++ programs. When using a strict Hungarian naming convention, you can look at any variable and know everything about the variable: where the variable was initiated, its data type, what data the variable holds, and so on. Some development environments, on the other hand, suggest their own take-off from strict Hungarian: Visual Basic being one example.

In order to stick with the "spirit" of Java, we suggest using a rather simple naming convention. It states:

☐ Prefix all variables with an identifier for the type of variable.

☐ For a multiword variable, capitalize the first letter of each word.

That's it (except for a few more suggestions later on). By following a few simple principles, you will most likely find your code easy to read and maintain, but also very easy to write, because you don't have to remember a complicated naming convention.

The following are some examples of naming conventions for the primitive data types, as well as for three of the Java class libraries that you'll find used in this book:

Type	Prefix	Definition	Notes
byte	si	byte siCount;	Similar to C++ Short Int
short	w	short wCount;	Similar to C++ WORD
int	i	int iCount;	
long	l	long lCount;	
float	f	float fCount;	
double	d	double dCount;	
char	c	char cItem;	
Font	fnt	Font fntBasic;	
OvalShape	ovl	OvalShape ovlMyShape;	
String	s	String sName;	

Comments

Java has three kinds of comments. /*and */surround multiline comments, as in C or C++. All text between the two delimiters is ignored:

```
/* I don't know how I wrote this next part; I was working
   really late one night and it just sort of appeared. I
   suspect the code elves did it for me. It might be wise
   not to try and change it.
*/
```

These comments cannot be nested; that is, you cannot have a comment inside a comment.

Double-slashes (//) can be used for a single line of comment that is also borrowed from C++. All the text up to the end of the line is ignored:

```
int iVices = 7; // are there really only 7 vices?
```

The final type of comment begins with /** and ends with */. The contents of these special comments are used by the javadoc system, but are otherwise used identically to the first type of comment. Javadoc is used to generate API documentation from the code. You won't learn about javadoc in this book; you can find out more information about it from the documentation that came with Sun's Java Developer's Kit or from Sun's Java home page (http://java.sun.com).

Literals

Literals are used to indicate simple values in your Java programs.

 Literal is a programming language term, which essentially means that what you type is what you get. For example, if you type 4 in a Java program, you automatically get an integer with the value 4. If you type 'a', you get a character with the value a.

Literals might seem intuitive most of the time, but there are some special literals in Java that are used for different kinds of numbers, characters, strings, and Boolean values.

Number Literals

There are several integer literals. 4, for example, is a decimal integer literal of type int. (Although you can assign it to a variable of type byte or short because it's small enough to fit into those types.) A decimal integer literal larger than an int is automatically of type long. You also can force a smaller number to a long by appending an L or ⌐ to that number. For example, 4L is a long integer of value 4. Negative integers are preceded by a minus sign—for example, -45.

Integers can also be expressed as octal or hexadecimal: a leading 0 indicates that a number is octal—for example, 0777 or 0004. A leading 0x (or 0X) means that it is in hex (0xFF, 0XAF45). Hexadecimal numbers can contain regular digits (0–9) or uppercase or lowercase hex digits (a–f or A–F).

Octal is base 8, meaning the only valid digits are 0-7.

Hexadecimal is base 16, which uses all the digits 0-9 and the letters A-F to represent values.

Floating-point literals usually have two parts: the integer part and the decimal part—for example, .5677777. Floating-point literals result in a floating-point number of type double, regardless of the precision of that number. You can force the number to the type float by appending the letter f (or F) to that number, for example, 2.56F.

You can use exponents in floating-point literals using the letter e or E, followed by the exponent (which can be a negative number): 10e45 or .36E-2.

Boolean Literals

Boolean literals consist of the keywords true and false. These keywords can be used anywhere you need to test a positive or negative state, or to declare the only possible value for a Boolean variable, for example, bYes=true.

Character Literals

Character literals are expressed by a single character surrounded by single quotes: 'a', '#', '3', and so on. Characters are stored as 16-bit Unicode characters. Table 4.2 lists the special codes that can represent non-printable characters, as well as characters from the Unicode character set. The letter d in the octal, hex, and Unicode escapes represents a number or a hexadecimal digit (a–f or A–F).

Table 4.2. Character escape codes.

Escape	Meaning
\n	Newline
\t	Tab
\b	Backspace
\r	Carriage return
\f	Formfeed
\\	Backslash
\'	Single quote
\"	Double quote
\ddd	Octal
\xdd	Hexadecimal
\udddd	Unicode character

TECHNICAL NOTE

C and C++ programmers should note that Java does not include character codes for \a (bell) or \v (vertical tab).

String Literals

A combination of characters is a string. Strings in Java are instances of the class String. Strings are not simple arrays of characters as they are in C or C++, although they do have many array-like characteristics. For example, you can test their length and access and change individual characters. Because string objects are real objects in Java, they have methods that enable you to combine, test, and modify strings very easily.

String literals consist of a series of characters inside double quotes:

```
"Hi, I'm a string literal."
"I like Visual J++"
""
```

Note that the last string listed in the preceding code is an empty string. This is a perfectly legal string in Visual J++.

Strings can contain character constants such as Newline, tab, and Unicode characters:

```
"A string with a \t tab in it"
"Nested strings are \"strings inside of\" other strings"
"This string brought to you by Java\u2122"
```

In the last example, the Unicode code sequence for \u2122 produces a trademark symbol (™).

NOTE

> Just because you can represent a character using a Unicode escape sequence in your program, doesn't mean your computer can display that character. The computer or operating system you or someone else is running might not support Unicode, or the font you're using might not have a glyph (picture) for that character. Unicode escape code support in Java provides only the means to encode special characters. The system your program runs on must provide the support for Unicode.

When you use a string literal in your Java program, Java automatically creates an instance of the class `String` for you with the value you give it. Strings are unusual in this respect; the other literals do not behave in this way (none of the primitive base types are actual objects), and creating a new object usually involves explicitly creating a new instance of a class. You'll learn more about strings, the `String` class, and the things you can do with strings later today and tomorrow.

Expressions and Operators

Expressions are the simplest form of statement in Java that actually accomplish something.

Expressions are statements that return a value.

Operators are special symbols that are commonly used in expressions.

Arithmetic and tests for equality and magnitude are common examples of expressions. Because they return a value, you can assign that result to a variable or test that value in other Java statements.

Operators in Java include arithmetic, various forms of assignment, increment and decrement, and logical operations. This section describes all these things.

Arithmetic

Java has five operators for basic arithmetic. (See Table 4.3.)

Table 4.3. Arithmetic operators.

Operator	Meaning	Example
+	Addition	3 + 4
–	Subtraction	5 – 7
*	Multiplication	5 * 5
/	Division	14 / 7
%	Modulus	20 % 7

Each operator takes two operands, one on either side of the operator. The subtraction operator (–) can also be used to negate a single operand.

Integer division results in an integer. Because integers don't have decimal fractions, any remainder is ignored. The expression 31 / 9, for example, results in 3 (9 goes into 31 only 3 times).

Modulus (%) gives the remainder once the operands have been evenly divided. For example, 31 % 9 results in 4 because 9 goes into 31 three times, with 4 left over.

Note that, for integers, the result type of most operations is an int, regardless of the original type of the operands. If either (or both) operands is of type long, the result is of type long. If one operand is an integer and another is a floating-point number, the result is a floating-point. (If you're interested in the details of how Java promotes and converts numeric types from one type to another, you might want to check out the Java Language Specification at Sun's official Java Web site; we're not going to cover that much detail here.)

Listing 4.1 is an example of simple arithmetic.

TYPE   **Listing 4.1. Simple arithmetic.**

```
1: class ArithmeticTest
2: {
3:     public static void main (String args[])
4:     {
5:         short siX = 6;
```

```
 6:        int iY = 4;
 7:        float fA = 12.5f;
 8:        float fB = 7f;
 9:
10:        System.out.println("x is " + siX + ", y is " + iY);
11:        System.out.println("x + y = " + (siX + iY));
12:        System.out.println("x - y = " + (siX - iY));
13:        System.out.println("x / y = " + (siX / iY));
14:        System.out.println("x % y = " + (siX % iY));
15:
16:        System.out.println("a is " + fA + ", b is " + fB;
17:        System.out.println("a / b = " + (fA / fB));
18:    }
19:
20: }
```

The following is a listing of the output that you would receive if you ran the preceding program using JVIEW:

```
x is 6, y is 4
x + y = 10
x - y = 2
x / y = 1
x % y = 2
a is 12.5, b is 7
a / b = 1.78571
```

ANALYSIS In this simple Java application (note the main() method), you initially define four variables in lines 3 through 6: siX and iY, which are integers (type int), and fA and fB, which are floating-point numbers (type float). Keep in mind that the default type for floating-point literals (such as 12.5) is double, so to make sure these are numbers of type float, you have to use an f after each one (lines 5 and 6).

The remainder of the program merely does some math with integers and floating-point numbers and prints out the results.

There is one other thing to mention about this program: the method System.out.println(). You've seen this method on previous days, but you haven't really learned exactly what it does. The System.out.println() method merely prints a message to the standard output of your system—to the screen, to a special window, or maybe just to a special log file, depending on your system and the development environment you're running. The System.out.println() method takes a single argument—a string—but you can use + to concatenate values into a string, as you'll learn later today.

More About Assignment

Variable assignment is a form of expression; in fact, because one assignment expression results in a value, you can string them together like this:

```
iX = iY = iZ = 0;
```

In this example, all three variables now have the value 0.

The right side of an assignment expression is always evaluated before the assignment takes place. This means that expressions such as x = x + 2 do the right thing; 2 is added to the value of x, and then that new value is reassigned to x. In fact, this sort of operation is so common that Java has several operators to do a shorthand version of this, borrowed from C and C++. Table 4.4 shows these shorthand assignment operators.

Table 4.4. Assignment operators.

Expression	Meaning
x += y	x = x + y
x --= y	x = x − y
x *= y	x = x * y
x /= y	x = x / y

Incrementing and Decrementing

As in C and C++, the ++ and -- operators are used to increment or decrement a value by 1. For example, x++ increments the value of x by 1 just as if you had used the expression x = x + 1. Similarly, x-- decrements the value of x by 1. (Unlike C and C++, Java allows x to be floating point.)

These increment and decrement operators can be prefixed or postfixed; that is, the ++ or -- can appear before or after the value it increments or decrements. For simple increment or decrement expressions, which one you use isn't overly important. In complex assignments, in which you are assigning the result of an increment or decrement expression, which one you use does make a difference.

Take, for example, the following two expressions:

```
y = x++;
y = ++x;
```

These two expressions give very different results because of the difference between prefix and postfix. When you use postfix operators (x++ or x--), y gets the value of x before x is changed;

using prefix, the value of x is assigned to y after the change has occurred. Listing 4.2 is a Java example of how all this works.

TYPE **Listing 4.2. Test of prefix and postfix increment operators.**

```
1: class PrePostFixTest
2: {
3:
4:     public static void main (String args[])
5:     {
6:        int ix = 0;
7:        int iy = 0;
8:
9:        System.out.println("x and y are " + ix + " and " + iy );
10:       ix++;
11:       System.out.println("x++ results in " + ix);
12:       ++x;
13:       System.out.println("++x results in " + ix);
14:       System.out.println("Resetting x back to 0.");
15:       ix = 0;
16:       System.out.println("------");
17:       iy = ix++;
18:       System.out.println("y = x++ (postfix) results in:");
19:       System.out.println("x is " + ix);
20:       System.out.println("y is " + iy);
21:       System.out.println("------");
22:
23:       y = ++x;
24:       System.out.println("y = ++x (prefix) results in:");
25:       System.out.println("x is " + ix);
26:       System.out.println("y is " + iy);
27:       System.out.println("------");
28:
29:    }
30:
31: }
```

The following is the output from the preceding program:

```
x and y are 0 and 0
x++ results in 1
++x results in 2
Resetting x back to 0.
------
y = x++ (postfix) results in:
x is 1
y is 0
------
y = ++x (prefix) results in:
x is 2
y is 2
------
```

In the first part of this example, you increment ix alone using both prefix and postfix increment operators. In each, ix is incremented by 1 each time. In this simple form, using either prefix or postfix works the same way.

In the second part of this example, you use the expression iy = ix++, in which the postfix increment operator is used. In this result, the value of ix is incremented *after* that value is assigned to iy. Hence the result: iy is assigned the original value of ix (0), and then ix is incremented by 1.

In the third part, you use the prefix expression iy = ++ix. Here, the reverse occurs: ix is incremented before its value is assigned to iy. Because ix is 1 from the previous step, its value is incremented (to 2), and then that value is assigned to iy. Both ix and iy end up being 2.

TECHNICAL NOTE

Technically, this description is not entirely correct. In reality, Java *always* completely evaluates all expressions on the right of an expression before assigning that value to a variable, so the concept of "assigning ix to iy before ix is incremented" isn't precisely right. Instead, Java takes the value of ix and "remembers" it, evaluates (increments) ix, and *then* assigns the original value of ix to iy. Although in most simple cases this distinction might not be important, for more complex expressions with side effects it might change the behavior of the expression overall. See the Language Specification for more detailed information for expression evaluation in Java.

Comparisons

Java has several expressions for testing equality and magnitude. All of these expressions return a Boolean value, either true or false. Table 4.5 shows the comparison operators:

Table 4.5. Comparison operators.

Operator	Meaning	Example
==	Equal	x == 3
!=	Not equal	x != 3
<	Less than	x < 3
>	Greater than	x > 3
<=	Less than or equal to	x <= 3
>=	Greater than or equal to	x >= 3

Logical Operators

Expressions that result in Boolean values (for example, the comparison operators) can be combined by using logical operators that represent the logical combinations AND, OR, XOR, and logical NOT.

For AND combinations, use either the & or &&. The expression will be true only if both expressions are also true; if either expression is false, the entire expression is false. The difference between the two operators is in expression evaluation. Using &, both sides of the expression are evaluated regardless of the outcome. Using &&, if the left side of the expression is false, the entire expression returns false, and the right side of the expression is never evaluated.

For OR expressions, use either ¦ or ¦¦. OR expressions result in true if either or both of the operands is also true; if both operands are false, the expression is false. As with & and &&, the single ¦ evaluates both sides of the expression regardless of the outcome; with ¦¦, if the left expression is true, the expression returns true and the right side is never evaluated.

In addition, there is the XOR operator ^, which returns true only if its operands are different (one true and one false, or vice versa) and false otherwise (even if both are true).

In general, only the && and ¦¦ are commonly used as actual logical combinations. &, ¦, and ^ are more commonly used for bitwise logical operations.

For NOT, use the ! operator with a single expression argument. The value of the NOT expression is the negation of the expression; if x is true, !x is false.

Bitwise Operators

Finally, here's a short summary of the bitwise operators in Java. These are all inherited from C and C++ and are used to perform operations on individual bits in integers. This book does not go into bitwise operations; it's an advanced topic covered better in books on C or C++. Table 4.6 summarizes the bitwise operators.

Table 4.6. Bitwise operators.

Operator	Meaning
&	Bitwise AND
¦	Bitwise OR
^	Bitwise XOR
<<	Left shift
>>	Right shift

continues

Table 4.6. continued

Operator	Meaning
>>>	Zero fill right shift
~	Bitwise complement
<<=	Left shift assignment (x = x << y)
>>=	Right shift assignment (x = x >> y)
>>>=	Zero fill right shift assignment (x = x >>> y)
x&=y	AND assignment (x = x & y)
x¦=y	OR assignment (x + x | y)
x^=y	XOR assignment (x = x ^ y)

Operator Precedence

Operator precedence determines the order in which expressions are evaluated. This, in some cases, can determine the overall value of the expression. For example, take the following expression:

```
y = 6 + 4 / 2;
```

Depending on whether the 6 + 4 expression or the 4 / 2 expression is evaluated first, the value of y can end up being 5 or 8. Operator precedence determines the order in which expressions are evaluated, so you can predict the outcome of an expression. In general, increment and decrement are evaluated before arithmetic, arithmetic expressions are evaluated before comparisons, and comparisons are evaluated before logical expressions. Assignment expressions are evaluated last.

Table 4.7 shows the specific precedence of the various operators in Java. Operators further up in the table are evaluated first; operators on the same line have the same precedence and are evaluated left to right based on how they appear in the expression itself. For example, given that same expression y = 6 + 4 / 2, you now know, according to this table, that division is evaluated before addition, so the value of y will be 8.

Table 4.7. Operator precedence.

Operator	Notes
. [] ()	Parentheses () group expressions; dot (.) is used for access to methods and variables within objects and classes (discussed tomorrow); [] is used for arrays (discussed later on in the week)

Operator	Notes
++ —— ! ~ instanceof	Returns true or false based on whether the object is an instance of the named class or any of that class' superclasses (discussed tomorrow)
new (type)expression	The new operator is used for creating new instances of classes; () in this case is for casting a value to another type (you'll learn about both of these tomorrow)
* / %	Multiplication, division, modulus
+ —	Addition, subtraction
<< >> >>>	Bitwise left and right shift
< > <= >=	Relational comparison tests
== !=	Equality
&	AND
^	XOR
¦	OR
&&	Logical AND
¦¦	Logical OR
? :	Shorthand for if...then...else (Discussed on Day 5)
= += —= *= /= %= ^=	Various assignments
&= ¦= <<= >>= >>>=	

You can always change the order in which expressions are evaluated by using parentheses around the expressions you want to evaluate first. You can nest parentheses to make sure expressions evaluate in the order you want them to, but the innermost parenthetical expression is evaluated first. The following expression results in a value of 5, because the 6 + 4 expression is evaluated first, and then the result of that expression (10) is divided by 2:

```
y = (6 + 4) / 2;
```

Parentheses also can be useful in cases where the precedence of an expression isn't immediately clear. In other words, they can make your code easier to read. Adding parentheses doesn't hurt, so if they help you figure out how expressions are evaluated, go ahead and use them.

String Arithmetic

One special expression in Java is the use of the addition operator (+) to create and concatenate strings. In most of the previous examples shown today and in earlier lessons, you've seen lots of lines that looked something like this:

```
System.out.println(name + " is a " + color " beetle");
```

The output of that line (to the standard output) is a single string, with the values of the variables (name and color) inserted in the appropriate spots in the string. So, what's going on here?

The + operator, when used with strings and other objects, creates a single string that contains the concatenation of all its operands. If any of the operands in a string concatenation is not a string, it is automatically converted to a string, making it easy to create these sorts of output lines.

TECHNICAL NOTE

An object or type can be converted to a String object if you implement the method toString(). All objects have a default string representation, but most classes override toString() to provide a more meaningful printable representation.

String concatenation makes lines such as the previous one especially easy to construct. To create a string, just add all the parts together—the descriptions plus the variables—and output it to the standard output, to the screen, to an applet, or anywhere.

The += operator, which you learned about earlier, also works for strings. For example, take the following expression:

```
sMyName += " Jr.";
```

This expression is equivalent to this:

```
sMyName = sMyName + " Jr.";
```

just as it would be for numbers. In this case, it changes the value of sMyName, which might be something like John Smith having a Jr. at the end—John Smith Jr.

Summary

As you learned in the last two lessons, a Java program is made up primarily of classes and objects. Classes and objects, in turn, are made up of methods and variables, and methods are made up of statements and expressions. It is those last two things that you've learned about today: the basic building blocks that enable you to create classes and methods and build them up to a full-fledged Java program.

Today, you learned about variables, how to declare them and assign values to them; literals for easily creating numbers, characters, and strings; and operators for arithmetic, tests, and other simple operations. With this basic syntax, you can move on tomorrow to learning about working with objects and building simple useful Java programs.

To finish up this summary, Table 4.8 is a list of all the operators you learned about today so that you can refer back to them.

Table 4.8. Operator summary.

Operator	Meaning
+	Addition
—	Subtraction
*	Multiplication
/	Division
%	Modulus
<	Less than
>	Greater than
<=	Less than or equal to
>=	Greater than or equal to
==	Equal
!=	Not equal
&&	Logical AND
¦¦	Logical OR
!	Logical NOT
&	AND

continues

4

Table 4.8. continued

Operator	Meaning
¦	OR
^	XOR
<<	Left shift
>>	Right shift
>>>	Zero fill right shift
~	Complement
=	Assignment
++	Increment
- -	Decrement
+=	Add and assign
— =	Subtract and assign
*=	Multiply and assign
/=	Divide and assign
%=	Modulus and assign
&=	AND and assign
¦=	OR and assign
<<=	Left shift and assign
^=	XOR and assign
>>=	Right shift and assign
>>>=	Zero fill right shift and assign

Q&A

Q I didn't see any way to define constants.

A You can't create local constants in Java; you can create constant instance and class
variables only. You'll learn how to do this tomorrow.

**Q What happens if you assign an integer value to a variable that is too large for
that variable to hold?**

A Logically, you would think that the variable is just converted to the next larger
type, but this isn't what happens. What does happen is called *overflow*. This means

that if a number becomes too big for its variable, that number wraps around to the smallest possible negative number for that type and starts counting upward toward zero again.

Because this can result in some very confusing (and wrong) results, make sure that you declare the right integer type for all your numbers. If there's a chance a number will overflow its type, use the next larger type instead.

Q How can you find out the type of a given variable?

A If you're using the base types (`int`, `float`, `boolean`, and so on), you can't. If you care about the type, you can convert the value to some other type by using casting. (You'll learn about this tomorrow.)

If you're using class types, you can use the `instanceof` operator, which you'll learn more about tomorrow.

Q Why does Java have all these shorthand operators for arithmetic and assignment? It's really hard to read that way.

A The syntax of Java is based on C++, and therefore on C. One of C's implicit goals is the capability of doing very powerful things with a minimum of typing. Because of this, shorthand operators, such as the wide array of assignments, are common.

There's no rule that says you have to use these operators in your own programs, however. If you find your code to be more readable using the long form, no one will come to your house and make you change it.

4

Day 5

Working with Objects

We'll start today's lesson with an obvious statement: Because Java is an object-oriented language, you're going to be dealing with a lot of objects. You'll create them, modify them, move them around, change their variables, call their methods, combine them with other objects—and, of course, develop classes and use your own objects in the mix.

Today, therefore, you'll learn all about the Java object in its natural habitat. Today's topics include

- ☐ Creating instances of classes (objects)
- ☐ Testing and modifying class variables and data members in your new instance
- ☐ Calling methods in that object
- ☐ Casting (converting) objects and other data types from one class to another
- ☐ Other odds and ends about working with objects
- ☐ An overview of the Java class libraries

Creating New Objects

When you write a VJ++ program, you define a set of classes. As you learned on Day 3, "Object-Oriented Programming and Java," classes are templates for objects; for the most part, you merely use the class to create instances and then work with those instances. In this section, therefore, you'll learn how to create a new object from any given class.

Remember strings from yesterday? You learned that using a string literal—a series of characters enclosed in double-quotes—creates a new instance of the class String with the value of that string.

The String class is unusual in that respect—although it's a class, there's an easy way to create instances of that class using a literal. The other classes don't have that shortcut; to create instances of other classes you have to create them by using the new operator.

NOTE

> What about the literals for numbers and characters? Don't they create objects, too? Actually, they don't. Even though the primitive data types for numbers and characters create numbers and characters, for reasons of efficiency, they aren't actually objects. If you need to treat them like objects, you can put object-wrappers around them. (You'll learn how to do this later.)

Using new

To create a new object, you use new with the name of the class you want to create an instance of and then parentheses after that:

```
String str = new String();
Random r = new Random();
Motorcycle m2 = new Motorcycle();
Motorcycle m3;
m3 = new Motorcycle();
```

NOTE

> Notice how m2 and m3 are both instances of the class Motorcycle.

The parentheses are important; don't leave them off. The parentheses can be empty, in which case the most simple, basic object is created; or the parentheses can contain arguments that determine the initial values of data members or other initial qualities of that object. The number and type of arguments you can use with new are defined by the class itself by using a special method called a constructor; you'll learn about how to create constructors in your own classes later in the week.

WARNING

> Some classes might not allow you to create instances without any arguments. This is dependent on whether or not there is a constructor that accepts no parameters. You will learn later on how to check a class to make sure you are performing a valid initialization of an object.

For example, take the Date class, which creates date objects. Listing 5.1 is a Java application that shows three different ways of creating a Date object using new. You can test this program yourself. Create a new Project Workspace named CreateDates; open a new text file; type in the code; save it as CreateDates; insert it into your application; and then build and execute it using JVIEW.

TYPE | **Listing 5.1. Colleen's Date program.**

```
1: import java.util.Date;
2:
3: class CreateDates
4: {
5:
6:     public static void main(String args[])
7:     {
8:         Date d1, d2, d3;
9:
10:        d1 = new Date();
11:        System.out.println("Date 1: " + d1);
12:
13:         d2 = new Date(70, 9, 16, 8, 30);
14:         System.out.println("Date 2: " + d2);
15:
16          d3 = new Date("June 5 1959 3:24 PM");
17:         System.out.println("Date 3: " + d3);
18:     }
19: }
```

The preceding application produces the following output.

```
Date 1: Tue Feb 13 09:36:56 PST 1996
Date 2: Wed Sep 16 08:30:00 PDT 1970
Date 3: Fri Jun 05 15:24:00 PST 1959
```

5

In the preceding example, three different dates are created by using different arguments to new. The first instance (line 8) uses new with no arguments, which creates a Date object for today's date, as the first line of the output shows.

The second Date object you create in this example has five integer arguments. The arguments represent a date: year, month, day, hours, and seconds. And, as the output shows, this creates a Date object for that particular date: Wednesday, September 16, 1970, at 8:30 AM.

The third version of Date takes one argument, a string, representing the date as a text string. When the Date object is created, that string is parsed, and a Date object with that date and time is created. (See the third line of output.) The date string can take many different formats; see the JDK documentation for the Date class (part of the java.util package) for information about what strings you can use.

What new Does

What does new do? When you use the new operator, several things happen: First, the new instance of the given class is created, and memory is allocated for it. In addition (and most importantly), when the new object is created, a special method defined in the given class is called. This special method is called a constructor.

NEW TERM *Constructors* are special methods for creating and initializing new instances of classes. Constructors initialize the new object and its variables, create any other objects the object needs, and generally perform any other operations the object needs to initialize itself.

Multiple constructor definitions in a class can each have a different number or type of argument; then, when you use new, you can specify different arguments in the argument list, and the right constructor for those arguments will be called. That's how each of those Date objects returned the same date output even though they were supplied different input.

When you create your own classes, you can define as many constructors as you need to implement that class' behavior. This is an example of function overloading. You'll learn how to create constructors on Day 7, "Creating Classes and Applications in Java."

A Note on Memory Management

Memory management in Java is dynamic and automatic. When you create a new object in Java, Java automatically allocates the right amount of memory for that object in the heap. You don't have to allocate any memory for any objects explicitly; Java does it for you.

What happens when you're finished with that object? How do you de-allocate the memory that object uses? The answer is, again: Memory management is automatic. Once you finish with an object, that object no longer has any live references to it. It won't be assigned to any variables you're still using or stored in any arrays. Java has a garbage collector that looks for unused objects and reclaims the memory that those objects are using. You don't have to do any explicit freeing of memory; you just have to make sure you're not still holding onto an object you want to get rid of. You'll learn more specific details about the Java garbage collector and how it works on Day 21, "Integrating Applets and ActiveX Controls with Scripting."

Accessing and Setting Class Variables and Data Members

Now you have your very own object, and that object might have class variables or data members defined in it. How do you work with those variables? Easy! Class variables and data members behave in exactly the same ways as the local variables you learned about yesterday; you just refer to them in a slightly different way than you do regular variables in your code.

Getting Values

To get to the value of a data member, you use dot notation.

With *dot notation*, a data member or class variable name has two parts: the object on the left side of the dot and the variable on the right side of the dot.

For example, if you have an object assigned to the variable myObject, and that object has a variable called m_var, you refer to that variable's value like this:

```
myObject.m_var;
```

This form for accessing variables is an expression (it returns a value), and both sides of the dot are also expressions. This means that you can nest data member access. If that m_var data member itself holds an object, and that object has its own data member called m_bState, you can refer to it like this:

```
myObject.m_var.m_bState;
```

Dot expressions are evaluated left to right, so you start with myObject's variable m_var, which points to another object with the variable m_bState. You end up with the value of that state variable.

NOTE

If you refer back to Table 4.7 (in yesterday's lesson) you'll also see that dot expressions are evaluated at the highest level of operator precedence.

5

Changing Values

Assigning a value to that variable is equally easy—just tack an assignment operator on the right side of the expression:

```
myObject.m_var.m_bState = true;
```

Listing 5.2 is an example of a program that tests and modifies the data members in a Point object. Point is part of the java.awt package and refers to a coordinate point with an x and a y value. The following is another Java application you can experiment with and test using JVIEW.

TYPE   **Listing 5.2. The TestPoint class.**

```
 1: import java.awt.Point;
 2:
 3: class TestPoint
 4: {
 5:
 6:     public static void main(String args[])
 7:     {
 8:         Point pntPoint = new Point(10,10);
 9:
10:         System.out.println("X is " + pntPoint.x);
11:         System.out.println("Y is " + pntPoint.y);
12:
13:         System.out.println("Setting X to 5.");
14:         pntPoint.x = 5;
15:         System.out.println("Setting Y to 15.");
16:         pntPoint.y = 15;
17:
18:         System.out.println("X is " + pntPoint.x);
19:         System.out.println("Y is " + pntPoint.y);
20:
21:     }
22: }
```

The preceding application produces the following output.

```
X is 10
Y is 10
Setting X to 5.
Setting Y to 15.
X is 5
Y is 15
```

ANALYSIS   In this example, you first create an instance of Point where X and Y are both 10. (See line 8.) Lines 10 and 11 print out those individual values, and you can see dot notation at work there. Lines 13 through 16 change the values of those variables to 5 and 15, respectively. Finally, lines 18 and 19 print out the values of X and Y again to show how they've changed.

Class Variables

Class variables, as you learned before, are variables that are defined and stored in the class itself. Their values, therefore, apply to the class and to all its instances.

With data members, each new instance of the class gets a new copy of the data members that the class defines. Each instance can then change the values of its data members without affecting any other object's data members. With class variables, there is only one copy of that variable. Every instance of the class has access to that variable, but there is only one value. Changing the value of that variable changes it for all the instances of that class.

You define class variables by including the static keyword before the variable itself. You'll learn more about this on Day 6, "Arrays, Conditionals, and Loops," but, for now, here is an example. Take the following partial class definition:

```
class FamilyMember
{
    static String c_sSurname = "Johnson";
    String m_sName;
    int m_iAge;
    ...
}
```

Instances of the class FamilyMember each have their own values for m_sName and m_iAge. But the class variable c_sSurname has only one value for all family members. Change c_sSurname, and all the instances of FamilyMember are affected.

To access class variables, you use the same dot notation as you do with data members. To get or change the value of the class variable, you can use either the instance or the name of the class on the left side of the dot. Both the lines of output in this example print the same value:

```
FamilyMember dad = new FamilyMember()
System.out.println("Family's surname is: " + dad.surname);
System.out.println("Family's surname is: " + FamilyMember.surname);
```

Because you can use an instance to change the value of a class variable, it's easy to become confused about class variables and where their values are coming from. (Remember, the value of a class variable affects all the instances.) For this reason, it's a good idea to use the name of the class when you refer to a class variable—it makes your code easier to read and strange results easier to debug.

NOTE

If you think back to yesterday when we talked about variables and how you name them, you will recall that we suggested a rather simple convention: sVar for Strings, iVar for int, and so on and so forth. Today, if you look at the code examples, you probably will notice that we have added two new prefixes to the code examples. These are m_ and c_. These two new prefixes are used for data members (m_) and class variables (c_). By using these two prefixes along with the variable type prefixes (from yesterday), it should be rather easy to look at a variable and be able to tell what data type the variable is and whether the variable is a data member, class variable, or local variable.

Calling Methods

Calling a method in objects is similar to referring to its data members: method calls also use dot notation. The object whose method you're calling is on the left side of the dot; the name of the method and its arguments is on the right side of the dot:

```
myObject.methodOne(arg1, arg2, arg3);
```

Note that all methods must have parentheses after them, even if that method takes no arguments:

```
myObject.methodNoArgs();
```

If the method you've called results in an object that itself has methods, you can nest methods as you would variables:

NOTE

It is important to be careful when nesting methods and variables. Too many levels of nesting make for very complicated and hard-to-maintain code.

```
myObject.getClass().getName();
```

You can combine nested method calls and data member references as well:

```
myObject.m_var.methodTwo(arg1, arg2);
```

System.out.println(), the method you've been using all through the book thus far, is a great example of nesting variables and methods. The System class (part of the java.lang package) describes system-specific behavior. System.out is a class variable that contains an instance of the class PrintStream that points to the standard output of the system. PrintStream instances have a println() method that prints a string to that output stream.

Listing 5.3 shows an example of calling some methods defined in the String class. Strings include methods for string tests and modification, similar to what you would expect in a string library in other languages. The following is another Java application you can experiment with and test using JVIEW.

TYPE | **Listing 5.3. Several uses of string methods.**

```
 1: class TestString
 2: {
 3:
 4:     public static void main(String args[])
 5:     {
 6:         String sStr = "Now is the winter of our discontent";
 7:
 8:         System.out.println("The string is: " + sStr);
 9:         System.out.println("Length of this string: "
10:                 + sStr.length());
11:         System.out.println("The character at position 5: "
12:                 + sStr.charAt(5));
13:         System.out.println("The substring from 11 to 17: "
14:                 + sStr.substring(11, 17));
15:         System.out.println("The index of the character d: "
16:                 + sStr.indexOf('d'));
17:         System.out.print("The index of the beginning of the ");
18:         System.out.println("substring \"winter\":"
19:                 + sStr.indexOf("winter"));
20:         System.out.println("The string in upper case: "
21:                 + sStr.toUpperCase());
22:     }
23: }
```

The preceding application produces the following output.

```
The string is: Now is the winter of our discontent
Length of this string: 35
The character at position 5: s
The substring from positions 11 to 17: winter
The index of the character d: 25
The index of the beginning of the substring "winter": 11
The string in upper case: NOW IS THE WINTER OF OUR DISCONTENT
```

ANALYSIS In line 6, you create a new instance of String by using a string literal. It's easier than using new and then putting the characters in individually. The remainder of the program simply calls different string methods to do different operations on that string:

- ☐ Line 8 prints the value of the string created in line 4: "Now is the winter of our discontent".

- ☐ Line 9 calls the length() method in the new String object. This string has 35 characters.

☐ Line 11 calls the charAt() method, which returns the character at the given position in the string. Note that string positions start at 0, so the character at position 5 is s.

☐ Line 13 calls the substring() method, which takes two integers indicating a range and returns the substring at those starting and ending points. The substring() method can also be called with only one argument, which returns the substring from that position to the end of the string.

☐ Line 15 calls the indexOf() method, which returns the position of the first instance of the given character (here, 'd').

☐ Line 17 shows a different use of the indexOf() method, which takes a string argument and returns the index of the beginning of that string. Notice also that print() is used instead of println(). Whereas println() causes a carriage return and line feed, print() does not.

☐ Finally, line 20 uses the toUpperCase() method to return a copy of the string in all uppercase.

Class Methods

Class methods, like class variables, apply to the class as a whole and not to its instances. Class methods are commonly used for general utility methods that might not operate directly on an instance of that class, but fit with that class conceptually. For example, the String class contains a class method called valueOf(), which can take one of many different types of arguments, such as integers, Booleans, other objects, and so on. The valueOf() method then returns a new instance of String containing the string value of the argument it was given. This method doesn't operate directly on an existing instance of String, but getting a string from another object or data type is definitely a String-like operation and it makes sense to define it in the String class.

Class methods can also be useful for gathering general methods together in one place (the class). For example, the Math class, defined in the java.lang package, contains a large set of mathematical operations as class methods—there are no instances of the class Math, but you can still use its methods with numeric or Boolean arguments.

To call a class method, use dot notation as you do with instance methods. As with class variables, you can use either an instance of the class or the class itself on the left site of the dot. However, for the same reasons noted in the discussion on class variables, using the name of the class for class variables makes your code easier to read. The last two lines in this example produce the same result:

```
String s1, s2;
s1 = "dummy";
s2 = s1.valueOf(5);
s2 = String.valueOf(5);
```

References to Objects

As you work with objects, one important thing going on behind the scenes is the use of references to those objects. When you assign objects to variables, or pass objects as arguments to methods, you are passing references to those objects, not the objects themselves or copies of those objects.

An example should make this clearer. Examine the following snippet of code:

```
import java.awt.Point;

class ReferencesTest
{
    public static void main (String args[])
    {
        Point pnt1, pnt2;
        pnt1 = new Point(100, 100);
        pnt2 = pnt1;

        pnt1.x = 200;
        pnt1.y = 200;
        System.out.println("Point1: " + pnt1.x + ", " + pnt1.y);
        System.out.println("Point2: " + pnt2.x + ", " + pnt2.y);
    }
}
```

In this program, you declare two variables of type Point, and assign a new Point object to pnt1. Then you assign the value of pnt1 to pnt2.

Now, here's the challenge. After changing pnt1's x and y data members, what will pnt2 look like?

Here's the output of that program:

```
Point1: 200, 200
Point2: 200, 200
```

As you can see, pnt2 was also changed. When you assign the value of pnt1 to pnt2, you actually create a reference from pnt2 to the same object that pnt1 refers. Change the object that pnt2 refers to, and you also change the object that pnt1 points to, because both are references to the same object.

The fact that VJ++ uses references becomes particularly important when you pass arguments to methods. You'll learn more about this later on today, but keep these references in mind.

5

TECHNICAL NOTE

There are no explicit pointers or pointer arithmetic in Java—just references. However, with these references, and with Java arrays, you have most of the capabilities that you have with pointers, without the confusion and lurking bugs that explicit pointers can create.

Casting and Converting Objects and Primitive Types

Sometimes in your Java programs you might have a value stored somewhere that is not the data type that you want. Maybe it's an instance of the wrong class, or perhaps it's a `float` and you want it to be an `int`. To convert the value of one type to another, you use a mechanism called casting.

NEW TERM   *Casting* is a mechanism of converting the value of an object or primitive data type into another object or primitive data type. The result of a cast is a new reference or value. This is also commonly referred to as typecasting.

NOTE

Casting doesn't affect the original object or value.

Although the concept of casting is a simple one, in Java, the rules for what types can be converted to what other types are complicated by the fact that Java has both primitive types (`int`, `float`, `boolean`), and object types (`String`, `Point`, `Window`, and so on). There are three forms of casts and conversions to talk about in this section:

- ☐ Casting between primitive types: `int` to `float` to `boolean`
- ☐ Casting between object types: an instance of a class to an instance of another class
- ☐ Converting primitive types to objects and then extracting primitive values back out of those objects

Casting Primitive Types

Casting between primitive types enables you to "convert" the value of one type to another primitive type—for example, to assign a number of one type to a variable of another type. Casting between primitive types most commonly occurs with numeric types.

> Boolean values cannot be cast to any other primitive type.

Often, if the type you are casting to is "larger" than the type of the value you're converting, you might not have to use an explicit cast. You can often automatically treat a byte or a character as an int, for example, or an int as a long, an int as a float, or anything as a double. In most cases, because the larger type provides more precision than the smaller, no loss of information occurs when the value is cast. The exception is casting integers to floating-point values; casting an int or a long to a float, or a long to a double might cause some loss of precision.

To convert a large value to smaller type, you must use an explicit cast, because converting that value might result in a loss of precision. Explicit casts look like this:

```
(typename) value
```

In this form, *typename* is the name of the type you're converting to (for example: short, int, float, boolean), and *value* is the expression that you want to convert. The following example divides the values of x by the value of y and casts the result to an iTemp that is declared as an int:

```
int iTemp = (int) (x / y);
```

Note that because the precedence of casting is higher than that of arithmetic, you have to use parentheses so that the result of the division is what gets cast to iTemp.

The following is another example of simple primitive casting:

```
...
    long lVar = 4543;
    int ivar = (int) lVar;
...
```

In this example, the long value of 4543 is converted to an integer value of the same 4543. As you can see, casting primitives is fairly straightforward.

Casting Objects

Instances of classes can also be cast to instances of other classes, with one restriction: The class of the object you're casting and the class you're casting it to must be related by inheritance; that is, you can cast an object only to an instance of its class' sub—or superclass—not to any random class.

Analogous to converting a primitive value to a larger type, some objects might not need to be cast explicitly. In particular, because subclasses contain all the information in the superclass, you can use an instance of a subclass anywhere a superclass is expected. Suppose you have a method that takes two arguments: one of type Object, and one of type Number. You don't have to pass instances of those particular classes to that method. For the Object argument, you can pass any subclass of Object (any object, in other words), and for the Number argument you can pass in any instance of any subclass of Number (Integer, bcolean, Float, and so on).

Casting an object to an instance of one of that object's superclasses loses the information the original subclass provided and requires a specific cast. To cast an object to another class, you use the same casting operation that you used for base types:

```
(classname) object
```

In this case, *classname* is the name of the class you want to cast the object to, and *object* is a reference to the object you're casting (the original). Note that casting creates a reference to the old object of the type classname; the old object still continues to exist as it did before.

Here's an (fictitious) example of a cast of an instance of the class GreenApple to an instance of the class Apple (where GreenApple is theoretically a subclass of Apple):

```
GreenApple a;
Apple a2;
a = new GreenApple();
a2 = (Apple) a;
```

In addition to casting objects to classes, you can also cast objects to interfaces—but only if that object's class or one of its superclasses actually implements that interface. Casting an object to an interface then enables you to call one of that interface's methods even if that object's class does not directly implement that interface. You'll learn more about interfaces in Week 3.

Converting Primitive Types to Objects and Vice Versa

Now you know how to cast a primitive type to another primitive type and how to cast between classes. How can you cast one to the other?

You can't! Primitive types and objects are very different things in Java and you can't automatically cast or convert between the two. However, the java.lang package includes several special classes that correspond to each primitive data type: Integer for ints, Float for floats, Boolean for booleans, and so on.

Using class methods defined in these classes, you can create an object equivalent for all the primitive types using new. The following line of code creates an instance of the Integer class with the value 35:

```
Integer intTemp = new Integer(35);
```

NOTE Notice that the new variable prefix int is created here. This is used so you can instantly tell that intTemp is an object of data type integer.

Now that you have a primitive-type object (intTemp), you can treat it exactly as any other object variable: For example, you can call any Java function that requires a parameter of type object. Then, when you want the primitive values back again, there are methods for that as well—for example, the intValue() method extracts an int primitive value from an Integer object:

```
int iInt = intTemp.intValue();  // returns 35
```

See the VJ++ Books Online for detailed information on these special classes and for specifics on the methods for converting primitives to and from objects.

Odds and Ends

This section is a catchall for other information about working with objects, in particular:

☐ Comparing objects
☐ Copying objects
☐ Finding out the class of any given object
☐ Testing to see whether an object is an instance of a given class

Comparing Objects

Yesterday, you learned about operators for comparing values: equals, not equals, less than, and so on. Most of these operators work only on primitive types, not on objects. For the most part, the operators that you learned about yesterday do not in any way work on objects.

The exception to this rule is with the operators for equality: == (equal) and != (not equal). These operators, when used with objects, test whether the two operands (objects) refer to exactly the same object. Here is an example:

```
...
  Apple a = new Apple();
  Fruit b;
  b = a;
  if (a == b)
  {
      //Code executed when equality is true goes here
  }
```

The preceding example shows two objects, a and b, which both reference the same object created on the first line. In the preceding case, the line starting with //Code executed (replaced by actual VJ++ statements) would be executed because a does equal the same object as b. Don't worry about the if statement in this example; you will get to it tomorrow.

What should you do if you want to be able to compare instances of your class and have meaningful results? You have to implement special methods in your class, and you have to call those methods using those method names.

TECHNICAL NOTE

Java does not have the concept of operator overloading—that is, the capability of defining the behavior of the built-in operators by defining methods in your own classes. The built-in operators remain defined only for numbers. Don't confuse the concept of operator overload with function overloading: Java supports the latter, not the former.

A good example of this is the String class. It is possible to have two strings, two independent objects in memory with the same values—that is, the same characters in the same order. According to the == operator, however, those two String objects will not be equal, because, although their contents are the same, they are not the same object.

The String class, therefore, defines a method called equals() that tests each character in the string and returns true if the two strings have the same values. Listing 5.4 is another Java application you can experiment with and test using JVIEW.

TYPE **Listing 5.4. A test of string equality.**

```
 1: class EqualsTest
 2: {
 3:     public static void main(String args[])
 4:     {
 5:         String sStr1, sStr2;
 6:         sStr1 = "she sells sea shells by the sea shore.";
 7:         sStr2 = sStr1;
 8:
 9:         System.out.println("String1: " + sStr1);
10:         System.out.println("String2: " + sStr2);
11:         System.out.println("Same object? " + (sStr1 == sStr2));
12:
13:         sStr2 = new String(sStr1);
14:
15:         System.out.println("String1: " + sStr1);
16:         System.out.println("String2: " + sStr2);
17:         System.out.println("Same object? " + (sStr1 == sStr2));
18:         System.out.println("Same value? " + sStr1.equals(sStr2));
19:     }
20: }
```

5

The preceding application produces the following output.

```
String1: she sells sea shells by the sea shore.
String2: she sells sea shells by the sea shore.
Same object? true
String1: she sells sea shells by the sea shore.
String2: she sells sea shells by the sea shore.
Same object? false
Same value? true
```

ANALYSIS The first part of this program (lines 5 through 7) declares two variables, sStr1 and sStr2, assigns the literal she sells sea shells by the sea shore. to sStr1, and then assigns that value to sStr2. As you know from object references, now sStr1 and sStr2 point to the same object, and the test at line 11 proves that.

In the second part, you create a new string object with the value of sStr1. Now you have two different string objects with the same value. Testing them to see whether they're the same object by using the == operator (line 17) returns the expected answer, as does testing them using the equals method (line 18) to compare their values.

TECHNICAL NOTE

> Why can't you just use another literal when you change sStr2, rather than using new? String literals are optimized in Java—if you create a string using a literal, and then use another literal with the same characters, Java knows enough to give you the first String object back. Both strings are the same objects—to create two separate objects you have to go out of your way.

Determining the Class of an Object

Want to find out the class of an object? Here's the way to do it for an object assigned to the variable obj:

```
String sName = obj.getClass().getName();
```

What does this do? The getClass() method is defined in the Object class, and, as such, is available for all objects. The result of that method is a Class object (where Class is itself a class), which has a method called getName(). getName() returns a string representing the name of the class.

Another test that might be useful to you is the instanceof operator. instanceof has two operands: an object on the left and the name of a class on the right. The expression returns true or false based on whether the object is an instance of the named class or any of that class' subclasses:

```
"dummy" instanceof String // true
Point pntPt = new Point(10, 10);
pntPt instanceof String // false
```

The `instanceof` operator can also be used for interfaces; if an object implements an interface, the `instanceof` operator with that interface name on the right side returns true. You'll learn all about interfaces in Week 3.

The Java Class Library

To finish up today, look at some of the components that make up the Java class libraries. Actually, you've had a bit of experience with these libraries during the past five days, so they shouldn't seem all that different.

NOTE
There can be different class libraries available to you—the VJ++ developer— than those available to other developers and the user. The standard Java class libraries included with the JDK are the same ones included with VJ++, other development environments, and on a user's computer. However, there are specific class libraries that are currently only available with VJ++.

The Java class library provides the set of classes that are guaranteed to be supported in any commercial Java environment, for example, in Microsoft Internet Explorer 3.0 or in Netscape 2.0x. Those classes are in the Java package and include all the classes you've seen so far in this book, plus many more classes you'll learn about later on in this book (and even more that we can't teach you about in 21 days).

VJ++ comes with full online documentation (Books Online) for all of the Java class libraries, which includes descriptions of each class' data members, methods, constructors, interfaces, and so on. A shorter summary of the Java API is in Appendix C, "The Java Class Library," as well. Exploring the Java class library and its methods and data members is a great way to figure out what Java can and cannot do, as well as a starting point for your own development.

Here are the class packages that are part of the Java class library:

- [ ] `java.lang`: Classes that apply to the language itself, which includes the `Object` class, the `String` class, and the `System` class. It also contains the special classes for the primitive types (`Integer`, `Character`, `Float`, and so on).

- [ ] `java.util`: Utility classes, such as `Date`, as well as simple collection classes, such as `Vector` and `Hashtable`.

- [ ] `java.io`: Input and output classes for writing to and reading from streams (such as standard input and output) and for handling files.
- [ ] `java.net`: Classes for networking support, including `Socket` and `URL` (a class to represent references to documents on the World Wide Web).
- [ ] `java.awt`: (the Abstract Window Toolkit): Classes to implement a graphical user interface, including classes for `Window`, `Menu`, `Button`, `Font`, `Checkbox`, and so on. This package also includes classes for processing images (in the `java.awt.image` package).
- [ ] `java.applet`: Classes to implement Java applets, including the `Applet` class itself, as well as the `AudioClip` interface.

Although the additional classes available to you as a VJ++ developer are incredibly useful, be careful. They are not part of the standard Java library and there is no guarantee that they will be available to other people across the Internet trying to run your Java program. You'll need to do a little extra planning and programming to help ensure that your Microsoft extensions to the Java language are executed properly on the user's computer. This is particularly important for applets, because applets are expected to be able to run on any platform, using any Java-capable Internet browser. Only classes inside the `Java` package are guaranteed to be available on all browsers and Java environments.

If you want the highest level of usability without the extra work, a good rule of thumb would be: For Internet applets, stick to the basic Java classes. For intranet applications, use any and all classes that you want; it's relatively easy to distribute across an intranet.

Summary

Objects, objects everywhere. Today, you learned all about how to deal with objects: how to create them, how to find out and change the values of their variables, and how to call their methods. You also learned how to copy and compare them, and how to convert them into other objects. Finally, you learned a bit about the Java class libraries—which give you a whole slew of classes to play with in your own programs.

You now have the fundamentals of how to deal with the most simple things in the Java language. All you have left are arrays, conditionals, and loops, which you'll learn about tomorrow. Then you'll learn how to define and use classes in Java applications on Day 7, and launch directly into applets next week.

Remember, with just about everything you do in your VJ++ programs, no matter how complex they become, or how much the language evolves, you'll always be writing in objects.

5

Q&A

Q **I'm confused about the differences between objects and the primitive data types, such as `int` and `boolean`. What are they?**

A The primitive types in the language (`byte`, `short`, `int`, `long`, `float`, `double`, `boolean` and `char`) represent the smallest things in the language. They are not objects, but they can be assigned to variables and passed in and out of methods like objects. However, most of the operations that work exclusively on objects will not work on them.

Objects are instances of classes and, as such, are much more complex data types than simple numbers and characters. Often, objects contain numbers and characters as data members or class variables.

Q **In the section on calling methods, you had examples of calling a method with a different number of arguments each time—and it gave a different kind of result. How is that possible?**

A That's called *method overloading*. Overloading enables the same function name to have different behaviors based on the arguments it's called with—and the number and type of arguments can vary. When you define methods in your own classes, you define separate method signatures with different sets of arguments and different definitions. When a method is called, Java figures out which definition to execute based on the number and type of arguments with which you called it.

You'll learn all about this on Day 6.

Q **No operator overloading in Java? Why not? I thought Java was based on C++, and C++ has operator overloading.**

A Java was indeed based on C++, but it was also designed to be simple, so many of C++'s features have been removed. The argument against operator overloading is that, because the operator can be defined to mean anything, it makes it very difficult to figure out what any given operator is doing at any one time. This can result in entirely unreadable code. When you use a method, you know it can mean many things to many classes, but when you use an operator you would like to know that it always means the same thing. Given the potential for abuse, the designers of Java felt it was one of the C++ features that was best left out.

Day 6

Arrays, Conditionals, and Loops

At this point you have enough information to write some extremely simple Java programs, but as you've seen, they don't do very much. The really good stuff in Java, or in any programming language, results when you have arrays—used to store values—and loop and conditional control-flow constructs—used to execute different bits of a program based on a test criteria. Today, you'll find out about the following:

- ☐ Arrays, one of the most useful objects in Java, which enable you to collect objects (your own or from the VJ++ class library) and primitive data types into an easy-to-manage table

- ☐ Block statements, for grouping together related statements

- ☐ `if` and `switch`, for conditional tests

- ☐ `for` and `while` loops, for repeating statements (iteration)

Arrays

Arrays in Java are objects. Because arrays are objects, they can be passed to other objects. In VJ++ programs, you treat arrays just like any other object.

NEW TERM *Arrays* are a means to store a list of related items. Each item you want to store in an array is held in an *element*. When you declare an array you give it a data type, variable name, and size. The data type determines what kind of item the array will hold, the variable name is how you'll reference the array, and the size determines the number of elements in the array. Arrays can be used to store static information, like the days of the week, or variable information, like user input from a Web page.

Any of the data types (primitive or objects) can be used to create an array, but an array declaration (and, therefore, the elements) can contain only one data type. For instance, you can have an array of integers, an array of strings, or an array of arrays, but you can't have an array that contains, for example, both strings and integers.

To create an array in Java, you use three steps:

1. Declare a variable to hold the array.
2. Create a new array object and assign it to the array variable.
3. Store things in that array.

Declaring Array Variables

The first step to creating an array is to create a variable that will hold the array. Naming an array variable follows the same conventions as any other variable. The array name should indicate the type of item the array will hold. What makes an array variable different (and, therefore, treated as an array variable) is the use of empty brackets. The following are typical array variable declarations:

```
String sDaysOfTheWeek[];

Point pntHits[];

int iTemp[];
```

An alternate method of defining an array variable is to put the brackets after the data type instead of after the variable. So, the preceding three declarations could be written like this:

```
String[] sDaysOfTheWeek;

Point[] pntHits;

int[] iTemp;
```

It doesn't matter which one you use. Whichever way you do choose, keep it consistent. In all of the examples in this book, the first method of defining arrays will be used, where the brackets follow the array variable name rather than the data type.

Creating Array Objects

The second step is to create an array object and assign it to the variable. There are two ways to do this:

- ☐ Using new
- ☐ Directly initializing the contents of that array

The first way is to use the new operator to create a new instance of an array:

```
String sNames[] = new String[10];
```

That line creates a new array of Strings with 10 elements. When you create a new array object using this form (new), you must declare the array's size.

Array objects can contain primitive types such as integers or Booleans, just as they can contain objects:

```
int iTemp[] = new int[99];
```

When you create an array object using new, all its elements are initialized for you: 0 for numeric arrays, false for Boolean, '\0' for character arrays, and null for objects. You can also create and initialize an array at the same time. Instead of using new to create the new array object, enclose all the elements of the array inside a set of braces, and separate each element with a comma:

```
String sDaysOfTheWeeks[] = { "Monday", "Tuesday", "Wednesday",
    "Thursday", "Friday", "Saturday", "Sunday" };
```

Each of the elements you use to initialize the array must be of the same data type, as well as the same data type as the variable that holds that array. This means that if the data type is String, the elements must all be strings, too.

At runtime, an array is automatically created; its size will be based upon the number of items used when it was declared. The preceding example creates an array of String objects named sDaysOfTheWeek, which contains seven elements.

Accessing Array Elements

Once you have an array that is populated with initial values, you can use the values stored in the array elements just like you would any other variable. You can use an element as part of a conditional test, extract a value to use in a calculation or to display on the screen, and change

6

the value of the element. The difference between a variable (which can store only one value at a time) and an array variable is how you reference each element in the array to extract only the data contained in a specific element.

To get at a value stored within an array, you must supply two pieces of information: the name of the array (surprise!) and the number of the element. The element number is called the array `subscript`. The `subscript` is enclosed in brackets and follows the array name, like this:

```
sDaysOfTheWeeks[subscript];
```

> Arrays in Java are zero-based. This means that the first subscripted element is 0 and the last is *one less* than the size of the array.

The `sDaysOfTheWeek` part of this expression is the variable holding the array object. The `subscript` expression specifies the element to access within the array. Array subscripts are zero-based, meaning they start with 0, as they do in C and C++. So, an array with 10 elements has 10 array elements accessed by using subscripts 0 to 9. If you're not used to working with arrays (or those in another language), the point of Java arrays being zero-based is very important in a number of ways—for example:

- [ ] When you declare the size of your array, you'll set the size to one *less* than the number of elements you'll need. For example, to declare the "Days of the Week" array with 7 elements using `new`, the declaration would be `String sDaysOfTheWeek[] = new String[6]`. At first this might be quite confusing, but it's very important, as you'll soon see.

- [ ] When you reference an element in the array, you'll also think in terms of one less. For example, `sDaysOfTheWeek[0]= "Monday"`, where the first day of the week is zero, not one as you might expect.

- [ ] When you're incrementing through the elements of the array, you'll begin at zero and end at the size minus one.

Note that all array subscripts are checked at compile-time and runtime to make sure that they are inside the boundaries of the array: Greater than or equal to 0, but one less than the array's length. In Java it is impossible to access or assign a value to an array element that is outside of the boundaries of the array. Note the following two statements, for example:

```
String[] sArr = new String[10];
sArr[10] = "eggplant";
```

`sArr[10]` doesn't exist. The largest element in the `sArr` array is 9, which is one less than its size of 10. Any Java program with the `sArr[10]` statement in it will produce a compiler error.

If the array subscript is calculated at runtime (for example, as part of a loop) and references an element outside the boundaries of the array, the Java interpreter also produces an error—or, to be technically correct, it throws an exception. You'll learn more about exceptions later next week and on Day 19, "Introduction to JavaScript."

How can you keep from accidentally overrunning the end of an array in your own programs? You can test for the length of the array in your programs using the `length` data member; it's available for all array objects, regardless of data type:

```
int len = sArr.length // returns 10
```

Changing Array Elements

To assign a value to a specific array element, put an assignment statement after the array name expression:

```
iMyAarray[1] = 15;
sSentence[0] = "The";
sSentence[10] = sentence[0]
\\ Now sSentence[10] now equals, by reference,"The";
```

An important thing to note is that an array of objects in Java is an array of references to those objects. (It is similar in some ways to an array of pointers in C or C++.) When you assign a value to an element in an array, you're creating a reference to that object, just as you do for a plain variable. When you move values around inside arrays (as in that last line), you just reassign the reference. You don't copy the value from one element to the other, except for primitive data type arrays, such as `ints` or `floats` that *do copy* the values from one element to another.

Arrays of references to objects, as opposed to the objects themselves, are particularly useful because it means you can have multiple references to the same objects, both inside and outside arrays. For example, you can assign an object contained in an array to a variable and refer to that same object by using either the variable or the array element subscript.

Multidimensional Arrays

Java supports multidimensional arrays the same way as C-style multidimensional arrays. You can think of a multidimensional array as an array of arrays, and those arrays can contain arrays, and so on, for however many dimensions you need. Visually, whereas a single dimension array would resemble a one-column table, a multidimensional array would resemble more of a matrix, where there would be multiple columns. When you declare your array, you supply a size for each of the columns, and when you need to reference an element, you need to supply multiple subscripts, since a specific element can now be in any of the columns.

6

```
int iCoords[][] = new int[12][12];
iCoords[0][0] = 1;
iCoords[0][1] = 2;
iCoords[1][5] = 3;
```

See the following matrix for a depiction of what the double subscripted iCoords array might look like.

Depiction of Array iCoords

	[sub0]	[sub1]	[sub...]	[sub12]
[subscript0]	1			
[subscript1]	2			
[subscript2]				
[subscript3]				
[subscript4]				
[subscript5]		3		
[subscript6]				
[subscript7]				
[subscript8]				
[subscript9]				
[subscript10]				
[subscript11]				

NOTE

The sizing parameters in multidimensional arrays don't have to be equal–for example, int iCoords[][] = new int[12][5];. You can size a multidimensional array to suit whatever your needs require.

block **Statements**

A block statement is a group of statements surrounded by braces ({}). You can use a block anywhere a single statement would go. However, the block creates a local scope for the statements contained inside it. This means that you can declare and use local variables inside a block, and those variables will cease to exist after the statements inside the block are finished executing. For example, here's a block inside a method definition that declares a new variable iY. Because iY is now local to the block, you cannot use iY outside the block in which it was declared:

```
void testblock()
{
    int iX = 10;
    { // start of block
      int iY = 50;
      System.out.println("inside the block:");
      System.out.println("iX:" + iX);
      System.out.println("iY:" + iY);
    } // end of block
    System.out.println("iX:" + iX);
    System.out.println("iY:" + iY); \\ this line will produce a compiler error
}
```

`block` statements are not usually used alone in a method definition. Up to this point, you've mostly seen `blocks` surrounding class and method definitions, but another very common use of a `block` is in the control flow constructs you'll learn about in the remainder of today's lesson.

`if` Conditionals

The `if` conditional enables you to execute different sections of code based upon the result of a comparison test. The Java `if` conditional is nearly identical to `if` statements in C.

`if` conditionals contain the keyword `if`, followed by a Boolean test, followed by a statement (often a `block` statement) to execute if the test is true:

```
if (iX < iY)
    System.out.println("iX is smaller than iY");
```

An optional `else` keyword provides the statement to execute if the test is false:

```
if (iX < iY)
    System.out.println("iX is smaller than iY");
else
    System.out.println("iY is bigger");
```

TECHNICAL NOTE

The difference between `if` conditionals in Java and in C or C++ is that, in Java, the result of the test must return a Boolean value—either `true` or `false`—unlike in C, where the result of the test can also return an integer.

6

```
if (bEngineOn == true )
   System.out.println("Engine is already on.");
else
   {
   System.out.println("Now starting Engine.");
   if (gasLevel >= 1)
       bEngineOn = true;
   else
       System.out.println("Low on gas! Can't start engine.");
   }
```

The preceding example uses the test (bEngineOn == true). For Boolean tests of this type, a common shortcut is merely to include the first part of the expression, rather than explicitly testing its value against true or false:

```
if (bEngineOn)System.out.println("Engine is on.");
else
    System.out.println("Engine is off.");
```

The Conditional Operator

An alternative to using the if and else keywords in a conditional statement is to use the conditional operator, sometimes called the ternary operator.

 The *conditional operator* is a *ternary operator* because it has three terms. The conditional operator is an expression, meaning that it returns a value (unlike the more general if, which can result only in a statement or block being executed).

The conditional operator is most useful for very short or simple conditionals, and looks like this:

```
test ? trueresult : falseresult
```

The *test* is a conditional expression that returns either true or false, just like a test in an if statement. If the test evaluates to being true, the conditional operator returns the value of *trueresult*; if it's false, it returns the value of *falseresult*. For example, the following conditional expression tests the values of iX and iY, returns the smaller of the two, and assigns that value to the variable iSmaller:

```
int iSmaller = (iX < iY) ? iX : iY;
```

The conditional operator has a very low precedence; that is, it's usually evaluated only after all its subexpressions are evaluated. The only operators lower in precedence than conditional operators are the assignment operators. See the precedence chart in Day 3's lesson, "Object-Oriented Programming and Java," for a refresher on precedence of all the operators.

switch **Conditionals**

A common programming practice is to test a variable against some value. If its value doesn't match the test value, test it again against a different test value, and if it doesn't match that one, make another test, and so on. Using only if statements, this can become unwieldy, due to how the test expression is formatted and how many different test expressions you need to evaluate. For example, you might end up with a set of if statements like the following:

```
if (cOper == '+')
  addargs(iArg1, iArg2);
else if (cOper == '-')
   subargs(iArg1, iArg2);
else if (cOper == '*')
   multargs(iArg1, iArg2);
else if (cOper == '/')
   divargs(iArg1, iArg2);
```

WARNING

In other languages, both single quotes (') and double quotes (") can be used to delimit a string. In Java (as in C), single and double quote delimiters mean different things. A double quote is used to delimit a string, whereas a single quote is used to convert the single character inside the quotes to a data type word (a single byte representation of the character). Note also that, because a byte can only represent (store) a single character, the character inside the quotes can be only a single character or an escape sequence, for example, '\n'.

This form of an if statement is called a nested if because each else statement in turn contains yet another if, and so on, until all the possible tests have been made.

A common shorthand mechanism for avoiding nested ifs allows you to group test expressions and actions together into a single statement. This mechanism is the switch or case statement. Java only uses the keyword switch, and it behaves as it does in C:

```
switch (test)
   {
   case valueOne:
           resultOne;
     break;
   case valueTwo:
           resultTwo;
     break;
   case valueThree:
           resultThree;
     break;
   ...
   default: defaultresult;
   }
```

In the switch statement, a simple primitive data type (byte, char, short, or int) is compared with each of the case values in turn, starting with the first. If a test evaluates to true (the test equaling the value), the statement or statements between the case and break is executed. If no match is found after evaluating all of the case statements, the default statement is executed. The default statement is optional, so if none of the case statements evaluate to true and default doesn't exist, the switch statement completes without doing anything.

Note that the significant limitation of switch in Java is that the tests and values can be only primitive types, and then only primitive types that are castable to int. You cannot use larger primitive types (for example, long or float), strings, or other objects within a switch; you also cannot test for any relationship other than equality. This limits the usefulness of switch to all but the simplest comparisons, whereas nested ifs can work with any kind of test on any data type.

Here is a simple example of a switch statement similar to the nested if shown earlier:

```
switch (cOper)
    {
     case '+':  \\ remember this is not a string comparision, but instead it's a
     word
         addargs(iArg1, iArg2);
         break;
     case '*':
         subargs(iArg1, iArg2);
         break;
     case '-':
         multargs(iArg1, iArg2);
         break;
     case '/':
         divargs(iArg1, iArg2);
         break;
    }
```

Note the break statement included at the end of every case. A break is used to jump out of the switch statement without executing any of the other statements, including any more case statements. Unlike some other programming languages that have an assumed break when they reach another case statement, Java will continue to execute the statements inside the switch until a break is found or until the switch ends. At the very least, this will slow down the execution of your program; at worst, statements might be executed unintentionally, for example:

```
char cOper = '+';

switch (cOper)
{
    case '+': \\this evaluates to true
        addargs(iArg1, iArg2); \\ this executes
        \\no break here
    case '*':  \\ this doesn't get evaluated at all
        subargs(iArg1, iArg2); \\ this executes too
        \\ no break here
```

```
    case '-': \\ this doesn't get evaluated at all
        multargs(iArg1, iArg2); \\so does this
        break; \\ this breaks you out of the switch
    case '/':
        divargs(iArg1, iArg2);
        break;
}
```

Sometimes, this falling-through effect might be exactly what you want to do, but most times you'll want to make sure to include the break so that only the statements you want to be executed are executed.

One handy use of falling-through occurs when you want different test values to execute the same statements. In this instance, you can use multiple case lines with no result, and the switch will execute the first statement it finds. For example, in the following switch statement, the string "iX is an even number." is printed if iX has values of 2, 4, 6, or 8. All other values of iX print the string "iX is an odd number.".

```
switch (iX)
{
    case 2:
    case 4:
    case 6:
    case 8:
        System.out.println("iX is an even number.");
        break;
    default: System.out.println("iX is an odd number.");
}
```

for **Loops**

The for loop, as in C, repeats a statement or block of statements a given number of times until the test condition is satisfied. for loops are frequently used for simple iteration, in which you repeat a block of statements a certain number of times and then stop; but you can use for loops for just about any kind of loop.

The for loop in Java looks roughly like this:

```
for (initialization; test; increment)
{
    statements;
}
```

The statement that defines a for loop has three parts:

☐ initialization is an expression that initializes the start of the loop. If you have a loop index, this expression might declare and initialize it, for example, int iLoopIndex = 0. Variables that you declare in this part of the for loop are local to the loop itself; they cease to exist after the loop has finished executing.

☐   test is the test that occurs *after* each pass of the loop and *before* incrementing the loop index. The test must be a Boolean expression or function that returns a Boolean value—for example, iLoopIndex < 10. If the test is true, the loop executes. Once the test is false, the loop stops executing.

☐   increment is any expression or function call. Commonly, the increment is used to change the value of the loop index to bring the state of the loop closer to returning false and thus exiting the loop.

The statements part of the for loop are the statements that are executed each time the loop iterates. Just as with if, you can include either a single statement here or a block; the previous example used a block because that is more common. Here's an example of a for loop that initializes all the values of a strString array to null strings:

```
String strArray[] = new String[10];
int iLoopIndex;

for (iLoopIndex = 0; iLoopIndex < strArray.length; iLoopIndex++)
    strArray[iLoopIndex] = "";
```

Any of the definition parts (for example, iLoopIndex) of the for loop can be empty statements; that is, you can simply use a semicolon as a placeholder for the missing expression or statement, and that part of the for loop will be ignored. If you use a null statement in your for loop, you might have to initialize or increment the loop variables or loop indexes yourself elsewhere in the program.

You can also have an empty statement for the body of your for loop, if everything you want to do is in the first line of that loop. For example, here's one that finds the first prime number higher than 4000:

```
for (iPrimeSeed = 4001; notPrime(iPrimeSeed); iPrimeSeed += 2)
    ;
```

WARNING

A common mistake in C, which also occurs in Java, is to accidentally put a semicolon after the first line of the for loop, as in the following code fragment:

```
for (iX = 0; iX < 10; iX++); \\ends the loop performing
nothing System.\out.println("Loop!"); \\outside loop, prints
only once
```

Because the first semicolon ends the loop with an empty statement, the loop doesn't actually do anything. The println() function will be printed only once because it's actually outside the for loop entirely. Also, because it's a valid for loop construct, the compiler will not flag it as an error. Be careful not to make this mistake in your own Java programs. This same mistake can be made with if conditional tests too; be careful.

`while` **and** `do` **Loops**

Finally, there are `while` and `do` loops. `while` and `do` loops, like `for` loops, enable a block of Java code to be executed repeatedly until a specific condition is met. Whether you use a `for`, a `while`, or a `do` loop is mostly a matter of your programming style.

`while` and `do` loops perform exactly the same as in C and C++ except that in Java, the test condition must be a Boolean.

`while` **Loops**

The `while` loop is used to repeat a statement or block of statements as long as a particular condition is `true`. `while` loops look like this:

```
while (bCondition)
{
    // Body of Loop Statements
}
```

The `bCondition` is a Boolean expression. If it returns `true`, the `while` loop executes the statements in the body of the loop and then tests the condition again, repeating until the condition is `false`. As shown in the following example, the most common use of a `while` loop is to execute a block of statements, although a single statement can be used also.

Here's an example of a `while` loop that copies the elements of an array of integers (`iArray1`) to an array of `float`s (`iArray2`), casting each element to a `float` as it goes. There's a catch, though: If any of the elements in the first array are `0`, the loop will immediately exit at that point. To cover both conditions wherein all the elements have been copied or an element might be `0`, you can use a compound test with the `&&` operator:

```
int iCount = 0;
while ( iCount < iArray1.length && iArray1[iCount] !=0)
{
    iArray2[iCount] = (float) iArray1[iCount++];
}
```

If the condition is initially false the first time it is tested (for example, if the first element in that first array is `0`), the body of the `while` loop will never be executed. If you need to execute the loop at least once, you can do one of two things:

☐ Duplicate the body of the loop outside the `while` loop.

☐ Use a `do` loop (described in the following section).

The `do` loop is generally considered the better of the two solutions.

6

do **Loops**

The do loop is just like a while loop, except that do executes a given statement or block until the condition is false. The main difference is that while loops test the condition before looping, making it possible for the body of the loop to never execute if the condition is false the first time it's tested. do loops run the body of the loop *at least once* before testing the condition. do loops look like this:

```
do
{
    // The Body of the Loop
} while (condition);
```

Here, the statements that are executed with each iteration are the body of the loop part. It's shown here with a block statement because it's most commonly used that way, but you can substitute the braces for a single statement as you can with the other control-flow constructs. The condition is a Boolean test. If it returns true, the loop is run again. If it returns false, the loop exits. Keep in mind that with do loops, the body of the loop executes *at least once*.

Here's a simple example of a do loop that prints a message each time the loop iterates:

```
int iX = 1;
do
{
    System.out.println("Looping, round " + iX);
    iX++;
} while (iX <= 10);
```

Here's the output based upon the preceding code fragment:

```
Looping, round 1
Looping, round 2
Looping, round 3
Looping, round 4
Looping, round 5
Looping, round 6
Looping, round 7
Looping, round 8
Looping, round 9
Looping, round 10
```

NOTE

You'll notice in our examples that the do loop also contains a while loop. In most cases the code you write will include these do...while loops.

Breaking Out of Loops

In all the loops (for, while, and do), the loop ends when the condition you're testing is met. What happens if something odd occurs within the body of the loop and you want to exit the loop early? For that, you can use the break and continue keywords.

You've already seen break as part of the switch statement; it stops execution of the switch, and the program continues with the statement after the switch construct. The break keyword, when used with a loop, does the same thing. It immediately halts execution of the current loop. If you've nested loops within loops, execution picks up in the next outer loop; otherwise, the program merely continues executing the next statement after the loop.

NOTE

> Although nesting levels can be very deep, it would probably be unwise to nest further than five levels. A general practice is to nest only three or four levels deep, otherwise your Java code becomes unmanageable.

For example, remember the while loop that copied elements from an integer array into an array of floats? It did this until the end of the array or until a 0 was reached (while (iCount < iArray1.length && iArray1[iCount] !=0)). If you wanted to, you could test for the latter condition inside the body of the while loop and then use a break to exit the loop:

```
int iCount = 0;
while (iCount < iArray1.length)
{
    if (iArray1[iCount] == 0)
    {
        break;
    }
    iArray2[iCount] = (float) iArray1[iCount++];
}
```

continue is similar to break except that instead of halting execution of the loop entirely, the loop starts over at the next iteration. In do and while loops, this means the execution of the block starts over again; in for loops, the loop index is incremented and then the block is executed. continue is useful when you want to ignore subsequent statements and simply continue with the next iteration of the loop. With the previous example of copying one array to another, you can test for whether the current element is 0 and, if it is, restart the loop, so that the resulting array won't contain a zero. Note that because you're skipping elements in the first array, you now have to keep track of two different array index counters:

6

```
int iCount1 = 0;
int iCount2 = 0;
while (iCount < iArray1.length)
{
    if (iArray1[iCount] == 0)
        continue;

    iArray2[iCount2++] = (float) iArray1[iCount++];
}
```

Labeled Loops

Both break and continue can have an optional label that tells Java where to break to. Without a label, break jumps outside the current loop to (if one exists) a loop the next level out, or to the next statement outside the current loop. Whereas, continue restarts the current loop. Using labeled breaks and continues enables you to break outside nested loops or to continue a loop outside the current loop.

To create a labeled loop, simple add a label statement followed by a colon before the initial definition part of the loop. Then, when you need to jump out to a specific level, use break or continue, followed by the name of the label:

```
lblOut:
    for (int iX = 0; iX <10; iX++)
      {
        while (iY < 50)
          {
            if (iX * iY == 400)
                break lblOut;
            ...
          }
        ...
      }
\\ statements to be executed when the break lblOut is executed or the loops
    naturally exit.
```

In this fragment of code, the label lb10ut identifies the outer loop. Then, inside both the for and the while loop, when the particular condition is met, a break lbl0ut causes the execution to break out of both loops, instead of just the while loop.

Here's another example. The following code fragment contains a nested for loop. If the summed values of the two counters is greater than four, both loops are exited.

```
lblBothOut:
    for (int iX = 1; iX <= 5; iX++)
        for (int iJ = 1; iJ <= 3; iJ++)
          {
            System.out.println("iX is " + iX + ", iJ is " + iJ);
            if ((iX + iJ) > 4)
                break lblBothOut;
          }
System.out.println("end of loops");
```

Here's the output from this code:

```
iX is 1, iJ is 1
iX is 1, iJ is 2
iX is 1, iJ is 3
iX is 2, iJ is 1
iX is 2, iJ is 2
iX is 2, iJ is 3
end of loops
```

As you can see, the loop iterated until the sum of iX and iJ was greater than 4, and then both loops exited to the statement following the outermost for block, causing the final message to be printed.

NOTE

Labels, like GOTO statements in other languages, can lend themselves to abuse. We're not about to get trapped into the age-old argument of whether GOTOs are good or bad. Suffice it to say that if you can't think of any other way out of a coding situation, use labels.

Summary

Today, you learned about three main topics that you'll most likely use quite often in your own Java programs: arrays, conditionals, and loops.

You learned how to declare an array variable, create and assign an array object to that variable, and access and change elements within that array.

Conditionals include the if and switch statements, with which you can branch to different parts of your program based on a Boolean test.

Finally, you learned about the for, while, and do loops, each of which enables you to execute a portion of your program repeatedly until a given condition is met.

Now that you've learned the small stuff, all that's left is to go over the bigger issues of declaring classes, creating instances and class variables, defining methods, and learning how objects of these class types can communicate with each other. Get to bed early tonight, because tomorrow is going to be a wild ride.

6

Q&A

Q If arrays are objects, you use `new` to create them, and they have an data member `length`, where is the `Array` class? I didn't see it in the Java class libraries.

A Arrays are implemented sort of weirdly in Java. The `Array` class is constructed automatically when your Java program runs; `Array` provides the basic framework for arrays, including the `length` variable. Additionally, each primitive type and object has an implicit subclass of `Array` that represents an array of that class or object. When you create a new array object, it might not have an actual class, but it behaves as if it does.

Q Does Java have `GOTO`s?

A The Java language defines the keyword `GOTO`, but it is not currently used for anything. In other words, no, Java does not have `GOTO`s.

Q I declared a variable inside a block statement for an `if`. When the `if` was done, the definition of that variable vanished. Where did it go?

A In technical terms, block statements inside braces form a new lexical scope. What this means is that if you declare a variable inside a block, it's only visible and usable inside that block. Once the block finishes executing, all the variables you declared go away.

It's a good idea to declare most of your variables in the outermost `block` in which they'll be needed—usually at the top of a `block` statement. The exception might be very simple variables, such as index counters in `for` loops, where declaring them in the first line of the `for` loop is an acceptable shortcut.

You'll learn more about variables and scope tomorrow.

Q Why can't you use `switch` with strings?

A Strings are objects, and `switch` in Java works only for the primitive types `byte`, `char`, `short`, and `int`. To compare strings, you have to use nested `if`s, which enable more general expression tests, including string comparison.

Q It seems to me that a lot of `for` loops could be written as `while` loops, and vice versa.

A True. The `for` loop is actually a special case of `while` that enables you to iterate a loop a specific number of times. You could just as easily do this with a `while` and then increment a counter inside the loop. Either works equally well. This is mostly just a question of programming style and personal choice.

6

Day 7

Creating Classes and Applications in Java

In just about every lesson up to this point, you've been creating Java applications—writing classes, creating data members and methods, and running those applications to perform simple tasks. You've also focused on both the very broad (general object-oriented theory) and the very minute (arithmetic and other expressions). Today, you pull it all together and learn how and why to create classes by using the following basics:

☐ The parts of a class definition

☐ Declaring and using data members

☐ Defining and using methods

☐ Creating Java applications, including the `main()` method and how to pass arguments to a Java program from a command line

Defining Classes

Defining classes is pretty easy; you've seen how to do it numerous times in previous lessons. To define a class, use the `class` keyword and the name of the class:

```
class MyClassName
{
...
}
```

If this `class` is a subclass of another `class` (remember a subclass is a `class` that *inherits* the properties and methods of another `class`), use `extends` to indicate the superclass of this `class`:

```
class myClassName extends mySuperClassName
{
...
}
```

If this `class` implements a specific interface, use `implements` to refer to that interface:

```
class MyRunnableClassName implements Runnable
{
...
}
```

Both `extends` and `implements` are optional. You'll learn about using and defining interfaces on Day 18, "Packages, Interfaces, and Exception Handling."

 NOTE

> Take special note of the keyword `Runnable` in the preceding code. `Runnable` is an interface you use to declare that you want the class to run in a separate thread. The importance of `Runnable` will become apparent when threads are discussed on Day 11, "Simple Animation and Threads."

Creating Data Members and Class Variables

A class definition with nothing in it is pretty dull. Typically, when you create a class, you have something you want to add to that class to make it different from its superclasses (if the class has a superclass). Inside each class definition are declarations and definitions for variables and/or methods or both for the class. These include class properties and methods as well as instance properties and methods. In this section, you'll learn all about data members and class variables (properties); the next section talks about methods.

Defining Data Members

On Day 3,"Object-Oriented Programming and Java," you learned how to declare and initialize local variables—that is, variables inside method definitions. Data members, fortunately, are declared and defined in almost the same way as local variables; the main difference is where they're located in the class definition. Variables are considered data members if they are declared outside a method definition.

Although you can declare a data member *anywhere* in your class, except within a method, most data members are defined just after the first line of the class definition. This is customary among most programmers because it makes the code easier to read and easier to maintain. For example, Listing 7.1 shows a simple class definition for the class Bicycle, which inherits from the class PersonPoweredVehicle. This class definition contains four data members:

- ☐ m_sBikeType: the kind of bicycle this is, for example, Mountain or Street
- ☐ m_iChainGear: the number of gears in the front
- ☐ m_iRearCcgs: the number of minor gears on the rear axle
- ☐ m_iCurrentGearFront and m_iCurrentGearRear: the gears the bike is currently in, both front and rear

TYPE **Listing 7.1. The bicycle class.**

```
1: class Bicycle extends PersonPoweredVehicle
2: {
3:      String m_sBikeType;
4:      int m_iChainGear;
5:      int m_iRearCogs;
6:      int m_iCurrentGearFront;
7:      int m_iCcurrentGearRear;
8: }
```

NOTE

The preceding m_ (member) data member prefix is part of the naming convention...remember back on Day 5, "Working with Objects," when m_ was first introduced? Keep this in mind. Later today, when the this keyword is described, the use of this naming convention becomes quite apparent and handy.

7

Constants

Constants are useful for defining shared values for all the methods of an object—for giving meaningful names to object-wide values that will never change. In Java, you can create constants only for data members or class variables, not for local variables.

 A *constant variable* or *constant* is a variable whose value never changes while your program is running, which might seem strange given the meaning of the word variable.

To declare a constant, you use the `final` keyword before the variable declaration and include an initial value for that variable.

 TECHNICAL NOTE

> The only way to define constants in Java is by using the `final` keyword. Neither the C nor C++ constructs for `#define` and `const` are available in Java, although `const` is reserved to help catch its accidental use.

```
final float PI = 3.141592;
final boolean DEBUG = false;
final int MAXSIZE = 40000;
```

Notice the preceding lines of code. It would appear that we broke the naming convention for data members. After all, we have stressed that an `int` variable begins with an `i` and that a data member begins with an `m_`. Why then are the preceding variables in all capitals with no identifiers? The answer is simple: It is common practice in programming (specifically C & C++) to define constants in all capitals. The purpose of this is to make it very easy to tell which variables are constants and cannot be changed.

Constants can be useful for naming various states of an object and then testing for those states. For example, suppose you have a test label that can be aligned left, right, or center. You can define those values as constant integers:

```
final int LEFT = 0;
final int RIGHT = 1;
final int CENTER = 2;
```

The variable alignment is then also declared as an `int`:

```
int iAlignment;
```

Then, later in the body of a method definition, you can either set the alignment:

```
this.iAlignment = CENTER;
```

or test for a given alignment:

```
switch (this._Alignment)
{
    case LEFT: // deal with left alignment
            ...
            break;
    case RIGHT: // deal with right alignment
            ...
            break;
    case CENTER: // deal with center alignment
                ...
            break;
}
```

Class Variables

As you learned in previous lessons, class variables are global to a class and to all that class' instances. Remember that in VJ++ there is no concept of a *Global* variable: class variables are as close as VJ++ gets to Globals. Class variables are good for communicating between different objects within the same class, or for keeping track of global states among a set of objects.

To declare a class variable, use the static keyword in the class declaration:

```
static int c_iSum;
static final int i_iMaxObjects = 10;
```

NOTE

> Notice the c_ before the variables in the preceding example. As per the naming conventions, this is an easily recognizable identifier you can use when defining a class variable.

Class variables can be used in two different ways: They can be accessed via the class itself or they can be accessed via an instance of the class. Take, for example, the class SomeClass. Assume the class SomeClass has a class variable called c_iCount. Examine the following code fragment:

```
SomeClass myInstance;
myInstance.c_iCount = 14;
SomeClass.c_iCount = 14;
```

The last two lines are equivalent: they both set the value of the class variable c_iCount in the class SomeClass to 14.

Creating Methods

Methods, as you learned on Day 4, "Java Basics," define an object's behavior—what happens when that object is created and the various operations that object can perform during its

7

lifetime. In this section, you'll get a basic introduction to method definition and how methods work; tomorrow, you'll go into more detail about advanced things you can do with methods.

 NOTE

> Score points at your next water cooler conference: if someone mentions the word *method,* fire back "Oh, you mean a member function." Both terms are used interchangeably within the programming industry.

Defining Methods

Method definitions have four basic parts:

- ☐ The name of the method
- ☐ The type of object or primitive type the method returns
- ☐ A list of parameters
- ☐ The body of the method

The method's *signature* is a combination of the name of the method, the type of object or base type this method returns, and a list of parameters.

 NOTE

> To keep things simple today, we've left off two optional parts of the method definition: a modifier such as public or private, and the throws keyword, which indicates the exceptions a method can throw. You'll learn about these parts of a method definition on Day 20, "Introduction to VBScript."

In other languages, the name of the method (function, subroutine, or procedure) is enough to distinguish it from other methods in the program. In Java, you can have different methods that have the same name but a different return type or argument list. This is called method overloading, and you'll learn more about it tomorrow.

Here's what a basic method definition looks like:

```
returntype methodname(type1 arg1, type2 arg2, type3 arg3..)
{
    ...
}
```

The returntype is the primitive type or class of the value this method returns. It can be one of the primitive types, a class name, or void if the method does not return a value at all.

Note that if this method returns an array object, the array brackets can go either after the return type or after the parameter list; because the return type is considerably easier to read, it is used in the examples today (and throughout this book):

```java
int[] makeRange(int lower, int upper)
{
...
}
```

The method's parameter list is a set of variable declarations, separated by commas, inside parentheses. These parameters become local variables in the body of the method, whose values are the objects or values of primitives passed in when the method is called.

Inside the body of the method you can have statements, expressions, method calls to other methods within this class or to other objects, conditionals, loops, and so on—everything you've learned about in the previous lessons.

If your method has a real return type (that is, it has not been declared to return void), somewhere inside the body of the method, you need to return a value. Use the return keyword to do this. Listing 7.2 shows an example of a class that defines a makeRange() method. makeRange() takes two integers—a lower bound and an upper bound—and creates an array that contains all the integers between those two boundaries (inclusive).

TYPE **Listing 7.2. The RangeClass class.**

```java
 1: class RangeClass
 2: {
 3:     int[] makeRange(int iLower, int iUpper)
 4:     {
 5:         int iArr[] = new int[ (iUpper - iLower) + 1 ];
 6:
 7:         for (int i = 0; i < iArr.length; i++)
 8:         {
 9:             iArr[i] = iLower++;
10:         }
11:         return iArr;
12:     }
13:
14:     public static void main(String iArg[])
15:     {
16:         int iTheArray[];
17:         RangeClass theRange = new RangeClass();
18:         theArray = theRange.makeRange(1, 10);
19:         System.out.print("The array: [ ");
20:         for (int i = 0; i < iTheArray.length; i++)
21:         {
22:             System.out.print(iTheArray[i] + " ");
23:         }
24:         System.out.println("]");
25:     }
26: }
```

7

Here's the output of this program:

```
The array: [ 1 2 3 4 5 6 7 8 9 10 ]
```

 The `main()` method in this class tests the `makeRange()` method by creating a range where the lower and upper boundaries of the range are 1 and 10, respectively (see line 9), and then uses a `for` loop to print the values of the new array.

The `this` Keyword

In the body of a method definition, you might want to refer to the current object—the object the method was called on—to refer to that object's data members or to pass the current object as an argument to another method. To refer to the current object in these cases, you can use the `this` keyword. `this` refers to the current object, and you can use it anywhere that object might appear: in dot notation to refer to the object's data members, as an argument to a method, as the return value for the current method, and so on. Here's an example:

```
t = this.x;             // the x data member for this object
this.myMethod(this); // call the mymethod method, defined in
                        // this class, and pass it the current
                        // object
return this;            // return the current object
```

In many cases, however, you might be able to omit the `this` keyword. You can refer to both data members and method calls defined in the current class simply by name; the `this` is implicit in those references. So, the first two examples could be written like this:

```
t = x;             // the x data member for this object
myMethod(this); // call the myMethod method, defined in this
                   // class
```

 NOTE

> Omitting the `this` keyword for data members depends on whether there are no variables of the same name declared in the local scope. See the next section for details.

Omitting the `this` keyword when referring to data members and methods is accepted and often encouraged; however, it is not always the prudent thing to do. When you include the `this` keyword when referring to the local object, it makes your code more readable and easier to maintain. It also forces you, the programmer, to better understand your own logic. However, because a naming convention prefix for variables has been developed, which immediately identifies their scope, you rarely need to use the `this` keyword. So, for the purposes of this book, we've used only the `this` keyword when it's necessary.

Keep in mind that this is a reference to the current instance of a class, therefore you should only use it inside the body of an instance method definition. Class methods, or methods declared with the static keyword, cannot use this. Class methods will be explained in greater detail later today.

Variable Scope and Method Definitions

When you refer to a variable within your method definitions, Java checks for a definition of that variable first in the current scope (which might be a block), then in the outer scopes up to the current method definition. If that variable is not a local variable, Java then checks for a definition of that variable as a data member or class variable in the current class, and then, finally, in each superclass in turn.

Because of the way Java checks for the scope of a given variable, it is possible for you to create a variable in a lower scope so that a definition of that same variable "hides" the original value of that variable. This can introduce subtle and confusing bugs into your code.

For example, note this small Java program:

```java
class ScopeTest
{
    int iTest = 10;
    void printTest ()
    {
        int iTest = 20;
        System.out.println("test = " + iTest);
    }
}
```

In this class, you have two variables with the same name and definition: the first, a data member, has the name iTest and is initialized to the value 10. The second is a local variable with the same name, but with the value 20. Because the local variable hides the data member, the println() method will print that iTest as 20.

You can get around this particular problem by using this.test to refer to the data member, and just test to refer to the local variable.

NOTE

When you looked at the preceding lines of code, maybe you immediately thought, "Those guys really messed up; they didn't follow their own naming convention and, boy, did it get them in trouble." Well, this was done on purpose in order to demonstrate the this keyword. If the preceding code had been written with the naming convention, the first iTest would have actually been named m_iTest and the second iTest would never have hidden the first—not demonstrating the point at all.

7

A more insidious example of this occurs when you redefine a variable in a subclass that already occurs in a superclass. This can create very subtle bugs in your code. For example, you might call methods that are intended to change the value of a data member, but they change the wrong one. Another bug might occur when you cast an object from one class to another; the value of your data member might mysteriously change (because it was getting that value from the superclass instead of from your class). The best way to avoid this behavior is to make sure that when you define variables in a subclass, you're aware of the variables in each of that class' superclasses so you don't duplicate what's already there.

Passing Arguments to Methods

When you call a method with object parameters, the variables you pass into the body of the method are passed by reference, which means that whatever you do to those objects inside the method affects the original objects as well. This includes arrays and all of the objects that the arrays contain; when you pass an array into a method and modify its contents, the original array is affected. (Note that primitive types are passed by value.)

NOTE

> Please reread the preceding paragraph! Commit it to memory. Put a sticker on your monitor. It is very important to understand how VJ++ passes arguments. If you don't, your programs will behave in strange and mysterious ways.

Here's an example to demonstrate how this works. First, you have a simple class definition, which includes a single method called OneToZero(). (See Listing 7.3.)

TYPE   **Listing 7.3. The PassByReference class.**

```
1: class PassByReference
2: {
3:     int OneToZero(int iArg[])
4:     {
5:         int iCount = 0;
6:         for (int i = 0; i < iArg.length; i++)
7:         {
8:             if (iArg[i] == 1)
9:             {
10:                 iCount++;
11:                 iArg[i] = 0;
12:             }
13:         }
14:         return iCount;
15:     }
16: }
```

The `OneToZero()` method does two things:

☐ It counts the number of ones in the array and returns that value.

☐ If it finds a one, it substitutes a zero in its place in the array.

Listing 7.4 shows the `main()` method for the `PassByReference` class, which tests the `OneToZero()` method:

TYPE **Listing 7.4. The `main()` method in `PassByReference`.**

```
 1: public static void main (String arg[])
 2: {
 3:     int iArr[] = { 1, 3, 4, 5, 1, 1, 7 };
 4:     PassByReference test = new PassByReference();
 5:     int iNumOnes;
 6:     System.out.print("Values of the array: [ ");
 7:     for (int i = 0; i < iArr.length; i++)
 8:     {
 9:         System.out.print(iArr[i] + " ");
10:     }
11:     System.out.println("]");
12:     iNumOnes = test.OneToZero(arr);
13:     System.out.println("Number of Ones = " + iNumOnes);
14:     System.out.print("New values of the array: [ ");
15:     for (int i = 0; i < iArr.length; i++)
16:     {
17:         System.out.print(iArr[i] + " ");
18:     }
19:     System.out.println("]");
20: }
```

Here is the output of this program:

```
Values of the array: [ 1 3 4 5 1 1 7 ]
Number of Ones = 3
New values of the array: [ 0 3 4 5 0 0 7 ]
```

Go over the `main()` method line by line so that you can see what is going on.

ANALYSIS Lines 3 through 5 set up the initial variables for this example. The first one is an array of integers; the second one is an instance of the class `PassByReference`, which is stored in the variable test. The third is a simple integer to hold the number of ones in the array.

Lines 6 through 11 print out the initial values of the array; you can see the output of these lines in the first line of the output.

Line 12 is where the real work takes place; this is where you call the `OneToZero()` method, defined in the object test, and pass it to the array stored in `iArr`. This method returns the number of ones in the array, which you'll then assign to the variable `iNumOnes`.

7

Got it so far? Line 13 prints out the number of ones—that is, the value you got back from the OneToZero() method. It returns three, as you would expect.

The last bunch of lines print out the array values. Because a reference to the array object is passed to the method, changing the array inside that method changes the original copy of the array. Printing out the values in lines 15 through 18 proves this; see the last line of output, where all the 1s in the array have been changed to 0s.

Class Methods

Just as you have class variables and data members, you also have class and instance methods. The difference between the two types of methods are analogous. Class methods are available to any instance of the class, and to the class itself, and can be made available to other classes. Therefore, some class methods can be used anywhere regardless of whether an instance of the class exists or not.

For example, the Java class libraries include a class called Math. The Math class defines a whole set of math operations that can be used in any program or the various number types:

```
float fRoot = Math.sqrt(453.0);
System.out.print("The larger of x and y is " + Math.max(x, y));
```

To define a class method, use the static keyword in front of the method definition, just as you would create a class variable. For example, the preceding max class method might have a signature like this:

```
static int max(int arg1, int arg2)
{
...
}
```

Java supplies wrapper classes for each of the base types. For example, classes for Integer, Float, and Boolean. Using class methods defined in those classes, you can convert to and from objects and primitive types. For example, the parseInt() class method in the Integer class takes a string and a radix (base) and returns the value of that string as an integer:

```
int iCount = Integer.parseInt("42", 10); // returns 42
```

Most methods that operate on a particular object, utilize the object's data members, or that affect that object, should be defined as instance methods. Methods that provide some general utility but do not directly affect an instance of that class are best declared as class methods.

Creating Java Applications

Now that you know how to create classes, objects, data members, class variables and instance methods, all that's left is to put it all together into something that can actually run—in other words, to create a VJ++ application.

Applications, to refresh your memory, are Java programs that run on their own. Applications are different from applets, which require Explorer, Netscape, or another Java-capable browser to view them. Much of what you've been creating up to this point have been Java applications; next week you'll investigate more on how to create applets. (Applets require a bit more background in order to get them to interact with the browser and draw and update with the graphics system. You'll learn all of this next week.)

A Java application consists of one or more classes and can be as large or as small as you want it to be. (Sun's browser, HotJava, is one example of a Java application.) The main thing that you need to make a Java application run is one class that serves as the jumping-off point for the rest of your Java program. If your program is small enough, it might need only the one class.

The jumping-off class for your program needs one thing in particular: a `main()` method. When you run your compiled Java class (using the Java interpreter jview), the `main()` method is the first thing that gets called. None of this should be much of a surprise to you at this point; you've been creating Java applications with `main()` methods all along.

The signature for the `main()` method in a VJ++ application always looks like this:

```
public static void main(String args[]) {...}
```

Here's a run-down of the parts of the `main()` method:

- [ ] `public` means that this method is available to other classes and objects. The `main()` method must be declared `public`. You'll learn more about `public` and `private` methods in Week 3.
- [ ] `static` means that this is a class method.
- [ ] `void` means the `main()` method doesn't return anything.
- [ ] `main()` takes one parameter: an array of strings. This argument is used for command-line arguments, which you'll learn about in the next section.

The body of the `main()` method contains any code you need to get your application started: generally, the initialization of the class containing `main` and initializing variables or creating instances of any classes you might have declared.

When Java executes the `main()` method, keep in mind that `main()` is a class method; the class that holds it is not automatically instantiated when your program runs. If you want to treat that class as an object, you have to instantiate it in the `main()` method yourself. All the examples up to this point have done this. (See Listing 7.4, line 4, for an example of instantiation.)

NEW TERM *Instantiate* means to create an instance of itself.

7

Java Applications and Command-Line Arguments

Because Java applications are stand-alone programs, it's useful to be able to pass arguments or options to that program to determine how the program is going to run, or to enable a generic program to operate on many different kinds of input. Command-line arguments can be used for many different purposes: to turn on debugging input, to indicate a filename to read or write from, or to obtain any other information your VJ++ program depends upon.

Passing Arguments to Java Programs

To pass arguments to a Java program, you merely append them to the command line when you run your Java program:

```
jview Myprogram argumentOne 2 three
```

On the preceding command line are three arguments: argumentOne, the number 2, and three. Note that a space separates arguments, so the following command line produces three arguments:

```
jview myprogram Java is cool
```

To group arguments, surround them with double quotes. This command line produces one argument:

```
jview myprogram "Java is cool"
```

The double-quotes are stripped off before the argument gets to your Java program.

Handling Arguments in Your Java Program

How does Java handle arguments? It stores them in an array of strings, which is passed to the main() method in your Java program. Remember the signature for main():

```
public static void main (String args[]) {...}
```

Here, args is the name of the array of strings that contains the list of arguments. Although you can call the args variable anything you want, it is a convention to leave it as the default of args. Doing so makes it easier for others to maintain your code, because they will more than likely expect the command-line array to be in args.

Inside your main() method, you can handle the arguments from which your program started by iterating over the array of arguments, and then handling each of those arguments as the program needs. For example, Listing 7.5 is a really simple class that prints out the arguments it gets—one per line.

TYPE **Listing 7.5. The EchoArgs class.**

```
 1: class EchoArgs
 2: {
 3:     public static void main(String args[])
 4:     {
 5:         for (int i = 0; i < args.length; i++)
 6:         {
 7:             System.out.println("Argument " + i + ": " + args[i]);
 8:         }
 9:     }
10: }
```

The following is some sample input and output from the preceding program:

```
jview EchoArgs 1 2 3 jump

Argument 0: 1
Argument 1: 2
Argument 2: 3
Argument 3: jump

jview EchoArgs "Black and Gold" New Mexico 6

Argument 0: Black and Gold
Argument 1: New
Argument 2: Mexico
Argument 3: 6
```

Note how the arguments are grouped in the listing; putting quotes around Black and Gold causes that argument to be treated as one unit inside the argument array.

TECHNICAL NOTE

The array of arguments in Java is not analogous to argv in C and UNIX. In particular, arg[0], the first element in the array of arguments, is the first command-line argument after the name of the class, *not* the name of the program as it would be in C. Be careful of this as you write your Java programs.

An important thing to note about the arguments you pass into a VJ++ program is that those arguments will be stored in an array of strings (args). This means that any arguments you pass to your Java program are strings stored in the argument array. To treat them as non-strings, you'll have to convert them to whatever type you want them to be.

For example, suppose you have a very simple Java program called SumAverage that takes any number of numeric arguments and returns the sum and the average of those arguments. Listing 7.6 shows a first pass at this program.

7

Listing 7.6. First try at the SumAverage **class.**

```
1: class SumAverage
2: {
3:     public static void main (String args[])
4:     {
5:         int iSum = 0;
6:         for (int i = 0; i < args.length; i++)
7:         {
8:             iSum += args[i];
9:         }
10:        System.out.println("Sum is: " + iSum);
11:        System.out.println("Average is: " +
12:            (float)iSum / args.length);
13:    }
14: }
```

At first glance, this program seems rather straightforward; a for loop iterates over the array of arguments, summing them, and then the sum and the average are printed out as the last step.

What happens when you try and compile this? You get the following error:

```
SumAverage.java:9: Incompatible type for +=. Can't convert java.lang.String to
int.
    sum += args[i];
```

You get this error because the argument array is an array of strings. Even though you passed integers into the program from the command line, those integers were converted to strings before they were stored in the array. To be able to sum those integers, you have to convert them from strings to integers. There's a class method for the Integer class, called parseInt, that does just this. If you change line 8 to use that method, everything works just fine:

```
iSum += Integer.parseInt(args[i]);
```

Now, compiling the program produces no errors, and running it with various arguments returns the expected results. For example, jview SumAverage 1 2 3 returns the following output:

```
Sum is: 6
Average is: 2
```

Summary

Today, you put together everything you've come across in the preceding days of this week about how to create Java classes and use them in Java applications. This included the following:

☐ Data members and class variables, which hold the attributes of the class and its instances. You learned how to declare them, how they are different from regular local variables, and how to declare constants.

☐ Instance and class methods, which define a class' behavior. You learned how to define methods, including the parts of a method's signature, how to return values from a method, how arguments are passed in and out of methods, and how to use the `this` keyword to refer to the current object.

☐ Java applications—all about the `main()` method and how it works, as well as how to pass arguments into a Java application from a command line.

Q&A

Q I tried creating a constant variable inside a method and I got a compiler error when I tried it. What was I doing wrong?

A You can create only constant (`final`) class variables or data members; local variables cannot be constant.

Q `static` and `final` are not the most descriptive words for creating class variables, class methods, and constants. Why not use `class` and `const`?

A `static` comes from Java's C++ heritage; C++ uses the `static` keyword to retain memory for class variables and methods. (And, in fact, they aren't called class methods and variables in C++; `static` member functions and variables are more common terms.)

`final`, however, is new. `final` is used in a more general way for classes and methods to indicate that those things cannot be subclassed or overridden. Using the `final` keyword for variables is consistent with that behavior. `final` variables are not quite the same as constant variables in C++, which is why the `const` keyword is not used.

Q In my class, I have a data member called `name`. I also have a local variable called `name` in a method, which, because of variable scope, gets hidden by the local variable. Is there any way to get hold of the data member's value?

A The easiest way is not to name your local variables the same names as your data members. If you feel you must, you can use `this.name` to refer to the data member and `name` to refer to the local variable.

Q I want to pass command-line arguments to an applet. How do I do this?

A You're writing applets already? Been skipping ahead, have you? The answer is that you use HTML attributes to pass arguments to an applet, not the command line (you don't have a command line for applets). You'll learn how to do this next week.

Q **I wrote a program to take four arguments, but if I give it too few arguments, it crashes with a runtime error.**

A It is your responsibility to test for the number of arguments and the data type of those arguments your program expects; Java won't do it for you. If your program requires four arguments, you need to make sure that you have indeed been given four arguments, and return an error message if you haven't.

Day **8**

More About Methods

In a non–object-oriented programming language, functions are generally thought of as the most important elements: They are the means by which the program performs its operations. In an object-oriented language, the only way to write a function is to write a class method. Whereas classes and objects provide the framework, and class variables and data members provide a way of holding that class' or object's attributes and state, it is the methods that actually provide an object's behavior and define how that object interacts with other objects in the system.

TECHNICAL NOTE

> VJ++ doesn't allow you to define a function that is not a method of a class, whereas C++ does.

Yesterday, you learned a little bit about defining methods. With what you learned yesterday, you could create some simple VJ++ programs, but you'd still be missing some characteristics of methods that make them really powerful, and that make your objects and classes more efficient and easier to understand. Today, you'll learn about these additional characteristics of methods, including the following:

- ☐ Overloading methods—creating methods with multiple signatures and definitions but with the same name
- ☐ Creating constructor methods—methods that enable you to set up the initial state of an object when it is created
- ☐ Overriding methods—creating a different definition for a method than has already been defined in a superclass
- ☐ Finalizer methods—a way for an object to clean up after itself before it is removed from memory

Methods OverLoading

Yesterday, you learned how to create methods with a single name and a single signature. Methods in Java can also be overloaded; this means you can create methods that have the same name, but different signatures and different definitions. Method overloading enables instances of your class to have a simpler interface to other objects (no need for entirely different methods that do essentially the same thing) and to behave differently based on the input to that method.

When you call a method in an object and choose which method definition to execute, Java matches up the method name, number of arguments, and data type (int, String, byte, and so on) of those arguments.

To create an overloaded method, create several different method definitions in your class, all with the same name, but with different parameter lists (either in the number of arguments or the type of arguments). Java allows method overloading as long as each parameter list is unique for the same method name.

For example, you could have a Dates() class with ReturnDate methods to accept input parameters as a string, number, or a string and a Boolean. Each could return a date string formatted a specific way, or, as in the last parameter example, could return whether the data was a valid date or not.

Note that Java differentiates overloaded methods with the same name, based on the number and type of parameters to that method, not on its return type. If you try to create two methods with the same name and same parameter list, but different return types, you'll get a compiler error. The variable names you choose for each parameter to the method are irrelevant; all that matters is the number of arguments and the data type.

Here's an example of creating an overloaded method. Listing 8.1 shows a simple class definition for a class called MyRect, which defines a rectangular shape. The MyRect class has four data members to define the upper-left and lower-right corners of the rectangle: m_iX1, m_iY1, m_iX2, and m_iY2.

NOTE

> Why did we call it MyRect? Java's awt package has a class called Rectangle that implements much of this same behavior. We called this class MyRect to prevent confusion between the two classes.

TYPE **Listing 8.1. The MyRect class.**

```
class MyRect
{
    int m_iX1 = 0;
    int m_iY1 = 0;
    int m_iX2 = 0;
    int m_iY2 = 0;
}
```

When a new instance of the MyRect class is initially created, all its data members are initialized to 0. Now define a buildRect() method that takes four integer arguments (iNewX1, iNewY1, iNewX2, and iNewY2) and resizes the rectangle to have the appropriate values for its corners, returning the resulting rectangle object.

```
MyRect buildRect(int iNewX1, int iNewY1, int iNewX2, int iNewY2)
{
    m_iX1 = iNewX1;
    m_iY1 = iNewY1;
    m_iX2 = iNewX2;
    m_iY2 = iNewY2;
    return this;
}
```

What if you wanted to have the option of defining a rectangle's dimensions in a different way? For example, you could use Point objects rather than individual coordinates. You can overload buildRect() so that its parameter list takes two Point objects. Note that you'll need to import the Point class at the top of your source file so Java can find it.

```
import java.awt.Point;  // top of the source file

MyRect buildRect(Point pntTopLeft, Point pntBottomRight)
{
    m_iX1 = prtTopLeft.x;
    m_iY1 = prtTopLeft.y;
    m_iX2 = prtBottomRight.x;
    m_iY2 = prtBottomRight.y;
    return this;
}
```

NOTE A single point is represented by an x and y coordinate in two-dimensional space.

Perhaps you want to also have the ability to define the rectangle using a top corner, a width, and a height. To accomplish this, just create a different definition for `buildRect()`:

```
MyRect buildRect(Point pntTopLeft, int iWidth, int iHeight)
{
    m_iX1 = pntTopLeft.x;
    m_iY1 = pntTopLeft.y;
    m_iX2 = (m_iX1 + iWidth);
    m_iY2 = (m_iY1 + iHeight);
    return this;
}
```

To finish this example, create a method to print out the rectangle's coordinates, and a `main()` method to test it all (just to prove that this does indeed work). Listing 8.2 shows the completed class definition with all of its methods.

Create a new VJ++ project workspace for the following example. Open a new code window and type the application, save the file, add it to the project, compile it, and then test it using JVIEW.

TYPE **Listing 8.2. The complete `MyRect` class.**

```
import java.awt.Point;

class MyRect
{
    int m_iX1 = 0;
    int m_iY1 = 0;
    int m_iX2 = 0;
    int m_iY2 = 0;

    MyRect buildRect(int iNewX1, int iNewY1, int iNewX2, int iNewY2)
    {
        m_iX1 = iNewX1;
        m_iY1 = iNewY1;
        m_iX2 = iNewX2;
        m_iY2 = iNewY2;
        return this;
    }
    MyRect buildRect(Point pntTopLeft, Point pntBottomRight)
    {
        m_iX1 = pntTopLeft.x;
        m_iY1 = pntTopLeft.y;
        m_iX2 = pntBottomRight.x;
        m_iY2 = pntBottomRight.y;
```

8

```
        return this;
    }
    MyRect buildRect(Point pntTopLeft, int iWidth, int iHeight)
    {
        m_iX1 = pntTopLeft.x;
        m_iY1 = pntTopLeft.y;
        m_iX2 = (m_iX1 + iWidth);
        m_iY2 = (m_iY1 + iHeight);
        return this;
    }
    void printRect()
    {
        System.out.print("MyRect: <" + m_iX1 + ", " + m_iY1);
        System.out.println(", " + m_iX2 + ", " + m_iY2 + ">");
    }

    public static void main(String args[])
    {
        MyRect rect = new MyRect();
        System.out.println("Calling buildRect with coordinates 25,25 50,50:");
        rect.buildRect(25, 25, 50, 50);
        rect.printRect();
        System.out.println("-----");

        System.out.println("Calling buildRect w/points (10,10), (20,20):");
        rect.buildRect(new Point(10,10), new Point(20,20));
        rect.printRect();
        System.out.println("-----");

        System.out.print("Calling buildRect w/1 point (10,10),");
        System.out.println(" width (50) and height (50)");

        rect.buildRect(new Point(10,10), 50, 50);
        rect.printRect();
        System.out.println("-----");

    }
}  // end of class MyRect
```

Here's the output of the preceding VJ++ application:

```
Calling buildRect with coordinates 25,25 50,50:
MyRect: <25, 25, 50, 50>
-----
Calling buildRect w/points (10,10), (20,20):
MyRect: <10, 10, 20, 20>
-----
Calling buildRect w/1 point (10,10), width (50) and height (50)
MyRect: <10, 10, 60, 60>
-----
```

As you can see from the preceding example, all of the buildRect() methods work based on the arguments with which they are called. You can define as many versions of a method as you need to in your own classes to implement each unique behavior you need for that class.

Constructor Methods

In addition to regular methods, which are called by other methods within your own classes or from within other classes, you can also define constructor methods in your class definition. These methods are called only when a new instance (object) of your class is created.

 A *constructor method* is a special kind of method that determines how an object is initialized when it's created.

Unlike regular methods, you can't call a constructor method directly; instead, constructor methods are automatically called by Java when the new object is created. It's important to note here that only Java can call a constructor method. When you use new to create a new instance of a class, Java does three things:

☐ Allocates memory for the object

☐ Initializes that object's data members, either to their initial values, as defined in your program, or to some default (0 for numbers, null for objects, false for Booleans, '\0' for characters)

☐ Calls the class' constructor method, which might be one of several methods depending upon whether or not it is an overloaded method

Even if a class doesn't have any special constructor methods defined, no errors will be generated and you will still end up with an object. But you might have to set its data members, or call other methods that the class needs to initialize itself. All the examples you've created up to this point have not had constructor methods and, as you have seen, they have all (hopefully) worked quite well.

By defining constructor methods in your own classes, you can set initial values of data members, call methods based upon those variables, create new objects based on other classes, call methods in other objects, calculate initial properties of your object, or perform any operation that you can within a normal method. You can also overload constructors, as you would regular methods, to create an object that has specific properties based upon the arguments passed when new is called.

Basic Constructors

Constructors look a lot like regular methods, with two basic differences:

☐ Constructors always have the same name as the class.

☐ Constructors don't have a return type.

For example, Listing 8.3 shows a simple class called Person, with a constructor that initializes its data members based upon the arguments used when new is called. Person also includes a

8

method for the object to introduce itself, and a `main()` method to test each of the other two methods.

TYPE **Listing 8.3. The `Person` class.**

```
class Person
{
    String m_sName;
    int m_iAge;

    Person(String sNewName, int iNewAge)
    {
        m_sName = sNewName;
        m_iAge = iNewAge;
    }

    void printPerson()
    {
        System.out.print("Hi, my name is " + m_sName);
        System.out.println(". I am " + m_iAge + " years old.");
    }

    public static void main (String args[])
    {
        Person psrPerson;
        psrPerson = new Person("Dustin", 15);
        psrPerson.printPerson();
        System.out.println("----");
        psrPerson = new Person("Zachary", 10);
        psrPerson.printPerson();
        System.out.println("----");
    }
}
```

Here's the output for the preceding example program:

```
Hi, my name is Dustin. I am 15 years old.
----
Hi, my name is Zachary. I am 10 years old.
----
```

Calling Another Constructor

Some constructors you write might be a superset of another constructor defined in your class; they might have the same behavior plus a little bit more. Rather than duplicating identical behavior in multiple constructor methods in your class, it makes sense to be able to just call that first constructor from inside the body of the second constructor. Java provides a special syntax for doing this. To call a constructor defined on the current class, use this form:

```
this(arg1, arg2, arg3...);
```

The arguments used in the call to this are the arguments that would be used in a call to new. Yes, this seems confusing, and it is. Take a look at the following example and this concept should make more sense:

```
class Student
{
    String m_sName;
    int m_iAge;
    String m_sGrade = "na";

    Student(String sNewName, int iNewAge)
    {
        m_sName = sNewName;
        m_iAge = iNewAge;
        m_sGrade = "Incomplete";
    }

    Student(String sNewName, int iNewAge, String sGrade)
    {
        this(sNewName, iNewAge);
        m_sGrade = sGrade;
    }

    void printStudent()
    {
        System.out.println("Name " + m_sName + " Age " +
            m_iAge + " Grade " + m_sGrade);
    }

    public static void main (String args[])
    {
        Student stdStudent;
        stdStudent = new Student("Liz", 20, "A+");
        stdStudent.printStudent();
        System.out.println("----");
        stdStudent = new Student("John", 19);
        stdStudent.printStudent();
        System.out.println("----");
        stdStudent = new Student("Pete", 21, "C-");
        stdStudent.printStudent();
        System.out.println("----");
        stdStudent = new Student("David", 19, "D");
        stdStudent.printStudent();
        System.out.println("----");
    }
}
```

Can you guess what the output of this system will be? Try it. The answer is located at the end of this chapter.

Overloading Constructors

Like regular methods, constructors can also take varying numbers and data types as parameters. This flexibility enables you to create your object with the properties you want it to have, or to be able to calculate properties from different input forms.

For example, the buildRect() methods you defined in the MyRect class from Listing 8.2 would make excellent constructors. Why? Because what they're doing is initializing an object's data members to the appropriate values. So, instead of the original buildRect() method you defined (which took the four corner coordinate parameters), you can create a constructor instead. Listing 8.4 shows a new class called MyRect2 that has all the same functionality as the original MyRect, except it uses overloaded constructor methods instead of the buildRect() method.

TYPE   **Listing 8.4. The MyRect2 class (with constructors).**

```
import java.awt.Point;

class MyRect2
{
    int m_iX1 = 0;
    int m_iY1 = 0;
    int m_iX2 = 0;
    int m_iY2 = 0;

    MyRect2(int iNewX1, int iNewY1, int iNewX2, int iNewY2)
    {
        m_iX1 = iNewX1;
        m_iY1 = iNewY1;
        m_iX2 = iNewX2;
        m_iY2 = iNewY2;
    }

    MyRect2(Point pntTopLeft, Point pntBottomRight)
    {
        m_iX1 = pntTopLeft.x;
        m_iY1 = pntTopLeft.y;
        m_iX2 = pntBottomRight.x;
        m_iY2 = pntBottomRight.y;
    }

    MyRect2(Point topLeft, int w, int h)
    {
        m_iX1 = topLeft.x;
        m_iY1 = topLeft.y;
        m_iX2 = (m_iX1 + w);
        m_iY2 = (m_iY1 + h);
    }
```

continues

Listing 8.4. continued

```
void printRect()
{
    System.out.print("MyRect: <" + m_iX1 + ", " + m_iY1);
    System.out.println(", " + m_iX2 + ", " + m_iY2 + ">");
}

public static void main(String args[])
{
    MyRect2 rect;

    System.out.println("Calling MyRect2 with coordinates 25,25 50,50:");
    rect = new MyRect2(25, 25, 50,50);
    rect.printRect();
    System.out.println("-----");

    System.out.println("Calling MyRect2 w/points (10,10), (20,20):");
    rect= new MyRect2(new Point(10,10), new Point(20,20));
    rect.printRect();
    System.out.println("-----");

    System.out.print("Calling MyRect2 w/1 point (10,10),");
    System.out.println(" width (50) and height (50)");
    rect = new MyRect2(new Point(10,10), 50, 50);
    rect.printRect();
    System.out.println("-----");

}
} // end of class MyRect2
```

Here's the output for `MyRect2`. It's the same output as from the original `MyRect`; only the code to produce it has changed:

```
Calling MyRect2 with coordinates 25,25 50,50:
MyRect: <25, 25, 50, 50>
- - - - -
Calling MyRect2 w/points (10,10), (20,20):
MyRect: <10, 10, 20, 20>
- - - - -
Calling MyRect2 w/1 point (10,10), width (50) and height (50)
MyRect: <10, 10, 60, 60>
- - - - -
```

Overriding Methods

When you call a method on an object, Java looks for that method definition in the class of that object. If it doesn't find one, it passes the method call up the class hierarchy until a method definition is found. Method inheritance enables you to define and use methods repeatedly in subclasses without having to duplicate the code itself.

There might be times, however, when you want an object to respond to the same methods, but have different behavior than the original method in the superclass. In this case, you can override that method. Overriding a method involves defining a method in a subclass that has the same signature as a method in a superclass. Then, when that method is called, the method in the subclass is found and executed instead of the original method in the superclass.

Creating Methods that Override Existing Methods

To override a method, create a method in your subclass that has the same signature (name, return type, and parameter list) as a method defined by one of your class' superclasses. Because VJ++ executes the first method definition it finds that matches the signature, this effectively "hides" the original method definition. Listing 8.5 is a simple class with a method called printMe(), which prints out the name of the class and the values of its data members. It doesn't show how to override a method, but is a setup for the following examples that do.

TYPE **Listing 8.5. The PrintClass class.**

```
class PrintClass
{
    int m_iX = 0;
    int m_iY = 1;

    void printMe()
    {
        System.out.println("m_iX is " + m_iX + ", m_iY is " + m_iY);
        System.out.println("I am an instance of the class " +
        this.getClass().getName());
    }
}
```

Listing 8.6 shows a class called PrintSubClass that is a subclass of (extends) PrintClass. The only difference between PrintClass and PrintSubClass is that the latter has an m_iZ data member. Again, this is a setup for what's to follow.

TYPE **Listing 8.6. The PrintSubClass class.**

```
class PrintSubClass extends PrintClass
{
    int m_iZ = 3;

    public static void main(String args[])
    {
        PrintSubClass obj = new PrintSubClass();
        obj.printMe();
    }
}
```

Here's the output from `PrintSubClass`:

```
X is 0, Y is 1
I am an instance of the class PrintSubClass
```

In the `main()` method of `PrintSubClass`, you created a `PrintSubClass` object and called the `printMe()` method. Note that `PrintSubClass` doesn't define the `printMe()` method, so Java looks for it in each of `PrintSubClass`' superclasses—and finds it, in this case, in `PrintClass`. Unfortunately, because `printMe()` is still defined in `PrintClass`, it doesn't print the `m_iZ` data member.

Now create a third class. `PrintSubClass2` is nearly identical to `PrintSubClass`, but you override the `printMe()` method to include the `m_iZ` variable. Listing 8.7 shows this class and, in combination with the two previous examples, shows how to override a method.

TYPE **Listing 8.7. The `PrintSubClass2` class.**

```
class PrintSubClass2 extends PrintClass
{
    int m_iZ = 3;

    void printMe()
    {
        System.out.println("m_iX is " + m_iX + ", m_iY is " + m_iY +
                ", m_iZ is " + m_iZ);
        System.out.println("I am an instance of the class " +
                this.getClass().getName());
    }

    public static void main(String args[])
    {
        PrintSubClass2 obj = new PrintSubClass2();
        obj.printMe();
    }
}
```

Now when you instantiate this class and call the `printMe()` method, the version of `printMe()` you defined for `PrintSubClass2` is called instead of the one in the superclass `PrintClass` (as you can see in this output):

```
m_iX is 0, m_iY is 1, m_iZ is 3
I am an instance of the class PrintSubClass2
```

Calling the Original Method

Usually, there are two reasons why you want to override a method that a superclass has already implemented:

8

□ To replace the definition of that original method completely

□ To enhance the original method with additional behavior

You've already learned about the first one; by overriding a method and giving that method a new definition, you've hidden the original method definition. But sometimes you might just want to add behavior to the original definition rather than hide it and ignore its intended functionality. VJ++'s capability to do exactly that is particularly useful when you would otherwise end up duplicating behavior in both the original method and the method that overrides it. VJ++ gives you the ability to call the original method in the body of the overridden method so that you can add only what additional functionality is required.

To call the original method from inside a method definition, use the super keyword to pass the method call up the hierarchy of classes. Here is a quick example of the concept:

```
void myMethod (String a, String b)
{
    // do stuff here
    super.myMethod(a, b); // call the myMethod method in the superclass(s)
    // maybe do more stuff here
}
```

The super keyword, which is like the this keyword, is a placeholder for the preceding class' superclass. You can use it anywhere you can use this, but it refers to the superclass rather than to the current object.

For example, Listing 8.8 shows the printMe() methods used in the previous example.

TYPE   **Listing 8.8. The printMe methods.**

```
// from PrintClass
    void printMe()
    {
        System.out.println("m_iX is " + m_iX + ", m_iY is " + m_iY);
        System.out.println("I am an instance of the class" +
                this.getClass().getName());
    }

//from PrintSubClass2
    void printMe()
    {
        System.out.println("m_iX is " + m_iX + ", m_iY is " +
                m_iY + ", m_iZ is " + m_iZ);
        System.out.println("I am an instance of the class " +
                this.getClass().getName());
    }
```

Rather than duplicating most of the behavior of the superclass' method in the subclass, you can rearrange the superclass' method so that additional behavior can easily be added in its subclasses:

```
// from PrintClass
void printMe()
{
    System.out.println("I am an instance of the class" +
                   this.getClass().getName());
    System.out.println("m_iX is " + m_iX);
    System.out.println("m_iY is " + m_iY);
}
```

Then, in the subclass, when you override printMe, you can merely call the original method and then add the code to print the additional data members that have been added to the new class:

```
// From PrintSubClass2
void printMe()
{
    super.printMe();
    System.out.println("m_iZ is " + m_iZ);
}
```

The following is the output of calling printMe() on an instance of the subclass:

```
I am an instance of the class PrintSubClass2
m_iX is 0
m_iY is 1
m_iZ is 3
```

Overriding Constructors

Constructors cannot technically be overridden. Because they always have the same name as the current class, you're always creating new constructors instead of inheriting the ones defined in superclasses. Most of the time this is fine, because when your class' constructor is called, the constructor with the same signature as all of your superclasses is also called. This insures proper initialization of your inherited subclass.

However, when you're defining constructors for your own class, you might want to change how your object is initialized, not only by initializing new variables your class adds, but also by changing the contents of variables that are already there. You do this by explicitly calling your superclass' constructors, and then changing whatever you like.

To call a regular method in a superclass, you use super.methodname(arguments). This, of course, cannot work with constructors because there is not a method name to call. Instead, you use the super keyword again.

```
super(arg1, arg2, ...);
```

Similar to using this(...) in a constructor, super(...) calls the constructor method for the immediate superclass. (This might, in turn, call the constructor of its superclass, and so on.)

For example, Listing 8.9 shows a class called NamedPoint, which extends the class Point from Java's awt package. The Point class has only one constructor, which takes an x and a y argument and returns a Point object. NamedPoint has an additional data member (a string for the name) and defines a constructor to initialize x, y, and the name.

TYPE   **Listing 8.9. The NamedPoint class.**

```
1: import java.awt.Point;
2:
3: class NamedPoint extends Point
4: {
5:     String m_sName;
6:
7:     NamedPoint(int iX, int iY, String sName)
8:     {
9:         super(iX,iY);
10:        m_sName = sName;
11:    }
12: }
```

The constructor defined here for NamedPoint (lines 7 through 11) calls Point's constructor method to initialize Point's data members (x and y). Although you can just as easily initialize x and y yourself, you might not know what other things Point is doing to initialize itself, so it's always a good idea to pass constructors up the hierarchy to make sure everything is set up correctly.

Passing constructors up the hierarchy also helps to ensure that each class provides only the functionality specific to that class. For example, suppose you are developing Class B and Jeff is developing Class A. Also suppose that Class B is inherited from Class A. (Class A is Class B's superclass.) If Jeff needs to add a variable to Class A that needs to be initialized at startup, all Jeff has to do is modify Class A with the new data and the changes will automatically be reflected in Class B (via inheritance). However, if you have modified the constructor in Class B, so as not to call the original constructor in Class A, the new variable that Jeff defined for Class A will not be initialized and your application will not work until you modify Class B to incorporate the new variable.

Finalizer Methods

Finalizer methods are the opposite of constructor methods; whereas a constructor method is used to initialize an object, finalizer methods are called just before the object is garbage-collected and its memory reclaimed.

The finalizer method is simply finalize(). The class Object, from which all other classes in VJ++ are inherited, defines a default finalizer method, which does nothing. To create a finalizer method for your own classes, override the finalize() method using this signature:

```
protected void finalize()
{
    ...
}
```

Include any cleaning up you want to do for that object inside the body of that finalize() method. If necessary, you can also call super.finalize() to allow your class' superclasses to finalize your object.

You can always call the finalize() method yourself at any time; it's simply a method like any other. However, calling finalize() does not force an object to be removed from memory and garbage-collected. Only removing all references to an object will cause it to be marked for deletion.

Finalizer methods are best used for optimizing the removal of an object, such as removing references to other objects or releasing external resources that have been acquired. They might also be used for other behaviors that make it easier for that object to be removed. In most cases, you will not need to use finalize() at all. See Day 21 for more about garbage collection and finalize().

Summary

Today, you learned all kinds of techniques for using, reusing, defining, and redefining methods. You learned how to overload a method, so that the same method can have different behaviors based on the arguments with which it's called. You learned about constructor methods, which are used to initialize a new object when it's created. You learned about method inheritance and how to override methods that have been defined in a class' superclasses. Finally, you learned about finalizer methods that can be used to clean up after an object, just before that object is garbage-collected and its memory reclaimed.

Q&A

Q I created two methods with the following signatures:

```
int total(int arg1, int arg2, int arg3) {...}
float total(int arg1, int arg2, int arg3) {...}
```

The Java compiler complains when I try to compile the class with these method definitions. But their signatures are different. What have I done wrong?

A Method overloading in Java works only if the parameter lists are different—either in the number of arguments or the data type of the arguments. Return type is not relevant for method overloading. Java (like any non-cognitive machine) gets confused. It doesn't know which method to call when it sees two methods with exactly the same parameter list. So, instead of staying confused, the compiler throws it back to you, with your cognitive brain, for you to help Java out of its quandary.

Q Can I overload overridden methods? (In other words, can I create methods that have the same name as an inherited method, but a different parameter list?)

A Sure! As long as the parameter lists vary, it doesn't matter whether you've defined a new method name or one that you've inherited from a superclass.

A Answers to the code in the section, "Calling Another Constructor."

```
Name Liz Age 20 Grade A+
- - - -
Name John Age 19 Grade Incomplete
- - - -
Name Pete Age 21 Grade C-
- - - -
Name David Age 19 Grade D
- - - -
```

Day 9

Java Applet Basics

Okay, you Web jockeys and Internet mavens, this chapter's for you. Application developers, don't despair. Remember, applets and applications have a lot in common. You'll learn a lot in this chapter too; don't take the day off.

Much of Java's current popularity has come about because of Java-capable World Wide Web browsers and their support for applets—small programs that run inside a Web page and can be used to create dynamic, interactive Web applications. Applets, as we noted at the beginning of this book, are written in the Java language (VJ++ being a development environment for Java) and can be viewed in any browser that supports Java, including Microsoft's Internet Explorer 3.0 and Netscape's Navigator 2.0x. Learning how to create applets is probably the reason you bought this book, so we'll not take any more time.

NOTE From here on out, when we mention a browser or Web browser, we mean a Java-enabled browser. Otherwise, what is the point in developing applets?

For the past eight days, you focused on learning about the Java language itself, the VJ++ interface, and some of the VJ++ tools. Most of the little programs you have created thus far were Java applications, but now that you have the basics down, it's time to move on to creating and using applets. We'll begin with a discussion of some of the classes in the standard Java class library.

Today, you'll start with the basics:

- [ ] A short review of differences between Java applets and applications
- [ ] Getting started with applets: the basics of how an applet works and how to create your own simple applets
- [ ] Including an applet on a Web page by using the <APPLET> tag; discussing the various features of that tag
- [ ] Passing parameters to applets

How Applets and Applications Are Different

Although you have already explored the differences between Java applications and Java applets in the early part of this book, you can review them now.

In short, Java applications are stand-alone Java programs that can be run by using the VJ++ interpreter (JVIEW). Most everything you've done so far in this book have been Java applications, albeit simple ones.

Java applets, however, are run from inside a World Wide Web browser. A reference to an applet is embedded in a Web page using a special HTML tag. When a reader loads a Web page with an applet in it, the browser downloads that applet from the Web server and executes it on the local system (the one the browser is running on).

Because Java applets run inside a Java browser, they have the advantage of using the structure already provided by the browser. The browser provides an existing window to run the applet, an event-handler and graphics context, and the surrounding user interface. Even though Java applications can create this structure, they don't require it (you'll learn how to create Java applications that use applet-like graphics and User Interface (UI) features later on in this book).

The convenience of structure and UI capabilities that applets provide over applications, however, is offset by some restrictions placed upon applets. Given the fact that Java applets can be downloaded from any Web site and run on a user's personal system, restrictions are necessary to prevent an applet from causing system damage or security breaches. Without

9

these restrictions in place, Java applets could be written to contain viruses, or be used to compromise the security of the system that runs them. The restrictions on what an applet can do include the following:

☐ By default, applets can't read or write to the user's file system (the file system of the machine that the browser is running on). However, some browsers permit a user to maintain a list allowing specific directories to be accessed. Other browsers don't allow an applet to read or write to the file system at all, or if they do, not when the user is still connected to the network.

☐ Usually, applets can communicate only with the server that originally stored the applet. This restriction can be overridden by some browsers. For the sake of compatibility (and error-free runtime), though, you should not write applets that depend upon communicating with a different server.

☐ Applets can't run any programs on the user's system. This includes forking a process for UNIX systems and `CreateProcess` and `WinExec` for Windows systems.

☐ Applets can't load programs or shared libraries that are native to the local platform, including DLLs.

NOTE

The last preceding item is true for a pure Java-enabled browser. Microsoft has extended the abilities of Java by providing support for COM objects, which, in effect, allow an applet to load COM objects from DLLs and EXEs that reside on the user's local machine. You will learn a bit about COM on Day 15, "Com, ActiveX, and JDBC."

In addition, Java itself includes various forms of security and consistency checking in the Java compiler and interpreter to prevent unorthodox use of the language (you'll learn more about this on Day 21, "Integrating Applets and ActiveX Controls with Scripting"). This combination of restrictions and security features makes it more difficult for a rogue Java applet to do damage to the client's system.

NOTE

These restrictions help to prevent all the traditional ways of causing damage to a user's system. However, it's impossible to be absolutely sure that a clever programmer cannot work around these restrictions to violate privacy, use CPU resources, and generally be an annoyance. Sun has asked the Net to try and break Java's security and create an applet that can circumvent the restrictions. You'll learn about more issues in Java security on Day 21.

ActiveX in an Applet

Keep this in the back of your mind as we go through the basic applet exercise today. The applets you create with VJ++ can include ActiveX objects. ActiveX objects are powerful, object-oriented extensions to the standard Java classes. For example, ActiveX controls allow button bars, scrollbars, and Excel spreadsheets to be included on a Web page. However, if a Web page contains an applet that uses ActiveX, the user will need to download the extra Microsoft classes that support ActiveX. Although this can be easily accomplished by your applet's initialization class, the user might not want (or be able) to download the controls. The good news is that Microsoft Internet Explorer 3.0 automatically installs the extra classes; Netscape (and other browsers) will probably do the same in the future. Also, in a press release dated July 26, 1996, Microsoft announced it would give up control of the ActiveX technology and help to move its control to an independent body. This should help to make ActiveX more popular, resulting in a larger installed base. So, what you need to consider when designing your applets is whether or not to make your applets ActiveX- (and Microsoft) specific, or more versatile, allowing ActiveX to coexist with the mundane standard Java classes, non-Microsoft applications, and the variety of Web browsers out there. For more detailed information about ActiveX, pick up a copy of *ActiveX Programming Unleashed,* also published by Sams.net.

Creating Applets

The VJ++ programs you've created up to this point have been Java applications—simple programs using a single main() method that created objects, set data members, and ran methods. Today, and in the days following, you'll be creating applets exclusively. To do this, you'll need a good grasp of how an applet works, the sorts of features an applet has, and where to start when you first create your own applets.

In general, an applet works when a user accesses a Web page that contains an applet. The browser then creates a local copy of the class file specified by an <APPLET> tag contained in the HTML file. As the browser is copying the class file, it's also parsing the file. If the browser finds any import statements, and those classes aren't on the local machine, it copies those files too. Once the files are copied, the applet is loaded, and the browser creates an instance of the initial class (the one specified by the <APPLET> tag). It's important to note here that from this point on, the browser and applet execute methods from the instance of the class it created and not from the original class. The instance of the class is then run by the browser. The browser then automatically executes the init() and start() methods. The remainder of the methods in the class are executed by the applet.

You can already see how different the applet process is from the application process. Other than the browser, though, there is one major difference. When an application loads, JVIEW runs the main method within the initial class; it doesn't make an instance of the initial class before running the main method like an applet does.

To create an applet, you create a subclass of the class `Applet`, from the `java.Applet` package. The `Applet` class provides behavior that enables your applet to work within the browser itself. It also enables it to take advantage of the capabilities of the Abstract Windowing Toolkit (AWT) to draw to the screen when you include UI elements to handle mouse and keyword events. Although your applet can have as many helper classes as it needs, the `main` applet class is the one that triggers the execution of the applet.

NEW TERM   *AWT* is the Abstract Windowing Toolkit. It is a group of classes and containers you'll use when your programs require graphical user interface elements, such as buttons, lists, scrollbars, windows, and frames. The AWT will be covered in detail on Day 12, "Creating an Interface Using Visual J++" and Day 13, "More on Graphical Front Ends Using Visual J++."

NEW TERM   A *helper* is a class that doesn't contain the `main` method that started the current applet.

The initial `main` applet class always has a signature like the following, where `myClass` would be replaced with the name of your particular class:

```
public class myClass extends java.Applet.Applet
{
    ...
}
```

Note the `public` keyword. Java requires that your applet subclass be declared `public`. This is true only of the `main` applet class; any helper classes you create can be `public` or `private`. It's your choice. Public, private, and other forms of access control are described on Day 17, "Modifiers, Access Control, and Class Design," when we discuss modifiers.

Major Applet Activities

Hopefully you remember, when creating a basic Java application, your class has to have only one method, `main()`, with a specific signature. Then, when your application starts up, `main()` is executed, and then from `main()`, you can set up the behavior your program needs.

Applets are similar in this respect, but they are a bit more complicated, because they rely on a browser to operate. During the life of an applet, many different activities correspond to various events, for example, initialization, painting, and mouse actions. Each activity has a corresponding method, so when the event occurs, the applet depends upon the browser to call the methods specific to the event.

By default, however, all of the preceding methods do nothing, because the method corresponding to the event contains no default behavior. It's more or less an event placeholder. To provide behavior for an event, you must override each method in your applet's subclass, and give it the specific behavior you require. Java is structured this way because it's platform-independent. Also, keep in mind you don't have to override all of the events, only the ones you need.

In other words, all applets are subclasses of the class `applet`. Class `applet` has methods that handle events, but the methods in `applet` don't actually do anything. They are simply holders for your behavior-specific methods. Therefore, if you want your applet to do anything, you'll need to create member functions for each event trigger. By doing so, you will overload the methods in the superclass `applet`, superimposing your applet's methods behavior on top of each of its methods.

You'll learn about the various methods you might need to override as the week progresses, but, for a general overview, here are five of the more important applet execution method types: initialization, starting, stopping, destroying, and painting.

Initialization

Initialization occurs when the applet is first loaded (or reloaded). Initialization might include creating needed objects, setting up an initial state, loading images or fonts, or setting parameters. To provide initialization behavior, override the `init()` method:

```
public void init()
{
    ...
}
```

Starting

After an applet is initialized, it is started. Starting can also reoccur if the applet was previously stopped. For example, when a reader follows a link to a different page, the applet stops—when the reader comes back to the page, the applet restarts. Even though starting can occur several times during the life of an applet, initialization happens only once.

Functionality that you might include in the `start()` method could be starting an applet control thread, sending messages to helper objects, or simply telling the applet to begin running. You'll learn more about starting applets on Day 11, "Simple Animation and Threads."

To provide applet startup behavior, override the `start()` method:

```
public void start()
{
    ...
}
```

Stopping

Stopping and starting go hand in hand. When the reader triggers an event signaling they are leaving the page that contains the applet currently running, a call is automatically placed by the browser to the stop() method.

When the browser leaves the page, any threads the applet had started, but not finished, will continue to run. You'll learn more about threads in Day 11. By overriding stop(), you can suspend execution of the threads and then restart them if the applet is viewed again (started).

You stop the applet yourself by calling stop():

```
public void stop()
{
    ...
}
```

Destroying

Destroying sounds more violent than it is. Destroying enables the applet to clean up after itself. It does this just before the applet is freed from memory or the browser exits. For example, destroying kills any running threads and releases any other running objects. Generally, you won't need to override destroy() unless you need to release specific resources, such as threads the applet has created. To provide applet clean up behavior, override the destroy() method:

```
public void destroy()
{
    ...
}
```

TECHNICAL NOTE

How is destroy() different from finalize(), which was described on Day 8, "More About Methods"? First, destroy() applies only to applets and it applies to the applet as a whole; you destroy() when you exit the applet. finalize() is a more general purpose way a single object of any type can clean up after itself. In an applet, you can use both—finalize() inside a class to clean up after itself, and destroy() to clean up before the applet exits.

Painting

Painting is how an applet draws something on the screen, whether it is text, a line, a colored background, or an image. Painting can occur hundreds of times during an applet's life. For example, painting can occur after the applet is initialized, when the browser window is brought back to the foreground after being placed in the background by an overlapping window, when the browser window is moved to a different position, or repeatedly, when a Web page contains an animation. The `paint()` method looks like this:

```
public void paint(Graphics g)
{
    ...
}
```

Unlike the other methods in this section, `paint()` uses arguments: an instance of the class `Graphics` and a `context`. The `Graphics` object is created and passed automatically to `paint` by the browser, so you don't have to worry about it. However, you will have to make sure that the `Graphics` class (part of the `java.awt` package) gets imported into your applet code. This is usually and easily accomplished by using the `import` statement at the top of your applet file:

```
import java.awt.Graphics;
```

VJ++ Java Applet Wizard

On Day 2, "Introducing Visual J++," you created a simple applet called `HelloAgainApplet` (this was the one that displayed the big red `Hello Again`). That example was used to illustrate how to create a subclass. Today we're going to recreate that applet using the VJ++ Java Applet Wizard. Along the way, we will go over each of the pieces of Java code that the Java Applet Wizard automatically creates for you.

NOTE

> Don't be mad at us for not showing you the Wizard earlier. By knowing the basics first, you'll appreciate and understand what the Wizard does.

NOTE

> As we're going through the following Wizard windows, we won't be explaining every bit of detail. If you want specific information, you can get it (and we recommend that you do) by clicking Help.

New Project Workspace Window

To begin, open Microsoft Developer Studio, select File | New | Project Workspace, and click OK. When the New Project Workspace window appears, select Java Applet Wizard, and for the Name, type `NewHelloApplet` (this is the name of the main class). Notice VJ++

automatically creates a new Location (directory name) under the default project directory, based upon your applet's name. You should keep the location name that VJ++ creates. Also remember that Java expects (requires!) that the class name and its filename be the same— respecting the same upper- and lowercase letters in the class and filename. VJ++ and the Wizard take care of this for you. Make sure, under Platforms, that Java Virtual Machine is selected, and then click Create. (See Figure 9.1.)

Figure 9.1.

A completed New Project Workspace window.

Java Applet Wizard—Step 1 of 5

Notice that the Wizard can add the proper code to have your applet run as an applet (which requires a browser to run) or as both an applet and an application (a stand-alone program). In the Wizard window, select As an applet only. Leave the name of your applet class alone. The Wizard can also add explanatory comments and To Do comments. Both of these options are very helpful when you're working on your own and creating your own applets. Explanatory comments are disbursed throughout the applet, describing the function of each method. To Do indicators are placed in code sections where the Wizard can't determine the specific code to create, and you'll need to add your own. For your purposes, we'll elect not to generate comments, so they don't clutter up the workspace and prevent a clear view of the actual code. Select No, thank you, and then click Next. (See Figure 9.2.)

Figure 9.2.

A completed Step 1 of 5 window.

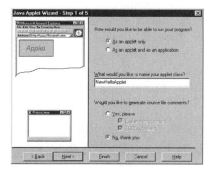

Java Applet Wizard—Step 2 of 5

The options in this window help you with testing your applet. The Wizard will create a skeleton HTML file containing a window in which to execute your applet. This is great for a couple of reasons. You might be a Java developer who doesn't know much about HTML, possibly because your company has HTML authors for that. Even if you do know HTML, you won't need to spend the time to create an HTML file simply for testing purposes. The initial applet size is measured in pixels (based on the values you supplied). Later, you can change the size by editing the values in the `init()` method of your source code, or it is also possible to create a dynamically sized window using the methods that determine screen size (`getScreenSize()`) and screen resolution (`getScreenResolution()`).

For now, you'll keep the default selections, and then click Next. (See Figure 9.3.)

Figure 9.3.

A completed Step 2 of 5 window.

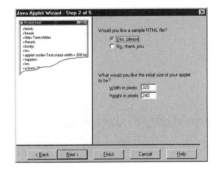

Java Applet Wizard—Step 3 of 5

These options handle how your applet behaves. Multithreaded, as discussed briefly earlier, allows your applet to spawn multiple processes that allow multiple things to appear to happen simultaneously. Displaying an animated image on a Web page is an example of multithreading. The multithreaded option adds a significant amount of code to your applet. Select No, thank you. Notice that when you elect not to have a multithreaded program, the options for animation and sample images become grey. These are unselectable now, because you must have support for multithreading to display an animation. If you didn't, your applet would display only the animated image and not give up any processing cycles to handle an exit event, which would be bad! Your last choice on this screen is to handle mouse events. More than likely, in your applets you'll choose to have these events handled. For your simple purposes, though, we'll choose not to support mouse events—leave the options unselected, and then click Next. (See Figure 9.4).

Java Applet Wizard—Step 4 of 5

The list box displayed in this window allows you to define the parameters that the HTML file will pass to your applet upon initialization. Read the text at the top of this window—it's good advice. An easy way to create a parameter is to click the New button (located to the left of the Delete button). Each time you click the New button, a row (representing a parameter definition) with default values is added to the Parameters table. To edit an item definition, double-click the item. For example, to change the name, double-click the name, and to change the description, double-click the description. To change the Type, after double-clicking the type, use the pull-down list box to select a valid data type. The Member variable stores the value read from the associated `<PARAM>.HTML` tag.

Figure 9.4.

A completed Step 3 of 5 window.

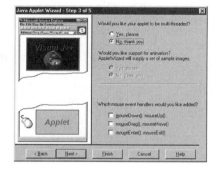

WARNING

In an early version of VJ++, the Wizard doesn't seem to check each parameter entry as valid. For example, we entered a data type of int with a value of 1.5 and, of course, we know that 1.5 is not a valid integer. We would hope that this will be corrected in the final release; however, you should be aware of it.

You're not going to pass any parameters to NewHelloApplet. If you've experimented with creating parameters (and we hope you did), use the Delete button to remove all the parameters you created, and then click Next. (See Figure 9.5.)

Figure 9.5.

A completed Step 4 of 5 window.

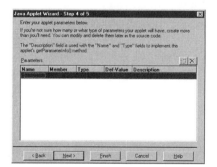

Java Applet Wizard—Step 5 of 5

This window displays a free-text scrollable list box. The default information shown in the box comes from VJ++ and information you have entered to personalize your copy of VJ++. When this window first displays, all the text is selected, so be careful! Read the message above the box to help explain why the information here can be useful. Note, the information you enter here is stored (hard coded) in the applet, not the HTML file.

Keep the default information displayed or type some new information of your own, but keep it short (Ogden Nash would probably be okay, whereas Tolstoy would not), and then click Finish. (See Figure 9.6.)

Figure 9.6.

A completed Step 5 of 5 window.

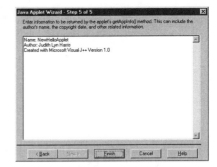

New Project Information

This window displays the information about your new applet based upon the choices and data you provided to the Wizard. The Wizard will use the information to build the basic Java program. Pay careful attention to the names of the files that will be created, and where the files will be located.

If you need to modify any of the information, first choose Cancel, which will redisplay the Step 5 of 5 window. From there, you can skip backwards through the windows by clicking Back. Click OK when you are ready to continue. (See Figure 9.7.)

Figure 9.7.

A New Project Informa-tion window.

Once the applet has been created, click the Class View tab to display your NewHelloApplet class structure. Click the plus (+) sign to the left of the class name to expand the outline. Your NewHelloApplet class should be displayed with a plus sign to its left. Click the plus sign to expand the outline again, and display the methods in your class.

In the Source window, at the very top of the source file, you will notice that the VJ++ Java Applet Wizard automatically added the import classes `java.applet.*` and `java.awt.*`. Remember that the * means to include all sub-libraries in the base library (`applet` and `awt`).

If you look further down in the code windows you'll find an `init()` method, a `destroy()` method, a `paint()` method, and `start()` and `stop()` methods. Of all these methods, the only one with any code in it is the `init()` member function. The code in that method is `resize()`, with two parameters (taken from the Wizard). This code resizes the applet's workspace (creates an embedded window of the specified size) within a Java-capable browser (more on that on Day 12).

There's a new method we've never discussed before in this applet: `getAppletInfo`. This method can be called by certain browsers when the user requests (via the browser) information about the currently running applet. You can also call this method in your applet during a `pageSetup()` method. This will include your requested information prior to a print method being called. The `getAppletInfo` is analogous to selecting Help | About in most Windows applications.

Modifying the Code for Your Own Use

To modify the VJ++ Java Applet Wizard's applet to resemble the `HelloAgain` applet created a few days ago is rather simple. First, if you look through the Source window, you won't see any references to a font object. As a result, any text drawn on the screen will be the default color and size. Change that. In the Source window, right below the class definition line, add the following line of code:

```
Font fntF = new Font("TimesRoman", Font.BOLD, 36);
```

The section of the window should now look like the following:

```
public class NewHelloApplet extends Applet
{
Font fntF = new Font("TimesRoman", Font.BOLD, 36);
```

Now that you have a font object defined, you can put it to work. The `paint` method is where the real work of this applet (what little work there is) really occurs. The `Graphics` object passed into the `paint()` method holds the graphics state, meaning the current features of the drawing surface. Add the following code to the `paint` method to complete this applet:

```
g.setFont(fntF);
   g.setColor(Color.red);
   g.drawString("Hello again!", 5, 50);
```

The `paint()` method should now look like the following:

```
public void paint(Graphics g)
{
   g.setFont(fntF);
   g.setColor(Color.red);
   g.drawString("Hello again!", 5, 50);
}
```

There you are! Now, compile and execute this applet. Notice how easy it is to have the VJ++ Java Applet Wizard create a skeleton applet and get it to work on a Web page. For you doubters out there, keep in mind that you didn't select multithreading or animation. If you had, the code the Wizard would have generated would have been quite impressive.

Take a few moments to look at the HTML page that the VJ++ Java Applet Wizard created for you. You can easily find the HTML file by selecting the Files tab in the Project Workspace window.

 NOTE

> When you compile an applet or application in Microsoft Developer Studio, errors are displayed in the Build output window located at the bottom of the screen. (Look for the Build tab.) When an error in your code is found, a line corresponding to each error displays. You can easily get to the specific line of your code that is in error by double-clicking the error line in the Build window displaying the error message. You will learn more about errors and debugging on Day 14, "Compiler Errors and Debugging."

Including an Applet on a Web Page

Remember, applets depend upon a browser in order to function. Unlike applications, they can't run as stand-alone programs. Once you've created an applet, it still needs a place to exist, live, and run! The safe and nurturing environment provided by a Web page and the HTML language allow you to let your applet go, to experience all that there is to see, and, most importantly, to be seen. The VJ++ Java Applet Wizard automatically created a simple HTML page for you. However, for testing purposes, it included only the necessary HTML tags to execute your applet. The HTML language, though, has a lot of specific tags that do a lot of wonderful things. The rest of today we're going to expand upon the `NewHelloApplet`, use some of the more common HTML tags, and show you how to make your applet available to the Web.

 NOTE

> The following section assumes you have at least a passing understanding of writing HTML pages. If you need help in this area, you might find the book *Teach Yourself Web Publishing with HTML in 14 Days* useful. It is also from Sams.net.

There is a special HTML tag for including applets in Web pages; Java-capable browsers use the information contained in that tag to locate the compiled class files and execute the applet itself. In this section, you'll learn about how to put Java applets in a Web page and how to serve those files to the Web at large.

The <APPLET> Tag

The <APPLET> tag is a special HTML tag used to include applets in a Web page. Java-capable browsers read this tag and then use the information contained in it to locate and execute your applet. Remember, your compiled applet will have the extension .class, whereas its source will have the extension .Java. The <APPLET> tag references the .class file.

To include an applet on a Web page, use the <APPLET> tag. Listing 9.1 shows a very simple example of a Web page containing an applet.

TYPE **Listing 9.1. A simple HTML page.**

```
1.  <html>
2.  <head>
3.  <title>This page has the NewHelloApplet</title>
4.  </head>
5.  <body>
6.  <hr>
7.  <applet
8.     code=NewHelloApplet.class
9.     width=320
10.    height=240 >
11.    There would be a way cool applet here if your browser supported Java
12. </applet>
13. <hr>
14. <a href="NewHelloApplet.java">The source.</a>
15. </body>
16. </html>
```

ANALYSIS There are three things to note about the <APPLET> tag in the preceding HTML page:

☐ The CODE attribute indicates the name of the compiled class file that contains this applet, including the .class extension. It is important to note that the .class extension is assumed and not required.

In this example, the class file and HTML file must be located in the same directory. To include applets located in a specific directory, use CODEBASE, which is described later today.

☐ WIDTH and HEIGHT are required. They are used to indicate the bounding box of the applet, meaning the dimensions of the embedded window containing the applet on the Web page.

It's very important to set the WIDTH and HEIGHT accurately. If your applet draws to an area outside the boundaries of the space you've provided, some browsers will not allow you (through your code) or a user to see or get to the parts of the applet that appear outside the bounding box.

☐ The text (line 11) between the <APPLET> and </APPLET> tags is displayed by browsers that do not understand the <APPLET> tag. Because your Web page might be viewed by different browsers, it's a very good idea to include alternate text. This allows a reader of your page who doesn't have a Java-enabled browser to see something other than a blank line. To satisfy those with less-fortunate browsers, include a simple statement that says, "There would be a way cool applet here if your browser supported Java."

The <APPLET> tag, like an <IMG> tag, is not in itself a paragraph, so it needs to be enclosed inside a more general text tag, such as <P>, or one of the heading tags (<H1>, <H2>, and so on).

Testing the Result

Click the File View tab and open the .html file for your applet. Edit line 3 and add line 11 to the file so it looks like Listing 9.1. Save the changes and then execute the applet. The browser loads and parses your HTML file. When it gets to the line containing the <APPLET> tag, it reserves the window space specified and then loads and executes the applet in that space. The only difference you should notice, because you're using a Java-enabled browser, is that a new window title displays.

Making Java Applets Available to the Web

Okay, you have a killer applet and you've tested it exhaustively on your local system. Everyone you've shown it to thinks you're the Web's equivalent to George Lucas. Now, how do you get the world to see your masterpiece?

Java applets are served by a Web server the same way that HTML files, images, and other media are. You don't need special server software to make Java applets available to the Web; you don't even need to configure your server to handle Java files. If you have a Web server up and running, or space on a Web server available to you, all you have to do is move your HTML and compiled class files to that server, as you would any other file.

If you don't have a Web server, you have to rent space on one, or set one up yourself. Microsoft NT 4.0 Server and NT 4.0 Workstation both have the capability and software to be Web servers. Also, Microsoft's GUI-based HTML authoring application Frontpage has the capability to turn a Windows NT 3.51 or 4.0 workstation into a mini-Web server—suitable for a small workgroup. Please note that Web server setup and administration, as well as other facets of Web publishing in general, are outside the scope of this book.

More About the <APPLET> Tag

In its simplest form, by using CODE, WIDTH, and HEIGHT, the <APPLET> tag merely creates a space of the appropriate size and then loads and runs the applet in that space. The <APPLET> tag, however, does include several attributes that can help you better integrate your applet into the overall design of your Web page.

NOTE The attributes available for the <APPLET> tag are almost identical to those for the HTML <IMG> tag.

ALIGN

The ALIGN attribute defines how the applet will be aligned in the browser window. This attribute can have one of nine values: LEFT, RIGHT, TOP, TEXTTOP, MIDDLE, ABSMIDDLE, BASELINE, BOTTOM, and ABSBOTTOM.

In the case of ALIGN=LEFT and ALIGN=RIGHT, the applet is placed at the left or right margins of the browser window, respectively, and any text outside of the applet window then flows to the left or to the right. The text will continue to flow in that space until reaching the bottom of the applet window, or until you use a line break tag (<BR>) with the CLEAR attribute starting the next line of text below the applet window. This is the same behavior as a desktop publishing package with an imbedded graphic, which allows the text to wrap around the graphic or not. The CLEAR attribute can have one of three values: CLEAR=LEFT starts the text at the next clear left margin, CLEAR=RIGHT does the same for the right margin, and CLEAR=ALL starts the text at the next line where both margins are clear.

For example, here's a fragment of HTML code that aligns an applet against the left margin, has some text flowing alongside it, and then breaks at the end of the paragraph so that the next bit of text starts below the applet:

```
<P><APPLET CODE="HelloAgainApplet" WIDTH=300 HEIGHT=200 ALIGN=LEFT>
Hello Again!</APPLET>
To the left of this paragraph is an applet. It's a
simple, unassuming applet in which a small string is
printed in red type, set in 36 point Times bold.
<BR CLEAR=ALL>
<P>In the next part of the page, we demonstrate how,
under certain conditions, styrofoam peanuts can be
used as a healthy snack.
```

Figure 9.8 shows how this applet and the text surrounding it might appear in a browser.

Figure 9.8.

An applet aligned left.

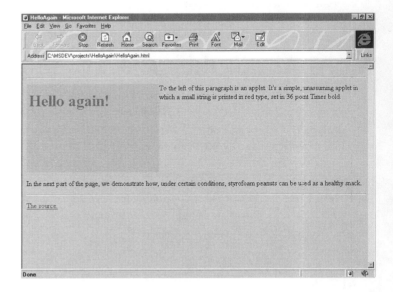

For smaller applets, you might want to include your applet within a single line of text. To do this, there are six values for ALIGN that determine how the applet is vertically aligned with the text:

☐ ALIGN=TEXTTTOP aligns the top of the applet with the top of the tallest text in the line.

☐ ALIGN=TOP aligns the applet with the topmost item in the line (which might be another applet, or an image, or the top of the text).

☐ ALIGN=ABSMIDDLE aligns the middle of the applet with the middle of the largest item in the line.

☐ ALIGN=MIDDLE aligns the middle of the applet with the middle of the baseline of the text.

☐ ALIGN=BASELINE aligns the bottom of the applet with the baseline of the text. ALIGN=BASELINE is the same as ALIGN=BOTTOM, but ALIGN=BASELINE is a more descriptive name.

☐ ALIGN=ABSBOTTOM aligns the bottom of the applet with the lowest item in the line (which might be the baseline of the text or another applet or image).

Figure 9.9 shows the various alignment options, where the line is an image and the arrow is a small applet.

Figure 9.9.
Applet alignment options.

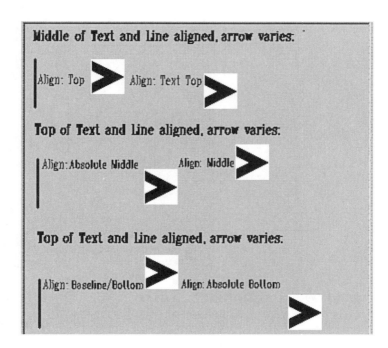

HSPACE **and** VSPACE

The HSPACE and VSPACE attributes are used to set the amount of space, in pixels, between an applet and its surrounding text. HSPACE controls the horizontal space (the space to the left and right of the applet). VSPACE controls the vertical space (the space above and below). For example, here's the preceding sample fragment of HTML with a vertical space of 50 and a horizontal space of 10:

```
<P><APPLET CODE="HelloAgainApplet" WIDTH=300 HEIGHT=200
ALIGN=LEFT VSPACE=50 HSPACE=10>Hello Again!</APPLET>
To the left of this paragraph is an applet. It's a
simple, unassuming applet in which a small string is
printed in red type, set in 36 point Times bold.
<BR CLEAR=ALL>
<P>In the next part of the page, we demonstrate how,
under certain conditions, styrofoam peanuts can be
used as a healthy snack.
```

The result in a typical Java browser might look like the result in Figure 9.10.

Figure 9.10.

Vertical and horizontal space.

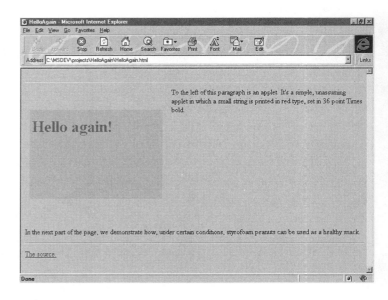

CODE **and** CODEBASE

CODE is used to indicate the name of the class file that holds the current applet. If CODE is used alone in the <APPLET> tag, the class file is searched for in the same directory as the HTML file that references it.

If you want to store your class files in a different directory than that of your HTML files, you have to tell the Java-capable browser where to find those class files. To do this, you use CODEBASE. CODE contains only the name of the class file; CODEBASE contains an alternate pathname where classes are contained. For example, if you store your class files in a directory called /classes, which is a child directory of the directory your HTML files are in, CODEBASE would be the following:

```
<APPLET CODE="myclass.class" CODEBASE="classes"
    WIDTH=100 HEIGHT=100></APPLET>
```

Passing Parameters to Applets

With Java applications, you can pass parameters to your main() routine by using arguments on the command line. You can then parse those arguments inside the body of your class. The application acts accordingly, based on the arguments it is given.

Applets, however, don't have a command line. How do you pass in different arguments to an applet? Applets can get different input from the HTML file that contains the <APPLET> tag through the use of applet parameters. To set up and handle parameters in an applet, you need two things:

☐ A special parameter tag in the HTML file

☐ Code in your applet to parse those parameters

Applet parameters come in two parts: a name, which is simply a name you pick, and a value, which determines the value of that particular parameter. For example, you can indicate the color of text in an applet by using a parameter with the name color and the value red. You can determine an animation's speed using a parameter with the name speed and the value 5.

In the HTML file that contains the embedded applet, you indicate each parameter using the <PARAM> tag, which has two attributes for the name and the value called (surprisingly enough), NAME and VALUE. The <PARAM> tag goes inside the opening and closing <APPLET> tags:

```
<APPLET CODE="MyApplet.class" WIDTH=100 HEIGHT=100>
<PARAM NAME=font VALUE="TimesRoman">
<PARAM NAME=size VALUE="36">
A Java Applet appears here.</APPLET>
```

This particular example defines two parameters to the MyApplet applet: one whose name is font and whose value is TimesRoman, and one whose name is size and whose value is 36.

Parameters are passed to your applet when it is loaded. In the init() method for your applet, you can then get hold of those parameters by using the getParameter() method. getParameter() takes one argument—a string representing the name of the parameter you're looking for—and returns a string containing the corresponding value of that parameter. (Like arguments in Java applications, all the parameter values are strings.) To get the value of the font parameter from the HTML file, you might have a line such as the following in your init() method:

```
String theFontName = getParameter("font");
```

NOTE
The names of the parameters, as specified in <PARAM>, and the names of the parameters in getParameter() must match identically, including having the same case. In other words, <PARAM NAME="name"> is different from <PARAM NAME="Name">. If your parameters are not being properly passed to your applet, make sure the parameter cases match.

If a parameter you expect has not been specified in the HTML file, getParameter() returns null. Most often, you will want to test for a null parameter and supply a reasonable default:

```
if (theFontName == null)
    theFontName = "Courier"
```

Keep in mind that getParameter() returns strings; if you want a parameter to be some other object or type, you have to convert it yourself. To parse the size parameter from that same HTML file and assign it to an integer variable called theSize, you might use the following lines:

```
int theSize;
String s = getParameter("size");
if (s == null)
    theSize = 12;
else theSize = Integer.parseInt(s);
```

Get it? Not yet? Try creating an example of an applet that uses this technique. You'll modify the HelloAgainApplet applet so that it says hello to a specific name, for example "Hello Jaren" or "Hello Mandy". The name is passed into the applet through an HTML parameter.

You can begin by copying the original HelloAgainApplet class:

```
import java.awt.Graphics;
import java.awt.Font;
import java.awt.Color;

public class MoreHelloApplet extends java.Applet.Applet {

    Font f = new Font("TimesRoman", Font.BOLD, 36);

    public void paint(Graphics g) {
        g.setFont(f);
        g.setColor(Color.red);
        g.drawString("Hello Again!", 5, 50);
    }
}
```

The first thing you need to add to this class is a place for the name. Because you'll need that name throughout the applet, add a data member for the name, just after the variable for the font:

```
String name;
```

To set a value for the name, you have to get its corresponding parameter. You set your variables to the parameter values inside the init() method. (The VJ++ Java Applet Wizard does this automatically when you define parameters for your applet.) The init() method is defined as public, with no arguments, and a return type of void. Make sure when you test for a parameter that you test for a null value; this way, you can supply a default value when no parameter is specified. The default, in this case, if a name isn't indicated, is to say hello to "Trevor":

```
public void init()
{
    name = getParameter("name");
```

```
    if (name == null)
    {
        name = "Trevor";
    }
}
```

One last thing to do, now that you have the name from the HTML parameters, is to modify the name so that it's a complete string; that is, to tack "Hello " onto the beginning, and an exclamation point onto the end. You could do this in the paint method just before printing the string to the screen. Here it's done only once, whereas in paint(), it's done every time the screen is repainted. In other words, it's slightly more efficient to do it inside init() instead:

```
name = "Hello " + name + "!";
```

And now, all that's left is to modify the paint() method. The original drawString() method looked like this:

```
g.drawString("Hello Again!", 5, 50);
```

To draw the new string you have stored in the name data member, all you need to do is substitute that variable for the literal string:

```
g.drawString(name, 5, 50);
```

Listing 9.2 shows the final result of the MoreHelloApplet class. Compile it so that you have a class file ready.

TYPE **Listing 9.2. The MoreHelloApplet class.**

```
1:   import java.awt.Graphics;
2:   import java.awt.Font;
3:   import java.awt.Color;
4:
5:   public class MoreHelloApplet extends java.Applet.Applet
6.   {
7:       Font f = new Font('TimesRoman", Font.BOLD, 36);
8:       String name;
9:
10:      public void init()
11:      {
12:          name = getParameter("name");
13:          if (name == null)
14:          {
15:              name = "Trevor";
16:          }
17:              name = "Hello " + name + "!";
18:      }
19:
```

continues

Listing 9.2. continued

```
20:     public void paint(Graphics g)
21:       {
22:         g.setFont(f);
23:         g.setColor(Color.red);
24:         g.drawString(name, 5, 50);
25:       }
26: }
```

Now, create the HTML file that will start the preceding applet. Listing 9.3 shows a new Web page for the MoreHelloApplet applet.

TYPE | **Listing 9.3. The HTML file for the MoreHelloApplet applet.**

```
 1:  <HTML>
 2:  <HEAD>
 3:  <TITLE>Hello!</TITLE>
 4:  </HEAD>
 5:  <BODY>
 6:  <P>
 7:  <APPLET CODE="MoreHelloApplet.class" WIDTH=300 HEIGHT=50>
 8:  <PARAM NAME=name VALUE="Jaren">
 9:  Hello to whoever you are!
10: </APPLET>
11: </BODY>
12: </HTML>
```

Note the <APPLET> tag, which points to the class file for the applet with the appropriate width and height (300 and 50). Just below it (line 8) is the <PARAM> tag, which you use to pass in the name. Here, the NAME parameter is simply name, and the VALUE is the string "Jaren".

Loading up this HTML file produces the result shown in Figure 9.11.

Now try a second example. Remember that in the code for MoreHelloApplet, if no name is specified, the default is the name "Trevor". Listing 9.4 creates an HTML file with no parameter tag for name.

TYPE | **Listing 9.4. Another HTML file for the MoreHelloApplet applet.**

```
 1:  <HTML>
 2:  <HEAD>
 3:  <TITLE>Hello!</TITLE>
 4:  </HEAD>
 5:  <BODY>
 6:  <P>
 7:  <APPLET CODE="MoreHelloApplet.class" WIDTH=300 HEIGHT=50>
 8:  Hello to whoever you are!
```

```
 9: </APPLET>
10: </BODY>
11: </HTML>
```

Figure 9.11.

The result of `MoreHelloApplet`, *first try.*

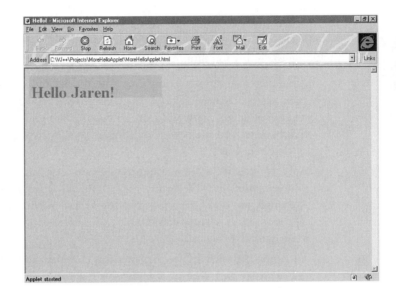

Here, because no name was supplied, the applet uses the default, and the result is what you might expect. (See Figure 9.12.)

Figure 9.12.

The result of `MoreHelloApplet`, *second try.*

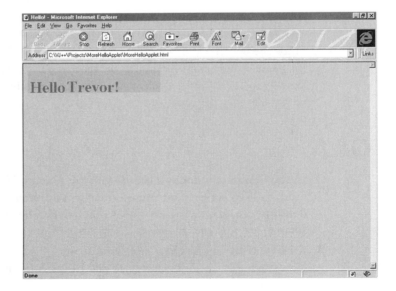

Summary

Applets are probably the most common use of the Java language today. They are more complicated than many Java applications because they are executed and drawn inline within Web pages; however, they can access the graphics, user interface, and event structure provided by the Web browser itself. Today, you learned the basics of creating applets, including the following things:

☐ All applets you develop using Java inherit from the Applet class part of the java.Applet package. The Applet class provides basic behavior for how the applet will be integrated with and react to the browser, and various forms of input from that browser and the person running it. By subclassing Applet, you have access to all that behavior.

☐ Applets have five main methods, which are used for the basic activities an applet performs during its life cycle: init(), start(), stop(), destroy(), and paint(). Although you don't need to override all these methods, these are the most common methods you'll see repeated in many of the applets you'll create in this book and in other sample programs.

☐ To run a compiled applet class file, you include it in an HTML Web page by using the <APPLET> tag. When a Java-capable browser comes across <APPLET>, it loads and runs the applet described in that tag. To publish Java applets on the World Wide Web alongside HTML files, you do not need special server software; any plain old Web server will do just fine.

☐ Unlike applications, applets do not have a common line on which to pass arguments, so those arguments must be passed into the applet through the HTML file that contains it. You indicate parameters in an HTML file by using the <PARAM> tag inside the opening and closing <APPLET> tags. <PARAM> has two attributes: NAME for the name of the parameter, and VALUE for its value. Inside the body of your applet (usually in init()), you can gain access to those parameters using the getParameter() method.

Q&A

Q **In the first part of today's lesson, you say that applets are downloaded from random Web servers and run on the client's system. What's to stop an applet developer from creating an applet that deletes all the files on that system, or in some other way compromises the security of the system?**

A Recall that Java applets have several restrictions that make it difficult for all of the more obvious malicious behavior to take place. For example, because Java applets cannot read or write files on the client system, they cannot delete files or read system files that might contain private information. Because they cannot run programs on the client's system without your express permission, they cannot, for example, run system programs pretending to be you. Nor can they run so many programs that your system crashes.

In addition, Java's architecture makes it difficult to circumvent these restrictions. The language itself, the Java compiler, and the Java interpreter all have checks to make sure that no one has tried to sneak in bogus code or play games with the system itself. You'll learn more about these checks at the end of this book.

Of course, no system can claim to be 100% secure, and the fact that Java applets are run on your system should make you suspicious—see Day 21 for more on security.

Q Wait a minute. If I can't read or write files or run programs on the system the applet is running on, doesn't that mean I basically can't do anything other than simple animation and flashy graphics?

A For everyone who doesn't believe that Java is secure enough, there is someone who believes that Java's security restrictions are too severe for just these reasons. Yes, Java applets are limited because of the security restrictions. But given the possibility for abuse, we believe that it's better to err on the side of being more conservative as far as security is concerned. Consider it a challenge.

Keep in mind, also, that ActiveX allows you to do more than just simple animation and graphics. We'll be discussing this on Day 21.

Q I noticed in my documentation that the `<APPLET>` tag also has a `NAME` attribute. You didn't discuss it here.

A `NAME` is used when you have multiple applets on a page that need to communicate with each other. You'll learn about this on Day 13.

Q I have an applet that takes parameters and an HTML file that passes it to those parameters. But when my applet runs, all I get are `null` values. What's going on here?

A Do the names of your parameters (in the `NAME` attribute) match exactly with the names you're testing for in `getParameter()`? They must be exact, including case, for the match to be made. Make sure, also, that your `<PARAM>` tags are inside the opening and closing `<APPLET>` tags, and that you haven't misspelled anything.

Day 10

Graphics, Fonts, and Color

A picture is worth a thousand words—a good graphic maybe more. And, if you're talking download time, certainly less time-consuming than a JPEG file. For the remainder of this week, you'll learn the sorts of things you can do with the built-in Java class libraries, and how you can combine them to produce interesting effects. You'll start today with learning how to produce lines and shapes using the built-in graphics primitives, how to print text using fonts, and how to use and modify color in your applets. Today, you'll specifically learn:

☐ How the graphics system works in Java: the Graphics class, the coordinate system used to draw to the screen, and how applets paint and repaint

☐ Using the Java graphics primitives, including drawing and filling lines, rectangles, ovals, and arcs

☐ Creating and using fonts, including how to draw characters and strings and how to find out the metrics of a given font to produce a better layout

☐ All about color in Java, including the Color class and how to set the foreground (drawing) and background color of your applet

NOTE

Today's lesson discusses many of the basic graphics, fonts, and color operations made available to you by the Java class library. However, today's lesson is intended to be an introduction and an overview more than an exhaustive description of all the features available. Be sure to check out the Java API documentation for more information on the classes described today.

The Graphics Class

With Java's graphics capabilities, you can draw lines, shapes, characters, and display images to the screen inside the applet window. You'll find that most of the graphics operations in Java are methods defined in the Graphics class. As a bonus, you don't have to create an instance of Graphics in order to draw something in your applet. An applet's paint() method (which you learned about yesterday) gives you a Graphics object. By using that object, results appear in the browser.

The Graphics class is part of the java.awt package, so if your applet does any painting (as it usually will), make sure you import that class at the beginning of your Java file:

```
import java.awt.Graphics;

public class MyClass extends java.applet.Applet
{
...
}
```

The Graphics Coordinate System

To draw an object on the screen, you call one of the drawing methods available in the Graphics class. All of the drawing methods have arguments that represent endpoints, corners, or starting locations of the object. These arguments are passed as values in the applet's coordinate system, for example, a line starting at the point 10,10 and ending at the point 20,20.

Java's coordinate system has the origin (0,0) in the top left corner. Positive x values are to the right, and positive y values are down. All pixel values are integers; there are no partial or fractional pixels. Figure 10.1 shows how you might draw a simple square by using this coordinate system.

Figure 10.1.

Drawing a square using the Java graphics coordinate system

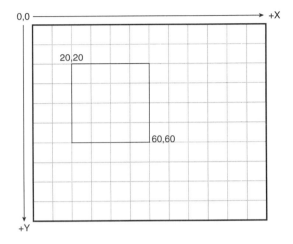

Java's coordinate system is different from many painting and layout programs that have their x and y in the bottom left. If you're not used to working with this upside-down graphics system, it might take some practice to become familiar with it.

Remember also, that these coordinates are relative to your applets, embedded window space inside the browser, and not the browser or screen as a whole.

Drawing and Filling

The `Graphics` class provides a set of simple built-in graphics primitives for drawing. These primitives include lines, rectangles, polygons, ovals, and arcs.

NOTE

> Bitmap images, such as JPEG and GIF files, can also be drawn by using the `Graphics` class. You'll learn about this tomorrow.

Lines

To draw straight lines, use the `drawLine()` method. `drawLine()` takes four arguments: the x and y coordinates of the starting point and the x and y coordinates of the ending point.

```
public void paint(Graphics g)
{
    g.drawLine(25,25,75,75);
}
```

Figure 10.2 shows the result of this fragment of code.

Figure 10.2.
A straight line.

Rectangles

The Java graphics primitives provide not just one, but three kinds of rectangles:

☐ Plain rectangles

☐ Rounded rectangles, which are rectangles with rounded corners

☐ Three-dimensional rectangles, which are drawn with a shaded border

For each of these rectangles, you have two methods to choose from: one that draws the rectangle in outline form and one that draws the rectangle filled with color.

To draw a plain rectangle, use either the drawRect() or fillRect() methods. Both take four arguments: the x and y coordinates of the top left corner of the rectangle, and the width and height of the rectangle to draw. For example, the following paint() method draws two squares: the left one is an outline and the right one is filled. (Figure 10.3 shows the results.)

```
public void paint(Graphics g)
{
    g.drawRect(20,20,60,60);
    g.fillRect(120,20,60,60);
}
```

Figure 10.3.
An outline rectangle and a filled rectangle.

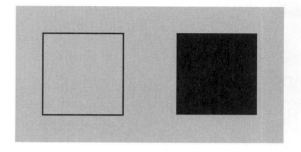

To draw a rectangle with rounded corners, the drawRoundRect() and fillRoundRect() methods are used. Drawing rounded rectangles is similar to regular rectangles, except that rounded rectangles have two extra arguments. These two extra arguments supply the width

and height values of the corner angles and also specify the starting point of the arc along the edges of the rectangle. The first argument describes the angle along the horizontal plane, the second describes the angle along the vertical plane. Larger values for the angle width and height make the overall rectangle more rounded; values equal to the width and height of the rectangle itself produce a circle. Figure 10.4 shows some examples of rounded corners.

Figure 10.4.

Some rectangles with rounded corners.

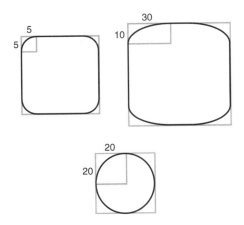

Here's a `paint()` method that draws two rounded rectangles: one as an outline with a rounded corner 10 pixels square; the other, filled, with a rounded corner 20 pixels square. (Figure 10.5 shows the resulting squares.)

```
public void paint(Graphics g)
{
    g.drawRoundRect(20,20,60,60,10,10);
    g.fillRoundRect(120,20,60,60,20,20);
}
```

Figure 10.5.

Two squares with rounded corners.

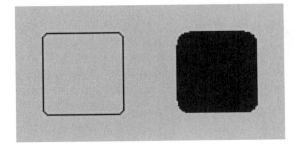

The final rectangle primitive creates three-dimensional rectangles. These rectangles aren't really 3D; if they were, you could make them pop out of the screen and bop somebody in the head. Instead, they have a shadow effect that makes them appear either raised or indented from the surface of the applet. Three-dimensional rectangles have five arguments—four arguments are for the x and y start position and the width and height of the rectangle, and the fifth argument is a Boolean indicating whether the 3D effect is to raise the rectangle (true) or indent it (false). As with the other rectangles, there are two different methods to draw (draw3DRect()) and fill (fill3DRect()). Here's a code fragment to produce an indented and a raised 3D rectangle. (Figure 10.6 shows the results.)

```
public void paint(Graphics g)
{
    g.draw3DRect(20,20,60,60,true);
    g.draw3DRect(120,20,60,60,false);
}
```

Figure 10.6.

A raised rectangle and an indented rectangle.

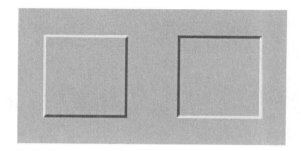

 NOTE

> Due to the very small line width in the current version of Visual J++, it is very difficult to see the 3D effect on 3D rectangles. If you seem to be having trouble with 3D rectangles, this might be why. Try drawing 3D rectangles using a color other than black. Sometimes this makes them easier to see.

Polygons

Polygons are shapes with multiple sides. In order to draw a polygon, you need sets of x and y coordinates. The drawing method starts at one xy set and draws a line to the second; it continues on from there and draws a line to the third xy set, and so on, until all the xy sets have been drawn.

As with rectangles, you can draw an outline or a filled polygon (using the drawPolygon() and fillPolygon() methods, respectively). When specifying the list of xy coordinates to the method, you have a choice of indicating them as either arrays of x and y coordinates or as an instance of the Polygon class.

Using the array method, the drawPolygon() and fillPolygon() methods take three arguments:

☐ An array of integers representing x coordinates

☐ An array of integers representing y coordinates

☐ An integer representing the total number of points

The x and y arrays must, of course, have the same number of elements.

The following is an example of drawing an outline polygon by using the array method. (Figure 10.7 shows the result.)

```
public void paint(Graphics g)
{
    int exes[] = { 39,94,97,142,53,58,26 };
    int whys[] = { 33,74,36,70,108,80,106 };
    int pts = exes.length;

    g.drawPolygon(exes,whys,pts);
}
```

Figure 10.7.

An outline polygon using arrays to specify the x and y points.

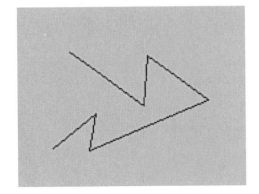

Java does not automatically close an outline polygon. If you want to complete the outline shape, you have to include the starting xy points of the polygon as the last elements of the arrays. When you're drawing a filled polygon, however, Java automatically joins the starting and ending points.

The second way of calling `drawPolygon()` and `fillPolygon()` is to use a `Polygon` object. The `Polygon` class is useful if you intend to add points to an existing polygon or if you're building a polygon on the fly. The `Polygon` class enables you to treat the polygon as an object rather than having to deal with the individual arrays.

To create a polygon object you can either create an empty polygon:

```
Polygon poly = new Polygon();
```

or create a polygon from a set of points using integer arrays, as in the previous example:

10

```
int exes[] = { 39,94,97,142,53,58,26 };
int whys[] = { 33,74,36,70,108,80,106 };
int pts = exes.length;
Polygon poly = new Polygon(exes,whys,pts);
```

Once you have a polygon object, you can append points to the polygon as you need to:

```
poly.addPoint(20,35);
```

Then, to draw the polygon, just use the polygon object as an argument to drawPolygon() or fillPolygon(). The following is the array example, rewritten using, instead, a Polygon object. Note that this code fragment fills the polygon, rather than just drawing its outline. (Figure 10.8 shows the output.)

```
public void paint(Graphics g)
{
    int iExes[] = { 39,94,97,142,53,58,26 };
    int iWhys[] = { 33,74,36,70,108,80,106 };
    int iPts = iExes.length;
    Polygon poly = new Polygon(iExes,iWhys,iPts);
    g.fillPolygon(poly);
}
```

Figure 10.8.
A filled polygon using the Polygon() *object.*

Ovals

Use ovals to draw ellipses or circles. Think of ovals as rectangles with overly rounded corners. You draw them using four arguments: the x and y of the top corner and the width and height of the oval itself. When you specify the top corner, it's actually a point outside the oval. If you think back to high school geometry of drawing an ellipse inside a rectangle, drawing an oval using the drawOval() method is quite similar.

As with the other drawing operations, the drawOval() method draws an outline of an oval, and the fillOval() method draws a filled oval.

Here's an example of two ovals, a circle and an ellipse. (Figure 10.9 shows how these two ovals appear on the screen.)

```
public void paint(Graphics g)
{
    g.drawOval(20,20,60,60);
    g.fillOval(120,20,100,60);
}
```

Figure 10.9.

A circle and an oval.

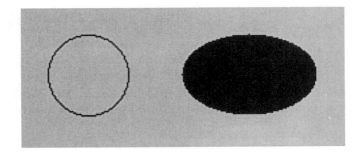

10

Arc

Of all the drawing operations, arcs are possibly the most complex to construct, which is why they're the last example. An arc is a part of an oval; in fact, the easiest way to think of an arc is as a section of a complete oval. Figure 10.10 shows some arcs.

Figure 10.10.

Some arcs.

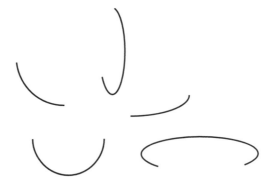

The drawArc() method takes six arguments: the x and y coordinates of the starting corner, the width and height, the starting angle of the arc, and the number of degrees to draw it before stopping. Once again, there is a drawArc method to draw the arc's outline and the fillArc() method to fill the arc. Filled arcs are drawn as if they were sections of a pie; instead of joining the two endpoints, both endpoints are joined to the center of the circle.

An important thing to understand about arcs is that you're actually formulating the arc as an oval and then drawing only some of it. The starting corner and width and height are not actually what's drawn on the screen as the arc; they're the width and height of the full ellipse of which the arc is only a part. Those first four arguments determine the size and shape of the arc; the last two arguments (for the degrees) determine the starting and ending points.

You'll start with a simple arc, a C shape on a circle as shown in Figure 10.11.

Figure 10.11.
A C shape on a circle.

To construct the method to draw this arc, the first thing you do is think of it as a complete circle. Then you find the x and y coordinates and the width and height of that circle. Those four values are the first four arguments of the drawArc() or fillArc() methods. Figure 10.12 shows how to get those values from the arc.

Figure 10.12.
Getting the x and y coordinates and width and height of a circle.

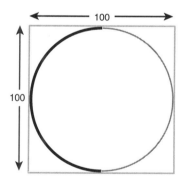

To get the last two arguments, think in degrees around the circle. Zero degrees is at 3 o'clock, 90 degrees is at 12 o'clock, 180 at 9 o'clock, and 270 at 6 o'clock. In this example, the starting point of the arc is the top of the C at 90 degrees; 90 then, is the fifth argument.

The sixth and last argument is another degree value indicating how far around the circle the arc sweeps and the direction to follow. (It's not the ending degree angle, as you might think.) In this case, because you're going halfway around the circle, you're sweeping 180 degrees; therefore, 180 is the last argument in the arc. The important part is that you're sweeping 180 degrees counterclockwise, which is the positive direction in Java. (Note that if you are drawing a backwards C, you sweep 180 degrees in the negative direction, and the last argument is -180.) See Figure 10.13 for the final illustration of how this works.

Figure 10.13.

An arc with a C.

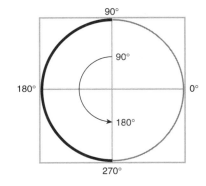

| **NOTE** | It doesn't really matter which side of the arc you start at; the shape of the arc has already been determined by the complete oval of which it's a section. Starting at either endpoint will work. |

Here's the code for this example; you'll draw an outline of the C and a filled C to its right, as shown in Figure 10.14:

```
public void paint(Graphics g)
{
    g.drawArc(20,20,60,60,90,180);
    g.fillArc(120,20,60,60,90,180);
}
```

Figure 10.14.

An outline C and a filled C.

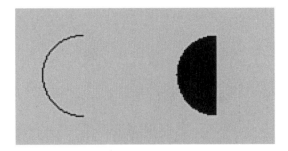

Arcs on ellipses are slightly more difficult than arcs on circles, but they use the same process. Now go through this same process to draw the arc shown in Figure 10.15.

Like the arc on the circle example, this arc is a piece of a complete oval, in this case, an elliptical oval. By completing the oval that this arc is a part of, you can get the starting points and the width and height arguments for the drawArc() or fillArc() method. (See Figure 10.16.)

Figure 10.15.
An arc on an ellipse.

Figure 10.16.
An elliptical oval.

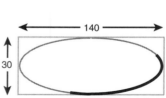

Then, all you need is to figure out the starting angle and the angle to sweep. This arc doesn't start on a nice boundary such as 90 or 180 degrees as in the circle, so you'll need a protractor. This arc starts somewhere around 25 degrees, and then sweeps clockwise about 130 degrees. (See Figure 10.17.)

Figure 10.17.
An arc on an elliptical oval.

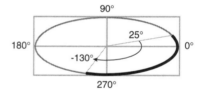

With all portions of the arc in place, you can write the code. Here's the Java code for this arc, using both the draw and fill methods. Note how filled arcs are drawn as if they were pie sections:

```java
public void paint(Graphics g)
{
    g.drawArc(10,20,150,50,25,-130);
    g.fillArc(10,80,150,50,25,-130);
}
```

Figure 10.18 shows the two elliptical arcs.

To summarize, here are the steps to construct arcs in Java:

- ☐ Think of the arc as a slice of a complete oval.
- ☐ Construct the full oval with the starting point and the width and height (to help determine the position, it might help to draw the full oval on the screen).
- ☐ Determine the starting angle for the beginning of the arc.
- ☐ Determine how far to sweep the arc and in which direction (counterclockwise indicates positive values, clockwise indicates negative values).

Figure 10.18.
Two elliptical arcs (outline and filled).

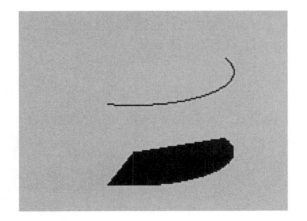

10

A Simple Graphics Example

Here's an example of an applet that uses many of the built-in graphics primitives to draw a rudimentary shape. In this case, it's a lamp with a spotted shade (or, depending upon your point of view, a sort of cubist mushroom). Listing 10.1 has the complete code for the lamp; Figure 10.19 shows the resulting applet.

TYPE **Listing 10.1. The Lamp class.**

```
 1: import java.awt.*;
 2:
 3: public class Lamp extends java.applet.Applet
 4:    {
 5:
 6:     public void paint(Graphics g)
 7:       {
 8:          // the lamp platform
 9:          g.fillRect(0,250,290,290);
10:
11:          // the base of the lamp
12:          g.drawLine(125,250,125,160);
13:          g.drawLine(175,250,175,160);
14:
15:          // the lamp shade, top and bottom edges
16:          g.drawArc(85,157,130,50,-65,312);
17:          g.drawArc(85,87,130,50,62,58);
18:
19:          // lamp shade, sides
20:          g.drawLine(85,177,119,89);
21:          g.drawLine(215,177,181,89);
22:
23:          // dots on the shade
24:          g.fillArc(78,120,40,40,63,-174);
```

continues

Listing 10.1. continued

```
25:          g.fillOval(120,96,40,40);
26:          g.fillArc(173,100,40,40,110,180);
27:    }
28: }
```

Figure 10.19.
The lamp applet.

Copying and Clearing

Once you've drawn a few things on the screen, you might want to move them around or clear the applet window. The Graphics class provides methods for doing both of these things.

The copyArea() method copies a rectangular area of the screen to another area of the screen. copyArea() takes six arguments: the x and y coordinates of the top corner of the rectangle to copy, the width and height of the rectangle, and the position to copy it to x and y coordinates. For example, the following line of code copies an area 100 pixels square to a position 100 pixels directly to its right:

```
g.copyArea(0,0,100,100,100,0);
```

To clear a rectangular area, use the `clearRect()` method. `clearRect()`, which takes the same four arguments as the `drawRect()` and `fillRect()` methods, fills the given rectangle with the current background color of the applet. (You'll learn how to set the current background color later on today.)

To clear the entire applet window, you can use the `size()` method, which returns a `Dimension` object representing the width and height of the applet. You can then get to the actual values for width and height by using the width and height data members:

```
g.clearRect(0,0,size().width,size().height);
```

Text and Fonts

The `Graphics` class, in conjunction with the `Font` and `FontMetrics` classes, enables you to print text on the screen. The `Font` class represents a given font—its name, style, and point size—and `FontMetrics` gives you information about a font (for example, the actual height or width of a given character) so that you can lay out text in your applet with better precision.

The text here is drawn to the screen once and intended to stay there. You'll learn about letting users enter text from the keyboard later this week.

Creating Font Objects

To draw text to the screen, first you need to create an instance of the `Font` class. Font objects represent an individual font, that is, its name, style (bold, italic), and point size. Font names are strings representing the family of the font, for example, `"TimesRoman"`, `"Courier"`, or `"Helvetica"`. Font styles are constants defined by the `Font` class; you can get to them using class variables, for example, `Font.PLAIN`, `Font.BOLD`, or `Font.ITALIC`. Finally, the point size is the size of the font, as defined by the font itself; the point size might or might not be the height of the characters.

To create an individual font object, use these three arguments to the `Font` class' new constructor:

```
Font f = new Font("TimesRoman", Font.BOLD, 24);
```

This example creates a font object for the "`TimesRoman`" `BOLD` font, in 24 points. Remember that like most Java classes, you have to import this class before you can use it.

Font styles are actually integer constants that can be added to create combined styles; for example, `Font.BOLD + Font.ITALIC` produces a font that is both bold and italic.

The fonts available to your applet depend upon the fonts installed on the system where the applet is running. If the font you use in your applet isn't available on the user's system, Java will substitute a default font (usually Courier). To be compatible with all systems accessing your applet through the Internet, it's a good idea to stick with the standard fonts such as `"TimesRoman"`, `"Helvetica"`, and `"Courier"`. If you'll be publishing your applet on an intranet, you'll probably have a wider variety of standard fonts to work with; check your system documentation to see which common fonts will be available on all platforms. Also, Microsoft's ActiveX components allow you to use TrueType fonts (more on that when you do ActiveX).

Your applet can also determine and use fonts on the fly; be careful, though—plan and test thoroughly. To do this, you use the `getFontList()` method, defined in the `java.awt.Toolkit` class. It returns a list of the fonts available on the user's system, from which you can perform some comparison checking and then make choices about which fonts to use. See the InfoView `getFontList()` and `getFontMetrics` topics if you're interested in trying this.

Drawing Characters and Strings

With a font object in hand, you can draw text on the screen using the methods `drawChars()` and `drawString()`. Before using either of these, you need to use the `setFont()` method to set the current font to your font object.

The current font is part of the graphics state that is kept track of by the active `Graphics` object. Each time you draw a character or a string to the screen, that text is drawn using the current font. To change to a different font, first change the current font. Here's a `paint()` method that creates a new font object, sets the current font to the one from the object, and then draws the string `"This is a big font."`, at the point `10,100` using the new current font.

```
public void paint(Graphics g)
{
    Font f = new Font("TimesRoman", Font.PLAIN, 72);
    g.setFont(f);
    g.drawString("This is a big font.", 10, 100);
}
```

If this looks familiar to you, it should. This is how the `Hello World` and `Hello Again` applets drew text to the applet window.

The latter two arguments to `drawString()` determine the point where the string will start. The x value is the start of the leftmost edge of the text; y is the baseline for the entire string.

NEW TERM *Baseline* is a typographic term. It refers to the common horizontal line on which all characters rest. A character (or parts of) ascend above the baseline; with characters such as g, j, p, q, and y, parts of the character descend below the baseline. Also, some very decorative or cursive fonts might have descenders (tails) for all of the characters in the font.

Similar to `drawString()` is the `drawChars()` method that, instead of taking a string as an argument, takes an array of characters. `drawChars()` has five arguments: the array of characters, an integer representing the first character in the array to draw, another integer for the last character in the array to draw (all characters between the first and last are drawn), and the x and y for the starting point. Most of the time, `drawString()` is more useful than `drawChars()`.

Listing 10.2 shows an applet that draws several lines of text in different fonts; Figure 10.20 shows the result.

TYPE   **Listing 10.2. Many different fonts.**

```
 1: import java.awt.Font;
 2: import java.awt.Graphics;
 3:
 4: public class ManyFonts extends java.applet.Applet
 5: {
 6:    public void paint(Graphics g)
 7:    {
 8:        Font f = new Font("TimesRoman", Font.PLAIN, 18);
 9:        Font fb = new Font("TimesRoman", Font.BOLD, 18);
10:        Font fi = new Font("TimesRoman", Font.ITALIC, 18);
11:        Font fbi = new Font("TimesRoman", Font.BOLD + Font.ITALIC, 18);
12:
13:        g.setFont(f);
14:        g.drawString("This is a plain font", 10, 25);
15:        g.setFont(fb);
16:        g.drawString("This is a bold font", 10, 50);
17:        g.setFont(fi);
18:        g.drawString("This is an italic font", 10, 75);
19:        g.setFont(fbi);
20:        g.drawString("This is a bold italic font", 10, 100);
21:    }
22:
23: }
```

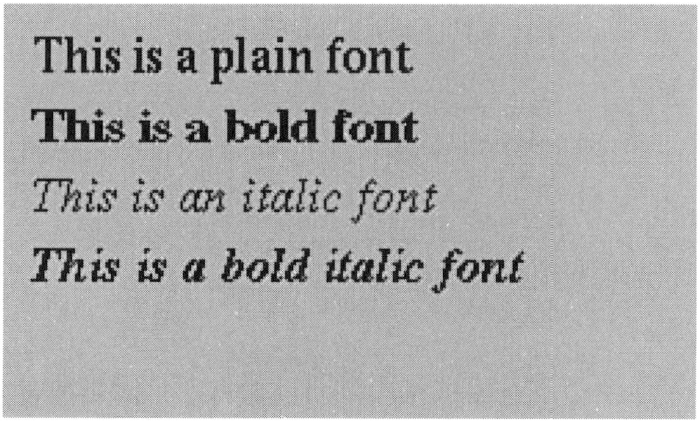

Figure 10.20.

The output of the ManyFonts *applet.*

This is a plain font

This is a bold font

This is an italic font

This is a bold italic font

Finding Out Information About a Font

Sometimes, you might want to make decisions in your Java program based on the qualities of the current font, for example, its point size, or the total height of its characters. You can find out some basic information about fonts and font objects by using simple methods on the `Graphics` and `Font` objects. Table 10.1 shows some of these methods:

Table 10.1. Font methods.

Method Name	In Object	Action
getFont()	Graphics	Returns the current font object as previously set by setFont()
getName()	Font	Returns the name of the font as a string
getSize()	Font	Returns the current font size (an integer)
getStyle()	Font	Returns the current style of the font (styles are integer constants: 0 is plain, 1 is bold, 2 is italic, 3 is bold italic)
isPlain()	Font	Returns true or false if the font's style is plain
isBold()	Font	Returns true or false if the font's style is bold
isItalic()	Font	Returns true or false if the font's style is italic

For more detailed information about the qualities of the current font (for example, the length or height of given characters), you need to work with font metrics. The `FontMetrics` class describes information specific to a given font: the leading between lines, the height and width of each character, and so on. To work with these sorts of values, you create a `FontMetrics` object based on the current font by using the applet method `getFontMetrics()`:

```
Font f = new Font("TimesRoman", Font.BOLD, 36);
FontMetrics fmetrics = getFontMetrics(f);
g.setfont(f);
```

Table 10.2 shows some of the things you can find out using font metrics. All these methods should be called on a `FontMetrics` object.

Table 10.2. Font metrics methods.

Method Name	Action
stringWidth(string)	Given a string, returns the full width of that string, in pixels
charWidth(char)	Given a character, returns the width of that character
getAscent()	Returns the ascent of the font—that is, the distance between the font's baseline and the top of the characters

Method Name	Action
getDescent()	Returns the descent of the font—that is, the distance between the font's baseline and the bottom of the characters (for characters such as p and q that drop below the baseline)
getLeading()	Returns the leading for the font—that is, the spacing between the descent of one line and the ascent of another line
getHeight()	Returns the total height of the font, which is the sum of the ascent, descent, and leading value

As an example of the sorts of information you can use with font metrics, Listing 10.3 shows the Java code for an applet that automatically centers a string horizontally and vertically inside an applet. The centering position is different depending on the font and font size; by using font metrics to find out the actual size of a string, you can draw the string in the appropriate place.

Note the applet.size() method here, which returns the width and height of the overall applet area as a Dimension object. You can then get to the individual width and height by using the width and height data members.

TYPE **Listing 10.3. Centering a string.**

```
 1: import java.awt.Font;
 2: import java.awt.Graphics;
 3: import java.awt.FontMetrics;
 4:
 5: public class Centered extends java.applet.Applet
 6: {
 7:
 8:     public void paint(Graphics g)
 9:     {
10:         Font f = new Font("TimesRoman", Font.PLAIN, 36);
11:         FontMetrics fm = getFontMetrics(f);
12:         g.setFont(f);
13:
14:         String s = "This is how the world ends.";
15:         int xstart = (size().width - fm.stringWidth(s)) / 2;
16:         int ystart = (size().height + fm.getHeight()) / 2;
17:
18:         g.drawString(s, xstart, ystart);
19:     }
20: }
```

Figure 10.21 shows the result (less interesting than if you actually compile and experiment with various applet and font sizes).

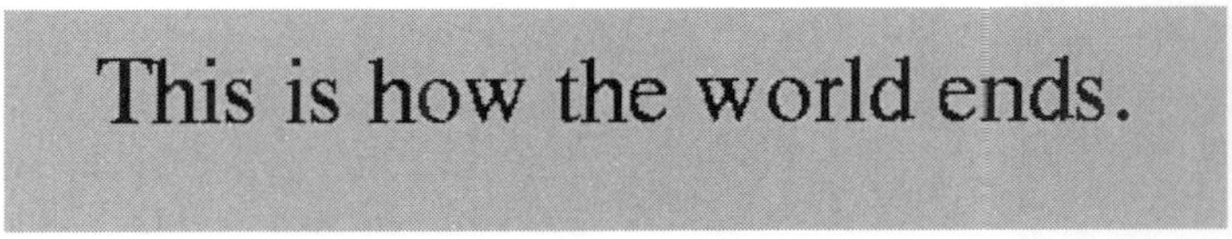

Figure 10.21.
The centered text.

> ## This is how the world ends.

Color

Drawing black on a gray background is all very nice, but being able to use different colors is much nicer. Java provides methods and behaviors for dealing with color in general through the Color class, and also provides methods for setting the current foreground and background colors so that you can draw with the colors you created.

Java's abstract color model uses 24-bit color, wherein a color is represented as a combination of red, green, and blue values. Each component of the color can have a number between 0 and 255. 0,0,0 is black, 255,255,255 is white, and Java can represent millions of colors between as well.

Java's abstract color model maps to the color model of the platform on which Java is running. The user's platform might have only 256 colors or fewer from which to choose. If a requested color in a color object is not available for display, the resulting color on the user's system might be mapped to another color or dithered. The resulting color depends upon how the color map was implemented by the browser. In other words, although Java provides the capability of managing millions of colors, in reality very few colors might actually be available to the user.

Using Color Objects

To draw an object in a particular color, you must create an instance of the Color class to represent that color. The Color class defines a set of standard color objects, stored in class variables, that enable you to quickly get a color object for some of the more popular colors. For example, Color.red gives you a Color object representing red (RGB values of 255, 0, and 0), Color.white gives you a white color (RGB values of 255, 255, and 255), and so on. Table 10.3 shows the standard colors defined by class variables in the Color class.

Table 10.3. Standard colors.

Color Name	RGB Value
Color.white	255,255,255
Color.black	0,0,0
Color.lightGray	192,192,192
Color.gray	128,128,128

Color Name	RGB Value
Color.darkGray	64,64,64
Color.red	255,0,0
Color.green	0,255,0
Color.blue	0,0,255
Color.yellow	255,255,0
Color.magenta	255,0,255
Color.cyan	0,255,255
Color.pink	255,175,175
Color.orange	255,200,0

10

If the color you want to draw in is not one of the standard color objects, fear not. You can create a color object for any combination of red, green, and blue, as long as you have the values of the color you want. Just create a new color object:

```
Color c = new Color(140,140,140);
```

This line of Java code creates a color object representing a dark gray. You can use any combination of red, green, and blue values to construct a color object.

Alternatively, you can also create a color object using three floats from 0.0 to 1.0:

```
Color c = new Color(0.55,0.55,0.55);
```

Testing and Setting the Current Colors

Just as you have to set the current font to the font with which you want to draw, to draw an object or text using a color object, you have to set the current color for the graphics context to be that color object. This allows you to set different colors for different objects. Use the setColor() method (a method for Graphics objects) to do this:

```
g.setColor(Color.green);
```

 The *Graphics Context* refers to the current settings of the active Java window. The Graphics Context includes font, background color, foreground color, and so on.

After setting the current color, all drawing operations will occur in that color.

In addition to setting the current color for the graphics context, you can also set the background and foreground colors for the applet itself by using the setBackground() and setForeground() methods. Both of these methods are defined in the java.awt.Component class, which Applet—and therefore, your classes—automatically inherits.

The setBackground() method sets the background color of the applet, which is usually defaulted to gray by the user's browser. It takes a single argument, a color object:

```
setBackground(Color.white);
```

The setForeground() method also takes a single color as an argument, and affects everything that has already been drawn by the applet, regardless of the color in which it had been originally drawn. You can use setForeground() to change the color of everything in the applet at once, rather than having to redraw everything:

```
setForeground(Color.black);
```

In addition to the setColor(), setForeground(), and setBackground() methods, there are corresponding get methods that enable you to retrieve the current graphics, background, and foreground colors. Those methods are getColor() (defined in Graphics objects), getForeground() (defined in Applet), and getBackground() (also in Applet). You can use these methods to choose colors based on existing colors in the applet:

```
setForeground(g.getColor());
```

A Single Color Example

Listing 10.4 shows the code for an applet that fills the applet's drawing area with square boxes, each of which is filled with a randomly chosen color. It's written so that it can handle any size applet and automatically populate the area with the right number of boxes.

TYPE   **Listing 10.4. Random color boxes.**

```
1:  import java.awt.Graphics;
2:  import java.awt.Color;
3:
4:  public class ColorBoxes extends java.applet.Applet
5:  {
6:
7:      public void paint(Graphics g)
8:      {
9:          int rval, gval, bval;
10:
11:         for (int j = 30; j < (size().height -25); j += 30)
12:         {
13:             for (int i = 5; i < (size().width -25); i += 30)
14:             {
15:                 rval = (int)Math.floor(Math.random() * 256);
16:                 gval = (int)Math.floor(Math.random() * 256);
17:                 bval = (int)Math.floor(Math.random() * 256);
18:                 g.setColor(new Color(rval,gval,bval));
19:                 g.fillRect(i, j, 25, 25);
20:                 g.setColor(Color.black);
```

10

```
21:                    g.drawRect(i-1, j-1, 25, 25);
22:            }
23:        }
24:    }
25: }
```

The two for loops are the heart of this example; the first one draws the rows, and the second draws the individual boxes within each row. When a box is drawn, the random color is calculated first, and then the box is drawn. Because some boxes tend to blend into the background of the applet, a black outline is drawn around each box.

Because the paint method generates new colors each time the applet is painted, you can regenerate the colors by moving the window around or by covering the applet's window with another one. Figure 10.22 shows the final applet (although the multicolored squares might be difficult to visualize in the picture shown).

Figure 10.22.

The random colors applet.

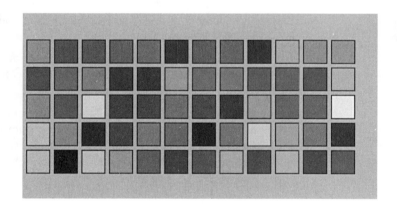

Summary

You present something on the screen by painting inside your applet: shapes, graphics, text, or images. Today, you learned the basics of how to paint, including using the graphics primitives to draw rudimentary shapes, using fonts and font metrics to draw text, and using Color objects to change the color of what you're drawing on the screen. It's this foundation in painting that enables you to do animation inside an applet (which basically involves just painting repeatedly to the screen) and to work with images, which you'll learn about tomorrow when the topic of discussion is animation.

Q&A

Q In all the examples you show and in all the tests I've made, the graphics primitives, such as `drawLine()` and `drawRect()`, produce lines that are one pixel wide. How can I draw thicker lines?

A In the current state of the Java Graphics class, you can't; no methods exist for changing the default line width. If you really need a thicker line, you have to draw multiple lines one pixel apart to produce that effect.

Q I wrote an applet to use Helvetica. It works fine on my system, but when I run it on my friend's system, everything is in Courier. Why?

A Your friend most likely doesn't have the Helvetica font installed on his or her system. When Java can't find a font, it substitutes a default font instead—in your case, Courier. The best way to deal with this is to query the font list using the `getFontList()` method in the `java.awt.Toolkit` class, and then use a font in the same font family as Helvetica.

Q I tried out that applet that draws boxes with random colors, but each time it draws, a lot of the boxes are the same color. If the colors are truly random, why is it doing this?

A There are two reasons. The first is that the random number generator we used in that code (from the `Math` class) isn't a very good random number generator; in fact, the documentation for that method says as much. For a better random number generator, use the `Random` class from the `java.util` package.

The second and more likely reason is that there just aren't enough colors available in your browser or on your system to draw all the colors that the applet is generating. If your system can't produce the wide range of colors available using the `Color` class, or if the browser has allocated too many colors for other things, you might end up with duplicate colors in the boxes. Remember, this behavior (for you and any potential user) is dependent upon how the system colors are set (16, 256, 64k, 16 million, and so on) and the browser implementation of the color mapper.

Day 11

Simple Animation and Threads

One of the coolest things that VJ++ can do extremely well is complex animation. After all, VJ++ is a Java development tool and Java is primarily used for the Internet where presentation—graphics and animation—are paramount.

Try the following: Using VJ++, create a new Project Workspace window by selecting New | Project Workspace from the menu. When the Wizards appear, select applet only, give it a name, and then click Create. On the next window, Step 1 of 5, select Finish. This will create a default project with animation and threads built in. Compile the project and view it using your browser. There it is, a fully multithreaded applet that does some pretty cool animation.

That sort of simple animation takes only a few methods to implement in Java, but these few methods are the basis for any Java applet that needs to update the screen dynamically. Starting with simple animation is a good way to build up to more complicated applets. Today, you'll learn the fundamentals of animation in VJ++: how the various parts of the system all work together so that you can create moving figures and dynamically updateable applets. Specifically, you'll explore the following:

- [ ] How a VJ++ animation works—the `paint()` and `repaint()` methods, starting and stopping dynamic applets, and how to use and override these methods in your own applets
- [ ] Threads—what they are and how they can make your applets more well-behaved with other applets and with the Java system in general
- [ ] Reducing animation flicker, a common problem in Java

Throughout today, you'll also work with lots of examples of real applets that create an animation or perform some sort of dynamic movement.

Creating Animation in VJ++

Animation in VJ++ involves two steps: constructing a frame of animation and then asking VJ++ to paint that frame, repeating as necessary to create the illusion of movement. The basic, static applets that you created yesterday taught you how to accomplish the first part; all that's left is how to tell Java to paint a frame.

Painting and Repainting

The `paint()` method, as you learned yesterday, is called by Java whenever the applet needs to be painted—when the applet is initially drawn, when the window containing it is moved, or when another window is moved over it. You can also, however, ask VJ++ to repaint the applet at a time you choose. So, to change the appearance of what is on the screen, you construct the image or frame you want to paint, and then ask VJ++ to paint this frame. If you do this repeatedly, and fast enough, you get animation inside your applet. That's all there is to it.

Where does all this take place? It doesn't take place in the `paint()` method itself. All `paint()` does is put dots on the screen. `paint()`, in other words, is responsible only for the current frame of the animation. The real work of changing what `paint()` does, of modifying the frame for an animation, actually occurs somewhere else in the definition of your applet.

In that "somewhere else," you construct the frame (set variables for `paint()` to use and create `Color`, `Font`, or other objects that `paint()` will need), and then call the `repaint()` method. `repaint()` is the function that causes VJ++ to call `paint()` and causes your frame to get drawn.

11

TECHNICAL NOTE

Because an applet can contain many different components that all need to be painted (as you'll learn later on this week), and, in fact, applets are embedded inside a larger Java application that also paints to the screen in similar ways, when you call repaint() (and therefore paint()) you're not actually immediately drawing to the screen as you do in other window or graphics toolkits. Instead, repaint() is a *request* for VJ++ to repaint your applet as soon as it can. Also, if too many repaint() requests are made in a short amount of time, the system might only call repaint() once for all of them. Much of the time, the delay between the call and the actual repaint is negligible.

Starting and Stopping an Applet's Execution

Remember start() and stop() from Day 9, "Java Applet Basics?" These are the methods that trigger your applet to start and stop running. You didn't use start() and stop() yesterday because the applets on that day did nothing except paint once. With animation and other Java applets that are actually processing and running over time, you'll need to make use of start() and stop() to trigger the start of your applet's execution, and to stop it from running when you leave the page that contains that applet. For most applets, you'll want to override start and stop for just this reason.

The start() method triggers the execution of the applet. You can either do all the applet's work inside that method, or you can call other object's methods in order to do so. Usually, start() is used to create and begin execution of a thread, so that the applet can run in its own time.

stop(), on the other hand, suspends an applet's execution, so when you move off the page on which the applet is displaying, it doesn't keep running and using up system resources. Most of the time when you create a start() method, you should also create a corresponding stop().

Putting It Together

Explaining how to do VJ++ animation is more of a task than actually showing you how it works in code. An example or two will help make the relationship between all these methods clearer.

11

Listing 11.1 shows a sample applet that, at first glance, uses basic applet animation to display the date and time and constantly updates it every second, creating a very simple animated digital clock. A frame from that clock is shown in Figure 11.1.

The words "at first glance" in the previous paragraph are very important; this applet doesn't work! However, despite the fact that it doesn't work, you can still learn a lot about basic animation by examining it. So, working through the code will still be valuable. In the next section, you'll learn just what's wrong with it.

See if you can figure out what's going on with the code before you skip ahead to the analysis.

TYPE   **Listing 11.1. The date and time applet.**

```
 1:  import java.awt.Graphics;
 2:  import java.awt.Font;
 3:  import java.util.Date;
 4:
 5:  public class DigitalClock extends java.applet.Applet
 6:  {
 7:      Font m_fntFont = new Font("TimesRoman", Font.BOLD, 24);
 8:      Date m_dteDate;
 9:
10:      public void start()
11:      {
12:          while (true)
13:          {
14:              m_dteDate = new Date();
15:              repaint();
16:              try
17:              {
18:                  Thread.sleep(1000);
19:              }
20:              catch (InterruptedException e)
21:              {   }
22:          }
23:      }
24:      public void paint(Graphics g)
25:      {
26:          g.setFont(m_fntFont);
27:          g.drawString(m_dteDate.toString(), 10, 50);
28:      }
29: }
```

Think you've got the basic idea? Now go through it, line by line.

ANALYSIS   Lines 7 and 8 define two basic data members: m_fntFont and m_dteDate, which hold objects representing the current font and the current date, respectively. More about these later.

Figure 11.1.

The digital clock.

Sun Nov 05 20:43:02 PST 1995

The start() method triggers the actual execution of the applet. Note the while loop inside this method; given that the test (true) always returns true, the loop never exits. A single animation frame is constructed inside that while loop with the following steps:

☐ The Date class represents a date and time (Date is part of the java.util package—note that it was specifically imported in line 3). Line 14 creates a new instance of the Date class, which holds the current date and time, and assigns it to the m_dteDate data member.

☐ The repaint() method is called.

☐ Lines 16 through 21, as complicated as they look, do nothing except pause for 1000 milliseconds (one second) before the loop repeats. The sleep() method there, part of the Thread class, is what causes the applet to pause. Without a specific sleep() method, the applet would run as fast as it possibly could, which, for most computer systems, would be too fast for the eye to see. Using sleep() enables you to control exactly how fast the animation takes place. try and catch enable Java to manage errors if they occur, and handle exceptions. They are described on Day 19, "Introduction to JavaScript."

On to the paint() method. Here, inside paint(), all that happens is the current font (in the variable m_fntFont) is set, and the date is printed to the screen. You have to call the toString() method to convert the date to a string. Because paint() is called repeatedly with whatever value happens to be in m_dteDate, the string is updated every second to reflect the new date.

NOTE

The toString() method is one of the most common VJ++ functions. If you run a Query on toString() (select Help | Search from the menu), you will get somewhere in the range of 100 topics found. This basically means that toString() is used to convert almost any non-string variable to a usable string.

There are a few things to note about this example. First, you might think it would be easier to create the new Date object inside the paint() method. That way you could use a local variable and not need a data member to pass the Date object around. Although doing things that way creates cleaner code, it also results in a less efficient program. The paint() method is called every time a frame needs to be changed. In this case, it's not that important, but in an animation that needs to change frames very quickly, the paint() method has to pause to create that new object every time. By leaving paint() to do what it does best—painting the screen—and calculating new objects beforehand, you can make painting as efficient as possible. This is precisely the same reason why the Font object is also in a data member.

Threads—What They Are and Why You Need Them

Depending on your experience with operating systems and with environments within those systems, you might or might not have run into the concept of threads. Start from the beginning with some definitions.

When a simple program runs, it starts executing, runs its initialization code, calls methods or procedures, and continues running and processing until its tasks are complete and the program terminates itself or is exited by a user. This type of program uses a single thread, where the thread is a single focus of control for the program.

Multithreading, as in Java, enables several different execution threads to run at the same time inside the same program, in parallel, without interfering with each other.

Here's a simple example: Suppose you have a long computation near the start of a program's execution. This long computation might not be needed until later in the program's execution. It's actually tangential to the main point of the program; it needs to get finished eventually, but not right away. In a single-threaded program, you have to wait for that computation to finish before the rest of the program can continue running. In a multithreaded system, you can put that computation into its own thread, enabling the rest of the program to continue running independently. Then, at some later point during the execution, the threads meet (for example, the computation stores a value in a variable where a comparison operation checks for a value) and the program continues on.

Now look at a real-world example, such as your car. If you consider your car to be a multithreaded program, you end up with a series of statements. When the car program is started, several threads are started—the engine thread, the radio thread, the air recirculating fan thread, and so on. Each of these threads basically runs independently of each other. If the engine thread stops, the radio and air recirculating fan threads won't necessarily stop (at least until the battery goes dead).

Using threads in Java, you can create an applet that runs in its own thread and will happily run all by itself without interfering with any other part of the system. Using threads, you can have lots of applets running at once on the same page. Be careful, though. Depending on how many threads you start, you might eventually tax the system so that all of them will run slower, yet they all will still run independently.

Even if you don't have the requirement to have lots of applets on a single page, using threads in your applets is good Java programming practice. The general rule of thumb for well-behaved applets is that whenever you have any bit of processing that is likely to continue for a long time (such as an animation loop, or a bit of code that takes a long time to execute), put it in its own thread.

The Problem with the Digital Clock Applet

The digital clock applet in the last section doesn't use threads. Instead, you put the `while` loop that cycles through the animation directly into the `start()` method so that when the applet starts running it keeps going until you quit the browser or applet viewer. Although this might seem like a good way to approach the problem, the digital clock won't work because the `while` loop in the `start()` method is monopolizing all the resources in the system, including painting. If you try compiling and running the digital clock applet, all you get is a blank screen. You also won't be able to stop the applet normally, because there's no way a `stop()` method can ever be called.

The solution to this problem is to rewrite the applet using threads. Threads enable this applet to animate on its own without interfering with other system operations, to be started and stopped (when you enter and exit the Web page), and to run it in parallel with other applets.

Writing Applets with Threads

How do you create an applet that uses threads? There are several things you need to do. Fortunately, none of them are difficult, and a lot of the basics of using threads in applets is just boilerplate code that you can copy and paste from one applet to another. Because it's so easy, there's almost no reason *not* to use threads in your applets.

There are four modifications you need to make to create an applet that uses threads:

1. Change the signature of your applet class to include the words implements Runnable.
2. Include a data member to hold this applet's thread.
3. Modify your start() method to do nothing but spawn a thread and start it running.
4. Create a run() method that contains the actual code that starts your applet running.

The first change is to the first line of your class definition. You've already got something like this:

```
public class MyAppletClass extends java.applet.Applet
{
...
}
```

You need to change it to the following:

```
public class MyAppletClass extends java.applet.Applet implements Runnable
{
...
}
```

When you include the Runnable keyword in your class definition, you'll have support for the Runnable interface in your applet. If you think way back to Day 4, "Java Basics," you'll remember that interfaces are a way to collect method names common to different classes, which can then be implemented inside different classes that need to implement that behavior. Here, the Runnable interface defines the behavior your applet needs to run a thread; in particular, it gives you a default definition for the run() method. By implementing Runnable you tell other objects (in particular, a Browser) that they can call the Run() method on your instances.

The second step is to add a data member to hold this applet's thread. Call it anything you like; it's a variable of the type Thread (Thread is a class in java.lang, so you don't have to import it):

```
Thread m_thRunner;
```

Third, add a start() method or modify the existing one so that it does nothing but create a new thread and start it running. Here's a typical example of a start() method:

```
public void start()
{
    if (m_thRunner == null)
    {
        m_thRunner = new Thread(this);
        m_thRunner.start();
    }
}
```

If you modify start() to do nothing but spawn a thread, where does the body of your applet go? It goes into a new method, run(), which looks like this:

```
public void run()
{
    // what your Applet actually does
}
```

run() can contain anything you want your class' thread to do: initialization code, the actual loop for your applet, or anything else that needs to run in its own thread. You also can create new objects and call methods from inside run(), and they'll run inside that thread. The run() method is the real heart of your applet.

Finally, now that you've got threads running and a start method to start them, you should add a stop() method to suspend execution of that thread (and, therefore, whatever the applet is doing at the time) when the browser leaves the page. stop(), like start(), is usually something along these lines:

```
public void stop()
{
  if (m_thRunner != null)
  {
      m_thRunner.stop();
      m_thRunner = null;
  }
}
```

The stop() method here does two things: it stops the thread from executing and also sets the thread's variable runner to null. Setting the variable to null makes the Thread object it previously contained available for garbage collection so that the applet can be removed from memory after a certain amount of time. If the reader comes back to this page and this applet, the start method creates a new thread and starts up the applet once again.

NOTE

All this stuff about start, stop, and creating threads can be confusing. The purpose of creating and destroying (setting the thread object to null) is to minimize the amount of memory that your applet takes when it's not the applet that's visible to the user. Even though you destroy and create new threads in the stop and start methods, you do not lose the values in your data members. Because you do not lose the data in your variables, you are not reinitializing your applet, just sort of pausing its execution.

And that's it! With four basic modifications, you can create a well-behaved applet that runs in its own thread.

Fixing the Digital Clock

Remember the problems you had with the digital clock applet at the beginning of this section? You'll now fix those problems so you can get an idea of how a real applet with threads looks. You'll follow the four steps outlined in the previous section.

First, modify the class definition to include the Runnable interface (the class is renamed to DigitalThreads instead of DigitalClock):

```
public class DigitalThreads extends java.applet.Applet implements Runnable
{
    ...
}
```

Second, add a data member for the Thread:

```
Thread m_thRunner;
```

For the third step, swap the way you did things. Because the bulk of the applet is currently in a method called start(), but you want it to be in a method called run(), rather than do a lot of copying and pasting, just rename the existing start() to run():

```
public void run()
{
   ...
}
```

Finally, add the boilerplate start() and stop() methods:

```
public void start()
{
   if (m_thRunner == null)
   {
       m_thRunner = new Thread(this);
       m_thRunner.start();
   }
}
public void stop()
{
   if (m_thRunner != null)
   {
       m_thRunner.stop();
       m_thRunner = null;
   }
}
```

You're finished! One applet converted to use threads in less than a minute flat. (Of course, this depends upon typing speed. Your actual time might vary—taxes and license not included.) The code for the final applet appears in Listing 11.2.

TYPE **Listing 11.2. The fixed digital clock applet.**

```
1:   import java.awt.Graphics;
2:   import java.awt.Font;
3:   import java.util.Date;
4:
5:   public class DigitalClock extends java.applet.Applet
6:   {
7:       Font m_fntFont = new Font("TimesRoman", Font.BOLD, 24);
8:       Date m_dteDate;
9:
10:      public void run()
11:      {
12:          while (true)
13:          {
14:              m_dteDate = new Date();
15:              repaint();
16:              try
17:              {
18:                  Thread.sleep(1000);
```

11

```
19:                }
20             catch (InterruptedException e)
21:            {   }
22:        }
23:    }
24:    public void paint(Graphics g)
25:    {
26:        g.setFont(m_fntFont);
27:        g.drawString(m_dteDate.toString(), 10, 50);
28:    }
29:    public void start()
30:    {
31:        if (m_thRunner == null)
32:        {
33:            m_thRunner = new Thread(this);
34:            m_thRunner.start();
35:        }
36:    }
37:    public void stop()
38:    {
39:        if (m_thRunner != null)
40:        {
41:            m_thRunner.stop();
42:            m_thRunner = null;
43:        }
44:    }
45: }
```

11

Reducing Animation Flicker

If you've been following along with this book and trying the examples as you go, rather than reading this book on an airplane, in the bathtub, or in another favorite reading place, you might have noticed that when the date program runs every once in a while, there's an annoying flicker in the animation. (Not that there's anything wrong with reading this book in the bathtub, but you won't see the flicker if you do that, so just trust me—there's a flicker.) This isn't a mistake or an error in the program; in fact, that flicker is a side effect of creating an animation in Java. Because it can be annoying, however, you'll learn how to reduce flicker in this part of today's lesson so that an animation runs cleaner and looks better on the screen.

Flicker and How to Avoid It

Flicker is caused by the way Java paints and repaints each frame of an applet. At the beginning of today's lesson, you learned that when you call the repaint() method, repaint() calls paint(). That's not precisely true. A call to paint() does indeed occur in response to a repaint(), but what actually happens are the following steps:

1. The call to repaint() results in a call to the method update().
2. The update() method clears the screen of any existing contents (in essence, fills it with the current background color), and then calls paint().
3. The paint() method then draws the contents of the current frame.

It's Step 2, the call to update(), that causes animation flicker. Because the screen is cleared between frames, the parts of the screen that don't change alternate rapidly between being painted and being cleared. Hence, you have flickering.

There are two major ways to avoid flicker in your Java applets:

☐ Override update() either not to clear the screen at all, or to clear only the parts of the screen you've changed.

☐ Override both update() and paint() and use double-buffering.

If the second way sounds complicated, that's because it is. Double-buffering involves drawing to an offscreen graphics surface and then copying that entire surface to the screen. Because it's more complicated, you'll explore that one tomorrow. Today, we'll cover the easier solution, overriding update().

How to Override Update

The cause of flickering lies in the update() method. To reduce flickering, therefore, override update(). Here's what the default version of update() does (in the Component class, which you'll learn more about on Day 13, "More on Graphical Front Ends Using Visual J++"):

```
public void update(Graphics g)
{
    g.setColor(getBackground());
    g.fillRect(0, 0, width, height);
    g.setColor(getForeground());
    paint(g);
}
```

Basically, update() clears the screen (or, to be exact, fills the applet's bounding rectangle with the background color), sets things back to normal, and then calls paint(). When you override update(), you have to keep these two things in mind and make sure that your version of update() does something similar. In the next two sections, you'll work through some examples of overriding update() in different ways to reduce flicker.

Solution One—Don't Clear the Screen

The first solution to reducing flicker is not to clear the screen at all. This works only for some applets. If your applet must redraw to the same area of the screen each time, this solution is for you. If your applet has a graphic that changes shape and/or moves around the screen, this solution is not the one to use.

The following is an example of an applet that flickers a lot. The ColorSwirl applet prints a single string to the screen ("All the swirly colors"), but that string is presented in different colors that dynamically fade into each other. This applet flickers terribly when it's run. Listing 11.3 shows the source for this applet, and Figure 11.2 shows the result.

TYPE Listing 11.3. The ColorSwirl applet.

```
 1:  import java.awt.Graphics;
 2:  import java.awt.Color;
 3:  import java.awt.Font;
 4:
 5:  public class ColorSwirl extends java.applet.Applet implements Runnable
 6:  {
 7:      Font m_fntF = new Font("TimesRoman",Font.BOLD,48);
 8:      Color m_clrColors[] = new Color[50];
 9:      Thread m_thThread;
10:
11:      public void start()
12:      {
13:          if (runThread == null)
14:          {
15:              m_thThread = new Thread(this);
16:              m_thThread.start();
17:          }
18:      }
19:
20:      public void stop()
21:      {
22:          if (m_thThread != null)
23:          {
24:              m_thThread.stop();
25:              m_thThread = null;
26:          }
27:      }
28:
29:      public void run()
30:      {
31:          // initialize the color array
32:          float fColor = 0;
33:          int i;
34:          for (i = 0; i < m_clrColors.length; i++)
35:          {
36:              m_clrColors[i] =
37:                  Color.getHSBColor(fColor, (float)1.0,(float)1.0);
38:              fColor += .02;
39:          }
40:
41:           // cycle through the colors
42:          i = 0;
43:          while (true)
```

continues

11

Listing 11.3. continued

```
44:         {
45:             setForeground(m_clrColors[i]);
46:             repaint();
47:             i++;
48:             try
49:             {
50:                 Thread.sleep(50);
51:             }
52:             catch (InterruptedException e)
53:             {   }
54:             if (i == m_clrColors.length )
55:             {
56:                 i = 0;
57:             }
58:         }
59:     }
60:
61:     public void paint(Graphics g)
62:     {
63:         g.setFont(m_fntF);
64:         g.drawString("All the Swirly Colors", 15, 50);
65:     }
66: }
```

Figure 11.2.
The ColorSwirl *applet.*

All the Swirly Colors

Compile and run this applet so you can observe the horrible screen flicker. Of course, if you're running a dual processor P6-300 (or whatever the hardware manufacturers are up to by the time this book is published), you might not notice the severity of the screen flicker and you might just have to take our word for it. Even so, keep in mind that the average user system might be 486-66!

There are three new things to note about this applet that might look strange to you:

☐ When the applet starts, the first thing you do (in lines 33 through 39) is to create an array of Color objects (m_clrColors) that contains all the colors that will be displayed. By creating all the colors beforehand, you can then just draw text in that color, one at a time; it's easier to precompute all the colors at once.

☐ To create the different colors, a method in the Color class called getHSBColor() creates a color object based upon values for hue, saturation, and brightness, rather than the standard red, green, and blue (RGB). By incrementing the hue value and keeping saturation and brightness constant, you can create a range of colors

11

without having to know the RGB for each one. If you don't understand this, don't worry about it; it's just an easy way to create the color array. You can learn more about `getHSBColor()` on your own by playing and using InfoView.

☐ The applet then cycles through the array of colors, setting the foreground to each one in turn and calling `repaint`. When it gets to the end of the array, it starts over again (line 54), thus repeating the process over and over ad infinitum.

Now that you understand what the applet does, fix the flicker. The flicker here results because each time the applet is painted, there's a moment where the screen is cleared. Instead of the text cycling neatly from red to a nice pink to purple, it's going from red to gray, to pink to gray, to purple to gray, and so on—not very nice looking at all.

Because the clearing of the screen is all that's causing the problem, the solution is easy: Override `update()` and remove the part where the screen gets cleared. It doesn't really need to get cleared anyhow, because nothing is changing except the color of the text. With the screen clearing behavior removed from `update()`, all update needs to do is call `paint()`. Here's what you should add to this applet to override the `update()` method:

```
public void update(Graphics g)
{
   paint(g);
}
```

With that—just one small, three-line addition—no more flicker. Wasn't that easy?

Solution Two—Redraw Only What You Have To

For some applets, it won't be quite that easy. Here's another example. In this applet, called Checkers, a red oval (a checker piece) moves from a black square to a white square and back again, as if on a checkerboard. Listing 11.4 shows the code for this applet, and Figure 11.3 shows the applet itself.

TYPE **Listing 11.4. The Checkers applet.**

```
 1:   import java.awt.Graphics;
 2:   import java.awt.Color;
 3:
 4:   public class Checkers extends java.applet.Applet implements Runnable
 5:   {
 6:        Thread m_thRunner;
 7:        int m_ixpos;
 8:
 9:        public void start()
10:        {
11:            if (m_thRunner == null)
12:            {
```

continues

Listing 11.4. continued

```
13:                    m_thRunner = new Thread(this);
14:                    m_thRunner.start();
15:           }
16:       }
17:
18:       public void stop()
19:       {
20:          if (m_thRunner != null)
21:          {
22:                  m_thRunner.stop();
23:                  m_thRunner = null;
24:          }
25:       }
26:
27:       public void run()
28:       {
29:           setBackground(Color.blue);
30:           while (true)
31:           {
32:               for (m_ixpos = 5; m_ixpos <= 105; m_ixpos+=4)
33:               {
34:                   repaint();
35:                   try
36:                   {
37:                       Thread.sleep(100);
38:                   }
39:                   catch (InterruptedException e)
40:                   {    }
41:               }
42:               for (m_ixpos = 105; m_ixpos > 5; m_ixpos -=4)
43:               {
44:                   repaint();
45:                   try
46:                   {
47:                       Thread.sleep(100);
48:                   }
49:                   catch (InterruptedException e)
50:                   {    }
51:               }
52:           }
53:       }
54:
55:       public void paint(Graphics g)
56:       {
57:           // Draw background
58:           g.setColor(Color.black);
59:           g.fillRect(0, 0, 100, 100);
60:           g.setColor(Color.white);
61:           g.fillRect(101, 0, 100, 100);
62:
63:           // Draw checker
64:           g.setColor(Color.red);
65:           g.fillOval(m_ixpos, 5, 90, 90);
66:       }
67: }
```

Figure 11.3.

The Checkers applet.

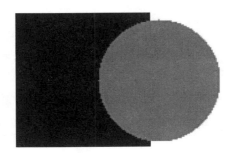

Here's a quick run-through of what this applet does: a data member, m_ixpos, keeps track of the current starting position of the checker (because it moves horizontally, the y stays constant and the x changes). In the run() method, you change the value of x and repaint, waiting 100 milliseconds between each move. The checker moves from one side of the screen to the other and then moves back (hence the two for loops in that method).

In the actual paint() method, the background squares are painted (one black and one white), and then the checker is drawn at its current position.

This applet, like the swirling colors applet, also has a terrible flicker. (In line 29, the background is blue to emphasize it, so if you run this applet you'll definitely see the flicker.)

However, the solution to solving the flicker problem for this applet is more difficult than for the last one, because you actually want to clear the screen before the next frame is drawn. Otherwise, the red checker won't have the appearance of leaving one position and moving to another; it'll just leave a red smear from one side of the checkerboard to the other.

How do you get around this? You still clear the screen, in order to get the animation effect; but, rather than clearing the entire screen, you clear only the part that you actually changed. By limiting the redraw to only a small area, you can eliminate much of the flicker you get from redrawing the entire screen.

To limit what gets redrawn, you need a couple of things. First, you need a way to restrict the drawing area so that each time paint() is called, only the part that needs to get redrawn actually gets redrawn. Fortunately, this is easy by using a mechanism called clipping.

 Clipping, part of the graphics class, enables you to restrict the drawing area to a small portion of the full screen; although the entire screen might get instructions to redraw, only the portions inside the clipping area are actually drawn.

The second thing you need is a way to keep track of the actual area to redraw. Both the left and right edges of the drawing area change for each frame of the animation (one side to draw the new oval, the other to erase the bit of the oval left over from the previous frame), so to keep track of those two x values, you need data members for both the left and the right side.

With those two concepts in mind, start modifying the Checkers applet to redraw only what needs to be redrawn. First, you'll add data members for the left and right edges of the drawing area. Call those data members m_ix1 and m_ix2 (u for update), where m_ix1 is the left side of the area to draw and m_ix2 the right.

```
int m_ix1,m_ix2;
```

Now modify the run() method so that it keeps track of the actual area to be drawn—which you would think is easy—just update each side for each iteration of the animation. Here, however, things can get complicated because of the way Java uses paint() and repaint().

The problem with updating the edges of the drawing area with each frame of the animation is that for every call to repaint() there might not be an individual corresponding paint(). If system resources get tight (because of other programs running on the system, or for any other reason), paint() might not get executed immediately and several calls to paint() might queue up waiting for their turn to change the pixels on the screen. In this case, rather than trying to make all those calls to paint() in order (and be potentially behind all the time), Java catches up by executing only the most recent call to paint() and skips all the others.

If you update the edges of the drawing area with each repaint(), and a couple of calls to paint() are skipped, you end up with bits of the drawing surface not being updated and bits of the oval left behind. There's a simple way around this: update the leading edge of the oval each time the frame updates, but only update the trailing edge if the most recent paint has actually occurred. This way, if a couple of calls to paint() get skipped, the drawing area will get larger for each frame—and when paint() finally gets caught up, everything will get repainted correctly.

Yes, this is horrifyingly complex. If I could have written this applet more simply, I would have. But without this mechanism, the applet will not get repainted correctly. Try stepping through it slowly in the code so you can get a better grasp of what's going on at each step.

Start with run(), where each frame of the animation takes place. Here's where you calculate each side of the drawing area based on the old position of the oval and the new position of the oval. When the oval is moving toward the left side of the screen, this is easy. The value of m_ix1 (the left side of the drawing area) is the previous oval's x position (xpos), and the value of m_ix2 is the x position of the current oval plus the width of that oval (90 pixels in this example).

To refresh your memory, here's what the old run() method looked like:

```
public void run()
{
    setBackground(Color.blue);
    while (true)
    {
```

```
        for (m_ixpos = 5; m_ixpos <= 105; m_ixpos+=4)
        {
            repaint();
            try
            {
                Thread.sleep(100);
            }
            catch (InterruptedException e)
            {    }
        }
        for (m_ixpos = 105; m_ixpos > 5; m_ixpos -=4)
        {
            repaint();
            try
            {
                Thread.sleep(100);
            }
            catch (InterruptedException e)
            {    }
        }
    }
```

In the first `for` loop in the `run()` method, where the oval is moving toward the right, you first update `m_ix2` (the right edge of the drawing area):

```
m_ix2 = m_ixpos + 90;
```

Then, after the `repaint()` has occurred, you update `m_ix1` to reflect the old x position of the oval. However, you want to update this value only if the paint actually happened. How can you tell if the paint actually happened? You can reset `m_ix1` in `paint()` to a given value (`0`), and then test to see whether you can update that value or whether you have to wait for the `paint()` to occur:

```
if (m_ix1 == 0)
{
    m_ix1 = m_ixpos;
}
```

Here's the new, completed `for` loop for when the oval is moving to the right:

```
for (m_ixpos = 5; m_ixpos <= 105; m_ixpos += 4)
{
    m_ix2 = m_ixpos + 90;
    repaint();
    try
    {
        Thread.sleep(100);
    }
    catch (InterruptedException e)
    {    }
    if (m_ix1 == 0)
    {
        m_ix1 = m_ixpos;
    }
}
```

11

When the oval is moving to the left, everything flips. m_ix1, the left side, is the leading edge of the oval that gets updated every time, and m_ix2, the right side, has to wait to make sure it gets updated. So, in the second for loop, you first update m_ix1 to be the x position of the current oval:

```
m_ix1 = m_ixpos;
```

Then, after the repaint() is called, you test to make sure the paint happened and update m_ix2:

```
if (m_ix2 == 0)
{
    m_ix2 = m_ixpos + 90;
}
```

Here's the new version of the second for loop inside run():

```
for (m_ixpos = 105; m_ixpos > 5; m_ixpos -= 4)
{
    m_ix1 = m_ixpos;
    repaint();
    try
    {
        Thread.sleep(100);
    }
    catch (InterruptedException e)
    {    }
    if (m_ix2 == 0)
    {
        m_ix2 = m_ixpos + 90;
    }
}
```

Those are the only modifications run() needs. Override update() to limit the region that is being painted to the left and right edges of the drawing area that you set inside run(). To clip the drawing area to a specific rectangle, use the clipRect() method. clipRect(), like drawRect(), fillRect(), and clearRect(), is defined for graphics objects and takes four arguments: x and y starting positions and the width and the height of the region.

Here's where m_ix1 and m_ix2 come into play. m_ix1 is the x point of the top corner of the region; then use m_ix2 to get the width of the region by subtracting m_ix1 from that value. Finally, to finish update(), you call paint():

```
public void update(Graphics g)
{
    g.clipRect(m_ix1, 5, m_ix2 - m_ix1, 95);
    paint(g);
}
```

With the clipping region in place, you don't have to do anything to the actual paint() method. paint() goes ahead and draws to the entire screen each time, but only the areas inside the clipping region actually get changed on screen.

You need to update the trailing edge of each drawing area inside paint() in case several calls to paint() are skipped. Because you're testing for a value of 0 inside run(), you merely reset m_ix1 and m_ix2 to 0 after drawing everything:

```
m_ix1 = m_ix2 = 0;
```

These are the only changes you have to make to this applet in order to draw only the parts of the applet that changed (and to manage the case where some frames don't get updated immediately). Although this doesn't totally eliminate flickering in the animation, it does reduce it a great deal. Try it and see. Listing 11.5 shows the final code for the Checkers applet.

TYPE **Listing 10.5. The final Checkers applet.**

```
1:    import java.awt.Graphics;
2:    import java.awt.Color;
3:
4:    public class Checkers extends java.applet.Applet implements Runnable
5:    {
6:        Thread m_thRunner;
7:        int m_ixpos;
8:        int m_ix1,m_ix2;
9:
10:       public void start()
11:       {
12:           if (m_thRunner == null)
13:           {
14:               m_thRunner = new Thread(this);
15:               m_thRunner.start();
16:           }
17:       }
18:
19:       public void stop()
20:       {
21:           if (m_thRunner != null)
22:           {
23:               m_thRunner.stop();
24:               m_thRunner = null;
25:           }
26:       }
27:
28:       public void run()
29:       {
30:           setBackground(Color.blue);
31:           while (true)
32:           {
33:               for (m_ixpos = 5; m_ixpos <= 105; m_ixpos+=4)
34:               {
35:                   m_ix2 = m_ixpos + 90;
36:                   repaint();
```

continues

Listing 10.5. continued

```
37:                    try
38:                    {
39:                        Thread.sleep(100);
38:                    }
39:                    catch (InterruptedException e)
40:                    {    }
41:                    if (m_ix1 == 0)
42:                    {
43:                        m_ix1 = m_ixpos;
44:                    }
45:                for (m_ixpos = 105; m_ixpos > 5; m_ixpos -=4)
46:                {
47:                    m_ix1 = m_ixpos;
48:                    repaint();
49:                    try
50:                    {
51:                        Thread.sleep(100);
52:                    }
53:                    catch (InterruptedException e)
54:                    {    }
55:                    if (m_ix2 == 0)
56:                    {
57:                        m_ix2 = m_ixpos + 90;
58:                    }
59:                }
60:            }
61:        }
62:        public void paint(Graphics g)
63:        {
64:            // Draw background
65:            g.setColor(Color.black);
66:            g.fillRect(0, 0, 100, 100);
67:            g.setColor(Color.white);
68:            g.fillRect(101, 0, 100, 100);
69:
70:            // Draw checker
71:            g.setColor(Color.red);
72:            g.fillOval(m_ixpos, 5, 90, 90);
73:            m_ix1 = m_ix2 = 0;
74:        }
75:        public void update(Graphics g)
76:        {
77:            g.clipRect(m_ix1, 5, m_ix2 - m_ix1, 95);
78:            paint(g);
79:        }
80:    }
```

Summary

Congratulations on getting through Day 11! This day was a bit rough; you've learned a lot, and it all might seem overwhelming. You learned about a plethora of methods to use and override: `start()`, `stop()`, `paint()`, `repaint()`, `run()`, and `update()`—and you got a solid foundation in creating and using threads.

After today, you're over the worst hurdles in terms of understanding applets. Other than handling bitmap images, which you'll learn about tomorrow, you now have the basic background to create just about any animation you want in Java.

Q&A

Q Why all the indirection with `paint()`, `repaint()`, `update()`, and all that? Why not have a simple paint method that just puts stuff on the screen when you want it there?

A The Java AWT toolkit enables you to nest drawable surfaces within other drawable surfaces. When a `paint()` takes place, all the parts of the system are redrawn, starting from the outermost surface and moving downward into the most nested one. Because the drawing of your applet takes place at the same time everything else is drawn, your applet doesn't get any special treatment; your applet will be painted when everything else is painted. Although with this system you sacrifice some of the immediacy of instant painting, it enables your applet to coexist with the rest of the system more cleanly.

Q Are Java threads like threads on other systems?

A Java threads have been influenced by other thread systems, and if you're used to working with threads, many of the concepts in Java threads will be very familiar to you. You learned the basics today; you'll learn more next week on Day 20, "Introduction to VBScript."

Q When an applet uses threads, I just have to tell the thread to start and it starts, and tell it to stop and it stops? That's it? I don't have to test anything in my loops or keep track of its state? It just stops?

A It just stops. When you put your applet into a thread, Java can control the execution of your applet much more readily. By causing the thread to stop, your applet just stops running, and then resumes when the thread starts up again. Yes, it's all automatic. Neat, isn't it?

Q **The Swirling Colors applet seems to display only five or six colors. What's going on here?**

A This is the same problem that you ran into yesterday wherein, on some systems, there might not be enough colors to be able to display all of them reliably. If you're running into this problem, other than upgrading your hardware, you might try quitting other applications running on your system that use color. Other browsers or color tools in particular might be hogging colors that Java wants to be able to use.

Q **Even with the changes you made, the Checkers applet still flickers.**

A And, unfortunately, it will continue to do so. Reducing the size of the drawing area by using clipping does significantly reduce the flickering, but it doesn't stop it entirely. For many applets, using either of the methods described today might be enough to reduce animation flicker to the point where your applet looks good. To get totally flicker-free animation, you'll need to use a technique called double-buffering, which you'll learn about tomorrow.

Day 12

Creating an Interface Using Visual J++

For the past five days you've concentrated on creating applets that do very simple things: display text, play an animation or a sound, or enable very basic interactions with the user. After you get past that point, however, you might want to start creating more complex applets that behave like real applications embedded in a Web page—applets that start to look like typical GUI applications with buttons, menus, text fields, and other elements of a real application.

For the next two days you'll learn how to create a visual front end with Visual J++. The tool you will use to create all your front ends is the Resource Editor, which is the same resource editor used by Visual C++ users in Microsoft Developer Studio. The Resource Editor provides an easy-to-use, graphical interface that allows you to drag and drop visual objects, resize them, and set their properties. The Resource Editor creates files called resource templates.

A *resource template* is a file that holds all of the visual elements you design when using the Resource Editor.

Resource Editor

To create a resource template for use with your Visual J++ application, select File | New from the menubar. In the dialog box that appears, select Resource Template and click OK. (See Figure 12.1.)

Figure 12.1.

Visual J++ New dialog box.

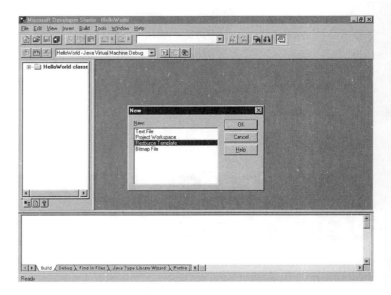

After you have created a Resource Template, you can add resources to it. To do so, select Insert | Resource from the Microsoft Developer Studio menu. For now, select Dialog from the Insert Resource window. (See Figure 12.2.)

Using the item on the Controls toolbar, experiment with drawing controls, sizing them, grouping them, and changing their properties. When you have a good idea how to manipulate a dialog and its controls, continue with the next section to learn about what you can really do with a resource and how it relates to the Abstract Window Toolkit.

Figure 12.2.

The Insert Resource window.

AWT Overview

Java's Abstract Window Toolkit, or AWT, was designed to provide the standard graphical user interface (GUI) elements such as buttons, lists, menus, and text areas. You've actually been using the AWT all along, as you might have guessed from the classes you've been importing. The applet class and most of the classes you've been using this week are all integral parts of the AWT.

The AWT provides the following:

- ☐ A full set of UI widgets and other components, including windows, menus, buttons, checkboxes, text fields, scrollbars, and scrolling lists

- ☐ Support for UI containers, which can comprise other embedded containers or UI widgets

- ☐ An event system for managing system and user events between and among parts of the AWT

- ☐ Mechanisms for laying out components in a way that enables platform-independent UI design

12

Today you'll learn how to use all these components in your Java applets. Tomorrow you'll learn how to create windows, menus, and pop-up dialogs, which enable you to pop up separate windows from the browser window. Also, you can use the AWT in stand-alone applications, so everything you've learned about applets so far this week can still be used with applications. Therefore, if you find the framework of the Web browser too limiting, you can take your AWT background and start writing full-fledged Java applications.

Today, however, you'll continue focusing on applets.

NOTE

Today's lesson is the most complex so far. There's a lot to cover and a lot of code to go through, so if it becomes overwhelming, you might want to take a little more time for this one.

The basic idea behind the AWT is that a Java window is a set of nested components, starting from the outermost window and progressing down to the smallest UI component. Components can include things you can actually see on the screen, such as windows, menubars, buttons, and text fields, and they can also include containers that in turn can contain other components. Figure 12.3 shows how a sample page in a Java browser might include several different components, all of which are managed through the AWT.

Figure 12.3.

A sample page in a Java browser.

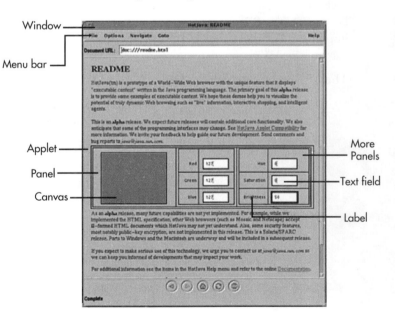

This nesting of components within containers within other components creates a hierarchy of components, from the smallest checkbox inside an applet to the overall window on the screen. The hierarchy of components determines the arrangement of items on the screen and inside other items, the order in which they are painted, and how events are passed from one component to another.

The following are the major components you can work with in the AWT:

- ☐ *Containers.* Containers are generic AWT components that can contain other components, including other containers. The most common form of container is the panel, which represents a container that can be displayed on the screen. Applets are a form of panel. (In fact, the Applet class is a subclass of the Panel class.)

- ☐ *Canvases.* A canvas is a simple drawing surface. Although you can draw on panels (as you've been doing all along), canvases are good for painting images or performing other graphics operations.

- ☐ *UI components.* These can include buttons, lists, simple pop-up menus, checkboxes, and text fields, as well as other typical elements of a user interface.

- ☐ *Window construction components.* These include windows, frames, menubars, and dialog boxes. These are listed separately from the other UI components because you'll use these less often—particularly in applets. In applets, the browser provides the main window and menubar, so you don't have to use these. However, your applet may create a new window, or you may want to write a Java application that needs to use these components.

The classes inside the java.awt package are written and organized to mirror the abstract structure of containers, components, and individual UI components. Figure 12.4 shows some of the class hierarchy that makes up the main classes in the AWT.

Figure 12.4.

Examples of class hierarchy.

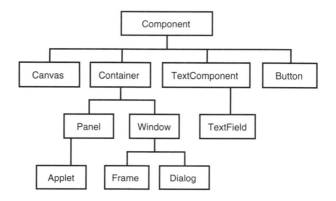

The root of most of the AWT components is the class `Component`, which provides basic display and event handling features. The classes `Container`, `Canvas`, `TextComponent`, and many of the other UI components inherit from `Component`. Inheriting from the `Container` class are objects that can contain other AWT components—the `Panel` and `Window` classes, in particular. Note that the `java.applet.Applet` class, even though it lives in its own package, inherits from `Panel`, so your applets are an integral part of the hierarchy of components in the AWT system.

A GUI-based application that you write by using the AWT can be as complex as you like, with dozens of nested containers and components inside each other. AWT was designed so that each component can play its part in the overall AWT system without needing to duplicate or keep track of the behavior of any other part in the system.

Creating a Simple Dialog Resource

The simplest form of an AWT component is the basic UI component. You can create and add these to your applet without needing to know anything about creating containers or panels—your applet, even before you start painting and drawing and handling events, is already an AWT container. Because an applet is a container, you can put other AWT components—such as UI components or other containers—into it.

When creating a Java applet using Visual J++, it's easy to create the basic AWT components: you simply create a dialog box in the resource editor and then attach it to the applets frame.

Start by creating a new applet to work with. Create a new Project Workspace using the Java Applet Wizard. Name your Project `UITest`. Make sure that you select Yes to create a multithreaded applet and select No for animation support.

To create a new Resource Template, do the following:

1. Select File | New | Resource Template.
2. Right-click the `Templ1` folder.
3. Select Insert | Dialog and click OK.
4. From the Controls Toolbar, choose the Edit Box control.
5. In the upper-left of the dialog box create an Edit Box.
6. Underneath it, create another one.
7. From the Controls Toolbar, choose the Static Text control.
8. In the top-middle of the dialog box, create a Static Text control.
9. Underneath it, create another one.

To access the properties of the controls you have just added, double-click on the controls or use the right mouse to pop up the menu and select properties.

1. Check the properties of the first edit box control you created and make sure the ID is IDC_EDIT1.

2. Check the properties of the second edit box control you created and make sure the ID is IDC_EDIT2.

3. Check the properties of the first static text control you created and change the ID to IDC_STATIC1.

4. Check the properties of the second static text control you created and change the ID to IDC_STATIC2.

5. Check the properties of the OK button control and change the ID to IDBUTTON1, and the caption to OK 1.

6. Check the properties of the Cancel button control and change the ID to IDBUTTON2, and the caption to OK 2.

7. To change the properties of the dialog box itself, double-click on any empty spot on the dialog box.

8. Change the ID to IDMyDialog.

When completed, your dialog box should look similar to the one in Figure 12.5. Granted, we knew what we were creating ahead of time, so your dialog box might not look at all like the one in the figure. Please resize, realign, or relocate the objects as necessary so your dialog box resembles Figure 12.5. When you're finished, save the Resource Template as UITest.rct.

Figure 12.5.

Completed dialog box.

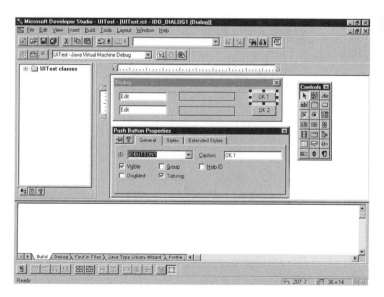

Java Resource Wizard

You might be wondering how in the world you are going to use these resources within your Visual J++ applet. The answer is simple: You aren't! (Well, at least directly you won't.) Instead, Visual J++ converts the work you just did in the Resource Editor into native Java classes, which you then use in your project.

To convert the resource you just completed to Java code, start the Java Resource Wizard by selecting it from the Tools menu. (See Figure 12.6.)

Figure 12.6.

Java Resource Wizard.

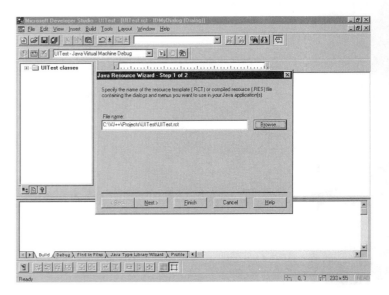

Use the Browse button to select the file UITest.rct and click Finish. Another dialog box appears, letting you know what Java classes were created for you.

WARNING

The files that the Java Resource Wizard creates should not be manually edited. If you need to make a change to a Java Resource Wizard generated file, you should go back to the Resource Editor, make the change, and then rerun the Java Resource Wizard. We can't stress this point enough. Not only would you have to update the resource files, but also any dependencies in the .class files. Then if, at any time in the future, you used the Resource Editor to change anything else, your manual edits would more than likely be overwritten by the Resource Wizard.

Using Classes Generated by Java Resource Wizard

Now that you have created native Java classes, the first step is to include the .java files in your project. Select Insert | Insert Files into Project from the menu and select DialogLayout.java and IDMyDialog.java from the list of available files. (See Figure 12.7.)

Figure 12.7.

Insert Files into Project window.

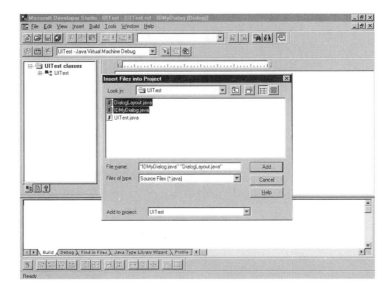

At the top of the UITest class before the public class line, add the following import statement:

```
import IDMyDialog;
```

To create a member variable of type IDMyDialog, add the following line inside the class definition of UITest, just after the Thread declaration:

```
IDMyDialog m_dlg;
```

In the init() method of UITest, remove the resize(*xx,xx*) line and add the following lines to create an instance of m_dlg and to draw the controls that we created:

```
m_dlg = new IDMyDialog( this );
m_dlg.CreateControls();
```

Finally, in the paint(Graphics g) method, comment out the drawString line:

```
// g.drawString("Running: " + Math.random(), 10, 20);
```

You are ready to test your applet, so compile and run it. Your display should look like the one in Figure 12.8.

12

Figure 12.8.

The simple IDMyDialog *applet.*

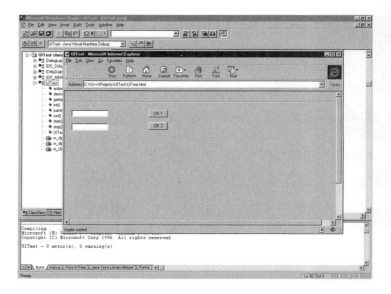

The Basic User Interface Components

Now that you have created a Dialog resource with some visual controls on it, it will be helpful to know what each control does, what its properties and methods are, and how to use them.

Note also that each of these components has an action associated with it—that is, something that the component does when it's activated. Actions generally trigger events or other activities in your applet (often called *callbacks* in other window toolkits). In this section, you'll focus on creating the components themselves; later in today's lesson you'll learn about adding actions to them.

As you read through the rest of this section, you might be asking why we're not teaching you how to create the UI controls without using the Resource Editor and why we're explaining all the methods available for each type of control. The reasoning is simple: the Resource Editor and Java Resource Wizard are quick and simple methods to design complex screens. Also, the Resource Editor and Java Resource Wizard simply create the control using the default properties that you set using the Resource Editor control properties. All manipulation of the controls must be done via Java code and must be written by you. However, there are times when it isn't practical to use the Java Resource Wizard and you will want to create the controls yourself via code. This section will provide you with the basics of UI controls, so you'll be able to create controls without the Resource Editor and Java Resource Wizard when need be.

Labels

The simplest form of UI component is the label.

NEW TERM *Labels* are text strings that you can use to label other UI components.

The advantages a label has over an ordinary text string are that it follows the layout of the given panel, and you don't have to worry about repainting it every time the panel is redrawn. Labels also can be easily aligned within a panel, enabling you to attach labels to other UI components without knowing exact pixel positions.

To create a label via code without using the Resource Editor, use one of the following constructors:

- ☐ Label() creates an empty label, with its text aligned left.
- ☐ Label(*String*) creates a label with the given text string, also aligned left.
- ☐ Label(*String, int*) creates a label with the given text string and the given alignment. The available alignments are stored in class variables in Label, making them easier to remember: Label.RIGHT, Label.LEFT, and Label.CENTER.

The label's font is determined by the overall font for the component as set by the setFont() method.

Once you have a label object, you can use methods defined in the Label class to get and set the values of the text as shown in Table 12.1.

Table 12.1. Label methods.

Method	Action
getText()	Returns a string containing this label's text.
setText(*String*)	Changes the text of this label.
getAlignment()	Returns an integer representing the alignment of this label: 0 is Label.LEFT; 1 is Label.CENTER; 2 is Label.RIGHT. setAlignment(*int*) changes the alignment of this label to the given integer; use the class variables above.

Buttons

The second user interface component to explore is the button.

Buttons are simple UI components that trigger some action in your interface when they are pressed. For example, a calculator applet might have buttons for each number and operator, or a dialog box might have buttons for OK and Cancel.

To create a button via code without using the Resource Editor, use one of the following constructors:

- ☐ `Button()` creates an empty button with no label.
- ☐ `Button(String)` creates a button with the given string object as a label.

Once you have a button object, you can get the value of the button's label by using the `getLabel()` method, and you can set the label using the `setLabel(String)` method.

Text Fields

Along with labels and buttons, text fields are the most common type of user interface control. Where a label is generally used when displaying a description and a button is used for capturing a specific action from the user, a text field is used to capture text data that the user enters.

To create a text field via code, without using the Resource Editor, use one of the following constructors:

- ☐ `TextField()` creates an empty text field 0 characters wide.
- ☐ `TextField(int)` creates an empty text field with the given width in characters.
- ☐ `TextField(String)` creates a text field 0 characters wide, initialized with the given string.
- ☐ `TextField(String, int)` creates a text field with the given width in characters and containing the given string. If the string is longer than the width, you can select and drag portions of the text within the field and the box will scroll left or right.

 TIP

Text fields include only the editable field itself. You usually need to include a label along with the text field to indicate what belongs in that text field.

 NOTE

Text fields are different from text areas; text fields are limited in size and are best used for one-line items, whereas text areas have scrollbars and are better for larger text windows. Both can be edited and enable selections with the mouse. You'll learn about text areas later today.

You can also create a text field that obscures the characters typed into it—for example, for password fields. To accomplish this using the Resource Editor, select the Styles tab in the properties page and check the Password box. (See Figure 12.9.)

Figure 12.9.

Styles tab in Edit Properties window.

To accomplish this using code, create the text field (either by code or by the Resource Editor) and then use the `setEchoCharacter()` method to set the character that is echoed on the screen. An example follows:

```
TextField tf = new TextField(30);
tf.setEchoCharacter('*');
```

Text fields inherit from the class `TextComponent` and have a whole suite of methods, both inherited from that class and defined in its own class, that might be useful to you in your Java programs. Table 12.2 shows a selection of those methods.

Table 12.2. Text field methods.

Method	Action
`getText()`	Returns the text this text field contains (as a string)
`setText(String)`	Puts the given text string into the field
`getColumns()`	Returns the width of this text field
`select(int, int)`	Selects the text between the two integer positions (Positions start from `0`.)

continues

Table 12.2. continued

Method	Action
selectAll()	Selects all the text in the field
isEditable()	Returns true or false based on whether the text is editable or not
setEditable(*boolean*)	true (the default) enables text to be edited; false freezes the text
getEchoChar()	Returns the character used for masking input
echoCharIsSet()	Returns true or false whether the field has a masking character or not

The remaining methods not shown in the table can be found using InfoView and searching on the topic TextComponent and TextField.

Checkboxes

Checkboxes can be selected or deselected to indicate multiple options.

NEW TERM *Checkboxes* are user interface components that have two states: on and off (or checked and unchecked, selected and unselected, true and false, and so on). Unlike buttons, checkboxes usually don't trigger direct actions in a UI, but instead, are used to indicate optional features of some other action.

You can create a checkbox via code, without using the Resource Editor, using one of the following constructors:

☐ Checkbox() creates an empty checkbox, unselected.

☐ Checkbox(*String*) creates a checkbox with the given string as a label.

☐ Checkbox(*String, null, boolean*) creates a checkbox that is either selected or unselected based on whether the *boolean* argument is true or false, respectively. (The *null* is used as a placeholder for a group argument. Only radio buttons have groups, as you'll learn in the next section.)

Table 12.3 lists the checkbox methods.

Table 12.3. Checkbox methods.

Method	Action
getLabel()	Returns a string containing this checkbox's label
setLabel(*String*)	Changes the text of the checkbox's label
getState()	Returns true or false, based on whether the checkbox is selected or not
setState(*boolean*)	Changes the checkbox's state to selected (true) or unselected (false)

Radio Buttons

Radio buttons are a variation of the checkbox.

NEW TERM *Radio buttons* have an appearance similar to checkboxes, but only one in the series can be selected at a time. Whereas checkboxes display a square box that is either checked or blank, radio buttons display a circle that is either filled or blank. Also, unlike checkboxes, radio buttons provide for a mutually exclusive option selection.

To create a series of radio buttons via code, without using the Resource Editor, first create an instance of CheckboxGroup:

```
CheckboxGroup cbg = new CheckboxGroup();
```

Then create and add the individual checkboxes, using the group as the second argument, and a true or false to determine whether that checkbox is selected. (Only one in the series can be selected.)

```
add(new Checkbox("Yes", cbg, true);
add(new Checkbox("no", cbg, false);
```

All the checkbox methods defined in the previous section can be used with the checkboxes in the group. Also, you can use the getCheckboxGroup() and setCheckboxGroup() methods to access and change the group of any given checkbox.

Finally, the getCurrent() and setCurrent(*Checkbox*) methods, defined in the checkbox group, can be used to get or set the currently selected checkbox.

12

Choice Menus

The choice menu is a more complex UI component than a label, button, or checkbox.

 Choice menus are pop-up (or pull-down) menus that allow the user to select an item from that menu. The menu then displays that choice on the screen.

 In other languages, choice menus are typically called *combo boxes*. The Visual J++ Resource Editor also calls them combo boxes.

To create a choice menu without using the Resource Editor, create an instance of the `Choice` and then use the `addItem()` method to add individual items to it in the order in which they should appear:

```
Choice c = new Choice();
c.addItem("Apples");
c.addItem("Oranges");
c.addItem("Strawberries");
```

Finally, add the entire choice menu to the panel in the usual way using the `add` method:

```
add(c);
```

Even if you use the Resource Editor to create the choice menu, you must programmatically add the individual items to the menu as follows:

```
m_dlg.IDC_COMBO1.addItem("Apples");
m_dlg.IDC_COMBO1.addItem("Oranges");
m_dlg.IDC_COMBO1.addItem("Strawberries");
```

Figure 12.10 shows a simple choice menu generated from the code in the preceding example.

 TIP   Choice menus enable only one selection per menu. If you want to select multiple items, use a scrolling list instead.

After your choice menu is created, regardless of whether it's added to a panel or not, you can continue to add items to that menu by using the `addItem()` method. Table 12.4 shows some other methods that may be useful in working with choice menus.

Figure 12.10.

A simple choice menu.

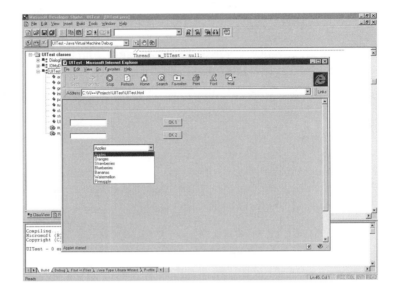

Table 12.4. Choice menu methods.

Method	Action
getItem(*int*)	Returns the string item at the given position. (Items inside a choice begin at 0, same as arrays.)
countItems()	Returns the number of items in the menu.
getSelectedIndex()	Returns the index position of the item that's selected.
getSelectedItem()	Returns the currently selected item as a string.
select(*int*)	Selects the item at the given position.
select(*String*)	Selects the item with the given string.

Panels and Layout

An AWT panel can contain UI components or other panels. The question now is how those components are actually arranged and displayed on the screen.

In other windowing systems, UI components are often arranged using hard-coded pixel measurements—put text field tf at 10,30, for example—the same way you used the graphics operations to paint squares and ovals on the screen on Day 10, "Graphics, Fonts, and Colors."

In the AWT, the window may be displayed on many different windowing systems on many different screens and with many different kinds of fonts with different font metrics. Therefore, you need a more flexible method of arranging components on the screen so that a layout that looks nice on one platform isn't a jumbled unusable mess on another.

For just this purpose, Java has layout managers, insets, and hints that each component can provide for helping lay out the screen.

Note that the nice thing about AWT components and user interface items is that you don't have to paint them: the AWT system manages all that for you. If you have graphic components or images, or you want to create an animation inside a panel, you still have to do that by hand, but for most of the basic components, all you have to do is put them on the screen and Java will handle the rest.

Layout Managers

When using the Resource Editor to design your user interfaces, which is the suggested manner, the Resource Editor creates a file called `DialogLayout.java`. This file manages all of the layout information for all of your dialogs. Thus, Visual J++ shields you from one of the more complex aspects of Java programming.

NOTE

When you create UI control without using the Resource Editor and Java Resource Wizard, you must specify and control the layout manager that you want to use for your controls. The rest of this section is designed to give you a brief overview of Layout Manager. For more information on layout managers, you can search the Sun Samples in the Visual J++ Books Online.

The actual appearance of the AWT components on the screen is determined by two things: the order in which they are added to the panel that holds them and the layout manager that the panel is currently using to lay out the screen. The layout manager determines how portions of the screen will be sectioned and how components within that panel will be placed.

Note that each panel on the screen can have its own layout manager. By nesting panels within panels and using the appropriate layout manager for each one, you can often arrange your UI to group and arrange components in a way that is both functionally useful—and also looks good on a variety of platforms and windowing systems. You'll learn about nesting panels in a section later in this chapter.

The AWT provides five basic layout managers: `FlowLayout`, `GridLayout`, `GridBagLayout`, `BorderLayout`, and `CardLayout`. To create a layout manager for a given panel, use the `setLayout()` method for that panel:

```
public void init()
{
    setLayout(new FlowLayout());
}
```

Setting the default layout manager, like creating the user interface components, is best done during the applet's initialization, which is why we've done it that way.

After the layout manager is set, you can start adding components to the panel. The order in which components are added is often significant, and depends upon which layout manager is currently active. Read on for further information about the specific layout managers and how they present components within the panel to which they apply.

The following sections describe the five basic Java AWT layout managers.

The `FlowLayout` Class

The `FlowLayout` class is the most basic of layouts. Using the flow layout, components are added to the panel one at a time, row by row. If a component doesn't fit onto a row, it's wrapped onto the next row. The flow layout also has an alignment argument, which determines the alignment of each row. By default, each row is center-aligned.

To create a basic flow layout with a centered alignment, use the following line of code in your panel's initialization. (Because this is the default panel layout, you don't need to include this line, but you might want to because it makes code maintenance easier.)

```
setLayout(new FlowLayout());
```

To create a flow layout with an alignment other than centered, add the `FlowLayout.RIGHT` or `FlowLayout.LEFT` class variable as an argument:

```
setLayout(new FlowLayout(FlowLayout.LEFT));
```

You can also set horizontal and vertical gap values by using flow layouts. The *gap* is the number of pixels between components in a panel; by default, the horizontal and vertical gap values are three pixels, which can be very close indeed. The horizontal gap spreads out components to the left and to the right, and the vertical gap spreads out the top and bottom of each component.

```
setLayout(new FlowLayout(FlowLayout.LEFT), 10, 10);
```

12

Grid and Grid Bag Layouts

Grid layouts use a layout that offers more control over the placement of components inside a panel. Using a grid layout, you portion off the area of the panel into rows and columns. Each component you then add to the panel is placed in a "cell" of the grid, starting from the top row and progressing through each row from left to right. (Here's where the order of calls to the add() method are very significant to how the screen is laid out.) By using grid layouts and nested grids, you can often approximate the use of hard-coded pixel values to place your UI components precisely where you want them.

To create a grid layout, indicate the number of rows and columns you want the grid to have when you create a new instance of the GridLayout class:

```
setLayout(new GridLayout(3, 3));
```

Grid layouts can also have a horizontal and vertical gap between components; to create gaps, add those pixel values:

```
setLayout(new GridLayout(3, 3, 10, 15));
```

Grid bag layouts, as implemented by the GridBagLayout class, are variations on grid layouts. Like grid layouts, grid bag layouts enable you to lay out your user interface elements in a rectangular grid, but with grid bag layouts you have much more control over the presentation of each element in the grid. Grid bag layouts use a helper class, GridBagConstraints, to indicate how each cell in the grid is to be formatted.

Border Layouts

Border layouts behave differently from flow and grid layouts. When you add a component to a panel that uses a border layout, you indicate its placement as a geographic direction: north, south, east, west, and center. The components around all the edges are laid out with as much size as they need; the component in the center, if any, gets any space left over.

To use a border layout, you create it as you do the other layouts:

```
setLayout(new BorderLayout());
```

Then you add the individual components by using a special add() method: the first argument to add() is a string indicating the position of the component within the layout:

```
add("North", new TextField("Title", 50));
add("South", new TextField("Status", 50));
```

You can also use this form of add() for the other layout managers; the string argument will just be ignored if it's not needed.

Border layouts can also have horizontal and vertical gaps. Note that the north and south components extend to the edge of the panel, so the gap will result in less space for the east, right, and center components. To add gaps to a border layout, include those pixel values as before:

```
setLayout(new BorderLayout(10, 10));
```

Card Layouts

Card layouts are different from the other layouts. Unlike with the other three layouts, when you add components to a card layout, they are not all displayed on the screen at once. Card layouts are used to produce slide shows of components, one at a time.

Generally, when you create a card layout, the components you add to it will be other container components—usually panels. You can then use different layouts for those individual "cards" so that each screen has its own look.

When you add each "card" to the panel, you can give it a name. Then you can use methods defined on the CardLayout class to move back and forth between different cards in the layout.

For example, here's how to create a card layout containing three cards:

```
setLayout(new CardLayout());
Panel one = new Panel()
add("first", one);
Panel two = new Panel()
add("second", two);
Panel three = new Panel()
add("third", three);
show(this, "second");
```

Using Layouts with a Resource Editor Created Dialog

Although you do not need to, it is very easy to use layouts with Resource Editor and Java Resource Wizard created classes. Go back to the UITest applet and add the following new data member to the class:

```
IDMyDialog m_dlg2;
```

Replace all the code in the init() method with the following code:

```
setLayout(new GridLayout(1,2,10,10);
Panel pnl1 = new Panel();
Panel pn12 = new Panel();
add(p1);
add(p2);
m_dlg = new IDMyDialog( p1 );
m_dlg2 = new IDMyDialog( p2 );
m_dlg.CreateControls();
m_dlg2.CreateControls();
```

12

When you run this applet now, you should have two separate copies of the dialog box IDMyDialog created on the screen, as shown in Figure 12.11. Try using some of the other layout managers to see what the results are.

Figure 12.11.

IDMyDialog *applet version 2.*

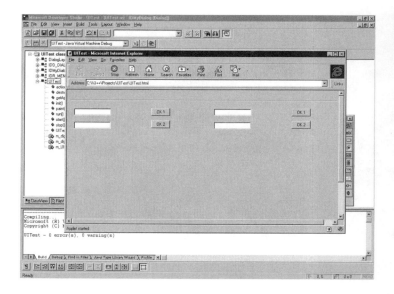

Insets

Whereas horizontal gap and vertical gap are used to determine the amount of space between components in a panel, insets are used to determine the amount of space around the panel itself. The Insets class provides values for the top, bottom, left, and right insets, which are then used when the panel itself is drawn.

To include an inset, override the insets() method in the class (the Applet class or other class that serves as a panel):

```
public Insets insets()
{
    return new Insets(10, 10, 10, 10);
}
```

The arguments to the Insets constructor provide pixel insets for the top, bottom, left, and right edges of the panel. This particular example provides an inset of 10 pixels on all four sides of the panel.

12

Nesting Panels and Components

Adding UI components to individual applets is fun, but applets begin to turn into lots of fun when you begin working with nested panels. By nesting different panels inside your applet, and panels inside those panels, you can create different layouts for different parts of the overall applet area, isolate background and foreground colors and fonts to individual parts of an applet, and manage the design of your UI components much more cleanly and simply. The more complex the layout of your applet, the more likely you're going to want to use nested panels.

Nested Panels

Panels, as you've already learned, are components that can actually be displayed onscreen; Panel's superclass Container provides the generic behavior for holding other components inside it. The Applet class, from which all your applets inherit, is a subclass of Panel. To nest other panels inside an applet, you merely create a new panel and add it to the applet, just as you would add any other UI component:

```
setLayout(new GridLayout(1, 2, 10, 10));
Panel panel1 = new Panel();
Panel panel2 = new Panel();
add(panel1);
add(panel2);
```

You can then set up an independent layout for those subpanels and add AWT components to them (including still more subpanels) by calling the add() method in the appropriate panel:

```
panel1.setLayout(new FlowLayout());
panel1.add(new Button("Up"));
panel1.add(new Button("Down"));
```

Although you can do all this in a single class, it's common in applets that make heavy use of the panels to factor out the layout and behavior of the subpanels into separate classes, and to communicate between the panels by using method calls. You'll look at an extensive example of this later in today's lesson.

Events and Nested Panels

When you create applets with nested panels, those panels form a hierarchy from the outermost panel (the applet, usually) to the innermost UI component. This hierarchy is important to how each component in an applet interacts with the other components in the

12

applet or with the browser that contains that applet. In particular, the component hierarchy determines the order in which components are painted to the screen.

More importantly, the hierarchy also affects event handling, particularly for user input events such as mouse and keyboard events.

Events are received by the innermost component in the component hierarchy and passed up the chain to the root. Suppose, for example, that you have an applet with a subpanel that can handle mouse events (using the `mouseDown()` and `mouseUp()` methods) and that subpanel contains a button. Clicking on the button means that the button receives the event before the panel does; if the button isn't interested in the `mouseDown()` method, the event gets passed to the panel, which can then process it or pass it further up the hierarchy.

Remember the discussion about the basic event methods yesterday? You learned that the basic event methods all return Boolean values. Those Boolean values become important when you're talking about handling events or passing them on.

An event-handling method, whether it is the set of basic event methods or the more generic `handleEvent()`, can do one of three things, given any random event:

- ☐ Not be interested in the event (which is usually true only for `handleEvent()`, which receives all the events generated by the system). If this is the case, the event is passed up the hierarchy until a component processes it (or it is ignored altogether). In this case, the event-handling method should return `false`.

- ☐ Intercept the event, process it, and return `true`. In this case, the event stops with that event method. You will learn a great deal more about events and the like in tomorrow's lesson.

- ☐ Intercept the method, process it, and pass it on to the next event handler. This is a more unusual case, but you may create a user interface by using nested components that will want to do this. In this case, the event method should return `false` to pass the event on to the next handler in the chain.

More UI Components

After you master the basic UI components and how to add them to panels and manage their events, you can add more UI components. In this section, you'll learn about text areas, scrolling lists, scrollbars, and canvases.

Text Areas

Text areas are like text fields, except they have more functionality for handling large amounts of text. Because text fields are limited in size and don't scroll, they are better for one-line responses and text entry; text areas can be any given width and height and have scrollbars by default, so you can deal with larger amounts of text more easily.

When creating a text area using the Resource Editor, you use the text box control. To make a text box a text area, you simply modify the property page for the control and select the multiline checkbox. Even though the Resource Editor treats the controls the same, the Java Resource Wizard treats them differently depending on whether they are multiline or not.

To create a text area, without using the Resource Wizard, use one of the following constructors:

- ☐ `TextArea()` creates an empty text area 0 rows long and 0 characters wide. Given that a text area with no dimensions can't be displayed, you should make sure you change the dimensions of this new text area before adding it to a panel (or just use the next constructor instead).

- ☐ `TextArea(int, int)` creates an empty text area with the given number of rows and columns (characters).

- ☐ `TextArea(String)` creates a text area displaying the given string, 0 rows by 0 columns.

- ☐ `TextArea(String, int, int)` creates a text area displaying the given string and with the given dimensions.

Both text areas and text fields inherit from the `TextComponent` class, so a lot of the behavior for text fields (particularly getting and setting text and selections) is usable on text areas as well. (See Table 12.5.) Text areas also have a number of their own methods that you might find useful.

Table 12.5. Text area methods.

Method	Action
`getColumns()`	Returns the width of the text area, in characters or columns
`getRows()`	Returns the number of rows in the text area (not the number of rows of text that the text area contains)
`insertText(String, int)`	Inserts the string at the given position in the text (text positions start at 0)
`replaceText(String, int, int)`	Replaces the text between the given integer positions with the new string

continues

Table 12.5. continued

Method	Action
setLineIncrement(*int inc*)	Changes the increment for how far to scroll when the end-points of the scrollbar are selected. The default is 1.
getLineIncrement()	Returns the increment for how far to scroll when the end-points of the scrollbar are selected.
setPageIncrement(*int inc*)	Changes the increment for how far to scroll when the inside range of the scrollbar is selected. The default is 10.
getPageIncrement()	Returns the increment for how far to scroll when the inside range of the scrollbar is selected.

NOTE

For a quick example of a text area, go into the Resource Editor and resize one of the two text boxes that you are using for the UITest applet. Make sure to modify the properties to make the text box multiline and to add both horizontal and vertical scrollbars.

Scrolling Lists

Remember the choice menu, which enables you to choose one of several different options? A scrolling list is functionally similar to a choice menu in that it enables you to pick several options from a list. Scrolling lists differ in two significant ways:

☐ Scrolling lists are not pop-up menus. They're lists of items in which you can choose one or more items from a list. If the number of items is larger than the list box, a scrollbar is automatically provided so that you can see the other items (think of a File list box).

☐ A scrolling list can be defined to accept only one item at a time (exclusive), or multiple items (non-exclusive).

When you use the Resource Editor, a scrolling list is identified by the term List Box. To change the type of selection that the list box accepts, change the Selection value under the Styles tab of the List Box Properties page.

To create a scrolling list without using the Resource Editor, create an instance of the List class and then add individual items to that list. The List class has two constructors:

☐ List() creates an empty scrolling list that enables only one selection at a time.

☐ List(*int, boolean*) creates a scrolling list with the given number of visible lines on the screen. (The number of actual items you can add to the list is unlimited. This constructor limits only the number displayed at one time.) The Boolean argument indicates whether this list enables multiple selections (true) or not (false).

After creating a List object, add items to it using the addItem() method as shown in the following code:

```
List lst = new List(5, true);
lst.addItem("Hamlet");
lst.addItem("Ophelia");
add(lst);
```

Table 12.6 shows some of the methods available to scrolling lists. See the API documentation for a complete set.

Table 12.6. Scrolling list methods.

Method	Action
getItem(*int*)	Returns the string item at the given position
countItems()	Returns the number of items in the menu
getSelectedIndex()	Returns the index position of the item that's selected (used for lists that enable only single selections)
getSelectedIndexes()	Returns an array of index positions (used for lists that enable multiple selections)
getSelectedItem()	Returns the currently selected item as a string
getSelectedItems()	Returns an array of strings containing all the selected items
select(*int*)	Selects the item at the given position
select(*String*)	Selects the item with that string

Scrollbars and Sliders

Text areas and scrolling lists come with their own scrollbars, which are built into those UI components and enable you to manage both the body of the area or the list and its scrollbar as a single unit. You can also create individual scrollbars, or sliders, to manipulate a range of values.

12

Scrollbars are used to select a value between a maximum and a minimum value. To change the current value of that scrollbar, you can use three different parts of the scrollbar. (See Figure 12.12.)

☐ Arrows on either end, which increment or decrement the values by some small unit (1 by default).

☐ A range in the middle, which increments or decrements the value by a larger amount (10 by default).

☐ A box in the middle, often called an *elevator* or *thumb*, whose position shows where the current value is located within the range of values. Moving this box with the mouse causes an absolute change in the value, based on the position of the box within the scrollbar.

Figure 12.12.

Scrollbar parts.

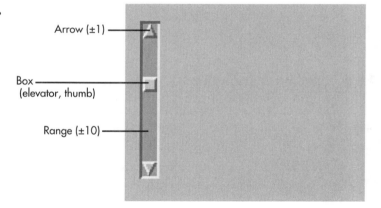

Choosing any of these visual elements causes a change in the scrollbar's value; you don't have to update anything or handle any events. All you have to do is give the scrollbar a maximum and minimum value, and Java will handle the rest.

Using the Resource Editor, it is very easy to create either a vertical or horizontal scrollbar. Simply draw a control of type Vertical Scroll Bar or Horizontal Scroll Bar. There is one limitation, however: The minimum value of the scrollbar will always be 0, and the maximum will always be 99.

NOTE

Take note of the preceding paragraph. Whenever you create a scrollbar using the resource editor, the maximum and minimum values will ALWAYS be 0 and 99 respectively. The only way to change these values is to modify the class that the Java Resource Wizard generates, which is not recommended.

To create a scrollbar without using the Resource Editor, you can use one of three constructors:

- [ ] `Scrollbar()` creates a scrollbar with `0`, `0` as its initial maximum and initial minimum values, in a vertical orientation.

- [ ] `Scrollbar(int)` creates a scrollbar with `0`, `0` as its initial maximum and initial minimum values. The argument represents an orientation, for which you can use the class variables `Scrollbar.HORIZONTAL` and `Scrollbar.VERTICAL`.

- [ ] `Scrollbar(int, int, int, int, int)` creates a scrollbar with the following arguments. (Each is an integer and must be presented in this order.)

    The first argument is the orientation of the scrollbar: `Scrollbar.HORIZONTAL` or `Scrollbar.VERTICAL`.

    The second argument is the initial value of the scrollbar, which should be a value between the scrollbar's maximum and minimum values.

    The third argument is the overall width (or height, depending on the orientation) of the scrollbar's box. In user interface design, a larger box implies that a larger amount of the total range is currently showing (applies best to things such as windows and text areas).

    The fourth and fifth arguments are the minimum and maximum values for the scrollbar.

The `Scrollbar` class provides several methods for managing the values within scrollbars. (See Table 12.7.)

Table 12.7. Scrollbar methods.

Method	Action
`getMaximum()`	Returns the maximum value
`getMinimum()`	Returns the minimum value
`getOrientation()`	Returns the orientation of this scrollbar: `0` is `Scrollbar.HORIZONTAL`; `1` is `Scrollbar.VERTICAL`
`getValue()`	Returns the scrollbar's current value
`setValue(int)`	Sets the current value of the scrollbar

Canvases

Although you can draw on most AWT components, such as panels, canvases do little *except* let you draw on them. They can't contain other components, but they can accept events, and you can create an animation and display images on them. Canvases, in other words, could have been used for much of what you learned about earlier this week, but not for most of what you learned today.

NEW TERM   A *canvas* is a component that you can draw on.

To create a canvas, use the `Canvas` class and add it to a panel as you would any other component:

```
Canvas can = new Canvas();
add(can);
```

Summary

The Java AWT, or Abstract Window Toolkit, is a package of Java classes and interfaces for creating full-fledged access to a windows-based graphical user interface system, with mechanisms for graphics display, event management, text and graphics primitives, user interface components, and cross-platform layout. Applets are also an integral part of the AWT toolkit.

The Resource Editor and Java Resource Wizard are tools provided with Visual J++ to make dealing with the AWT even easier. For the most part, using a dialog box (or almost any other component) created in the Resource Wizard is much simpler than creating all of the controls, the panels, the sizing, and the placement by writing the Java code yourself.

Today has been a big day; the lesson has brought together everything you've learned up to this point about simple applet management and added a lot more about creating applets, panels, and user interface components. The one major thing left to learn is how to make your application do something. Right now, you can create some very nice-looking screens, but they don't do much. Tomorrow, we will change that.

Q&A

Q You've mentioned a lot about the `Component` and `Container` classes, but it looks like the only `Container` objects that ever get created are `Panel`s. What do the `Component` and `Container` classes give me?

A Those classes factor out the behavior for components (generic AWT components) and containers (components that can contain other components). Although you don't necessarily create direct instances of these classes, you can create subclasses of them if you want to add behavior to the AWT that the default classes do not provide. As with most of the Java classes, whenever you need a superclass' behavior, don't hesitate to extend that class by using your own subclass.

Q Can I put a UI component at a specific x and y position on the screen?

A By using the existing layout managers supplied with the AWT toolkit, no. This is actually a good thing because you don't know what kind of display environment your applet will be run under, what kind of fonts are installed, or what kind of fonts are being currently used. By using the layout managers provided with the AWT, you can be reasonably sure that every portion of your window will be viewable, readable, and usable (fonts may cause you trouble). You can't guarantee anything like that with hard-coded layouts.

Q I was exploring the AWT package, and I saw this subpackage called peer. There are also references to the peer classes sprinkled throughout the API documentation. What do peers do?

A Peers are responsible for the platform-specific parts of the AWT. For example, when you create a Java AWT window, you have an instance of the Window class that provides generic window behavior, and then you have an instance of a class implementing WindowPeer that creates the specific window for that platform—a motif window under X Window, a Macintosh-style window under the Macintosh, or a Windows 95 window under Windows 95. These "peer" classes also handle communication between the window system and the Java window itself. By separating the generic component behavior (the AWT classes) from the actual system implementation and appearance (the peer classes), you can focus on providing behavior in your Java application and let the Java implementation deal with the platform-specific details.

Q There's a whole lot of functionality in the AWT that you haven't talked about here. Why?

A Given that even a basic introduction took this long, we figured that if we put in even more detail than we already have, this chapter and the next could easily be a book unto themselves. In that regard, our mission is to give you the basics, plus some of the extra stuff. We hope, because the AWT is so feature-packed, that if we point you in the right direction your inquisitive nature will fill in the missing details.

As it is, I've left windows, menus, and dialogs until tomorrow, so you'll have to wait for those. But you can find out about a lot of the other features of AWT merely by exploring the API documentation. Start with the Applet class and examine the sorts of methods you can call. Then look at Panel, from which applet inherits—you have all that class' functionality as well. The superclass of Panel is Container, which provides still more interesting detail. Component comes next. Explore the API and see what you can do with it. You might find something interesting.

12

Day 13

More on Graphical Front Ends Using Visual J++

Up until now, your applets and applications have not done much. They have displayed some nice interfaces and you have learned how to manipulate them in your code. Today, we are going to bring your Visual J++ applets and applications to life using dialogs and handling events to manipulate data. Today you'll learn about the following:

☐ Creating windows, menus, and dialog boxes

☐ Handling window, mouse, and keyboard events

NOTE
This chapter is very long and covers a lot of material. You might want to budget some extra time for this day.

Windows, Menus, and Dialog Boxes

Today, you'll finish up the last bits of the AWT that didn't fit into yesterday's lesson. In addition to all the graphics, events, UI, and layout mechanisms that the AWT provides, it also provides windows, menus, and dialog boxes, which enable you to create fully featured applications either as part of your applet or independently for stand-alone Java applications.

Frames

The AWT Window class enables you to create windows that are independent of the browser window containing the applet—that is, separate pop-up windows with their own titles, resize handles, and menubars.

NOTE
> It's important to note here that the Window class has nothing to do with Microsoft Windows. The Window class is a generic class that handles windows on any platform.

The Window class provides basic behavior for windows. Most commonly, instead of using the Window class, you'll use Window's subclasses, Frame and Dialog. The Frame class enables you to create a fully functioning window with a menubar. Dialog is a more limited window for dialog boxes. You'll learn more about dialog boxes later in this section.

To create a frame, use one of the following constructors:

☐ new Frame() creates a basic frame without a title.

☐ new Frame(*String*) creates a basic frame with the given title.

Like panels, frames are containers. You can add other components to them just as you would regular panels, using the add() method. The default layout for windows is BorderLayout:

```
win = new Frame("My Cool Window");
win.setLayout(new BorderLayout(10, 20));
win.add("North", new Button("Start"));
win.add("Center", new Button("Move"));
```

To set a size for the new window, use the resize() method. To set a location for where the window appears, use the move() method. Note that the location() method can tell you where the applet window is on the screen so that you can pop up the extra window in a position relative to that window (all these methods are defined for all containers, so you can use them for applets, windows, and the components inside them, subject to the current layout):

```
win.resize(100, 200);
Dimension d = location();
win.move(d.width + 50, d.height + 50);
```

When you initially create a window, it's invisible. You need to use the `show()` method to make the window appear on the screen (you can use `hide()` to hide it again):

```
win.show();
```

The following is an example of a simple applet that displays a simple pop-up window. This applet depends on the MyFrame class that you will also need to create. The MyFrame Class should be a separate .java file called MyFrame.java. Save this project because you will be extending it throughout this chapter.

Now start by creating a new applet to work with. Create a new Project Workspace using the Java Applet Wizard. Name your Project UIApp. Make sure that you select Yes to create a multithreaded applet and select No for animation support.

Once your Project Workspace is created, create a new text file and enter the following code to create the class MyFrame. Save this as MyFrame.java and insert into the project (Insert | Files into Project from the menu). You can omit the comments if you so wish.

```
import java.applet.*;
import java.awt.*;

class MyFrame extends Frame
{
    MyFrame(String title)
    {
        super(title); // Call the parent class function to set the title
        resize(300,300); // set default size
        this.show(); // show the frame
    }
}
```

In the UIApp.java file before the class definition, import the MyFrame class:

```
import MyFrame;
```

Add a new data member called m_frmFrame that is of type MyFrame:

```
MyFrame m_frmFrame;
```

In the UIApp applet init() method, add the following code:

```
m_frmFrame = new MyFrame( "My Frame Test" );
```

Compile and run the applet. A single blank pop-up window should be displayed. As you can tell, all this applet does now is display a simple window. By the way, the only way you can stop this applet is to select File | Close (or Exit) from your browser's menu. Keep reading and some cool functionality will be added.

13

Menus

Each new window you create can have its own menubar along the top of the screen. Each menubar can have a number of menus, and each menu, in turn, can have menu items. The AWT provides classes for all these things called, respectively, MenuBar, Menu, and MenuItem. Creating a menu system using plain Java code is akin to pulling teeth, although you might be forced to do so if you ever need to maintain older code or code developed with another development environment. Luckily, Visual J++ makes it extremely easy by using the Resource Editor.

 NOTE | If you still wish to create a menu without using the Resource Editor, you can use the Java API documentation included with Visual J++.

Creating a Menu Resource Item

The first step in creating a Menu Resource, like other resources, is to create a Resource Template (File | New | Resource Template) just as you did yesterday. Save this new Resource Template, in the UIApp project directory, as UIApp.rct. To insert a new Menu resource into the template, do the following:

1. Right-click the UIApp folder and select Insert.
2. Select Menu and click OK (an empty menubar displays).
3. Right-click (or double-click) the empty Menu item and select Properties.
4. Type File for the Caption (notice that you can't give the menu item an ID), and then close the window.
5. Click the File Menu item, a box displays below it; double-click the empty box, the properties window displays.
6. Type MN_EXIT for the ID and Exit for the Caption (see Figure 13.1), and then close the window.
7. Double-click any empty space on your menubar, type MyMenu for the ID, and then close the window.

Save the Resource Template. Run the Java Resource Wizard (Tools | Java Resource Wizard). Insert the newly created file MyMenu.java into your UIApp project.

13

Figure 13.1.

A Menu Item Properties dialog box.

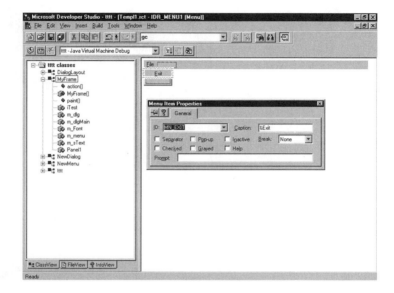

Using your Newly Created Menu Item

Add the following code to the MyFrame Class. At the top of the file add the line:

```
import MyMenu;
```

Under the MyFrame class definition add the line:

```
MyMenu m_mnuMine;
```

Under the constructor MyFrame(*String title*) add these lines of code:

```
m_menuMine = new MyMenu( this );
m_menuMine.CreateMenu();
```

Your window—with a menu—will now display. (See Figure 13.2.) Even though you've easily created the window and menu item, it doesn't do very much, other than display. That's because there hasn't been any action assigned to the Exit menu item. Later in this chapter, we'll assign an action to the menu item event. Try adding some other items to your menu and experimenting with the property page settings.

Some browsers enable you to indicate a special help menu, which will display on the right side of the window's menubar. You can indicate that a specific menu is the help menu by calling the setHelpMenu method of the class MenuBar. You can view the MyMenu file created by the Java Resource Wizard to determine what data members represent which menu items.

```
mb.setHelpMenu(ID_HELP);
```

13

Figure 13.2.

My Frame window showing the File menu item.

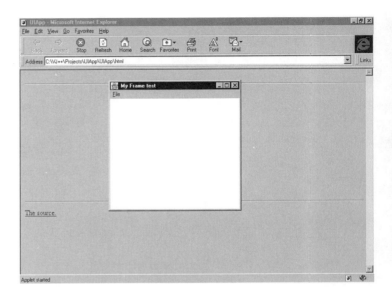

If, for any reason, you want to prevent a user from selecting a menu item or menu command, you can use the `disable()` command on the menu ID (and the `enable()` command to make it available again). When a menu item or command is disabled, it still appears on the menu; it is, however, grayed-out and unselectable by the user:

```
ID_HELP.disable();
```

Pop-ups, Separator Bars, and a Little More

When you use many Windows applications such as word-processing, spreadsheet, databases, and mail systems, the menu systems are quite elaborate. Often you open a single menu and if you select a given item, another menu opens. A simple example of this is the Start menu in Windows 95 or Windows NT 4.0. This kind of menu is called a pop-up menu.

To create a pop-up in Visual J++, it is a simple matter of setting properties in the Resource Editor. Follow the preceding steps listed (in the Creating a Menu Resource Item section) to create a new menu resource. Create a new child menu under the File menu and label it Test. View the properties of the Test item and check the Pop-up box. Immediately, a new pop-up menu appears to which you can add more menu items.

Another menu item that is often used to make menu systems easier to read is a separator bar. As with all pop-ups, adding a separator bar is as simple as checking a box in the properties page of a menu item. In this same little Test resource, add a new menu item under the Test item. Don't bother with a label or an ID, but simply view the properties and check Separator box. There you go: instant Separator bar.

Dialog Boxes

Dialog boxes are functionally similar to frames in that they pop up new windows on the screen. However, dialog boxes are intended to be used for transient windows—for example, windows that let you know about warnings, windows that ask you for specific information, and so on. Dialog boxes don't usually have titlebars (although you can create a dialog box with a titlebar) or many of the more general features that windows have. Dialog boxes can also be made non-resizable or modal.

NEW TERM A *modal dialog box* prevents input to any of the other windows in the applet or application until that dialog box is dismissed.

The AWT provides two kinds of dialog boxes: the `Dialog` class, which provides a generic dialog box, and `FileDialog`, which produces a platform-specific dialog box to choose files to save or open.

To create a generic dialog box, use one of these constructors:

☐ `Dialog(Frame, boolean)` creates an initially invisible dialog box, attached to the current frame, which is either modal (`true`) or not (`false`).

☐ `Dialog(Frame, String, boolean)` is the same as the previous constructor, with the addition of a titlebar and a title indicated by the *string* argument.

Note that because you have to give a dialog box a `Frame` argument, you can attach dialog boxes only to windows that already exist independent of the applet itself.

The dialog box window, like the frame window, is a panel on which you can lay out and draw UI components and perform graphic operations, just as you would any other panel. Like other windows, the dialog box is initially invisible, but you can show it with `show()` and hide it with `hide()`.

Now add a dialog box to that same example with the pop-up window that we have been working with: `UIApp`. You are simply going to modify the `MyFrame` class to attach a dialog box that you will define in the Resource Editor. You are also going to attach a dialog box to the Frame itself.

To create the `DLG_GetData` dialog box, do the following.

1. Open `UIApp.rct` (or simply switch to the already open window).
2. From the menubar, select Insert | Resource | Dialog.
3. Select the Cancel button and press Delete.
4. Select the OK button and drag it down to the middle of the right side.(You can also use Ctrl+F9 to center the button.)

13

5. Double-click the OK button; the Properties window displays. The ID should be IDOK and the Caption should be OK.

6. Double-click any empty space in the dialog box; the Properties window displays. Change the Dialog box ID to DLG_GetData.

7. Click the Font button, change the Size to 14 (you might need to resize the window to see the changes), and then close the window.

8. From the Controls Toolbar, select the Edit Box control.

9. Click and drag to draw an Edit box on the Dialog box, and then press Ctrl+F9.

10. Double-click the Edit box and change the ID to ID_DATA.

See Figure 13.3 for the completed dialog box.

TIP

The default font size for dialog boxes is 8 point. This is quite small! Setting the font on the dialog box to 14 sets the font size for all controls to 14 point.

Figure 13.3.

Completed DLG_GetData *Dialog box, showing the Edit Box control and OK Button control.*

Now you're going to create a new dialog box called DLG_ShowData. This new dialog box will be created in the same UIApp.rct file as DLG_GetData.

To create the DLG_ShowData, do the following:

1. Open UIApp.rct (or simply switch to the already open window).

2. From the menubar, select Insert | Resource | Dialog.

3. Delete the OK and Cancel buttons.

4. Change the Dialog box ID to DLG_ShowData.

5. Click the Font button, change the Size to 14.

6. Create an Edit Control in the dialog.

7. Change the ID of the Edit box ID_DISPLAY_DATA.

There should be three resources in the resource file: DLG_ShowData, DLG_GetData, and MyMenu. To complete the Resource phase of this example, do the following:

1. Save the resource file.

2. Run the Java Resource Wizard.

3. Insert the DLG_GetData.java and DLG_ShowData.java files into the project.

In the MyFrame class, add the following lines of code:

```
import DLG_GetData;
import DLG_ShowData;
```

Under the MyFrame class definition add the lines:

```
Font m_Font;
DLG_GetData m_dlgGet;
DLG_ShowData m_dlgShow;
Dialog m_dlgGetDlg;
```

In the constructor of MyFrame, before Show(), add the following lines of code:

```
m_Font = new Font("Arial", Font.PLAIN, 18);
setFont(m_Font);
// Create the ShowData dialog on the Frame;
setBackground(Color.lightGray);
m_dlgShow = new DLG_ShowData( this );
m_dlgShow.CreateControls();
// Create the GetData dialog Box
m_dlgGetDlg = new Dialog ( this, "Data Dialog", false);
// Create new generic Dialog object
m_dlgGetDlg.setBackground(color.lightGray);
m_dlgGetDlg.resize(300,300);
m_dlgGetDlg.setFont( m_Font );
// Create the Resource File generated Dialog
m_dlgGet = new DLG_GetData(m_dlgGetDlg);
m_dlgGet.CreateControls();
// display the two windows;
show()
m_dlgGetDlg.show();
```

NOTE

It might seem unnecessary to add the line of code m_dlgGetDlg.setFont(m_Font);. But, without it, the applet doesn't run. This might be a bug in VJ++—we don't know.

To see all of your great work, compile and then run it. (See Figure 13.4.)

Figure 13.4.

The GetData *and* ShowData *dialog boxes in IE.*

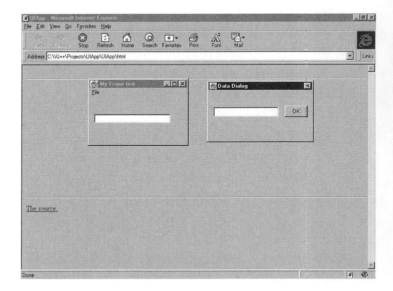

File Dialogs

FileDialog provides a basic file open/save dialog box that enables you to access the file system. The FileDialog class is system-independent, but depending upon the platform. the standard Open File dialog is brought up.

NOTE

For applets, you can bring up the file dialog box, but due to security restrictions you can't do anything with it (or, if you can do anything, access to any files on the local system is severely restricted). FileDialog is much more useful in stand-alone applications.

To create a file dialog, use the following constructors:

☐ FileDialog(*Frame*, *String*) creates an Open File dialog, attached to the given frame, with the given title. This form creates a dialog to load a file.

☐ FileDialog(*Frame*, *String*, *int*) also creates a file dialog box, but that integer argument is used to determine whether the dialog is for loading a file or saving a file (the only difference is the label on the buttons; the file dialog box does not actually open or save anything). The possible options for the mode argument are FileDialog.LOAD and FileDialog.SAVE.

After you create a `FileDialog` instance, use `show()` to display it:

```
FileDialog fd = new FileDialog(this, "FileDialog");
fd.show();
```

When the user chooses a file in the file dialog and dismisses it, you can then access the filename they chose by using the `getDirectory()` and `getFile()` methods; both return strings indicating the values the user chose. You can then open that file by using the stream and file handling methods (which you'll learn about next week) to read from or write to that file.

Handling UI Actions and Events

Java events are part of the Java AWT package. An event is the way that the AWT communicates to you, as the programmer, and to other Java AWT components that something has happened. That something can be input from the user (mouse movements or clicks, keypresses), changes in the system environment (a window opening or closing, the window being scrolled up or down), or a host of other things that might, in some way, be interesting to the operation of the program.

In other words, whenever just about anything happens to a Java AWT component, including an applet, an event is generated. Some events are handled by the AWT or by the browser without your needing to do anything. `paint()` methods, for example, are generated and handled by the browser—all you have to do is tell the AWT what you want painted when it gets to your part of the window. Some events, however (for example, a mouse click inside the boundaries of your applet), you might need to know about. Writing your Java programs to handle these kinds of events enables you to get input from the user and have your applet change its behavior based on that input.

Mouse Clicks

Now start with the most common event you might be interested in: mouse clicks. Mouse-click events occur when the user clicks the mouse somewhere in the body of your applet. You can intercept mouse clicks to do very simple things—for example, to toggle the sound on and off in your applet, to move to the next slide in a presentation, or to clear the screen and start over—or you can use mouse clicks in conjunction with mouse movements to perform more complex motions inside your applet.

mouseDown and mouseUp

When you click the mouse once, the AWT generates two events: a `mouseDown` event when the mouse button is pressed, and a `mouseUp` event when the button is released. Why two individual events for a single mouse action? Because you might want to do different things

13

for the "down" and the "up." For example, look at a pull-down menu. The mouseDown extends the menu, and the mouseUp selects an item (with mouseDrags between—but you'll learn about that one later today). If you have only one event for both actions (mouseUp and mouseDown), you cannot implement that sort of user interaction.

Handling mouse events in your applet is easy—all you have to do is override the proper method definition in your applet. That method will be called when that particular event occurs. Here's an example of the method signature for a mouseDown event:

```
public boolean mouseDown(Event evt, int x, int y)
{
...
}
```

The mouseDown() method (and the mouseUp() method as well) takes three parameters: the event itself and the x and y coordinates where the mouseDown or mouseUp event occurred.

The event argument is an instance of the class Event. All system events generate an instance of the Event class, which contains information about where and when the event took place, the kind of event it is, and other information that you might want to know about this event. Sometimes having a handle to that event object is useful, as you'll discover later in this section.

The x and the y coordinates of the event, as passed in through the x and y arguments, are particularly nice to know because you can use them to determine precisely where the mouse click took place.

For example, here's a simple method that grabs the current x and y positions when a mouseDown event occurs:

```
public boolean mouseDown(Event evt, int x, int y)
{
    m_iMousex = x;
    m_iMousey = y;
    return true;
}
```

By including this method in an applet, every time the user clicks the mouse inside your applet, the data members m_iMousex and m_iMousey will be updated.

Note that this method, unlike the other system methods you've studied thus far, returns a Boolean value instead of not returning anything (void). This will become important later today when you create user interfaces and then manage input to these interfaces; having an event handler return true or false determines whether a given UI component can intercept an event or whether it needs to pass it on to the enclosing component. The general rule is that if your method deals with the event, it should return true.

The second half of the mouse click is the mouseUp() method, which is called when the mouse button is released. To handle a mouseUp event, add the mouseUp() method to your applet. mouseUp() looks just like mouseDown():

```
public boolean mouseUp(Event evt, int x, int y)
{
    ....
}
```

A Spots **Applet Example**

In this section, you'll create an example of an applet that uses mouse events—mouseDown events in particular. The Spots applet starts with a blank screen and then sits and waits. When you click the mouse on that screen, a blue dot is drawn. You can place up to ten dots on the screen. Figure 13.5 shows the Spots applet.

Figure 13.5.

The Spots *applet.*

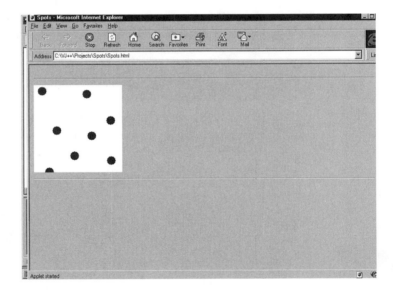

Start from the beginning and build this applet, starting from the initial class definition:

NOTE

Because this is a very simple applet, we are not going to use the Resource Editor at all. Leave the UIApp running while you complete this next exercise; however, you're going to use it later today.

13

Create a new Project Workspace and name it Spots. Create a new text file and add the following lines of code to it.

```
import java.awt.Graphics;
import java.awt.Color;
import java.awt.Event;

public class Spots extends java.applet.Applet
{
    final int MAXSPOTS = 10;
    int m_iXspots[] = new int[MAXSPOTS];
    int m_iYspots[] = new int[MAXSPOTS];
    int m_iCurrspots = 0;
}
```

This class uses three other AWT classes: Graphics, Color, and Event. That last class, Event, needs to be imported in any applets that use events. The class has four instance variables: a constant to determine the maximum number of spots that can be drawn, two arrays to store the x and y coordinates of the spots that have already been drawn, and an integer to keep track of the number of the current spot.

NOTE

This class doesn't include the `implements Runnable` words in its definition. As you'll see later as you build this applet, it also doesn't have a `run()` method. Why not? Because it doesn't actually do anything on its own—all it does is wait for input and then do stuff when input happens. There's no need for threads if your applet isn't actively doing something all the time.

Start with the init() method, which has one line, to set the background to white:

```
public void init()
{
        setBackground(Color.white);
}
```

Set the background in init(), instead of in paint(), because you really need to set the background only once. Also, since paint() is called repeatedly each time a new spot is added, setting the background color in the paint() method unnecessarily slows down that method. Putting it here is a much better idea.

The main action of this applet occurs on the mouseDown() method, so add that one now:

```
public boolean mouseDown(Event evt, int x, int y)
{
    if (m_iCurrspots < MAXSPOTS)
            addspot(x,y);
    return true;
}
```

13

When the mouse click occurs, the mouseDown() method tests to see whether there are less than ten spots. If so, it calls the addspot() method (which you'll write soon). If not, it just prints an error message. Finally, it returns true, because all the event methods have to return a Boolean value (usually true).

What does addspot() do? It adds the coordinates of the spot to the arrays that store the coordinates, increments the currspots variable, and then calls repaint():

```
void addspot(int x, int y)
{
        m_iXspots[currspots] = x;
        m_iYspots[currspots] = y;
        m_iCurrspots++;
        repaint();
}
```

You might be wondering why you have to keep track of all the past spots in addition to the current spot. The reason is because of repaint(): Each time you paint the screen, you have to paint all the old spots in addition to the newest spot. Otherwise, each time you painted a new spot, the older spots would get erased. Now, on to the paint() method:

```
public void paint(Graphics g)
{
    g.setColor(Color.blue);
    for (int i = 0; i < m_iCurrspots; i++)
    {
        g.fillOval(m_iXspots[i] -10, m_iYspots[i] - 10, 20, 20);
    }
}
```

Inside paint, you just loop through the spots you've stored in the m_iXspots and m_iYspots arrays, painting each one (actually, painting them a little to the right and upward so that the spots are painted around the mouse pointer rather than below and to the right).

That's it! That's all you need to create an applet that handles mouse clicks. Everything else is handled for you. You have to add the appropriate behavior to mouseDown() or mouseUp() to intercept and handle that event. Listing 13.1 shows the full text for the Spots applet.

TYPE | **Listing 13.1. The Spots applet.**

```
1: import java.awt.Graphics;
2: import java.awt.Color;
3: import java.awt.Event;
4:
5: public class Spots extends java.applet.Applet
6: {
7:     final int MAXSPOTS = 10;
8:     int m_iXspots[] = new int[MAXSPOTS];
```

continues

Listing 13.1. continued

```
 9:     int m_iYspots[] = new int[MAXSPOTS];
10:     int m_iCurrspots = 0;
11:
12:     public void init()
13:     {
14:         setBackground(Color.white);
15:     }
16:
17:     public boolean mouseDown(Event evt, int x, int y)
18:     {
19:         if (m_iCurrspots < MAXSPOTS)
20:             addspot(x,y);
21:         return true;
22:     }
23:
24:     void addspot(int x,int y)
25:     {
26:         m_iXspots[m_iCurrspots] = x;
27:         m_iYspots[m_iCurrspots] = y;
28:         m_iCurrspots++;
29:         repaint();
30:     }
31:
32:     public void paint(Graphics g)
33:     {
34:         g.setColor(Color.blue);
35:         for (int i = 0; i < m_iCurrspots; i++)
36:         {
37:             g.fillOval(m_iXspots[i] - 10, m_iYspots[i] - 10, 20, 20);
38:         }
39:     }
40: }
```

Mouse Movements

Every time the mouse is moved a single pixel in any direction, a mouse movement event is generated. There are two mouse movement events: mouse drags, where the movement occurs with the mouse button pressed down, and plain mouse movements, where the mouse button isn't pressed.

To manage mouse movement events, use the mouseDrag() and mouseMove() methods.

mouseDrag **and** mouseMove

The mouseDrag() and mouseMove() methods, when included in your applet code, intercept and handle mouse movement events. The mouseMove() method, for plain mouse pointer movements without the mouse button pressed, looks much like the mouse-click methods:

```
public boolean mouseMove(Event evt, int x, int y)
{
    ...
}
```

The `mouseDrag()` method handles mouse movements made with the mouse button pressed down (a complete dragging movement consists of a `mouseDown` event, a series of `mouseDrag` events for each pixel the mouse is moved, and a `mouseUp` event when the button is released). The `mouseDrag()` method looks like this:

```
public boolean mouseDrag(Event evt, int x, int y)
{
    ...
}
```

mouseEnter **and** mouseExit

Finally, there are the `mouseEnter()` and `mouseExit()` methods. These two methods are called when the mouse pointer enters the applet or when it exits the applet. (In case you're wondering why you might need to know this, it's more useful on components of user interfaces that you might put inside an applet. You'll learn more about UI tomorrow.)

Both `mouseEnter()` and `mouseExit()` have similar signatures—three arguments: the event object and the x and y coordinates of the point where the mouse entered or exited the applet.

```
public boolean mouseEnter(Event evt, int x, int y)
{
    ...
}
```

```
public boolean mouseExit(Event evt, int x, int y)
{
    ...
}
```

Keyboard Events

Keyboard events are generated whenever users press a key on the keyboard. By using key events, you can get hold of the values of the keys that were pressed to perform an action or merely to get character input from the users of your applet.

The keyDown **and** keyUp **Methods**

To capture a keyboard event, use the `keyDown()` method:

```
public boolean keyDown(Event evt, int key)
{
    ...
}
```

13

The keys generated by keyDown events (and passed into keyDown() as the key argument) are integers representing ASCII character values, which include alphanumeric characters, function keys, tabs, returns, and so on. To use them as characters (for example, to print them), you need to cast them to characters:

```
currentchar = (char)key;
```

Here's a simple example of a keyDown() method that does nothing but set the data member m_cLastKey to the character value of the key you just typed.

```
public boolean keyDown(Event evt, int key)
{
    m_cLastKey = (char)key;
    return true;
}
```

As with mouse clicks, each keyDown event also has a corresponding keyUp event. To intercept keyUp events, use the keyUp() method:

```
public booklean keyUp(Event evt, int key)
{
    ...
}
```

Default Keys

The Event class provides a set of class variables that refer to several standard non-alphanumeric keys, such as the arrow keys. If your interface uses these keys, you can provide more readable code by testing for these names in your keyDown() method rather than testing for their numeric values. For example, to test whether the up arrow was pressed, you might use the following code fragment:

```
if (key == Event.UP)
{
    ...
}
```

Because the values these class variables hold are integers, you also can use the switch statement to test for them.

Table 13.1 shows the standard event class variables for various keys and the actual keys they represent.

Table 13.1. Standard keys defined by the event class.

Class Variable	Represented Key
Event.HOME	The Home key
Event.END	The End key
Event.PGUP	The Page Up key
Event.PGDN	The Page Down key
Event.UP	The up arrow
Event.DOWN	The down arrow
Event.LEFT	The left arrow
Event.RIGHT	The right arrow

An Example of Entering, Displaying, and Moving Characters

Now look at an applet that demonstrates keyboard events. This one enables you to type a character, it then displays that character in the center of the applet window. You then can move that character around on the screen by using the arrow keys. Typing another character at any time changes the character as it's currently displayed. Figure 13.6 shows an example.

Figure 13.6.

The Keys *applet.*

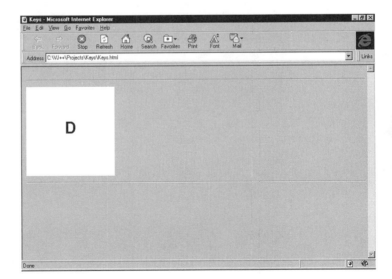

This applet is actually less complicated than the previous applets you've used. This one has only three methods: init(), keyDown(), and paint(). The data members are also simpler, because the only things you need to keep track of are the x and y positions of the current character and the values of that character itself. Here's the top of this class definition:

```
import java.awt.Graphics;
import java.awt.Event;
import java.awt.Font;
import java.awt.Color;

public class Keys extends java.applet.Applet
{
    char m_cCurrkey;
    int m_iCurrx;
    int m_iCurry;
}
```

The init() method is responsible for three things: setting the background color, setting the applet's font (here, 36 point Helvetica bold), and setting the beginning position for the character (the middle of the screen, minus a few points to nudge it up and to the right):

```
public void init()
{
    m_iCurrx = (size().width / 2) - 8;  // default
    m_iCurry = (size().height / 2) - 16;
    setBackground(Color.white);
    setFont(new Font("Helvetica", Font.BOLD, 36));
}
```

Because this applet's behavior is based on keyboard input, the keyDown() method is where most of the work of the applet takes place:

```
public boolean keyDown(Event evt, int key)
{
    switch (key)
        {
        case Event.DOWN:
            m_iCurry += 5;
            break;
        case Event.UP:
            m_iCurry -= 5;
            break;
        case Event.LEFT:
            m_iCurrx -= 5;
            break;
        case Event.RIGHT:
            m_iCurrx += 5;
            break;
        default:
            m_cCurrkey = (char)key;
        }
        repaint();
        return true;
}
```

In the center of the keyDown() applet is a switch statement that tests for different key events. If the event is an arrow key, the appropriate change is made to the character's position. If the event is any other key, the character itself is changed. The method finishes up with a repaint() and returns true.

The paint() method here is almost trivial; just display the current character at the current position. However, note that when the applet starts up, there's no initial character and nothing to draw, so you have to take that into account. The m_cCurrkey variable is initialized to 0, so you paint the applet only if m_cCurrkey has an actual value:

```
public void paint(Graphics g)
{
   if (m_cCurrkey != 0)
   {
      g.drawString(String.valueOf(m_cCurrkey), m_iCurrx,m_iCurry);
   }
}
```

Listing 13.2 shows the complete source for the Keys applet:

TYPE **Listing 13.2. The Keys applet.**

```
1: import java.awt.Graphics;
2: import java.awt.Event;
3: import java.awt.Font;
4: import java.awt.Color;
5:
6: public class Keys extends java.applet.Applet
7: {
8:    char m_cCurrkey;
9:     int m_iCurrx;
10:     int m_iCurry;
11:
12:     public void init()
13:         {
14:        m_iCurrx = (size().width / 2) -8;  // default
15:        m_iCurry = (size().height / 2) -16;
16:
17:        setBackground(Color.white);
18:        setFont(new Font("Helvetica",Font.BOLD,36));
19:     }
20:
21:     public boolean keyDown(Event evt, int key)
22:     {
23:        switch (key)
24:        {
25:          case Event.DOWN:
26:            m_iCurry += 5;
27:            break;
28:          case Event.UP:
29:            m_iCurry -= 5;
```

continues

Listing 13.2. continued

```
30:                    break;
31:                case Event.LEFT:
32:                    m_iCurrx -= 5;
33:                    break;
34:                case Event.RIGHT:
35:                    m_iCurrx += 5;
36:                    break;
37:                default:
38:                    m_cCurrkey = (char)key;
39:            }
40:
41:            repaint();
42:            return true;
43:        }
44:
45:        public void paint(Graphics g)
46:        {
47:            if (m_cCurrkey != 0)
48:            {
49:                g.drawString(String.valueOf(m_cCurrkey), m_iCurrx,m_iCurry);
50:            }
51:        }
52: }
```

Testing for Modifier Keys

Shift, control, and meta are modifier keys. They don't generate key events themselves, but when you get an ordinary mouse or keyboard event, you can test to see whether those keys were held down when the event occurred. Sometimes it might be obvious—shifted alphanumeric keys produce different key events than unshifted ones, for example. For other events, however—mouse events in particular—you might want to handle an event with a modifier key held down differently from a regular version of that event.

NOTE

In the Windows environment, there is no equivalent to a meta key, so when running a Java program on a Windows system, the metaDown() event will never be triggered by a key press. Even though there is no meta on a Windows system, the metaDown() event is triggered when the right mouse button is clicked.

13

The Event class provides three methods for testing whether or not a modifier key is held down: shiftDown(), metaDown(), and controlDown(). All return Boolean values based on whether that modifier key is indeed held down. You can use these three methods in any of the event handling methods (mouse or keyboard) by calling them on the event object passed into that method:

```
public boolean mouseDown(Event evt, int x, int y )
{
    if (evt.shiftDown())
        // handle shift-click
    else // handle regular click
}
```

The AWT Event Handler

The default methods you've learned about today for handling basic events in applets are actually called by a generic event handler method called handleEvent(). The handleEvent() method is how the AWT generically deals with events that occur between application components and events based upon user input.

In the default handleEvent() method, basic events are processed and the methods you learned about today are called. To handle events other than those mentioned here, to change the default event handling behavior, or to create and pass your own events, you need to override handleEvent() in your own Java programs. The handleEvent() method looks like this:

```
public boolean handleEvent(Event evt)
{
    ...
}
```

To test for specific events, examine the ID data member of the Event object that gets passed in. The event ID is an integer, but fortunately, the Event class defines a whole set of event IDs as class variables that you can test for in the body of the handleEvent(). Because these class variables are integer constants, a switch statement works particularly well. For example, here's a simple handleEvent() method to print out debugging information about mouse events:

```
public boolean handleEvent(Event evt)
{
    switch (evt.id)
    {
      case Event.MOUSE_DOWN:
        System.out.println("MouseDown: " +
                evt.x + "," + evt.y);
```

13

```
      return true;
    case Event.MOUSE_UP:
      System.out.println("MouseUp: " +
             evt.x + "," + evt.y);
      return true;
    case Event.MOUSE_MOVE:
      System.out.println("MouseMove: " +
             evt.x + "," + evt.y);
      return true;
    case Event.MOUSE_DRAG:
      System.out.println("MouseDown: " +
             evt.x + "," + evt.y);
      return true;
    default:
      return false;
  }
}
```

You can test for the following keyboard events:

☐ Event.KEY_PRESS is generated when a key is pressed (the same as the keyDown()
method).

☐ Event.KEY_RELEASE is generated when a key is released.

☐ Event.KEY_ACTION and Event.KEY_ACTION_RELEASE are generated when a key is
pressed and released.

You can test for these mouse events:

☐ Event.MOUSE_DOWN is generated when the mouse button is pressed (the same as the
mouseDown() method).

☐ Event.MOUSE_UP is generated when the mouse button is released (the same as the
mouseUp() method).

☐ Event.MOUSE_MOVE is generated when the mouse is moved (the same as the
mouseMove() method).

☐ Event.MOUSE_DRAG is generated when the mouse is moved with the button pressed
(the same as the mouseDrag() method).

☐ Event.MOUSE_ENTER is generated when the mouse enters the applet (or a component
of that applet). You can also use the mouseEnter() method.

☐ Event.MOUSE_EXIT is generated when the mouse exits the applet. You can also use
the mouseExit() method.

Note that if you override handleEvent() in your class, none of the default event handling
methods you learned about today will get called unless you explicitly call them in the body
of handleEvent(), so be careful if you decide to do this. One way to get around this is to test

for the event you're interested in, and if that event isn't it, to call `super.handleEvent()` so that the superclass that defines `handleEvent()` can process things. Here's an example of how to do this:

```
public boolean handleEvent(Event evt)
{
    if (evt.id == Event.MOUSE_DOWN)
    {
        // process the mouse down
        return true;
    }
    else
    {
        return super.handleEvent(evt);
    }
}
```

In addition to these events, the `Event` class has a whole suite of methods for handling the UI components. You'll learn more about these events in the next section.

Handling UI Component Actions and Events

Now put everything you have learned today together. You have learned how to display windows and dialog boxes, and you have the basics of event handling under your belt. Now it's time to add some life to the `UIApp` that you created earlier today:

1. Open `UIApp.rct` (or simply switch to the already open window).

2. Double-click the `MyMenu` item to open the menu resource. (Expand the outline if the `MyMenu` item is not displayed.)

3. Open the properties page for the blank box displayed to the right of the File menu; make the Caption Edit, and then close the Properties box.

4. Open the properties page for the blank box under the Edit menu. Make the Caption `GetData` and the ID `MN_GETDATA` (see Figure 13.7), and then close the properties box.

5. Save the resource file and then run the Java Resource Wizard.

For your UI components to do something when they are activated, you need to hook up the UI's action with an operation. Testing for an action by a UI component is a form of event management—the things you learned yesterday about events will come in handy here. In

13

particular, UI components produce the special kind of event called an action. To intercept an action by any UI component, you define an `action()` method in your applet or class:

```
public boolean action(Event evt, Object arg)
{
    ...
}
```

Figure 13.7.

GetData *Properties box.*

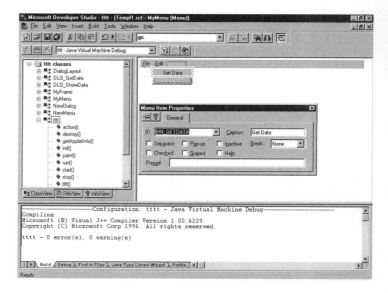

The `action()` method should look familiar to the basic mouse and keyboard event methods. Like those methods, it gets passed the event object that represents this event. It also gets an extra object, which can be of any type. What's that second argument for?

The second argument to the action method depends upon the UI component that's generating the event. The basic definition is that it's any arbitrary argument—when a component generates an event, it can pass along any extra information that might be needed later. Because that extra information might be useful for you, it's passed on through the `action()` method.

All the basic UI components (except for labels, which have no action) have different actions and arguments:

☐ Buttons create actions when they are selected, and a button's argument is the label of the button.

☐ Checkboxes, both exclusive and nonexclusive, generate actions when a box is checked. The argument is always `true`.

☐ Choice menus generate an action when a menu item is selected, and the argument is that item.

☐ Text fields create actions when the user presses Return inside that text field. Note that if the user tabs to a different text field or uses the mouse to change the input focus, an action is not generated. Only a Return triggers the action.

Note that with actions, unlike with ordinary events, you can have many different kinds of objects generating the event, as opposed to a single event such as a mouseDown. To deal with those different UI components and the actions they generate, you have to test for the type of object that sent/created the event in the first place inside the body of your action() method. That object is stored in the event's target data member and you can use the instanceof operator to find out what kind of UI component sent it, as shown in the following code sample:

```
public boolean action(Event evt, Object arg)
{
    if (evt.target instanceof TextField)
    {
        handleText(evt.target);
    }
    else if (evt.target instanceof Choice)
    {
        handleChoice(arg);
    }
...
}
```

Although you can handle UI actions in the body of the action() method, it's much more common simply to define a handler method and call that method from action() instead. Here, there are two handler methods: one to handle the action on the text field (handleText()) and one to handle the action on the choice menu (handleChoice()). Depending upon the action you want to handle, you might also want to pass on the argument from the action, the UI component that sent it, or any other information that the event might contain.

Now make the UIApp do something other than look pretty. In the MyFrame class, add the following method:

```
public boolean action(Event evt, Object arg)
{
    if (evt.target instanceof Button)
    {
        String Val = (String)arg;
        if ( Val.compareTo("OK") == 0)
        {
            m_dlgShow.ID_DISPLAY_DATA.setText(m_dlgGet.ID_DATA.getText());
            m_dlgGetDlg.hide();
            return true;
        }
    }
    return false;
}
```

13

The preceding code traps the event on the OK button in the dialog box. It then checks to see if the caption is OK, and if so, sets the text in the Frame to the same data as the text in the dialog box.

Menu Actions

The act of selecting a menu item causes an action event to be generated. You can handle that action the same way you handle other `action` methods—by overriding `action()`. Both regular menu items and checkbox menu items have actions that generate an extra argument representing the label for that menu. You can use that label to determine which action to take. Note, also, that because `CheckBoxMenuItem` is a subclass of `MenuItem`, you don't have to treat menu items of type `CheckBoxMenuItem` as a special case. Here is an example:

```
public boolean action(Event evt, Object arg)
{
    if (evt.target instanceof MenuItem)
    {
        String label = (String)arg;
        if (label.equals("Show Coordinates")) toggleCoords();
        else if (label.equals("Fill")) fillcurrentArea();
        return true;
    }
    else return false;
}
```

Now add some more functionality to the UPApp. In the `MyFrame` class, change the action method to read like the following:

```
public boolean action(Event evt, Object arg)
{
    String sVal = (String)arg;
    if (evt.target instanceof Button)
    {
        if ( sVal.compareTo("OK") == 0)
        {
            m_dlgShow.ID_DISPLAY_DATA.setText(m_dlgGet.ID_DATA.getText());
            m_dlgGetDlg.hide();
            return true;
        }
    }
    if (evt.target instanceof MenuItem)
    {
        if (sVal.equals ("Get Data"))
        {
            m_dlgGet.ID_DATA.setText(m_dlgShow.ID_DISPLAY_DATA.getText());
            m_dlgGetDlg.show();
            return true;
        }
        if (sVal.equals ("&Exit"))
        {
            m_dlgGetDlg.hide();
            hide();
```

```
            return true;
        }
    }
    return false;
}
```

Recompile your project, and then execute it. Now the UIApp applet should actually do something. When it starts, the frame window and the dialog box are displayed. When you enter some text in the text field and click OK, the text value of the frame is set to the same value as in the text field of the dialog box. If you change the text in the frame, and then select Edit | Get Data from the menu, the dialog box is displayed again. You can then change the text in the dialog box and continue to repeat the procedures. From the menu of the frame, you can also select File | Exit to close the windows. .

Window Events

Today, you learned about writing your own event handler methods, and you noted that the Event class defines many standard events for which you can test. Window events are part of that list, so if you use windows, these events might be of interest to you. Table 13.2 shows those events.

Table 13.2. Window events from the Event class.

WINDOW_DESTROY	Generated when a window is destroyed (for example, when the browser or applet viewer has quit)
WINDOW_EXPOSE	Generated when the window is brought forward from behind other windows
WINDOW_ICONIFY	Generated when the window is minimized to an icon
WINDOW_DEICONIFY	Generated when the window is restored from an icon
WINDOW_MOVED	Generated when the window is moved

More UI Events

To intercept a specific event, you need to test for that event's ID. The available IDs are defined as class variables in the Event class, so you can test for them by name. You learned about some of the basic events today; Table 13.3 shows additional events that might be useful to you for some of the more common components; other events can be found in the InfoView topic "1.14 Class Event."

13

Table 13.3. Additional events.

Event ID	What It Represents
ACTION_EVENT	Generated when a UI component action occurs
KEY_ACTION	Generated when text field action occurs
LIST_DESELECT	Generated when an item in a scrolling list is deselected
LIST_SELECT	Generated when an item in a scrolling list is selected
SCROLL_ABSOLUTE	Generated when a scrollbar's box has been moved
SCROLL_LINE_DOWN	Generated when a scrollbar's bottom or left endpoint (button) is selected
SCROLL_LINE_UP	Generated when a scrollbar's top or right endpoint (button) is selected
SCROLL_PAGE_DOWN	Generated when the scrollbar's field below (or to the left of) the box is selected
SCROLL_PAGE_UP	Generated when the scrollbar's field above (or to the right of) the box is selected

Summary

Today you finished exploring applets and the AWT by learning about two important concepts. First, you learned about windows, frames, menus, and dialogs, which enable you to create a framework for your applets—or enable your Java applications to take advantage of applet features.

The second topic was how to handle menu actions and events. Most of the time, all you need to do is stick the right method in your applet code, and your applet intercepts and handles that method. The following are some of the basic events you can manage in this way:

☐ Mouse clicks: mouseUp() and mouseDown() methods cover each part of a mouse click.

☐ Mouse movements: the mouseMove() and mouseDrag() methods are for mouse movement with the mouse button released and pressed, respectively. The mouseEnter() and mouseExit() methods are for when the mouse enters and exits the applet area.

☐ The keyDown() and keyUp() methods are for when a key on the keyboard is pressed.

Q&A

Q **When I created a dialog box resource, I noticed that a new button bar displayed. What's it used for?**

A The button bar that appears at the bottom of the screen has a number of alignment options that make it easy to align the buttons on your newly created dialog box. Options are also available for sizing the dialog box buttons. At least one control (and in several cases two or more controls) must be selected before the option(s) become active. Experiment with the options on the button bar. The option on the extreme left of the toolbar (it looks like a light switch) that might be a particular interest allows you to run the dialog box to test its appearance and behavior.

Q **On the Controls Toolbar, I saw a number of controls I didn't use. What are they used for?**

A There are a number of options available on the Controls Toolbar that make designing a dialog box very easy. The options allow you to easily add check boxes, radio buttons, or a combination boxes with drop-down lists. There are options for adding scroll bars, hot keys, and sliders. Pictures and animation can also be added using options provided on this rather extensive toolbar. Experiment with the many options and see what you can come up with.

Q **The pop-up windows I create using VJ++ display a warning in my browser that an applet window is running. What does this mean and why does this warning display?**

A Depending on the browser that's used, the applet warning varies; however, the purpose for the warning is the same. The warning displays to tell you (and any users of your applet) that the window being displayed was generated by an applet and not by the browser itself. This security feature is a good thing; it keeps an applet programmer from popping up a window that masquerades as a browser window and, for example, asks users for their passwords. There's nothing you can do to hide or obscure the warning.

Q **What good is having a File dialog box if you can't read or write files from the local file system?**

A Depending on the browser, applets often can't read or write from the local file system, but you can use AWT components in Java applications as well as applets, and the File dialog box is very useful for applications.

Q **The `mouseDown()` and `mouseUp()` methods seem to apply only to a single mouse button. How can I determine which button on the mouse has been pressed?**

A At the moment, you can't. AWT assumes that you're using a one button mouse , or if you have a mouse with multiple buttons, that it's using only the left one.

13

Although this assumption limits the kinds of actions you can perform in your applet, it does provide a cross-platform solution. Different systems have different mice, so writing your applet to do something specific with the right mouse button isn't a good idea if the people running your applet are using Macintoshes and have only a one button mouse. If you really want to have different mouse actions perform different things, test for modifier keys (Alt | Shift) in your `mouseDown()` and `mouseUp()` methods.

Day 14

Compiler Errors and Debugging

After today's lesson, you'll be two-thirds of the way through learning Visual J++. You've covered a lot of topics so far, and today you will learn about compiler errors and debugging. The topic of debugging is fairly advanced, but very important. If you've never used a professional debugger before, today's activity will be extremely valuable. For those of you with more programming experience, you'll have a chance to see how VJ++ handles errors.

When writing applications or applets, it stands to reason that you will have errors. What do you do when a program won't compile; how do you find the error? What do you do when a program does compile, but you get a random program error? Today's lesson will answer these questions. In today's lesson, you will learn:

☐ How to deal with compiler errors
☐ How to deal with runtime errors

NOTE

Today's examples are intentionally written with errors in order to show what happens when errors occur and how to correct them. If you try the examples, remember to write the code exactly as it's stated in this book, even if you recognize the errors. This will help you better understand the logic behind debugging.

Compiler Errors

Compiler errors are errors that prevent your `.java` files from compiling into `.class` files. The errors can be wide-ranging from all the appropriate files not being included in the project, to spelling, capitalization, punctuation errors, and so on.

To demonstrate how to deal with compiler errors, create a project workspace for an applet only. Make it multithreaded with no animation. You can name your project `TestDebug`.

Now, create a resource file and name the dialog `DlgButtons`. Save the resource file as `TestDebug.rct`, and name the buttons: `ID_HIDE`, `ID_SHOW`, and `ID_DESTROY`, respectively. (See Figure 14.1.)

Figure 14.1.

The `DlgButtons` *dialog box.*

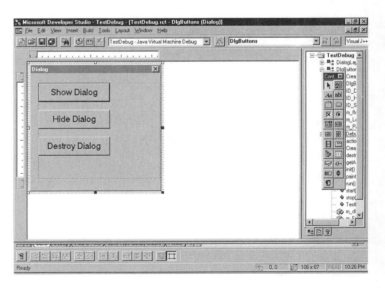

Type the following code exactly as it is shown. Remember to include the exact punctuation (no matter how obvious an error it might seem).

Add the following code in the header:

```
import DlgButtons;
DlgButtons m_dlg;
Frame m_Frame;
```

Remove the existing text in the Init method:

```
m_dlg = new DlgButtons();
m_dlg.CreateControls();
CreateMyframe();
```

Now, create a new method called CreateMyFrame:

```
void CreateMyFrame()
{
    m_Frame = new Frame( "Debug Frame );
    m_Frame.resize(200,200);
    m_Frame.show();
}
```

Create another new method:

```
public boolean action(Event evt, Object arg)
{
    String sVal = (String)arg;
    if (evt.target instanceof Button)
    {
        if ( sVal.compareTo("Hide Dialog") == 0)
        {
            if (m_Frame.isShowing())
            {
                m_Frame.Hide();
            }
            return true;
        }
        else if ( sVal.compareTo("Show Dialog") == 0)
        {
            if (m_Frame.isShowing())
            {
                m_Frame.show();
            }
            return true;
        }
        else if ( sVal.compareTo("Destroy Dialog") == 0)
        {
            if (m_Frame != null)
            {
                m_Frame.dispose();
                m_Frame = null;
            }
        }
    }
    return false;
}
```

14

Compile the TestDebug project. Remember that the project has errors, so it's not meant to compile. So unless you did something wrong (or right in this case), the first time you attempt to compile this, you will get errors in the Output window. Figure 14.2 shows the Output window as you should see it after you attempt to compile the project.

Figure 14.2.

The Output window for the project TestDebug.

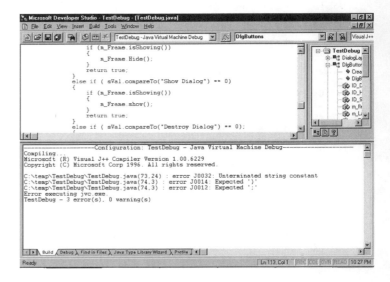

Notice that the output information can be very cryptic. But if you double-click any of the lines in the Output window, the offending line in the code window will automatically be displayed.

 NOTE

It is common for a single error to cause multiple lines of compiler errors to be displayed in the Output window. For example, if you incorrectly declared something, such as a class or variable, that was used numerous times throughout the program, this one mistake would cause numerous errors to be reported. Because of this, it is suggested that you always start the debugging process from the top line and work your way down. It is important also to look for patterns or similarities among the error messages to see where they are pointing to in the physical code.

Now we'll demonstrate how VJ++ assists you with finding the errors. Double-click the first error message in the Output window, which is as follows:

```
C:\VJ++\Projects\TestDebug\TestDebug.java(73,24) : error J0032: Unterminated
➡ string constant
```

 14

Notice that VJ++ uses an arrow to direct your attention to the code within the Source window where the mistake has been made. The cursor is also inserted within the line of code so that the error can be corrected. In this case, your attention is drawn to the following line:

```
m_Frame = new Frame( "Debug Frame );
```

The error Unterminated string constant is simple enough. It indicates that a string was not terminated. This might not make sense at first glance because the line ends with the necessary semicolon. However, if you look closer, you will notice that the code has unbalanced quotation marks. Without the terminating quotation mark, the compiler thinks that everything on the line after the D in Debug is part of the string literal. To correct this error, simply add an end quotation mark so that the line will now read:

```
m_Frame = new Frame( "Debug Frame" );
```

Now recompile and you will see a completely different list of bugs. This lets you know that the other two (now missing) errors that were listed the first time you compiled were related to the Unterminated string constant error and by fixing the missing quotation mark, both errors disappear. Wow, that's two for one! This happened because the missing quotation mark caused the additional errors to be generated when the compiler was trying to understand how the line of code preceding the quote and following the quote would work together.

TECHNICAL NOTE

> When error messages occur, it is best to start at the top and correct the first error, recompile, and see which errors you get the second time around. Sometimes, one error can have an effect on other parts of the code, which will generate additional errors. Newcomers to programming might assume that if there is one error in the code, only one error message would be shown by the compiler, and that the compiler would only display the lines that had actual errors. Unfortunately, compilers have yet to be developed with that level of logic and intelligence. At first, you should follow the fix one error and recompile rule. Once you become familiar with error patterns, you will soon be able to correct multiple errors without having to recompile after each correction.

Figure 14.3 shows the TestDebug project after the second compile.

This time you get an error that Hide is not a member of the class Frame. The problem is that the correct method is hide, not Hide. Remember, capitalization counts!

14

Figure 14.3.

The Output window for TestDebug *on the second try.*

Fix this error and recompile, and then only two errors remain. This time the errors were not caused by the capitalization of Hide. Go ahead and fix these errors. Hint: one of the errors is a spelling error and the other is a bad method call. (Check the DlgButtons class for the correct method format.)

When you are finished, your entire (correct) program should look something like this:

```java
import java.applet.*;
import java.awt.*;
import DlgButtons;

public class TestDebug extends Applet implements Runnable
{
    Thread m_TestDebug = null;
    DlgButtons m_dlg;
    Frame m_Frame;
    public TestDebug()
    {
    }
    public String getAppletInfo()
    {
        return "Name: TestDebug\r\n" +
        "Author: Your Name\r\n" +
        "Created with Microsoft Visual J++ Version 1.0";
    }
    public void init()
    {
        m_dlg = new DlgButtons( this );
        m_dlg.CreateControls();
        CreateMyFrame();
    }
```

```
 public void destroy()
{
}
public void paint(Graphics g)
{
}
public void start()
{
    if (m_TestDebug == null)
    {
       m_TestDebug = new Thread(this);
       m_TestDebug.start();
    }
}

public void stop()
{
   if  (m_TestDebug != null)
   {
       m_TestDebug.stop();
       m_TestDebug = null;
   }
}
 public void run()
 {
     while (true)
     {
         try
         {
             repaint();
             Thread.sleep(50);
         }
         catch (InterruptedException e)
         {
             stop();
         }
     }
 }
 void CreateMyFrame()
 {
     m_Frame = new Frame( "Debug Frame" );
     m_Frame.resize(200,200);
     m_Frame.show();
 }

public boolean action(Event evt, Object arg)
{
    String sVal = (String)arg;
    if (evt.target instanceof Button)
    {
        if ( sVal.compareTo("Hide Dialog") == 0)
        {
            if (m_Frame.isShowing())
            {
                m_Frame.hide();
            }
```

14

```
            return true;
        }
        else if ( sVal.compareTo("Show Dialog") == 0)
        {
            if (m_Frame.isShowing())
            {
                m_Frame.show();
            }
            return true;
        }
        else if ( sVal.compareTo("Destroy Dialog") == 0)
        {
            if (m_Frame != null)
            {
                m_Frame.dispose();
                m_Frame = null;
            }
        }
    }
    return false;
}
```

Now your program compiles, but will it run? If you typed everything in correctly, your program will run. It won't "blow up," but there will still be some problems. To help determine what these problems are, you can use Microsoft Developer Studio debugger tools.

Microsoft Developer Studio Debugger

When debugging your program, you will typically use breakpoints to halt the execution of your program. To enable a breakpoint on a line of code, set your cursor on the line and press F9. To use advanced features of breakpoints such as conditional breakpoints and breakpoints that are skipped the first *n* number of times, press ALT+F9 or select Edit | Breakpoints from the menu. Figure 14.4 is an example of the Breakpoints dialog box.

Once you have breakpoints defined in your applet or application, you start the debugging process by either pressing F5 or by using the Build | Debug menu command. You also need to make sure your program was compiled using the Java Virtual Machine Debug setting; debug cannot debug a non-debug version (Java Virtual Machine Release) of your program.

WARNING

Up until now, you've been running your programs using Build | Execute—stop it! That's bad…very bad in this chapter. Even if you select Build | Execute (CTRL+F5) using a debug version of your program, the program will not run in debug mode; you must use Build | Debug (F5).

Figure 14.4.

An example of the Breakpoints dialog box.

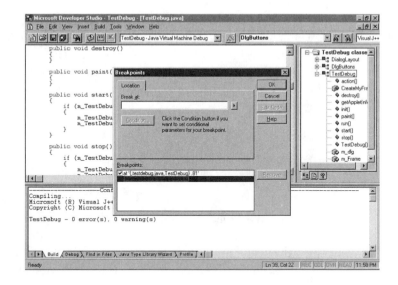

Debugging Your Applet

Now take your TestDebug applet and run it to see what works and what doesn't work. Go ahead and run your applet. You should get output similar to Figure 14.5.

Figure 14.5.

The TestDebug applet running in Internet Explorer.

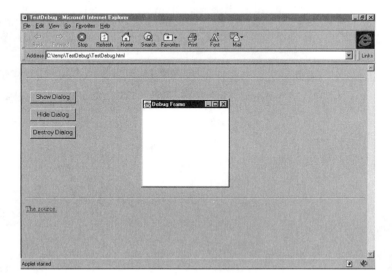

As soon as you click any of the buttons on the page, no matter which button is pressed, the Frame window goes away and will not display again. Now, we'll analyze this. The window displays, so that section of code is probably correct. The window hides (or destroys), so the code is working, but not properly. And, the Show event is not being recalled, so it's not working either. You now need to step through the code to discover the problems one at a time.

In your program, go to the following segment of code:

```
public boolean action(Event evt, Object arg)
{
    String sVal = (String)arg;
    if (evt.target instanceof Button)
    {
        if ( sVal.compareTo("Hide Dialog") == 0)
```

Because you could probably assume that the problem with the Window not reappearing when you hit the Show Dialog button lies in the action method, you should start there. Highlight the first if line and set a breakpoint. A red dot will appear on the left margin that indicates a breakpoint is set on this line. Your code window should look something like Figure 14.6.

NOTE

The red dot that appears on the left margin in your program is one of the many color coding features that Microsoft Developer Studio uses to identify certain items. Remember, if you change the default Windows system colors, the colors that are displayed will change.

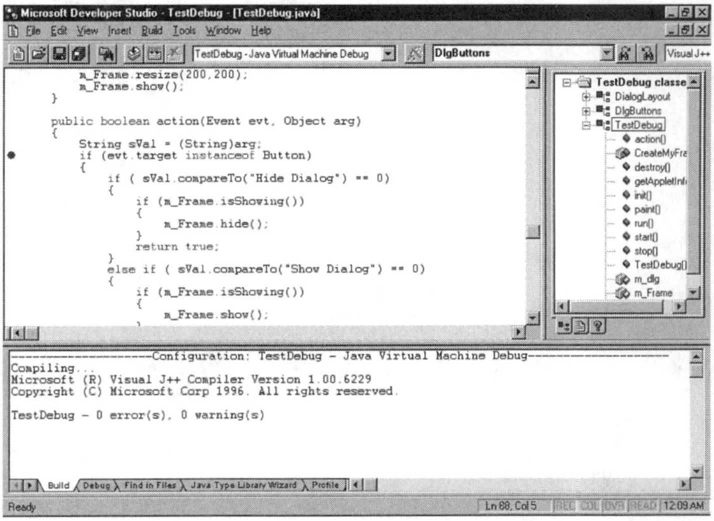

Figure 14.6.

The code for TestDebug *showing a breakpoint set.*

Now start the debugger by pressing F5.

Your program will start, the browser will be displayed containing the applet and its three buttons on the page, and the Dialog window will be displayed. To get the program to the state where it doesn't work right, click Hide Dialog.

After you click Hide Dialog, Microsoft Developer Studio will return to the foreground and the cursor will be placed on the line where the breakpoint was set. This is nifty, huh? But, you know this line is fine; it's just your starting point for stepping through the debug session. For now, press F5, or select Debug | Go from the menu. Use Ctrl+Esc to get back to the browser. Now click Show Dialog. You will once again be returned to the action method in the code window.

Now you will want to step through the code to find out why the Dialog is not being displayed properly.

From the View menu, select Watch and then select Variables to display both the Watch and Variables windows.

The Watch window displays variables (both objects and non-objects). You define the variables you want to watch by adding them to the Watch window. The Variables window displays all variables that the current line affects or that were affected by the previous line of code. If you arrange your Variables window on the bottom left of your screen and the Watch window on the bottom right, your window should now resemble Figure 14.7.

Figure 14.7.

Microsoft Developer Studio with Variable and Watch windows displayed.

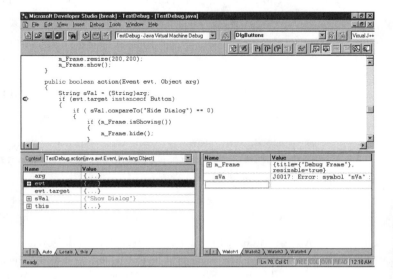

Now to step through the code. You use the Step Into, Step Over, and Step Out debugging commands from the menu or their hot keys F10, F11, Shift+F11, respectively, to move through the code. For your purposes, you will be using only Step Into (F10).

NOTE

> If this is the first professional debugger that you have used, Step Into, Step Over, and Step Out can be somewhat confusing. Step Into is used when you want to follow the code into the selected method. Step Over is used when you want to remain in the current method. Step Out is used when you want to stop following the code in the current method.

Step to the next line of code. You should be at the following:

```
if ( sVal.compareTo("Hide Dialog") == 0)
```

Now step two more times and you should be at the following:

```
if (m_Frame.isShowing())
```

At this point, you should be in the right function, so now see what the program does next. Step once more with F10. Oops, suddenly you are on the return true; line. What happened? Why was the Frame.show() line skipped? Go back and try to figure out what went wrong.

Look at the following code fragment and think about what the if statement is asking:

```
if (m_Frame.isShowing())
{
    m_Frame.show();
}
return true;
```

You could equate the preceding code fragment to the following pseudo-code:

```
If the m_Frame is showing now, execute the code m_Frame.show().
```

Are you curious? Why show something that's already showing? But, more importantly, the code only executes when m_Frame is showing, not when it is not showing, which is not the correct purpose of the test.

If you simply change the line to read if (!m_Frame.isShowing()), the code will make sense because it will show the frame when m_Frame is not showing.

So now that you have found that logic error, what do you do? Simply let your program finish gracefully by pressing Debug | Go from the menu and then closing your browser. If this doesn't work, select Debug | Stop Debugging from the menu. Go ahead and make the change, recompile your program, and rerun the applet.

14

When you run your program now, there still seems to be a problem. For some reason, when you click the Destroy Dialog button, you are never able to show the dialog again. Using what you've learned about debugging, setting breakpoints, and stepping through your code, see if you can find a solution to make the Show Dialog button work properly once the Destroy Dialog button has been clicked. The following is the corrected Source Code segment:

```
void CreateMyFrame()
{
    else if ( sVal.compareTo("Show Dialog") == 0)
    {
        if (m_Frame == null)
        {
            CreateMyFrame();
        }
        else if (!m_Frame.isShowing())
        {
            m_Frame.show();
        }
    return true;
    }
}
```

Summary

Today you learned to use the Microsoft Developer Studio Integrated Debugger. You experimented with the two ways to use the debugger: at compile time to check compiler errors, which consist mainly of syntax or improper usage errors, and at runtime to check logic errors, which consist mainly of faulty construction. Today we have shown you most of the tools and the most common methods of debugging programs.

Debugging code has never been a simple undertaking. There are so many different kinds of errors that can occur, ranging from simple typing errors to major logic errors. However, as you've seen, Visual J++ provides you with a wide variety of tools to help you debug your programs. The more you use Visual J++, the more comfortable you will become with the debugger.

Learning how to debug is necessary, but debugging should not be the only tool in your tool chest. Careful planning and execution go much further in helping to create solid code than a debugger ever will.

Regardless of whether you take the preceding advice to heart or not, remember that the manner in which you view your classes, the logic you use to write them, and the methods that you use to debug classes are personal choices and preferences.

14

Q&A

Q It seems like there are an awful lot of places I can do things wrong. What would be good methodology to help me to produce bug-free programs?

A I wish I had an answer for you; this has been the goal of programmers for years. From past experience, the single most important element in producing logic error-free programs is to design the class hierarchies and program flows before writing any code.

The best advice for creating typo and syntax error-free programs is to use the abilities of the IDE you are using. When using Microsoft Developer Studio, for example, the cursor will automatically jump to the correct tab (indent level) based upon how you terminate the previous line. If you don't terminate a line with a semicolon, Microsoft Developer Studio will automatically indent the next line. This should be a clue to you. If Microsoft Developer Studio indents a line that should not be indented, the chances are pretty good that there is a syntax error in the preceding line.

Microsoft Developer Studio also color codes certain types of text such as keywords and comments. These colors are configurable by selecting Tools | Options from the menu and modifying the information under the Format tab.

Q As I am debugging my program, suppose I want to see the value of a variable that is not on the current affected line of code. Because I just want to check the value of this variable once, I also do not want to add it to the Watch window. How do I do this?

A As with most new Microsoft products these days, there is a great deal of functionality available by using the right mouse button. If you click on a variable with the right mouse button, a rather large pop-up window appears allowing you to jump to all sorts of other windows. It just so happens that one of the options on this pop-up is QuickWatch *xxx* (where *xxx* is the name of the variable you clicked). This action will bring up a detailed window (similar to a Watch window) that displays all data about the variable you clicked on.

Q What's the difference between Debug and Release mode? When do I use each?

A Typically, you would compile your program as a Debug version while you are developing your project. You must use the Debug version when you need to step through your code and check for variable values or for logic errors. Because all of the Debug-related information is stored in this version's file, the Debug version is larger and less efficient. Therefore, when you are satisfied with your program and its behavior, you would then compile a Release version for General Distribution.

Day 15

COM, ActiveX, and JDBC

The concepts of COM, ActiveX, and JDBC are rather complex. To go into great detail about these three would require us to describe a plethora of other supporting concepts in order to fully explain the ideas we're trying to get across. It could easily take several days to cover these topics in enough detail to make them useful to you. These concepts also are more Microsoft- and intranet-, not Java-, specific than the other chapters in the book. Also, due to the enormous amount of information available on these subjects, much of which is changing on a regular basis, most of the information provided here will be an overview so as not to be outdated by the time you read it. Our hope, therefore, is that by the end of today, you'll have a good grasp of what COM, ActiveX, and JDBC are, how they can be used, and why you might want to consider using them. And finally, you'll learn about Visual J++'s capabilities in the following areas:

☐ How Visual J++ works with COM and other ActiveX objects

☐ Using Visual J++ to access databases using DAO, RDO, and JDBC

NOTE

Because there is so much information to cover in one day, the information presented today will not include any of the complex examples that would require a discussion of the connection between COM and OLE. Although whole books are devoted to OLE, providing examples of COM without having the space to go into the detail necessary to explain how the examples relate to OLE would certainly be much more confusing.

TIP

Much of the information contained in today's chapter is Microsoft-specific and can be found in Books Online (which is installed when you install VJ++) or on Microsoft's Visual J++ Web site (`http://microsoft.com/visualj/`) or on Microsoft's ActiveX Web site (`http://www.microsoft.com/activex/default.htm`). Please refer to those for additional information. We would also suggest that you visit these Web sites frequently to get the latest information concerning these technologies. As already mentioned, the information on these subjects can (and often does) change regularly.

Component Object Model (COM)

Microsoft has been working with objects in one way or another in its operating systems for some time now. One of the first objects that appeared in Microsoft operating systems was OLE automation within the Office Suite. Next came OCXs (OLE-based custom controls). After OCXs, Microsoft came out with a new specification called ActiveX. And of course, the OLE automation within the Office Suite of products (now called ActiveX objects) is still there. Eventually, Microsoft informed us, NT will become a completely object-based operating system.

Since the beginning of OLE, Microsoft has been basing all of its objects on the Component Object Model. Although the different objects all have their subtle differences, OLE, OCXs, and ActiveXs are all formed from the same mold called COM.

Microsoft defines the COM as the following:

"The Component Object Model is a specification that describes the process of communicating through interfaces, acquiring access to interfaces through the QueryInterface method,

15

determining pointer lifetime through reference counting, and re-using objects through aggregation."

What does the preceding quote really mean? Well, to help clear it up some more, here are a couple more Microsoft definitions that can be found in VC++ 4.x Books Online:

An object is defined as:

"An item in the system that exposes interfaces to manipulate the data or properties of the object. An object is created by directly or indirectly calling the `CoCreateInstance()` application programming interface (API), which in turn creates a new instance of the object and returns a pointer to a requested interface."

An interface is defined as:

"A group of related functions. Communication between two objects in a system occurs by calling the functions in an interface through a pointer to that interface. An interface pointer is originally obtained at the time the object is created."

Pretty interesting reading. Do the preceding two definitions resemble anything from the beginning of this book?

Notice how a COM object and a COM interface sound a lot like your typical everyday Java objects and Java methods.

☐ Java and COM are very complementary to one another.

☐ A Java program can be created as a COM object.

☐ A COM object can be used by a Java program.

Calling COM Objects from Visual J++

Visual J++ has the capability to use almost any COM object that is currently installed on your computer. Before Visual J++ can use a COM object, though, it must be run through the Type Library Wizard. The Type Library Wizard takes all of the exposed methods in the COM object and creates a usable Java `*.class` file.

Microsoft defines a type library as "a mechanism defined by COM to store type information; each type library contains complete type information about one or more COM entities, including classes, interfaces, dispinterfaces, and others." For more information about type libraries, see Type Libraries and the Object Description Language, or the Win32 SDK. Once again, this information is available in the VC++ Books Online packaged with VC++ 4.x.

Running the Type Library Wizard

In order to use a COM class from Java, you must first import it; this means creating a Java class that represents the COM class in the context of Java. Visual J++ includes the Java Type Library Wizard for this purpose.

The following steps show how to import a COM class for use in Java:

1. From the Tools menu, choose Java Type Library Wizard.

   The check box list displays all the type libraries registered on your machine. This list reflects the entries beneath the \HKEY_CLASSES_ROOT\TypeLib key of the system registry. (See Figure 15.1.)

Figure 15.1.

Java Type Library Wizard dialog box.

2. Choose the type library that describes the COM class(es) you want to use.

3. Choose OK.

In the Output window, the Type Library Wizard displays the import statement(s) appropriate for each package it has created. You can use these import statements in your Java source code; this allows you to refer to classes in those packages by their short names. Figure 15.2 shows the output statements as well as the summary.txt file created for comdlg32.ocx when run through the Type Library Wizard.

Figure 15.2.

Output statements produced from the Type Library Wizard.

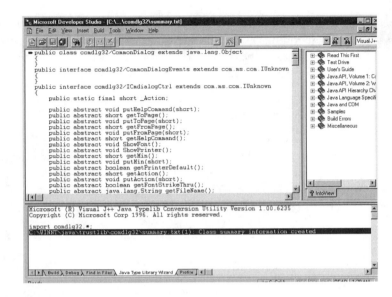

The Type Library Wizard also displays the complete path of the newly created file named SUMMARY.TXT. By double-clicking on this line, you can open the text file in Microsoft Developer Studio. This file lists the Java signatures of all the methods for the COM interfaces and classes described by the type library. You can then call all of these methods from your Java program.

To find out how to use the interfaces available from a particular programmable control or automation server, you'll need to consult the documentation provided by the vendor.

What the Type Library Wizard Generates

For each type library imported, the Java Type Library Wizard creates a directory below the trusted library directory having the same name as the type library. The Java Type Library Wizard fills that directory with .class files, one for each COM class and/or interface described in the type library. All the generated classes and interfaces are part of a Java package having the same name as the type library file. (If the type library contains an importlib statement, the Java Type Library Wizard creates a separate Java package in a separate directory for the imported type library.)

Each .class file generated by the Java Type Library Wizard contains a special attribute identifying it as a wrapper for a COM class. When the Java support in Internet Explorer sees this attribute on a class, it translates all Java method invocations on the class into COM function invocations on the COM class. For a COM interface that defines properties, the corresponding Java interface defines two methods for each property, named get*property* and put*property*. If the COM interface defines methods with the propget or propput attributes, the Java interface versions of those methods have get or put before their names.

Once you have run the Java Type Library Wizard for a given type library, you don't need to re-run the wizard unless the type library has changed.

Once the Java Type Library Wizard has generated .class files for a type library, your Java program has no further need for the type library. When distributing an applet that uses COM, your Java program needs only its own .class files, and the .DLL, .EXE, or .OCX files that implement the COM services, along with the generated .class files for the COM services. You must also be sure to register the COM object appropriately.

NOTE
From the command line, you can use the JavaTLB tool to generate Java class wrappers out of type library information. Simply type javatlb *filename*, where *filename* is the name of the .TLB file (or .OCX, .DLL, or .EXE file) containing the type library information. This will create the appropriate directory and .class files under the trusted library directory.

If you include COM objects with Java applets embedded on a Web page, the .OCX or .DLL files that implement the COM object should have digital signatures. Digital signatures allow users to trust your applet, allowing it to run on their system. In order to do this, the Java applets need to be packaged into a digitally signed cabinet (.CAB) file. For more information on .CAB files and digital signatures, see "Creating a Signed .CAB File" later in today's lesson.

Using a COM Object in Java

For this section, you're going to use one of the examples that Microsoft ships with Visual J++. This example is called the javabeep applet. This applet consists of the following:

- [ ] A javabeep.class file
- [ ] Beeper.dll
- [ ] javabeep.html
- [ ] Associated project files

NOTE

COM components can generally access any system resource on the machine on which they run. Because Java is a secure environment, browsers will only allow trusted Java .class files to access COM components. Obviously, when you design and build a Visual J++ program that uses COM, you'll want to test your applet. To make this possible, the browser allows applets that use COM to access system resources when run from within Microsoft Developer Studio only. If you try to execute a COM-enabled applet outside of Microsoft Developer Studio it will not run.

For the following exercise you'll need to copy some files from your VJ++ CD-ROM to your hard drive. Find the msdev\samples\microsoft\javabeep directory on the CD-ROM. Copy all the files (and subdirectory and files) in the javabeep directory to a directory named \projects\samples\microsoft\javabeep on your hard drive. If you don't have a directory with this name already, please create it.

NOTE

After you copy the project from the CD-ROM, if the javabeep.java file is named Javabeep.jav, you will need to rename the file to javabeep.java (lowercase the J and add the final a) so that the project will compile properly.

Once all the files are copied, fire up Microsoft Developer Studio. Open the javabeep.mdp Project Workspace, and compile the project. Figure 15.3 shows what the compiler output should look like.

Examine the output in the Build window. Notice that the second line says that a class library is being created from beeper.dll (just as if you ran the Java Type Library Wizard). How does this Project Workspace know to create class information for beeper.dll? It knows because the beeper.dll file is included in the project. Click the FileView tab in the Project Workspace window to see the list of files included in the project.

In the Build window, notice also that the file beeper.dll is being registered. This is not a Java registration, but rather standard Microsoft WIN32 OLE registration.

Figure 15.3.

Compiled javabeep *project as shown in Microsoft Developer Studio.*

Execute the javabeep applet. (Remember to execute it inside Microsoft Developer Studio.) After the applet loads, click anywhere in the applet window. Each time you click, a message displays at the point where the mouse cursor is and a beep is sounded.

NOTE

Netscape Navigator 2.x. does not support ActiveX or COM, so even though javabeep displays and the animation runs, javabeep does not play as it's supposed to. You can try running it using Navigator 3.0 using the NCompass ScriptActive plug-in, which can be found at http://www.ncompasslabs.com/binaries/download_plugin_pro.htm.

On your own, examine the source code for javabeep, and also look at the .html file. Notice that the HTML file doesn't contain any special code to run COM-enabled applets; all the code is in your .class file (and the supporting COM files called by your applet).

Exposing a Visual J++ Applet as a COM Object

Besides allowing Java programs to use COM objects, the Java Support in Internet Explorer also allows Java programs to expose their functionality as COM services. This lets you use Java for developing component software without requiring that your clients use Java; your clients can use any language that is compatible with COM, such as Microsoft Visual Basic or C++.

ActiveX Controls

Microsoft defines ActiveX as all component technologies built on Microsoft's Component Object Model, other than Object Linking and Embedding. It defines ActiveX control as the new name for programmable elements formerly known variously as OLE Controls, OCXs, or OLE Custom Controls. Controls previously built with the MFC Control Developer's Kit meet the ActiveX control specification.

You can embed both Java applets, COM objects, and ActiveX controls in the same Web page and use applet (or VBScript) handlers to connect them. For example, you can read values from an ActiveX control and pass them to a Java applet, or vice versa. (However, you cannot trigger events from the Java applet.)

Basically, the methods of using an ActiveX control are identical to the methods of using a generic COM object. The preceding beeper example uses an OLE-based DLL. The `beeper.dll` could just have easily been compiled using C++, as `beeper.ocx`.

You can download the ActiveX SDK from `http://www.microsoft.com/activex/` (which is accessible using the Web Favorites command on the VJ++ Help menu) for more detailed information on ActiveX.

Trusted and Untrusted Applets

Java applets typically run in a carefully constrained execution environment preventing them from interfering with your system. Using COM services, though, means that your programs will need to access resources on your (or the user's) system. To prevent Java applets from posing a security threat, the Java Support in Internet Explorer categorizes classes as either *trusted* or *untrusted*. Microsoft defines trusted and untrusted in Visual J++ Books Online as follows:

- [ ] Untrusted classes run within the constrained execution environment and cannot use COM services. All classes that aren't loaded from the class path—which includes classes downloaded off a network—are considered untrustworthy, unless they are packaged in a `.CAB` (cabinet) file that has a digital signature.

- [ ] Trusted classes include any class that's loaded from the class path, and those extracted from a `.CAB` file that has a digital signature. Trusted classes are the only classes that are allowed to use COM services. Trusted classes are also freed of the constraints in terms of Java code; for example, you can read and write files using pure Java code, if the applet is trusted.

You specify a `.CAB` file using the `CABBASE` parameter with the `<APPLET>` tag in the `.html` file.

Before we tell you how to create a `.CAB` file, it's important that you understand the following.

Internet Explorer (when executing the `.class`) behaves differently depending on whether the class is trusted or not. The primary difference is the way that Internet Explorer searches the class path. The InfoView topic in Visual J++ Books Online sums it up best:

There are four class path-related registry keys that are relevant to the security of Java applets. All of these keys are subkeys of `HKEY_LOCAL_MACHINE\Software\Microsoft\Java VM`:

- ☐ `Classpath`—contains classes available to all applets.
- ☐ `LibsDirectory`—contains libraries available to all applets.
- ☐ `TrustedClassPath`—contains classes available only to trusted applets.
- ☐ `TrustedLibsDirectory`—contains libraries available only to trusted applets.

 NOTE

> Everything that the Java Type Library Wizard generates is placed under the trusted library directory.

When executing a trusted applet, Internet Explorer looks in the following places (and in the following order) for classes referenced by the applet:

- ☐ The trusted class path
- ☐ The trusted library directory
- ☐ The class path
- ☐ The library directory

When executing an untrusted applet, Internet Explorer looks in the following places (and in the following order) for classes referenced by the applet:

- ☐ The class path
- ☐ The library directory

In addition to restricting the class search path, Internet Explorer Java Support also employs other security mechanisms. For example, any classes that are Java wrappers for COM classes are inaccessible to untrusted applets, even if those classes happen to be located in the regular class path or in the library directory.

The following summarizes the major differences between a trusted applet and an untrusted applet:

☐ A trusted applet can access any class, no matter where it originates, whether it implements COM services or not.

☐ An untrusted applet can access only pure Java classes, and only if they don't reside in the trusted class path or the trusted library directory.

Remember, too, that even though Java classes in your project directory are considered trusted when you launch Internet Explorer from the Developer Studio environment, this does not mean that an applet built using Visual J++ automatically qualifies as trusted. Outside of Microsoft Developer Studio, an applet must be packaged into a .CAB file and digitally signed in order to use COM services. This relaxed feature of Internet Explorer under Microsoft Developer Studio is there so you don't have to package your classes into a signed .CAB file just to execute and test them.

Creating a Signed .CAB File

The cab&sign directory on the Visual J++ CD-ROM contains two tools:

☐ CabDevKit.EXE

☐ CodeSignKit.EXE

Both of these are self-extracting executables that install the tools and documentation needed to, respectively, create a Cabinet (.CAB) file and digitally sign a file.

These executables are not installed by the Visual J++ setup program. You need to copy each of these executables into its own directory and run them to extract their respective tool kits.

You can also get all the tools needed for creating a .CAB file and digitally signing a file as part of the ActiveX Software Development Kit. You can download the ActiveX SDK from http://www.microsoft.com/activex/ (which is accessible using the Web Favorites command on the VJ++ Help menu).

See the respective documentation included with the tool kits for complete information on using these tools.

Ensuring that Java Support Is Up-to-Date on a User's Machine

If you are placing an applet that uses COM on an HTML page that is accessible from the Internet, you must ensure that any users who encounter that page have a version of the Java Support for Internet Explorer that fully supports Java/COM integration.

To do this, you must insert the following tag on the HTML page containing your applet (or on the introductory page of your Web site):

```
<OBJECT
CLASSID="clsid:08B0E5C0-4FCB-11CF-AAA5-00401C608500"
CODEBASE="http://www.microsoft.com/java/IE30Java.cab#Version=1,0,0,1'>
</OBJECT>
```

This tag (from <OBJECT to </OBJECT>) causes the user's Internet Explorer to check the version of its Java support. If the version installed on the user's machine is not up-to-date, Internet Explorer downloads the latest version of Java support from http://www.microsoft.com and updates the user's machine.

Database Access

This section deals with database access using Data Access Objects (DAO), Remote Data Objects (RDO), Open Database Connectivity (ODBC), and Java Database Connectivity (JDBC) PDQ ASAP. Wow, that's a lot of abbreviations! In short, all of these database tools are used in one way or another to allow you and the user access to data contained in tables. Using these tools in your Java programs, in most cases, also frees you from learning CGI and Perl.

Some differences exist for the tools. The most notable differences are the following:

- ☐ DAO and RDO are Microsoft-specific.
- ☐ DAO and RDO are specific to the Microsoft Java virtual machine.
- ☐ JDBC is pure Java and, as such, is portable.
- ☐ ODBC drivers are available for Microsoft, Macintosh, UNIX, Linux, and VAX platforms.
- ☐ DAO, RDO, and JDBC all rely on the ODBC drivers.

Data Access Objects (DAO)

Microsoft defines Data Access Objects (DAO) as a high-level set of objects that insulates developers from the physical details of reading and writing records. In a database application, for example, these objects include databases, table definitions, query definitions, fields, indexes, and so on. DAO would be used, for example, to access a local Microsoft Access database.

A Demonstration of DAO

The following Microsoft-supplied example demonstrates the use of Data Access Objects (DAO) from Java. This example requires that you have DAO installed on your machine. You can install DAO from Visual J++'s Setup program by choosing Custom Install and checking the Database Options checkbox.

The following steps show how to run this example:

1. Use InfoView to query on the phrase DAOSample: Demonstrates DAO.
2. Put the product CD-ROM in the drive.
3. Click the button in the InfoView topic window.
4. In the Sample Application dialog box, click the Copy All... button.
5. Specify the target directory for the sample project (or accept the default) and click OK.
6. Click Close to close the Sample Application dialog box.
7. In Internet Explorer, go to the directory in which you installed the example and double-click `readme.html` for further instructions on how to continue with the example.

NOTE

> Using Visual J++ version 1.0 build 4.20.6213, we noticed that the preceding example would not compile until we used the Java Type Library Wizard to register the Microsoft DAO *xxx* objects.

Remote Data Objects (RDO)

RDO is an alternative that in many scenarios performs better than DAO. Some future version of the DAO should include all of the positive features of RDO. RDO was designed explicitly for accessing data on remote servers such as Microsoft SQL Server version 6.0 or ORACLE®. The DAO developers designed it for accessing data from both remote servers and local workstations, for example, from xBase files, Microsoft Access files, and Paradox™ files.

Even though RDO can access Microsoft Access database on a local drive, it's a bad choice for reading data because it will go through all of the layers that the DAO uses, as well as its own layer. However, RDO is an excellent choice for reading data from Microsoft SQL Server 6.0

because the RDO developers put extra effort into tuning its performance with this database. Think of the RDO as a replacement for making DB-Library™ application programming interface (API) calls or ODBC API calls—it's a way to get performance without spending weeks coding API calls. If you're writing client/server applications with Microsoft SQL Server, RDO should be your first choice.

Why use RDO? The greatest advantage of RDO is that it does not use the Jet engine. The Jet engine is Microsoft's database engine that is used by DAO and consumes a large amount of resources and adds a lot of overhead. The RDO uses a thin layer of code over the ODBC layer and the driver manager that establishes connections to the database. This thin layer appears very similar to the DAO but without all of the resources required by Jet on the client PC. This small memory footprint results in a huge drop in the amount of memory required and reduces the code swapped to the hard drive on some workstations.

Java Database Connectivity (JDBC)

DAO and RDO are, arguably, incredibly Microsoft-specific database access methods. Fortunately for those of us who must write platform-independent systems, Sun has provided the world with an alternative: JDBC. JDBC is located in the base java class `java.sql.*`.

NOTE

> `java.sql` was not included with the version of Visual J++ that was available when writing this book. If your version of Visual J++ does not have the `java.sql` class, you should be able to download it from either Microsoft or from Sun (`http://java.sum.com`).

Because ODBC is generally the agreed upon defacto standard for database access, Sun simply wrote a Java-based API to access ODBC Drivers. The reason it's not practical to have Java use an ODBC Driver directly is that ODBC is a 'C' interface and Java does not directly support that interface.

The JDBC is the first platform-independent database driver available for Java. Because the JDBC is written as a very low level interface to an ODBC driver, it is likely that JDBC is simply the first of many various flavors of database access toolkits for Java that will evolve from JDBC. You would expect that some of these toolkits will include dynamic mapping of tables to Java classes and embedded SQL.

15

Summary

Well, we said it would be an overview! But, you should notice by what we did write that there's a whole lot to learn about ActiveX, COM, and database access using Java. We hope we answered some of your questions, and also gave you enough information to cause you to think about this powerful and exciting technology. To follow up, you should experiment on your own with the remaining examples on the VJ++ CD-ROM.

Q&A

Q How do I know if a particular browser supports ActiveX and COM?

A Currently, only Microsoft Internet Explorer and Netscape 3.0 (with the added ActiveX plug-in) do. You should be able to check the ActiveX Web site as well as other browser developer Web sites to see what level of support is offered. As mentioned earlier, the address for Microsoft's ActiveX Web site is http://www.microsoft.com/activex/default.htm.

Q Where do I go from here to write a database access Java program?

A First start by knowing your target audience. Is it Internet or intranet, or both? What is the platform? What are the requirements? Look at the Microsoft and Sun Web sites to get the latest information and implementation of the database classes. Other than gathering as much information as possible, we'd strongly recommend using (and understanding) the examples contained on the VJ++ CD. And, above all—design big, but start small!

Day 16

Connecting Java to a Network and Other Tidbits

With so many people networking at espresso bars, it's a natural that Java programs can be connected to a network. Okay, bad pun; let's move on. To enable your Java applets and applications to access files on another system, you use the classes in the java.net package.

These classes provide cross-platform abstracts for simple network operations, such as connecting to other systems and performing file read, write, and copy operations. To create and maintain the link to the other system on the network, the classes use basic UNIX-like sockets and common Web protocols. Using the java.net classes in conjunction with input and output streams (which you'll learn much more about later this week) makes reading and writing files over a network as easy as reading or writing files on a local disk.

Of course, there are restrictions due to the security implementation in Java. Even though your applet may use the network classes, the Java applet will not be allowed to read or write disk files on the user's machine, unless the user gives applets explicit permission. Moreover, depending on the browser being used, the user may not even be allowed to re-configure applet permissions. Microsoft Internet Explorer 3.0 and Netscape Navigator 2.0x both allow the user to configure applet settings.

NOTE   COM (and ActiveX, discussed on Day 15) do allow your applet to connect to another system. Only standard plain-vanilla Java does not. This chapter deals with the standard Java implementation of network access.

Although you may not (that is, aren't allowed to) connect to another system, you may still use the network classes to link to the same system in which the applet was stored. Even given these restrictions, you can still accomplish a great deal and use the Web or any other network to your advantage.

NOTE   Throughout this section, we'll be discussing networks, the Internet, and the Web. All the same principles apply, regardless of whether your applet is running on the Internet or an intranet. The added benefit of an intranet is that you may have more control of the runtime environment (that is, which browser(s) are being used and how they are configured to work with applets). Keep these ideas in mind as you work with this section.

This section describes three ways you can communicate with systems on a network:

- [ ] showDocument(), which enables an applet to tell the browser to load and link to another HTML page
- [ ] openStream(), a method that opens a connection to a URL, enabling your applet to extract data from that connection
- [ ] The socket classes—Socket and ServerSocket—which enable you to open standard host socket connections for reading and writing

Creating Links Inside Applets

Probably the easiest way to implement a network connection inside an applet is to tell the browser running that applet to load a new page. This technique is used frequently to create an animated image map that loads a new page when clicked.

To link to a new page, you create a new instance of the class URL. You saw some of this when you worked with images, but let's go over it a little more thoroughly here.

The URL class defines a Uniform Resource Locator. To create a new URL object, you can use one of four different forms:

- ☐ URL(*String*, *String*, *int*, *String*) creates a new URL object, given a protocol (HTTP, FTP, Gopher, file), a hostname (www.microsoft.com, ftp.netcom.com), a port number (80 for http), and a filename or pathname.

- ☐ URL(*String*, *String*, *String*) does the same thing as the previous form, except there is no port number given.

- ☐ URL(*URL*, *String*) creates a new URL object, given a base path and a relative path. For the base, you can use getDocumentBase() to return the URL of the current HTML file, or getCodeBase() to return the URL of the Java applet class file. The relative path will be appended to the base URL (just like with images and sounds).

- ☐ URL(*String*) creates a URL object from a URL string (which should include the protocol, hostname, optional port name, and filename).

For that last one (creating a URL from a string), you have to catch a malformed URL exception (we'll do Exceptions in more detail on Day 19), so surround the URL constructor with a try...catch:

```
String url = "http://www.yahoo.com/";
try
{ theURL = new URL(url);
}
catch ( MalformedURLException e)
{
    System.out.println("Bad URL: " + theURL);
}
```

Because using these methods is so easy, identifying the URL object is the hardest part. Once you identify one, all you have to do is pass it to the browser. You do this by using the following single line of code, where theURL is the URL object to link to:

```
getAppletContext().showDocument(theURL);
```

getAppletContext() returns the document (environment) where the applet is running. showDocument(*theURL*) replaces the Web page currently being viewed with the one located at that URL.

Listing 16.1 shows an applet that displays three buttons. An image of the running applet is shown in Figure 16.1. Clicking on one of the buttons causes the document to be loaded from the location to which the button refers.

TYPE **Listing 16.1. Bookmark buttons.**

```
1:import java.applet.*;
2:import java.awt.*;
3:import java.net.URL;
4:import java.net.MalformedURLException;
5:import DlgButtons;
6:
7:public class ButtonLink extends Applet implements Runnable
8:{
9:     Thread m_ButtonLink = null;
10:    Bookmark bmlist[] = new Bookmark[3];
11:    DlgButtons m_dlgButtons;
12:
13:    public void init()
14:    {
15:        bmlist[0] = new Bookmark("Microsoft's Home Page",
16:            "http://www.microsoft.com");
17:        bmlist[1] = new Bookmark("Yahoo",
18:            "http://www.yahoo.com");
19:        bmlist[2]= new Bookmark("VJ++ Updates",
20:            "http://www.microsoft.com/visualj/updates/");
21:        m_dlgButtons = new DlgButtons( this );
22:        m_dlgButtons.CreateControls();
23:        m_dlgButtons.ID_B1.setLabel(bmlist[0].name);
24:        m_dlgButtons.ID_B2.setLabel(bmlist[1].name);
25:        m_dlgButtons.ID_B3.setLabel(bmlist[2].name);
26:        resize(320, 240);
27:    }
28:
29:    public void start()
30:    {
31:        if (m_ButtonLink == null)
32:        {
33:            m_ButtonLink = new Thread(this);
34:            m_ButtonLink.start();
35:        }
36:    }
37:
38:    public void stop()
39:    {
40:        if (m_ButtonLink != null)
41:        {
42:            m_ButtonLink.stop();
43:            m_ButtonLink = null;
44:        }
45:    }
46:
47:    public void run()
48:    {
49:        while (true)
```

16

```
50:        {
51:            try
52:            {
53:                repaint();
54:                Thread.sleep(50);
55:            }
56:            catch (InterruptedException e)
57:            {
58:                stop();
59:            }
60:        }
61:    }
62:
63:    public boolean action(Event evt, Object arg)
64:    {
65:        if (evt.target instanceof Button)
66:        {
67:            LinkTo((String)arg);
68:            return true;
69:        }
70:        else return false;
71:    }
72:
73:    void LinkTo(String name)
74:    {
75:        URL theURL = null;
76:        for (int i = 0; i < bmlist.length; i++)
77:        {
78:            if (name.equals(bmlist[i].name))
79:            {
80:                theURL = bmlist[i].url;
81:            }
82:        }
83:        if (theURL != null)
84:        {
85:            getAppletContext().showDocument(theURL);
86:        }
87:    }
88:}
89:
90:class Bookmark
91:{
92:    String name;
93:    URL url;
94:    Bookmark(String name, String theURL)
95:    {
96:        this.name = name;
97:        try
98:        {
99:            this.url = new URL(theURL);
100:        }
101:        catch ( MalformedURLException e)
102:        {
103:            System.out.println("Bad URL: " + theURL);
104:        }
105:    }
106:}
```

16

Three classes make up this applet: The first implements the actual applet itself called ButtonLink, the second is a class representing a bookmark called BookMark, and the third is generated by the Java Resource Wizard to display the buttons and is called DlgButtons.

The DlgButtons dialog box resource is a very simple resource. The dialog box has only three buttons on it, which have IDs (not the captions) of ID_B1, ID_B2, and ID_B3, respectively. The captions for these three buttons are irrelevant at design time, since lines 15, 17, and 19 set the button captions.

This particular applet creates three bookmark instances and stores them in an array of bookmarks. (This applet could be easily modified to accept bookmarks as parameters from an HTML file.) For each bookmark, the label of one of the buttons in the DlgButtons instance, m_dlgButtons, is set to the value of the bookmark's name.

When the buttons are pressed, the action method calls the linkTo() method, which tells the browser to load the URL referenced by that bookmark.

Figure 16.1.

Bookmark buttons in Internet Explorer.

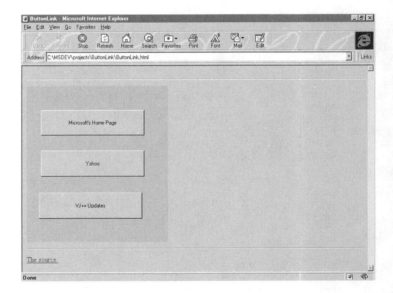

Opening Web Connections

Sometimes, instead of simply having a browser load a Web page, you might want to get hold of that file's contents so that your applet can use it. If the file you want to grab is stored on the Web, and can be accessed using the URL forms (HTTP, FTP, and so on from the last exercise), use them in your applet to get the file's contents. However, when the URL form won't do, the following methods might work for you.

NOTE Remember, due to Java's security implementation, applets can, by default, connect back only to the same host from which they were originally loaded. This means that if you have your applets stored on a system called www.myhost.com, the only machine your applet can open a connection to will be www.myhost.com (and that same hostname), so be careful with host aliases. If the file the applet wants to retrieve is on that same system, using URL connections is the easiest way to get it.

openStream()

URL defines a method called openStream(), which opens a network connection using the given URL and returns an instance of the class InputStream (part of the java.io package). If you convert that stream to a DataInputStream (with a BufferedInputStream in the middle for better performance), you can read characters and lines from that stream. (You'll learn all about streams on Day 20, "Introduction to VBScript.") For example, these lines open a connection to the URL stored in the variable theURL, and then read and echo each line of the file to the standard output:

```
try
{
    InputStream in = theURL.openStream();
    DataInputStream data = new DataInputStream(new BufferedInputStream(in);

    String line;
    while ((line = data.readLine()) != null)
    {
        System.out.println(line);
    }
}
catch (IOException e)
{
    System.out.println("IO Error: " + e.getMessage());
}
```

NOTE You need to wrap all those lines in a try...catch statement to catch IOExceptions generated.

Here's an example of an applet that uses the openStream() method to open a connection to a Web site, reads a file from that connection (Edgar Allen Poe's poem "The Raven"), and displays the result in a text area. Listing 16.2 shows the code; Figure 16.2 shows the result after the file has been read.

TYPE
Listing 16.2. The GetRaven class.

```
 1: import java.awt.*;
 2: import java.io.DataInputStream;
 3: import java.io.BufferedInputStream;
 4: import java.io.IOException;
 5: import java.net.URL;
 6: import java.net.URLConnection;
 7: import java.net.MalformedURLException;
 8:
 9: public class GetRaven extends java.applet.Applet implements Runnable
10: {
11:
12:     URL theURL;
13:     Thread runner;
14:     TextArea ta = new TextArea("Getting text...", 30, 70);
15:
16:     public void init()
17:     {
18:         String url = "http://www.lne.com/Web/Java/raven.txt";
19:         try
20:         {
21:             this.theURL = new URL(url);
22:         }
23:         catch
24:             ( MalformedURLException e)
25:         {
26:             System.out.println("Bad URL: " + theURL);
27:         }
28:         add(ta);
29:     }
30:
31:     public Insets insets()
32:     {
33:         return new Insets(10,10,10,10);
34:     }
35:
36:     public void start()
37:     {
38:         if (runner == null)
39:         {
40:             runner = new Thread(this);
41:             runner.start();
42:         }
43:     }
44:
45:     public void stop()
46:     {
47:         if (runner != null)
48:         {
49:             runner.stop();
50:             runner = null;
51:         }
52:     }
53:
```

16

```
54:    public void run()
55:    {
56:        InputStream conn;
57:        DataInputStream data;
58:        String line;
59:        StringBuffer buf = new StringBuffer();
60:
61:        try
62:        {
63:            conn = theURL.openStream();
64:            data = new DataInputStream(new BufferedInputStream(conn));
65:
66:            while ((line = data.readLine()) != null)
67:            {
68:                buf.append(line + "\n");
69:            }
70:
71:            ta.setText(buf.toString());
72:        }
73:        catch
74:            (IOException e)
75:        {
76:            System.out.println("IO Error:" + e.getMessage());
77:        }
78:    }
79: }
```

Figure 16.2.

The GetRaven *class.*

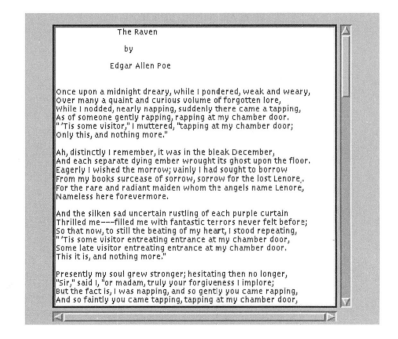

ANALYSIS   The init() method (lines 16 to 29) sets up the URL and the text area in which that file will be displayed. The URL could be easily passed into the applet via an HTML parameter; here, it's just hard-coded for simplicity.

Because it might take some time to load the file over the network, you should put that routine into its own thread and use the familiar start(), stop(), and run() methods to control that thread.

Inside run() (lines 54 to 78), the work takes place. Here, you initialize a bunch of variables and then open the connection to the URL (using the openStream() method in line 63). Once the connection is open, you set up an input stream in lines 64 to 68 and read from it, line by line, putting the result into an instance of StringBuffer (a string buffer is a modifiable string).

After all the data has been read, line 71 converts the StringBuffer object into a real string and then puts that result in the text area.

One other thing to note about this example is that the part of the code that opened a network connection, read from the file, and created a string is surrounded by a try and catch statement. If any errors occur while you're trying to read or process the file, these statements enable you to recover from them without the entire program crashing (in this case, the program exits with an error, because there's little else to be done if the applet can't read the file). try and catch give you the capability of handling and recovering from errors. You'll learn more about exceptions on Day 19.

The URLconnection **Class**

URL's openStream() method is actually a simplified use of the URLconnection class. URLconnection provides a way to retrieve files by using URLs—on Web or FTP sites, for example. URLconnection also enables you to create output streams if the protocol allows it.

To use a URL connection, you create a new instance of the class URLconnection, set its parameters (whether it enables writing, for example), and then use the connect() method to open the connection. Keep in mind that, with a URL connection, the class handles the protocol for you based on the first part of the URL, so you don't have to make specific requests to retrieve a file; all you have to do is read it.

Sockets

For network applications beyond what the URL and URLconnection classes offer (for example, for other protocols or for more general network applications), Java provides the Socket and ServerSocket classes as an abstraction of standard socket programming techniques.

NOTE

> I won't provide you with a full explanation of how socket programming works because there isn't enough space here to do it. See whether openStream() will meet your needs. If it doesn't and you haven't worked with sockets before, procure a book dedicated to socket programming. It should give you the background you need to work with Java's sockets.

The Socket class provides a client-side socket interface similar to standard UNIX sockets. To open a connection, create a new instance of Socket (where *hostname* is the host to connect to, and *portnum* is the port number):

```
Socket connection = new Socket(hostname, portnum);
```

NOTE

> If you use sockets in an applet, you are still subject to the Java security restrictions.

Once the socket is open, you can use input and output streams to read and write from that socket. (You'll learn all about input and output streams on Day 20.)

```
DataInputStream in = new DataInputStream(
    new BufferedInputStream(connection.getInputStream()));
DataOutputStream out= new DataOutputStream(
    new BufferedOutputStream(connection.getOutputStream()));
```

When you're done with the socket, don't forget to close it. (When you close the socket, you also close all the input and output streams you may have set up for that socket.)

```
connectior.close();
```

Server-side sockets work similarly, with the exception of the accept() method. A server socket listens on a TCP port for a connection from a client; when a client connects to that port, the accept() method accepts a connection from that client. By using both client and server sockets, you can create applications that communicate with each other over the network.

To create a server socket and bind it to a port, create a new instance of ServerSocket with a port number:

```
ServerSocket sconnection = new ServerSocket(8888);
```

To listen on that port (and to accept a connection from a client if one is made), use the `accept()` method:

```
sconnection.accept();
```

Once the socket connection is made, you can use input and output streams to read from and write to the client.

See the `java.net` package for more information about Java sockets.

Other Applet Hints

On this, the shortest day, let's finish with some small hints that didn't fit in anywhere else: using `showStatus()` to print messages in the browser's status window, providing applet information, and communicating between multiple applets on the same page.

The `showStatus()` Method

The `showStatus()` method, available in the applet class, enables you to display a string in the status bar of the browser. You can use this for printing error, link, help, or other status messages:

```
getAppletContext().showStatus("Change the color");
```

The `getAppletContext()` method enables your applet to access features of the browser that contains it. You already saw a use of this with links, wherein you could use the `showDocument()` method to tell the browser to load a page. `showStatus()` uses that same mechanism to print status messages.

> **NOTE**
>
> Even though `showStatus()` is a useful way of communicating optional information to your user, it may not be supported in all browsers, so don't depend on it for your applet's functionality or interface. If you need a more reliable method of communication, set up a label in your applet and update it with messages.

Applet Information

The AWT gives you a mechanism for associating information about your applet. Usually, there is a mechanism in most browsers to view the information you embed in your applet.

You can use this mechanism to include your name or your organization, version, date, or any other pertinent information in your applet. When you use the VJ++ Applet Wizard, this information is captured (on screen 7) and the method is automatically overridden.

To provide information about your applet, override the `getAppletInfo()` method:

```
public String getAppletInfo()
{
  return "Name: ButtonBookmarks\r\n" +
         "Author: Patrick J Winters\r\n" +
         "Created with Microsoft Visual J++ Version 1.0";
}
```

Communicating Between Applets

You might want to have an HTML page that has several different applets on it. To do this, include several different iterations of the applet tag; the browser will create different instances of your applet for each one that appears on the HTML page.

But, what if you also want communication between those applets? What if you want a change in one applet to affect the other applets?

The best way to do this is to use the applet context to get access to the different applets on the same page. You've already seen several uses of the `getAppletContext()` method; you can also use it to get a hold of the other applets on the page. For example, to call the `sendMessage()` method in all the applets on a page (including the current applet), use the `getApplets()` method and a `for` loop that looks something like the following:

```
for (Enumeration e = getAppletContext().getApplets();
        e.hasMoreElements();)
{
    Applet current = (Applet)(e.nextElement());
    current.sendMessage();
}
```

The `getApplets()` method returns an `Enumeration` object with a list of the applets on the page. Iterating over the `Enumeration` object in this way enables you to access each element in the `Enumeration` in turn.

If you want to call a method in a specific applet, it's only slightly more complicated: Give each of your applets a name in the HTML file and then refer to them by their name inside the body of the applet code.

To give an applet a name, use the NAME parameter in the HTML file:

```
<P>This applet sends information:
<APPLET CODE="MyApplet.class" WIDTH=100 HEIGHT=150 NAME="sender">
</APPLET>
<P>This applet receives information from the sender:
<APPLET CODE="MyApplet.class" WIDTH=100 HEIGHT=150 NAME="receiver">
</APPLET>
```

To get a reference to another applet on the same page, use the `getApplet()` method from the applet context using the name of that applet. This gives you a reference to the applet of that name. You can then refer to that applet as if it were just another object—call methods, set its instance variables, and so on:

```
// get ahold of the receiver applet
Applet receiver = getAppletContext().getApplet("receiver");
// tell it to update itself.
reciever.update(text, value);
```

In this example, you use the `getApplet()` method to get a reference to the applet with the name `receiver`. Given that reference, you can then call methods in that applet as if it were just another object in your own environment. Here, for example, if both applets have an `update()` method, you can tell `receiver` to update itself by using the information the current applet has.

Naming your applets and then referring to them by using the methods described in this section enables your applets to communicate and stay in sync with each other, providing uniform behavior for all the applets on your page.

Summary

Today and yesterday have been full of useful information about connecting to a network using Java and COM, and using Java methods for socket sessions.

Today you had a brief introduction to Java network connections through some of the classes in the `java.net` package. Applet network connections include things as simple as pointing the browser to another page from inside your applet, but can also include retrieving files from the Web by using standard Web protocols (HTTP, FTP, and so on). For more advanced network session capabilities, Java provides basic socket interfaces that can be used to implement many basic network-oriented applets: client/server interactions, chat sessions, and so on.

Finally, you finished up with the tidbits—small features of the Java AWT and of applets that didn't fit anywhere else, including `showStatus()`, providing information about your applet, and communicating between multiple applets on a single page.

Q&A

Q `showStatus()` **doesn't work in my browser. How can I give my readers status information?**

A As you learned in the section on `showStatus()`, whether or not a browser supports `showStatus()` is up to that browser. If you must have status-like behavior in your applet, consider creating a status label in the applet itself. Then update the label with the information you need to present.

Q It looks like the `openStream()` method and the `Socket` classes implement TCP sockets. Does Java support UPD (datagram) sockets?

A The JDK 1.0 provides two classes, `DatagramSocket` and `DatagramPacket`, which implement UDP sockets. The `DatagramSocket` class operates similarly to the `Socket` class. Use instances of `DatagramPacket` for each packet you send or receive over the socket.

See the `java.net` package in the API documentation for more information.

Q I've seen something called applet properties in the Java documentation. What are properties?

A Properties are features of applets and the applet environment that you can test for and make decisions in your code based on their values.

16

Day **17**

Modifiers, Access Control, and Class Design

Today, you'll start with advanced Java language concepts for organizing and designing individual classes:

☐ What a modifier is and how it's used

☐ Controlling access to methods and variables from outside a class to better encapsulate your code

☐ A special case of controlling access to methods and variables: instance variable accessor methods

☐ Using class variables and methods to store class-specific attributes and behavior

☐ Finalizing classes, methods, and variables so their values or definitions cannot be subclassed or overridden

☐ Creating abstract classes and methods for factoring common behavior into superclasses

Modifiers

The techniques for programming you'll learn today involve different strategies and ways of thinking about how a class is organized. But the one thing all these techniques have in common is that they all use special modifier keywords in the Java language.

You have already learned how to define classes, methods, and variables in Java. Modifiers are keywords you add to those definitions to change their meaning. Classes, methods, and variables with modifiers are still classes, methods, and variables, but the modifiers change their behavior or how Java treats those elements.

 Modifiers are special language keywords that modify the definition (and the behavior) of a class, method, or variable.

 You've already learned about a few of these modifiers earlier on in the book, but here we'll talk about them in detail so you can get the bigger picture of why modifiers work the way they do.

The Java language has a wide variety of modifiers, including the following:

- ☐ Modifiers for controlling access to a class, method, or variable: `public`, `protected`, and `private`
- ☐ The `static` modifier for creating class methods and variables
- ☐ The `abstract` modifier, for creating abstract classes and methods
- ☐ The `final` modifier, for finalizing the implementations of classes, methods, and variables
- ☐ The `synchronized` and `volatile` modifiers, which are used for threads

Some modifiers, as you can see, can apply to only classes and methods or only to methods and variables. To use a modifier, you simply place it before the class, method, or variable definition, for example:

```
public class MyApplet extends Java.applet.Applet { ... }

private boolean engineState;

static final double pi = 3.14159265

protected static final int MAXNUMELEMENTS = 128;

public static void main(String args[]) { ...}
```

The order of modifiers is irrelevant to their meaning; your order can vary and is really a matter of taste. Pick a style and then be consistent with it throughout all your classes. Here is the usual order:

`<access> static abstract synchronized volatile final native`

In this definition, *<access>* can be `public`, `protected`, or `private` (but only one of them).

All the modifiers are essentially optional; none have to appear in a declaration. Good object-oriented programming style, however, suggests adding as many as are needed to best describe the intended use of, and restrictions on, the thing you're declaring. In some special situations (inside an interface, for example, as described tomorrow), certain modifiers are implicitly defined for you, and you do not need to type them—they will be assumed to be there.

Controlling Access to Methods and Variables

The most important modifiers in the language, from the standpoint of class and object design, are those that allow you to control the visibility of, and access to, variables and methods inside your classes.

Why Access Control Is Important

Why would you care about controlling access to methods and variables inside your classes? Consider a PC, which is made up of a number of different components that, when combined, work together to create a useful, larger system.

Each component in a PC system works in a particular way, and has a specific way of interacting with the other components in the system. For example, a video card plugs into your motherboard using a standard socket and plug arrangement, as does your monitor to the back of the card. Your computer can then display information on the screen by using standard software interfaces.

The video card itself has a lot of other internal features and capabilities beyond the basic hardware and software interfaces. But as a user or consumer of the card, I don't need to know what every single chip does, nor do I need to touch them in order to get the card to work. Given the standard interfaces, the card figures everything out and does what it needs to do internally. And, in fact, the manufacturer of the card most likely doesn't want me to go in and start mucking with individual chips or capabilities of the card because I'm likely to screw something up. It's best if I just stick to the defined interface and let the internal workings stay hidden.

17

Classes and objects are the same way. Although a class can define lots of methods and variables, not all of them are useful to a consumer of that class, and some might even be harmful if they're used in the wrong way from how they were intended to be used.

Access control is about controlling visibility. When a method or variable is visible to another class, its methods can reference (call or modify) that method or variable. Protecting those methods and instance variables limits the visibility and the use of those methods and variables. Therefore, as a designer of a class or an entire hierarchy of classes, it is a good idea to define what the external appearance of a class is going to be, which variables and methods will be accessible for other users of that class, and which ones are for internal use only. This is called *encapsulation* and is an important feature of object-oriented design.

NEW TERM   *Encapsulation* is the process of hiding the internal parts of an object's implementation and allowing access to that object only through a defined interface.

You might note that, up to this point, not very much of this has been done in any of the examples; in fact, just about every variable and method you've created has been fairly promiscuous and had no access control whatsoever. The reason I approached the problem in this way is that it makes for simpler examples. As you become a more sophisticated programmer and create Java programs with lots of interrelated classes, you'll find that adding features such as encapsulation and protecting access to the internal workings of your classes makes for better designed programs overall.

The Four Ps of Protection

The Java language provides four levels of protection for methods and instance variables: public, private, protected, and package (actually, the latter isn't an explicit form of Java protection, but I've included it here because it's nicely alliterative). Before applying protection levels to your own code, you should know what each form means and understand the fundamental relationships that a method or variable within a class can have to the other classes in the system.

 NOTE   You can also protect entire classes using these modifiers. But class protection applies better once you know what packages are, so I'll postpone talking about that until tomorrow.

Package Protection

The first form of protection is the one you've been unconsciously using all this time: package protection. In C, there's the notion of hiding a name so that only the functions within a given source file can see it. Java doesn't have this kind of control; names will be happily found in other source files as long as Java knows where to find them. Instead of file-level protection, Java has the concept of packages, which are a group of classes related by purpose or function.

Methods and variables with package protection are visible to all other classes in the same package, but not outside that package. This is the kind of protection you've been using up to this point, and it's not much protection at all. Most of the time, you'll want to be more explicit when you define the protection for that class' methods and variables.

NEW TERM   *Package protection*, the default level of protection, means that your methods and variables are accessible to all the other classes in the same package.

Package protection isn't an explicit modifier you can add to your method or variable definitions; instead, it's the default protection you get when you don't add any protection modifiers to those definitions.

NOTE

You might not think you've been using packages at all up to this point, but actually, you have. In Java, if you don't explicitly put a class into a package, it'll be included in a default package that is essentially defined as all the classes in the same directory. So all the classes you put in a single directory are part of their own implicit package and can be used by other classes in that directory.

Private Protection

From the default protection you get with package protection, you can either become more restrictive or more loose in how you control the visibility and access to your methods and variables. The most restrictive form of protection is private, which limits the visibility of methods and instance variables to the class in which they're defined. A private instance variable, for example, can be used by methods inside the same class, but cannot be seen or used by any other class or object. Private methods, analogously, can be called by other methods inside that same class, but not by any other classes. In addition, neither private variables or private methods are inherited by subclasses.

NEW TERM   *Private protection* means that your methods and variables are accessible only to other methods in the same class.

To create a private method or instance variable, add the private modifier to its definition:

```
class  Writer {
    private boolean writersBlock = true;
    private String mood;
```

```
        private int income = 0;

        private void getIdea(Inspiration in) {
            . . .
        }

        Book createBook(int numDays, long numPages) {
          ...
        }
    }
```

In this snippet of code example, the internal data to the class Writer (the variables writersBlock, mood, income, and the method getIdea()) are all private. The only method accessible from outside the Writer class is the createBook() method. createBook() is the only thing other objects (editors?) can ask the Writer object to do; the other bits of data are implementation details that might affect how the book is written, but don't otherwise need to be visible or accessible from other sources.

The rule of thumb for private protection is that any data or behavior internal to the class, that other classes or subclasses should not be independently touching, should be private. Judicious use of private variables and methods is how you limit the functionality of a class to only those features you want visible outside that class—as with the example of the PC components. Remember that an object's primary job is to encapsulate its data—to hide it from the world and limit its manipulation. It separates design from implementation, minimizes the amount of information one class needs to know about another to get its job finished, and reduces the extent of the code changes you need to do if your internal implementation changes.

In addition to picking and choosing which methods you'll want to keep private and which will be accessible to others, a general rule of thumb is that all the instance variables in a class should be private, and that you should create special non-private methods to get or change those variables. You'll learn more about this rule and why it's important a little later in "Instance Variable Protection and Accessor Methods."

Public Protection

The diametric opposite of private protection, and the least restrictive form of protection, is public. A method or variable that is declared with the public modifier is accessible to the class in which it's defined, all the subclasses of that class, all the classes in the package, and to any other classes outside that package, anywhere in the entire universe of Java classes.

 Public protection means that your methods and variables are accessible to other methods anywhere inside or outside the current class or package.

Indicating that a method or variable is public isn't necessarily a bad thing. Just as hiding the data that is internal to your class using private helps encapsulate an object, using public methods defines precisely what the interface to instances of your class is. If you expect your classes to be reused by other programmers in other programs, the methods that they'll be using in your class should be public.

In many ways, public protection is very similar to the default package protection. Both allow methods and variables to be accessed by other classes in the same package. The difference occurs when you create packages of classes. Variables and methods with package protection can be used in classes that exist in the same package. But if someone imports your class into his or her own program from outside your package, those methods and variables will not be accessible unless they have been declared `public`. Once again, you'll learn more about packages tomorrow.

Public declarations work just like private ones; simply substitute the word `public` for `private`.

Protected Protection

The final form of protection available in Java concerns the relationship between a class and its present and future subclasses declared inside or outside a package. These subclasses are much closer to a particular class than to any other outside classes for the following reasons:

☐ Subclasses usually know more about the internal implementation of a superclass.

☐ Subclasses are often written by you or by someone to whom you've given your source code.

☐ Subclasses frequently need to modify or enhance the representation of the data within a parent class.

To support a special level of visibility reserved for subclasses somewhat less restrictive than private, Java has an intermediate level of access between package and private called, appropriately enough, protected. Protected methods and variables are accessible to any class inside the package, as they would be if they were package protected, but those methods and variables are also available to any subclasses of your class that have been defined outside your package.

NEW TERM   *Protected protection* means that your methods and variables are accessible to all classes inside the package, but only to subclasses outside the package.

TECHNICAL NOTE

In C++, the `protected` modifier means that only subclasses can access a method or variable, period. Java's meaning of `protected` is slightly different, also allowing any class inside the package to access those methods and variables.

Why would you need to do this? You might have methods in your class that are specific to its internal implementation—that is, not intended to be used by the general public—but that would be useful to subclasses for their own internal implementations. In this case, the developer of the subclass—be it you or someone else—can be trusted to be able to handle calling or overriding that method.

For example, say you had a class called AudioPlayer, which plays a digital audio file. AudioPlayer has a method called openSpeaker(), which is an internal method that interacts with the hardware to prepare the speaker for playing. openSpeaker() isn't important to anyone outside the AudioPlayer class, so at first glance you might want to make it private. A snippet of AudioPlayer might look something like the following:

```
class AudioPlayer {

  private boolean openSpeaker(Speaker sp)_ {
    // implementation details
  }
}
```

This works fine if AudioPlayer isn't going to be subclassed. But what if you were going to create a class called StereoAudioPlayer that is a subclass of AudioPlayer? This class would want access to the openSpeaker() method so that it can override it and provide stereo-specific speaker initialization. You still don't want the method generally available to random objects (and so it shouldn't be public), but you want the subclass to have access to it—so protected is just the solution.

TECHNICAL NOTE	In versions of Java up to 1.01, you could use private and protected together to create yet another form of protection that would restrict access to methods or variables solely to subclasses of a given class. As of 1.02, this capability has been removed from the language. Using this combination with Visual J++ will result in a compiler warning and the method or variable will default to protected only.

Modifier Icons in ClassView

The ClassView pane in the Visual J++ development environment has several icons to help you visually distinguish between public, private, and protected variables and methods. These icons are demonstrated in Figure 17.1.

The lock icon next to the DisplayImage method indicates that DisplayImage is private. The key icon next to the AProtectedMethod method indicates that it is protected. You can see that the other methods do not have any additional icons next to them and are therefore public.

The same icons apply to the member variables. As you can see by the lock icon, all of the member variables except m_Animal are private.

Figure 17.1.

Modifier icons in ClassView.

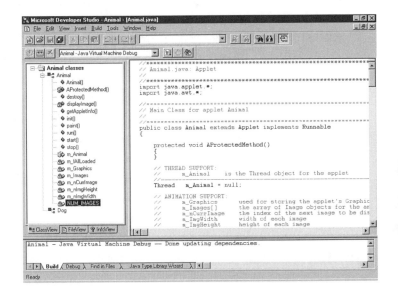

A Summary of Protection Forms

The differences between the various protection types can become very confusing, particularly in the case of protected methods and variables. Table 17.1, which summarizes exactly what is allowed where, will help clarify the differences from the least restrictive (public) to the most restrictive (private) forms of protection.

Table 17.1. Different protection schemes.

Visibility	public	protected	package	private
From the same class	yes	yes	yes	yes
From any class in the same package	yes	yes	yes	no
From any class outside the package	yes	no	no	no
From a subclass in the same package	yes	yes	yes	no
From a subclass outside the same package	yes	yes	no	no

Method Protection and Inheritance

Setting up protections in new classes with new methods is easy; you make your decisions based on your design and apply the right modifiers. When you create subclasses and override other methods, however, you have to take the protection of the original method into account.

The rule in Java is that you cannot override a method and make the new method more private than the original method (you can, however, make it more public).

☐ Methods declared `public` in a superclass must also be `public` in all subclasses (this, by the way, is the reason most of the applet methods are all `public`).

☐ Methods declared `protected` in a superclass must either be `protected` or `public` in subclasses; they cannot be `private`.

☐ Methods declared `private` are not inherited and therefore this rule doesn't apply.

☐ Methods declared without protection at all (the implicit package protection) can be declared more `private` in subclasses.

Instance Variable Protection and Accessor Methods

A good rule of thumb in object-oriented programming is that unless an instance variable is constant it should almost certainly be `private`. But, I hear you say, if instance variables are `private`, how can they be changed from outside the class? The answer is that they can't, which is precisely the point. Instead, if you create special methods that indirectly read or change the value of that instance variable, you can better control the interface of your classes and how those classes behave. You'll learn about how to do this in this section.

Why Non-Private Instance Variables Are a Bad Idea

In most cases, having someone else accessing or changing instance variables inside your object isn't a good idea. Take, for example, a class called `Circle`, whose partial definition looks like the following:

```
class Circle {
    int x, y, radius;

    Circle(int x, int y, int radius) {
        ...
    }

    void draw() {
        ...
    }
}
```

The `Circle` class has three instance variables for the x and y position of the center point and of the `radius`. A constructor builds the circle from those three values, and the `draw()` method draws the circle on the screen. So far, so good, right?

Now say you have a `Circle` object created and drawn on the screen. Then some other object comes along and changes the value of `radius`. Now what? Your circle doesn't know that the radius has changed. It doesn't know to redraw itself to take advantage of the new size of the circle. Changing the value of an instance variable doesn't in itself trigger any methods. You have to rely on the same random object that changed the radius to also call the `draw()` method, and that overly complicates the interface of your class, making it more prone to errors.

Another example of why it's better not to make instance variables publicly accessible is that it's not possible to prevent a non-constant instance variable from being changed. In other words, you could create a variable that you'd intended to be read-only, and perhaps your program was well-mannered and didn't go about changing that variable randomly—but because the variable is there and available, someone else might very well change it without understanding your methodology.

Why Accessor Methods Are a Better Idea

If all your instance variables are `private`, how do you give access to them to the outside world? The answer is to write special methods to read and change that variable (one for reading the value of the variable, one for changing it) rather than allowing it to be read and changed directly. These methods are sometimes called accessor methods, mutator methods (for changing the variable), or simply getters and setters.

NEW TERM   *Accessor methods* are special methods you implement to indirectly modify otherwise private instance variables.

Having a method to change a given instance variable means you can control the value that that variable is set to (to make sure it's within the boundaries you expect) as well as perform any other operations that might need to be finished if that variable changes, such as redrawing the circle.

Having two methods for reading and changing the variable also allows you to set up different protections for each. The method to read the value, for example, could be `public`, whereas the method to change the value can be `private` or `protected`, effectively creating a variable that's read-only except in a few cases (which is different from constant, which is read-only in all cases).

Using methods to access an instance variable is one of the most frequently used idioms in object-oriented programs. Applying it liberally throughout all your classes repays you numerous times over with more robust and reusable programs.

Creating Accessor Methods

Creating accessor methods for your instance variables simply involves creating two extra methods for each variable. There's nothing special about accessor methods; they're just like any other method.

Consider the following example:

```
class Circle {
   private int x, y radius;

   public int getRadius() {
     return radius;
   }
   public int setRadius(int value) {
       radius = value;
       draw();
       doOtherStuff();
       return radius;
   }

    ....
}
```

In this modified example of the Circle class, the accessor methods for the instance variable radius have the names set and get appended with the name of the variable. This is a naming convention popular among many programmers for accessor methods, so you always know which methods do what and to which variable. To access or change the value of the instance variable, therefore, you'd just call the following methods:

```
radius = theCircle.getRadius(); //get the value
theCircle.setRadius(4); //set the value (and redraw, etc)
```

Another convention for naming accessor methods is to use the same name for the methods as for the variable itself. In Java, it is legal for instance variables and methods to have the same name; Java knows how to perform the right operation from how they are used. Although this does make accessor methods shorter to type, there are two problems with using this convention:

☐ The fact that methods and variables can have the same names is a vague point in the Java specification and may not be treated the same with all compilers.

☐ I find using the same name for instance variables and methods makes my code more difficult to read and understand than using a more explicit name.

The convention you use is a question of personal taste. The most important thing is to choose a convention and stick with it throughout all of your classes so that your interfaces are consistent and understandable.

Using Accessor Methods

The point of declaring instance variables private and using accessor methods is so that external users of your class will be forced to use the methods you choose to modify your class' data. But the benefit of accessor methods isn't just for use by objects external to yours; they're also there for you. Just because you have access to the actual instance variable inside your own class doesn't mean you can avoid using accessor methods.

Consider that one of the good reasons to make instance variables private is to hide implementation details from outside your object. Protecting a variable with accessor methods means that other objects don't need to know about anything other than the accessor methods—you can happily change the internal implementation of your class without wreaking havoc on everyone who's used your class. The same is true of your code inside that class; by keeping variables separate from accessors, if you must change something about a given instance variable all you have to change are the accessor methods and not every single reference to the variable itself. In terms of code maintenance and reuse, what's good for the goose (external users of your class) is generally also good for the gander (you, as a user of your own class).

17

Class Variables and Methods

A class variable or method is one that exists only once, for the class. For example, a class variable is not created each time you create a new instance of the class. This is useful for variables that hold information that applies to the entire class.

To create a class variable or method, simply include the word static in front of the method name. The static modifier typically comes after any protection modifiers, such as this:

```
public class  Circle {
    public static float  pi = 3.14159265F;

    public float  area(float r) {
        return  pi * r * r;
    }
}
```

NOTE   The word static comes from C and C++. Although static has a specific meaning for where a method or variable is stored in a program's runtime memory in those languages, it simply means that it's stored in the class in Java. Whenever you see the word static, remember to substitute mentally the word class.

Both class variables and methods can be accessed using standard dot notation with either the class name or an object on the left side of the dot. However, the convention is to always use the name of the class, to clarify that a class variable is being used, and to help the reader to know instantly that the variable is global to all instances. Here are a few examples:

```
float circumference = 2 * Circle.pi * getRadius();
float randomNumer = Math.random();
```

TIP   Class variables, for the same reasons as instance variables, can also benefit from being declared private and having accessor methods get or set their values.

Listing 17.1 shows a class that uses class and instance variables to keep track of how many instances of that class have been created:

TYPE   **Listing 17.1. The** `CountInstances` **example.**

```
 1: public class  CountInstances {
 2:     private static int   numInstances = 0;
 3:
 4:     protected static int getNumInstances() {
 5:           return numInstances;
 6:     }
 7:
 8:     private static void  addInstance() {
 9:           numInstances++;
10:     }
11:
12:     CountInstances() {
13:           CountInstances.addInstance();
14:     }
15:
16:     public static void  main(String args[]) {
17:           System.out.println("Starting with " +
18:             CountInstances.getNumInstances() + " instances");
19:           for (int  i = 0;  i < 10;  ++i)
20:               new CountInstances();
21:         System.out.println("Created " +
22:             CountInstances.getNumInstances() + " instances");
23:     }
24:}
```

The following is the output:

```
Started with 0 instances
Creates 10 instances
```

This example has a number of features; You'll now go through it line by line.

ANALYSIS In line 2, you declare a `private` class variable to hold the number of instances (called `numInstances`). This is a class variable (declared `static`) because the number of instances is relevant to the class as a whole, not to any one instance. And it's private so that it follows the same rules as instance variable accessor methods.

Note the initialization of `numInstances` to `0` in that same line. Just as an instance variable is initialized when its instance is created, a class variable is initialized when its class is created. This class initialization happens essentially before anything else can happen to that class, or its instances, so the class in the example will work as planned.

In lines 4 through 6, you created a `get` method for that `private` instance variable to get its value (`getNumInstances()`). This method is also declared as a class method, as it applies directly to the class variable. The `getNumInstances()` method is declared `protected`, as opposed to `public`, because only this class and perhaps subclasses will be interested in that value; other random classes are therefore restricted from seeing it.

Note that there's no accessor method to set the value. The reason is that the value of the variable should only be incremented when a new instance is created; it should not be set to any random value. Instead of creating an accessor method, therefore, you'll create a special `private` method called `addInstance()` in lines 8 through 10 that increments the value of `numInstances` by one.

In lines 12 through 14, you have the constructor method for this class. Remember, constructors are called when a new object is created, which makes this the most logical place to call `addInstance()` and to increment the variable.

And finally, the `main()` method indicates that you can run this as a Java application and test all the other methods. In the `main()` method, you create ten instances of the `CountInstances` class, reporting after you're finished the value of the `numInstances` class variable (which, predictably, prints 10).

Finalizing Classes, Methods, and Variables

Although it's not the final modifier discussed in this chapter, the `final` modifier is used to finalize classes, methods, and variables. Finalizing a thing effectively freezes the implementation or value of that thing. More specifically, it does the following:

☐ When the `final` modifier is applied to a class, it means that the class cannot be subclassed.

☐ When applied to a variable, `final` means that the variable is constant.

☐ When applied to a method, `final` means that the method cannot be overridden by subclasses.

 Finalization (using the `final` modifier) freezes the implementation of a class, method, or variable.

Finalizing Classes

To finalize a class, add the `final` modifier to its definition. `final` typically goes after any protection modifiers such as `private` or `public`:

```
public final class  AFinalClass {
    . . .
}
```

You declare a class `final` for only two reasons:

☐ To prevent others from subclassing your class. If your class has all the capabilities it needs, and no one else should be able to extend its capabilities, that class should be `final`.

☐ For better efficiency, you want your program to be able to count on instances of only that one class (and no subclasses) being around in the system so that you can optimize for them.

The Java class library uses `final` classes extensively. Classes that have finalized for security reasons are `java.lang.System`, `java.net.InetAddress`, and `java.net.Socket`. A good example of the second reason is `java.lang.String`. Strings are so common in Java, and so central to it, that the runtime handles them specially (for security reasons as well).

In most cases, it will be a rare event for you to create a `final` class yourself because extendible classes are so much more useful than finalized classes, and the efficiency gains are minimal. You will, however, most likely have plenty of opportunity to be upset at certain system classes being `final` (making extending them more difficult).

Finalized Variables

A finalized variable means its value cannot be changed. This is effectively a constant. To declare constants in Java, use `final` variables with initial values:

```
public class  AnotherFinalClass {
    public static final int aConstantInt    = 123;
    public final String aConstantString = "Hello world!";
}
```

Local variables (those inside blocks of code surrounded by braces, for example, in `while` or `for` loops) can't be declared `final`.

Finalized Methods

Finalized methods are methods that cannot be overridden; that is, their implementations are frozen and cannot be redefined in subclasses.

```
public class  ClassWithFinalMethod {

    public final void  noOneGetsToDoThisButMe() {
        . . .
    }
}
```

The only reason to declare a method `final` is efficiency. Normally, method signatures and implementations are matched up when your Java program runs because that method can be found in the current class or in any subclass. When you call a method, therefore, Java checks the current class and each superclass in turn for that definition. Although this makes methods very flexible to define and use, it is also not very fast.

If you declare a method `final`, however, the compiler can then inline it (stick its definition) right in the middle of methods that call it, because it knows that no one else can ever subclass and override the method to change its meaning. Although you might not use `final` right away when writing a class, as you tune the system later, you might discover that a few methods have to be `final` to make your class fast enough. Almost all your methods will be fine, however, just as they are.

If you use accessor methods a lot (as recommended), changing your accessor methods to be `final` can be a quick way of speeding up your class. Because subclasses will rarely want to change the definitions of those accessor methods, there's little reason those methods should not be `final`.

The Java class library declares a lot of commonly used methods `final` so that you'll benefit from the speed-up. In the case of classes that are already `final`, this makes perfect sense and is a wise choice. The few `final` methods declared in non-`final` classes will annoy you—your subclasses can no longer override them. When efficiency becomes less of an issue for the Java environment, many of these `final` methods can be unfrozen again, restoring this lost flexibility to the system.

NOTE

> `private` methods are effectively `final`, as are all methods declared in a `final` class. Marking these latter methods `final` (as the Java library sometimes does) is legal, but redundant; the compiler already treats them as `final`.
>
> It's possible to use `final` methods for some of the same security reasons you use `final` classes, but it's a much rarer event.

abstract **Classes and Methods**

Whenever you arrange classes into an inheritance hierarchy, the presumption is that higher classes are more abstract and general, whereas lower subclasses are more concrete and specific. Often, as you design hierarchies of classes, you factor out common design and implementation into a shared superclass. That superclass won't have any instances; its sole reason for existing is to act as a common, shared repository for information that its subclasses use. These kinds of classes are called abstract classes, and you declare them using the abstract modifier.

```
public abstract class Fruit {
...
}
```

abstract classes can never be instantiated (you'll get a compiler error if you try), but they can contain anything a normal class can contain, including class and instance variables and methods with any kind of protection or finalization modifiers. In addition, abstract classes can also contain abstract methods. An abstract method is a method signature with no implementation; subclasses of the abstract class are expected to provide the implementation for that method. abstract methods, in this way, provide the same basic concept as abstract classes; they're a way of factoring common behavior into superclasses and then providing specific concrete uses of those behaviors in subclasses.

NEW TERM   *abstract classes* are classes whose sole purpose is to provide common information for subclasses. abstract classes can have no instances.

abstract methods are methods with signatures, but no implementation. Subclasses of the class that contain that abstract method must provide its actual implementation.

Like abstract classes, abstract methods give you the capability to factor common information into a general superclass and then reuse that class in different ways.

The opposite of abstract is concrete: concrete classes are classes that can be instantiated; concrete methods are those that have actual implementations.

abstract methods are declared with the abstract modifier, which usually goes after the protection modifiers but before either static or final. In addition, they have no body. abstract methods can only exist inside abstract classes; even if you have a class full of concrete methods, with only one abstract method, the whole class must be abstract.

Listing 17.2 shows two simple classes. One, called appropriately, MyFirstAbstractClass, has an instance variable and two methods. One of those methods, subclassesImplementMe(), is abstract. The other, doSomething(), is concrete and has a normal definition.

The second class is `AConcreteSubclass`, which is a subclass of `MyFirstAbstractClass`. It provides the implementation of `subclassesImplementMe()`, and inherits the remaining behavior from `MyFirstAbstractClass`.

TYPE | **Listing 17.2. An example of using `abstract`.**

```
public abstract class  MyFirstAbstractClass {
    int  anInstanceVariable;

    public abstract int  subclassesImplementMe(); // note no definition

    public void  doSomething() {
        . . .    // a normal method
    }
}

public class  AConcreteSubClass extends MyFirstAbstractClass {
    public int  subclassesImplementMe() {
        . . .    // we *must* implement this method here
    }
}
```

Here are some attempted uses of these classes:

```
Object  a = new MyFirstAbstractClass();    // illegal, is abstract
Object  c = new AConcreteSubClass();       // OK, a concrete subclass
```

Using an `abstract` class with no `abstract` methods—that is, one which provides nothing but a template for behavior—is better accomplished in Java by using an *interface* (discussed tomorrow). Whenever a design calls for an abstraction that includes instance state and/or a partial implementation, however, an `abstract` class is your only choice. .

Summary

Today, you learned how variables and methods can control their visibility and access by other classes via the four Ps of protection: `public`, `package`, `protected`, and `private`. You also learned that, although instance variables are most often declared `private`, declaring accessor methods allows you to control the reading and writing of them separately. Protection levels allow you, for example, to cleanly separate your public abstractions from their concrete representations.

You also learned how to create class variables and methods, which are associated with the class itself, and how to declare `final` variables, methods, and classes to represent constants and fast or secure methods and classes.

Finally, you discovered how to declare and use abstract classes, which cannot be instantiated, and abstract methods, which have no implementation and must be overridden in subclasses. Together, they provide a template for subclasses to fill in and act as a variant of the powerful interfaces of Java that you'll study tomorrow.

Q&A

Q Why are there so many different levels of protection in Java?

A Each level of protection, or visibility, provides a different view of your class to the outside world. One view is tailored for everyone, one for classes in your own package, another for your class and its subclasses only, one combining these last two, and the final one for just within your class. Each is a logically well-defined and useful separation that Java supports directly in the language (as opposed to, for example, accessor methods, which are a convention you must follow).

Q Won't using accessor methods everywhere slow down my Java code?

A Not always. As Java compilers improve and can create more optimizations, the use of accessor methods should not slow your code significantly, but if you're concerned about speed, you can always declare accessor methods to be final, and they'll be just as fast as direct instance variable accesses.

Q Are class (static) methods inherited just like instance methods?

A No. static (class) methods are now final by default. How, then, can you ever declare a non-final class method? The answer is that you can't! Inheritance of class methods is not allowed, breaking the symmetry with instance methods.

Q Based on what I've learned, it seems like private abstract methods and final abstract methods or classes don't make sense. Are they legal?

A Nope, they're compile-time errors, as you have guessed. To be useful, abstract methods must be overridden, and abstract classes must be subclassed, but neither of these two operations would be legal if they were also private or final.

Q I tried creating a private variable inside a method definition. It didn't work. What did I do wrong?

A Nothing. All the modifiers in this chapter, when you can use them with variables, only apply to class and instance variables. Local variables—those that appear inside the body of a method or loop—cannot use any of these modifiers.

Day **18**

Packages, Interfaces, and Exception Handling

Packages and interfaces are two capabilities that allow you greater control and flexibility in designing sets of interrelated classes. Packages allow you to combine groups of classes and control those classes available to the outside world; interfaces are a way of grouping abstract method definitions and sharing them among classes that might not necessarily acquire those methods through inheritance.

Exception handling provides a method for dealing with unexpected events that interrupt the normal operation of the program. There are specific statements built into the Java language to handle exceptions.

Today, you'll cover how to design with, use, and create your own packages, interfaces, and exception handlers. Specific topics you'll learn today include the following:

☐ A discussion of designing classes versus coding classes and how to approach each one

☐ What packages are and why they are useful for class design

☐ Using other people's packages in your own classes

☐ Creating your own packages

☐ What interfaces buy you in terms of code reuse and design

☐ Designing and working with interfaces

☐ Understanding and using exception handlers

Programming in the Large and Programming in the Small

When you examine a new language feature, you should ask yourself two questions:

1. How can I use it to better organize the methods and classes of my Java program?

2. How can I use it while writing the actual Java code?

The first is often called programming in the large, and the second, programming in the small. Bill Joy, a founder of Sun Microsystems, likes to say that Java feels like C when programming in the small and like SmallTalk when programming in the large. What he means is that while you're coding individual lines, Java is familiar and powerful like any C-like language, but while you're designing, it has the extensibility and expressive power of a pure object-oriented language such as SmallTalk.

The separation of designing from coding was one of the most fundamental advances in programming in the past few decades. Object-oriented languages such as Java implement a strong form of this separation. When you develop a Java program, you first design the classes and decide on the relationships between these classes; you then implement the Java code needed for each of the methods in your design. If you are careful enough with both of these processes, you can change your mind about aspects of the design without affecting anything but small, local pieces of your Java code. You can also change the implementation of any method without affecting the rest of the design.

As you begin to explore more advanced Java programming, however, you'll find that this simple model becomes too limiting. Today, you'll explore these limitations of programming in the large and in the small, which motivate the need for packages and interfaces. First, you'll start with packages.

What Are Packages?

Packages, as already mentioned in this book, are a way of organizing groups of classes. For example, the AWT package contains all the classes that are related to user interface design. A package contains any number of classes that are related in purpose, in scope, or by inheritance.

Why bother with packages? If your programs are small and use a limited number of classes, you might find that you don't need to explore packages at all. But the more Java programming you do, the more classes you'll end up with. And, although those classes might be individually well-designed, reusable, encapsulated, and with specific interfaces to other classes, you might find the need for a bigger organizational entity that allows you to group your classes.

Packages are useful for several reasons:

- [ ] Packages allow you to protect classes, variables and methods in larger ways than on a class-by-class basis, as you learned in yesterday's discussion. There will be more about protections with packages later in this chapter.

- [ ] Packages allow you to organize your classes into units. Just as you have folders or directories on your hard drive to organize your files and applications, packages allow you to organize your classes into groups so that you only use what you need for each program.

- [ ] Packages reduce problems with conflicts in names. As the number of Java classes grows, so does the likelihood that you'll use the same class name as someone else, opening up the possibility of naming clashes and errors if you try to integrate groups of classes into a single program. Packages allow you to hide classes so that conflicts can be avoided.

- [ ] Packages can be used to identify your classes. For example, if you implemented a set of classes to perform some purpose, you could name a package of those classes with a unique identifier that identified you or your organization.

While a package is usually a collection of classes, packages can also contain other packages, forming yet another level of organization somewhat analogous to the inheritance hierarchy. Each level usually represents a smaller, more specific grouping of classes. The Java class library itself is organized along these lines. The top level is called `java`; the next level includes names such as `io`, `net`, `util`, and `awt`. The last of these has an even lower level, which includes the package `image`.

18

NOTE

By convention, the first level of the hierarchy specifies the (globally unique) name to identify the author or owner of those packages. For example, Sun Microsystem's classes, which are not part of the standard Java environment, all begin with the prefix sun. Netscape includes classes with its implementation that are contained in the netscape package. The standard package, java, is an exception to this rule because it is so fundamental and it might someday be implemented by multiple companies.

More about package naming conventions later today when you create your own packages.

Using Packages

You've been using packages all along in this book. Every time you used the import command and referred to a class by its full package name (java.awt.Color, for example), you were using packages. Now I'll go into greater depth than in previous lessons by going over the specifics of how to use classes from other packages in your own programs (to make sure you've got it).

To use a class contained in a package, you can use one of three mechanisms:

- ☐ If the class you want to use is in the package java.lang (for example, System or Date), you can simply use the class name to refer to that class. The java.lang classes are automatically available to you in all your programs.
- ☐ If the class you want to use is in some other package, you can refer to that class by its full name, including any package names, such as java.awt.Font.
- ☐ For classes that you frequently use from other packages, you can import individual classes or a whole package of classes. Once a class or a package has been imported, you can refer to that class by its class name.

What about your own classes in your own programs that don't belong to any package? The rule is that if you don't specifically define your classes to belong to a package, they're put into a default unnamed package. You can refer to those classes by class name from anywhere in your classes.

Full Package and Class Names

To refer to a class in some other package, you can use its full name: the class name preceded by any package names. You do not have to import the class or the package to use it in the following way:

18

```
java.awt.Font f = new java.awt.Font()
```

For classes that you use only once or twice in your program, using the full name makes the most sense. If, however, you use that class multiple times, or if the package name is really long with lots of subpackages, you'll want to, instead, import that class to save yourself some typing.

The `import` Command

To import classes from a package, use the `import` command as you've done throughout this book. You can import an individual class in the following way:

```
import java.util.Vector;
```

Or you can import an entire package of classes using a * to replace the individual class names:

```
import java.awt.*
```

NOTE

> Actually, to be technically correct, this command doesn't import all the classes in a package; it only imports the classes that have been declared `public`. There is more on this in the section titled "Packages and Class Protection" later in this chapter.

Note that the asterisk (*) in this example is not like the one you might use at a command prompt to specify the contents of a directory or to indicate multiple files. For example, if you ask to list the contents of the directory `classes/java/awt/*`, that list includes all the `.class` files and subdirectories such as `image` and `peer`. Writing `import java.awt.*` does not import subpackages such as `image` and `peer`. To import all the classes in a complex package hierarchy, you must explicitly import each level of the hierarchy by hand. Also, you cannot indicate partial class names—for example, `L*` to import all the classes that begin with `L`. It's either all the classes in a package or a single class.

The import statements in your class definition go to the top of the file before any class definitions (but after the package definition, as you'll see in the next section).

You might have noticed that the Visual J++ Applet Wizard automatically imports the `java.applet.*` and `java.awt.*` packages by adding the appropriate import statements at the top of the generated source code.

18

So, should you take the time to import classes individually or just import them as a group? It depends on how specific you want to be. Importing a group of classes does not slow down your program or make it any larger. But importing a package does make it a little more confusing for readers of your code to figure out where your classes are coming from. Using individual imports or importing packages is mostly a question of your own coding style.

TECHNICAL NOTE

> Java's import command is not at all like the #include command in C-like languages. The C preprocessor takes the contents of all the included files (and, in turn, the files they include, and so on), and stuffs them at the spot where the #include was. The result is an enormous hunk of code that has far more lines than the original program did. Java's import tells the Java compiler and interpreter where (in which files) to find class, variable and method names and definitions. It doesn't bring anything into the current Java program.

Name Conflicts

Once you have imported a class or a package of classes, you can usually refer to a class name by its name without the package identifier. I say usually because there's one case where you might have to be more explicit: where there are multiple classes with the same name from different packages.

Here's an example. Suppose you import the classes from two packages from two different programmers (Joe and Eleanor):

```
import joesclasses.*;
import eleanorsclasses.*;
```

Inside Joe's package is a class called Name. Unfortunately, inside Eleanor's package there is also a class called Name that has an entirely different meaning and implementation. Whose version of Name ends up getting used if you refer to the Name class in your own program?

```
Name myName = new Name("Susan");
```

The answer is neither; the Java compiler will complain about a naming conflict and refuse to compile your program. In this case, despite the fact that you imported both classes, you still have to refer to the appropriate Name class by its full package name:

```
joesclasses.Name myName = new joesclasses.Name("Susan");
```

A Note About CLASSPATH and Where Classes Are Located

Before we go on to explain how to create your own packages of classes, we'd like to make a note about how Visual J++ finds packages and classes when it's compiling and running your classes.

For Visual J++ to be able to use a class, it has to be able to find it on the file system. Otherwise, you'll get an error that says the class does not exist. Visual J++ uses two things to find classes: the package name itself and the directories listed in your CLASSPATH variable.

Package names map to directory names on the file system, so the class java.applet.Applet will actually be found in the applet directory, which in turn will be inside the Java directory (java/applet/Applet.class, in other words).

Visual J++ then looks for those directories inside the directories listed in your CLASSPATH variable. The CLASSPATH variable is configured by selecting Settings from the Build menu. The CLASSPATH variable is defined under the tab General. Figure 18.1 shows the dialog box for setting the CLASSPATH variable. When you install Visual J++, the default location for the built-in classes is c:\windows\java\classes.

Figure 18.1.

Setting the CLASSPATH *variable.*

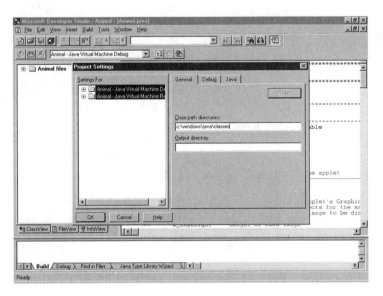

Creating Your Own Packages

Creating your own packages is a difficult process, involving many lines of code, long hours late at night with lots of coffee, and the ritual sacrifice of many goats. Just kidding. To create a package of classes, you have three basic steps to follow: picking a package name, creating the directory structure, and using `package` to add your class to a package.

Picking a Package Name

The first step is to decide what the name of your package is going to be. The name you choose for your package depends on how you are going to be using those classes. Perhaps your package will be named after you, or perhaps after the part of the Java system you're working on (`graphics` or `hardware_interfaces`). If you're intending your package to be distributed to the Net-at-large, or as part of a commercial product, you'll want to use a package name (or set of package names) that uniquely identifies you, your organization, or both.

One convention for naming packages that has been recommended by Sun is to use your Internet domain name, with the elements reversed. If you look in the `c:\windows\java\classes` directory, you will see that Microsoft has followed this suggestion and placed their classes in the `com.ms` structure. If your Internet domain name is `fooblitzky.eng.nonsense.edu`, your package name might be `edu.nonsense.eng.fooblitzky`. (You might add another package name on the end of that to refer to the product or specifically to you.)

The idea is to make sure your package name is unique. While packages can hide conflicting class names, the protection stops there. There's no way to make sure your package won't conflict with someone else's package if you both use the same common name.

By convention, package names tend to begin with a lowercase letter to distinguish them from class names. Therefore, for example, in the full name of the built-in `String` class, `java.lang.String`, it's easier to separate the package name from the class name visually. This convention helps reduce name conflicts.

Create the Directory Structure

Step two in creating packages is to create a directory structure on your disk that matches the package name. If your package has just one name (`mypackage`), you'll only have to create a directory for that one name. However, if the package name has several parts, you'll have to create directories within directories. For the package name edu.nonsense.eng.fooblitzky, you'll need to create an edu directory, create a nonsense directory inside edu, an eng directory inside nonsense, and a fooblitzky directory inside eng. Your classes and source files can then go inside the fooblitzky directory.

Use package to Add Your Class to a Package

The final step to putting your class inside packages is to add the package command to your source files. The package command says which class goes inside which package, and is used like the following:

```
package myclasses;
package edu.nonsense.eng.fooblitzky;
package java.awt;
```

The single package command, if any, must be the first line of code in your source file, after any comments or blank lines, and before any import commands.

As I mentioned earlier today, if your class doesn't have a package command in it, that class is contained in the default package, and can be used by any other class. But once you start using packages, you should make sure all your classes belong to some package to reduce the chance of confusion as to where your classes belong.

Creating Packages with the Visual J++ User Interface

The Visual J++ development environment will automate the preceding manual steps in creating your own packages. When you add a class using the graphical interface (as opposed to just typing it in), Visual J++ will automatically add the appropriate statements into your class and create the directory structure for you.

For example, if you want to create a new class called Dog that extends a class called Animal, you can simply right-click in the ClassView window and select Create New Class, as shown in Figure 18.2.

After you make this selection, a dialog box will appear that allows you to enter information about the class, such as the superclass, modifiers, and package information. In this case, name your class Dog and it will extend Animal. Also, create a package called myAnimals. Your new class, Dog, will be a member of the package myAnimals. The dialog box is shown in Figure 18.3.

Figure 18.2.

Creating a new class in Visual J++.

Figure 18.3.

The Create New Class dialog box.

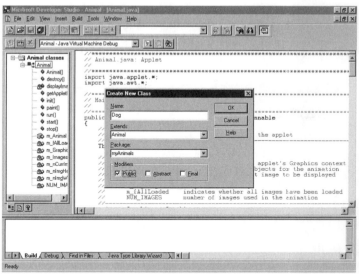

After you enter the class information, Visual J++ will automatically create a source code template for the class with the appropriate statements for creating a package. In this case, you created a package called myAnimals. Figure 18.4 shows the template that was created for your new class called Dog. As you can see, the statement

```
package myAnimals;
```

was added to the top of the code. In addition, if you save the project and look at your file structure, you will see that the file Dog.class has been created in a directory called myAnimals.

Figure 18.4.

The Source template for the Dog Class.

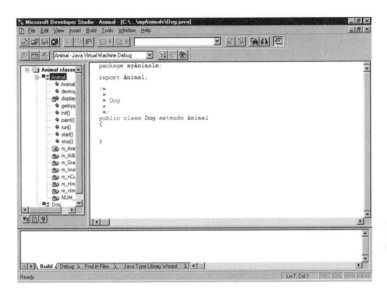

Packages and Class Protection

Yesterday you learned all about the four Ps of protection, and how they applied (primarily) to methods and variables and their relationship to other classes. When referring to classes and their relationship to other classes in other packages, you only have two Ps to worry about: package and public.

By default, classes have package protection, which means that the class is available to all the other classes in the same package, but is not visible or available outside that package (not even to subpackages). It cannot be imported or referred to by name; classes with package protection are hidden inside the package in which they are contained.

Package protection comes about when you define a class (as you have been doing throughout this book) like the following:

```
class TheHiddenClass extends AnotherHiddenClass {
...
}
```

To allow a class to be visible and importable outside your package, you'll want to make it have public protection by adding the `public` modifier to its definition:

```
public class TheVisibleClass {
...
}
```

`public` classes can be imported by other classes outside the package.

Note that when you use an `import` statement with an asterisk, you import only the `public` classes inside that package. Hidden classes remain hidden and are only used by the other classes in this package.

Why would you want to hide a class inside a package? For the same reason you want to hide variables and methods inside a class—so you can have utility classes and behavior that are only useful to your implementation, or so you can limit the interface of your program so that you can minimize the effect of larger changes. As you design your classes, you'll want to take the whole package into consideration and decide which classes will be public and which will be hidden.

Listing 18.1 shows two classes that illustrate this point. The first is a `public` class that implements a linked list; the second is a `private` node of that list.

TYPE **Listing 18.1. The `LinkedList` classes.**

```
package   collections;

public class  LinkedList {
    private Node   root;

    public  void  add(Object o) {
        root = new Node(o, root);
    }
    . . .
}

class   Node {                        // not public
    private Object  contents;
    private Node     next;

    Node(Object o, Node n) {
        contents = o;
        next      = n;
    }
    . . .
}
```

NOTE

> You'll note that I'm breaking a rule I mentioned earlier in this book:
> You can only have one class definition per file. In truth, the restriction
> is that you can include as many class definitions per file as you want,
> but only one of them can be public. In reality, I find that keeping one
> class definition per file is easier to maintain because I don't have to go
> searching around for the definition of a class.

The public `LinkedList` class provides a set of useful `public` methods (such as `add()`) to any
other classes that might want to use them. These other classes don't need to know about any
support classes `LinkedList` needs to get its job finished. `Node`, which is one of those support
classes, is therefore declared without a `public` modifier, and will not appear as part of the
public interface to the collections class.

NOTE

> Just because `Node` isn't public doesn't mean `LinkedList` won't have
> access to it once it has been imported into some other class. Think of
> protections not as hiding classes entirely, but more as checking the
> permissions of a given class to use other classes, variables, and methods.
> When you import and use `LinkedList`, the `node` class will also be loaded
> into the system. Only instances of `LinkedList`, though, will have
> permission to use it.

One of the great powers of hidden classes is that even if you use them to introduce a great
deal of complexity into the implementation of some `public` class, all the complexity is hidden
when that class is `imported` or used. Thus, creating a good package consists of defining a small,
clean set of `public` classes and methods for other classes to use, and then implementing them
by using any number of hidden (`package`) support classes.

What Are Interfaces?

Interfaces, like the `abstract` classes and methods you saw yesterday, provide templates of
behavior that other classes are expected to implement. Interfaces, however, provide far more
functionality to Java and to class and object design than simple `abstract` classes and methods.
You will now explore interfaces: what they are, why they're crucial to getting the most out
of the Java language for your own classes, and how to use and implement them.

The Problem of Single Inheritance

When you first began to design object-oriented programs, the concept of the class hierarchy probably seemed almost miraculous. Within that single tree, you can express a hierarchy of different types of objects; many simple to moderately complex relationships between objects and processes in the world; and any number of points along the axis, from abstract/general to concrete/specific. The strict hierarchy of classes appears, at first glance, to be simple, elegant, and easy to use.

After some deeper thought or more complex design experience, however, you might discover that the pure simplicity of the class hierarchy is restrictive, particularly when you have some behavior that needs to be used by classes in different branches of the same tree.

Now look at an example. Suppose you have a biological hierarchy, with `Animal` at the top, and the classes `Mammal` and `Bird` underneath. Things that define a mammal include bearing live young and having fur. Behavior or features of birds include having a beak and laying eggs. So far, so good, right? But how do you go about creating a class for the creature `Platypus`, which has fur, a beak, and lays eggs? You'd need to combine behavior from two classes to form the `Platypus` class. And, because classes can only have one immediate superclass in Java, this sort of problem cannot be solved elegantly.

Other OOP languages include the concept of multiple inheritance, which can solve this problem. With multiple inheritance, a class can inherit from more than one superclass, and get behavior and attributes from all its superclasses at once. Using multiple inheritance, you could simply factor the common behavior of egg laying creatures into a single class (`EggLayers`) and then create new classes that inherit from the primary superclass and the `EggLayer` class. For example, the `Platypus` class would inherit from both the `Mammal` class and the `EggLayer` class. In addition, a `BeakedCreature` class could be created, which could also be inherited by the `Platypus` class.

The problem with multiple inheritance is that it makes a programming language far more complex, and more difficult to learn, use, and implement. Questions of method invocation and how the class hierarchy is organized become far more complicated with multiple inheritance, and more open to confusion and ambiguity. And because one of the goals for Java was that it be simple, multiple inheritance was rejected in favor of the simpler single inheritance.

So, how do you solve the problem of needing common behavior that doesn't fit into the strict class hierarchy? Java, borrowing from Objective-C, has another hierarchy altogether. This is separate from the main class hierarchy of mixable behavior classes. When you create a new class, that class only has one primary superclass, but can pick and choose different common behaviors from the other hierarchy.

That other hierarchy is the interface hierarchy. A Java interface is a collection of abstract behaviors that can be mixed into any class to add behavior to that class that is not supplied by its superclasses. Specifically, a Java interface contains nothing but abstract method definitions and constants—no instance variables and no method implementations.

Interfaces are implemented and used throughout the Java class library whenever a behavior is expected to be implemented by a number of disparate classes. In the Java class hierarchy, for example, there are the interfaces, `java.lang.Runnable`, `java.util.Enumeration`, `java.util.Observable`, `java.awt.image.ImageConsumer`, and `java.awt.image.ImageProducer`. The interfaces in the standard Java class hierarchy might be useful to you in your own programs, so be sure to examine the API to see what's available to you.

Abstract Design and Concrete Implementation

Throughout this book you've gotten a taste of the difference between design and implementation in object-oriented programming, where the design of a thing is its abstract representation and its implementation is the concrete counterpart of the design. You saw this with methods, where a method's signature defines how its used, but the method implementation can occur anywhere in the class hierarchy. You saw this with abstract classes, where the class' design provides a template for behavior, but that behavior isn't implemented until further down in the hierarchy.

This distinction between the design and the implementation of a class or a method is a crucial part of object-oriented programming theory. Thinking in terms of design when you organize your classes allows you to get the big picture without being bogged down in implementation details. And having the overall design already defined when you actually start implementing allows you to concentrate on those details, solely on the class you're working on. This programming version of "think globally, act locally" provides a powerful way of thinking about how your classes, your programs, and your overall designs are organized, and how they interrelate with each other.

An interface is made up of a set of method signatures with no implementations, making it the embodiment of pure design. By mixing an interface in with your class, you're encompassing that design into your implementation. Therefore, that design can be safely included anywhere in the class hierarchy because there are no class-specific details of how an interface behaves—nothing to override, nothing to keep track of, just the name and arguments for a method.

What about abstract classes? Don't abstract classes provide this same behavior? Yes and no. abstract classes, and the abstract methods inside them, do provide a separation of design and implementation, allowing you to factor common behavior into an abstract superclass.

18

But abstract classes can, and often do, contain some concrete data (such as instance variables). And, you can have an abstract superclass with both abstract and regular methods, thereby confusing the distinction.

Even a pure abstract class with only an abstract method isn't as powerful as an interface. An abstract class is simply another class; it inherits from some other class, and has its place in the hierarchy. abstract classes cannot be shared across different parts of the class hierarchy the way interfaces can. They cannot be mixed into other classes that need their behavior. To attain the sort of flexibility of shared behavior across the class hierarchy, you need an interface.

You can think of the difference between the design and the implementation of any Java class as the difference between the interface hierarchy and the design hierarchy. The single inherited class hierarchy contains the implementations where the relationships between classes and behaviors are rigidly defined. The multiple inherited mixable interface hierarchy, however, contains the design, and can be freely used anywhere it's needed in the implementation. This is a powerful way of thinking about the organization of your program. Although it takes a little getting used to, it's also highly recommended.

Interfaces and Classes

Interfaces and classes, despite their different definitions, have a lot in common. Interfaces, like classes, are declared in source files, one interface to a file. Like classes, they also are compiled using the Java compiler into .class files. And, in most cases, anywhere you can use a class (as a data type for a variable, as the result of a cast, and so on), you can also use an interface.

Almost everywhere that there is a class name in any of this book's examples or discussions, you can substitute an interface name. Java programmers often say class when they actually mean class or interface. Interfaces complement and extend the power of classes, and the two can be treated almost exactly the same. One of the few differences between them is that an interface cannot be instantiated: new can create only an instance of a class.

Implementing and Using Interfaces

Now that you've grasped what interfaces are and why they're powerful (the programming in the large part), it's time to move on to actual bits of code (programming the small). There are two things you can do with interfaces: Use them in your own classes and define your own. First, you'll start with the former.

The `implements` **Keyword**

To use an interface, you include the `implements` keyword as part of your class definition. For example, to use an interface called `myInterface` with a class called `myApplet` you would use the following definition:

```
public class myApplet extends java.applet.Applet // java.applet.Applet is the
superclass
    implements myInterface {                   // but it also has myInterface
behavior
...
}
```

Because interfaces provide nothing but abstract method definitions, you have to implement those methods in your own classes using the same method signatures from the interface. Note that once you include an interface, you have to implement all the methods in that interface—you can't pick and choose the methods you need. By implementing an interface you're telling users of your class that you support all of that interface. (Note that this is another difference between interfaces and abstract classes—subclasses of the latter can pick which methods to implement or override, and can ignore others.)

Once your class implements an interface, subclasses of your class will inherit those new methods (and can override or overload them) just as if your superclass had actually defined them. If your class inherits from a superclass that implements a given interface, you don't have to include the `implements` keyword in your own class definition.

Now examine one simple example—creating the new class `GoldenRetriever`. Suppose you already have a good implementation of the class `Animal` and an interface, `Animallike`, that represents what `Animals` are expected to be able to do. You want a Golden Retriever to be an animal, but you also want it to have doglike characteristics, such as the ability to roll over. Here's how to express it all (don't worry about the definitions of these interfaces for now; you'll learn more about them later today):

```
interface AnimalLike {
    void  eat();
    void  sleep();
    . . .
}

class  Animal implements AnimalLike {
    private int age;
    private int weight;
    . . .
}

interface  Doglike {
    void  rollOver();
    void  messOnNeighborsLawn();
    . . .
}
```

```
class  GoldenRetriever extends Animal implements Doglike {
    . . . // eat()ing may cause me to messOnNeighborsLawn() (A unique behavior)
    . . .
}
```

Note that the class `GoldenRetriever` doesn't have to say `implements Animallike` because, by extending `Animal`, it already has! One of the nice things about this structure is that you can change your mind about what class `GoldenRetriever` extends (if a really great `Dog` class is suddenly implemented, for example), yet class `GoldenRetriever` will still understand the same two interfaces:

```
class  Dog implements Doglike {   // extends Object
    private int  ageInDogYears;
    . . .
}

class  GoldenRetriever extends Dog implements Animallike {
    . . .      // users of GoldenRetriever never need know about the change!
}
```

Implementing Multiple Interfaces

Unlike the single inherited class hierarchy, you can include as many interfaces as you need in your own classes and your class will implement the combined behavior of all the included interfaces. To include multiple interfaces in a class, just separate the names with commas:

```
class  GoldenRetriever extends Animal
    implements Doglike, Petlike {
. . .
}
```

Note that complications might arise from implementing multiple interfaces; what happens if two different interfaces both define the same method? There are three combinations of how this can be solved:

☐ If the two methods in each of the interfaces have identical signatures, you implement that one method in your class and that definition satisfies both interfaces.

☐ If the two methods have different parameter lists, this is a simple case of method overloading; you implement both method signatures and each definition satisfies its respective interface definition.

☐ If the two methods have the same parameter lists but differ in return type, you cannot create a method that satisfies both (remember, method overloading is triggered by parameter lists, not by return type). In this case, trying to compile a class that implements both interfaces will produce a compiler error. Running across this problem suggests that your interfaces have some design flaws that might need reexamining.

Other Uses of Interfaces

Remember that almost everywhere that you can use a class, you can use an interface instead. For example, you can declare a variable to be of an interface type like the following:

```
Runnable aRunnableObject = new MyAnimationClass()
```

When a variable is declared to be of an interface type, it simply means that any object the variable refers to is expected to have implemented that interface—that is, it is expected to understand all the methods that interface specifies. It assumes that a promise made between the designer of the interface and its eventual implementors has been kept. In this case, because ARunnableObject contains an object of the type Runnable, the assumption is that you can call aRunnableObject.run().

The important thing to realize here is that although aRunnableObject is expected to be able to have the run() method, you could write this code long before any classes that qualify are actually implemented (or even created!). In traditional object-oriented programming, you are forced to create a class with stub implementations to get the same effect.

You can also cast objects to an interface, just as you can cast objects to other classes. For example, go back to that definition of the GoldenRetriever class, which implemented both the Animallike interface (through its superclass, Animal) and the Doglike interface. Here, you'll cast instances of GoldenRetriever to both classes and interfaces:

```
GoldenRetriever   aGoldenRetriever   = new GoldenRetriever();
Animal            anAnimal      = (Animal)aGoldenRetriever;
Animallike        anAnimallike  = (Animallike)aGoldenRetriever;
Doglike           aDoglike = (Doglike)aGoldenRetriever;


anAnimal.eat();         // Animals eat
anAnimallike.sleep();   //  and sleep

aAnimallike.rollOver(); // things that are Animallike do not roll over
aDoglike.rollOver();    // but things that are Doglike do

aGoldenRetriever.eat();         // A Golden Retriever can do it all
aGoldenRetriever.sleep();
aGoldenRetriever.rollOver();
aGoldenRetriever.messOnNeighborsLawn();
```

Declarations and casts are used in this example to restrict a Golden Retriever's behavior to act like a mere animal or dog, but not both. This is shown by the objects anAnimal, anAnimallike, and aDoglike.

Finally, note that although interfaces are usually used to mix in behavior to other classes (method signatures), interfaces can also be used to mix in generally useful constants. For example, if an interface defined a set of constants, and then multiple classes used those

18

constants, the values of those constants could be globally changed without having to modify multiple classes. This is yet another example where the use of interfaces to separate design from implementation can make your code more general and more easily maintainable.

Creating Interfaces

After using interfaces for a while, the next step is to define your own interfaces. Interfaces look a lot like classes; they are declared in much of the same way, and can be arranged into a hierarchy. However, there are rules for declaring interfaces that must be followed.

New Interfaces

To create a new interface, you declare it like the following:

```
public interface Growable {
...
}
```

This is, effectively, the same as a class definition, with the word `interface` replacing the word `class`. Inside the interface definition you have methods and constants. The method definitions inside the interface are `public` and `abstract` methods; you can either declare them explicitly as such, or they will be turned into `public abstract` methods if you do not include those modifiers. You cannot declare a method inside an interface to be either `private` or `protected`.

```
public interface Growable {
    public abstract void growIt(); //explicitly public and abstract
    void growItBigger();            // effectively public and abstract
}
```

Note that, as with `abstract` methods in classes, methods inside interfaces do not have bodies. Remember, an interface is pure design; there is no implementation involved.

In addition to methods, interfaces can also have variables, but those variables must be declared `public`, `static`, and `final` (making them constant). As with methods, you can explicitly define a variable to be `public`, `static`, and `final`, or it will be implicitly defined as such if you don't use the following modifiers:

```
public interface Growable {
    public static final int increment = 10;
    long maxnum = 1000000;  // becomes public static and final

    public abstract void growIt(); //explicitly public and abstract
    void growItBigger();            // effectively public and abstract
}
```

Interfaces must have either public or package protection, just like classes. Note, however, that interfaces without the public modifier do not automatically convert their methods to public and abstract or their constants to public. A non-public interface also has non-public methods and constants that can only be used by classes and other interfaces in the same package.

Interfaces, like classes, can belong to a package by adding a package definition to the first line. Interfaces can also import other interfaces and classes from other packages, just as classes can.

Methods Inside Interfaces

Because methods inside interfaces are supposed to be abstract and apply to any kind of class, how can you define parameters for them? You don't know what class will be using them!

The answer lies in the fact that you can use an interface name anywhere a class name can be used, as you learned earlier today. By defining your method parameters to be interface types, you can create generic parameters that apply to any class that might use this interface.

For example, take the interface Animallike, which defines methods (with no arguments) for eat() and sleep(). There might also be a method for reproduce(), which has one argument: the animal itself. What type is that argument going to be? It can't be Animal because there might be a class that's Animallike (uses the interface) without actually being an animal. The solution is to declare the argument as Animallike in the following interface:

```
public interface Animallike {
    public abstract reproduce(Animallike self) {
        ...
    }
}
```

Then, in an actual implementation for this method in a class, you can take the generic Animallike argument and cast it to the appropriate object:

```
public class GoldenRetriever extends Animal {

    public reproduce(Animallike self) {
        GoldenRetriever aGoldenRetriever = (GoldenRetriever)self;
        ...
    }
}
```

Extending Interfaces

As with classes, interfaces can be organized into a hierarchy. When one interface inherits from another interface, that "subinterface" acquires all the method definitions and constants that

18

its "superinterface" defined. To extend an interface, you use the extends keyword like you do in a class definition:

```
public interface Doglike extends Petlike {
...
}
```

Note that unlike classes, the interface hierarchy has no equivalent of the Object class; the interface hierarchy is not rooted at any one point. Interfaces can either exist entirely on their own or inherit from another interface.

Note also that unlike the class hierarchy, the inheritance hierarchy is multiply inherited. For example, a single interface can extend as many classes as it needs to (separated by commas in the extends part of the definition), and the new interface will contain a combination of all its parent's methods and constants.

```
public interface Doglike extends Petlike, Friendlike {
...}
```

In multiply inherited interfaces, the rules for managing method name conflicts are the same as for classes that use multiple interfaces; methods that differ only in return type will result in a compiler error.

Exception Handling

The last topic covered today is exception handling. Exception handling is the capability of your program to respond in a predetermined way to runtime errors and exceptions. The exception handling capabilities of Java are provided by the statements try, catch, throw, and finally. The basic exception handling structure is the try...catch series of statements.

The try...catch Structure

The try...catch structure is best explained by first examining a simple example. Consider the following code:

```
public static double Divider (double numerator, double denominator) {
    try{
        double result = numerator / denominator;
        return result;
    }
    catch (ArithmeticException a) {
        System.out.print("An arithmetic exception occurred!");
        return 0;
    }
}
```

In this example, the method Divider will try the code inside of the try block. If result evaluates okay and the return statement executes without any problems, the method completes and control returns to the calling code. If, however, there is an exception inside this block, control will immediately jump to the catch statement. In this example, if the exception is of type ArithmeticException, a message will be displayed indicating that an arithmetic exception has occurred and 0 will be returned. For example, if a divide by zero is attempted, an ArithmeticException will occur and the message will be displayed.

If additional types of exceptions are possible, additional catch statements can be added. The only requirement is that each catch statement must have a unique type. When an exception occurs, the catch block with the associated type will be executed.

When an exception occurs it is said to be thrown. All exceptions are derived from the class Throwable.

If you list parent classes before subclasses, you can catch errors that did not match any of the types of subclasses. For example, if you introduce a catch of type Throwable, all errors not caught in previous catch statements will be caught because Throwable is the parent class of all exceptions. The example is expanded in the following code with a catch for Throwable at the end to catch all uncaught exceptions:

```
public static double Divider (double numerator, double denominator) {
    try{
        double result = numerator / denominator;
        return result;
    }
    catch (ArithmeticException a) {
        System.out.print("An arithmetic exception occurred!");
        return 0;
    }
    catch (Throwable t) {
        System.out.print("An unknown error has occurred!");
        return 0;
    }
}
```

The finally Statement

Sometimes there is something that must be performed, whether or not an exception occurs. Usually, this is to free some external resource after acquiring it, to close a file after opening it, or something similar. To be sure that these no-matter-what statements occur, even if there is an exception, you can use the finally statement.

18

NOTE
> The primary difference between exception handling in C++ and Java is the `finally` statement. The `finally` statement is not supported by C++.

The following example shows the use of the `finally` statement to make sure that an open file is closed. In this example, the statement `f.close()` will be executed, whether or not an exception occurs:

```
aFileClass f = new aFileClass();

try {
    f.open(aPathString)) {
    // additional file operations
    }
    catch (aFileOpenError x) {
        System.out.print("Error opening file");
    }
    catch (aFileWriteError x) {
        System.out.print("Error writing to file");
    }
    // additional catch statements as necessary
    catch (throwable x) {
        System.out.print("An unknown error has occurred");
    }
    finally {
        f.close();
    }
}
```

In the preceding example, if there are any exceptions or errors in the `try` block, the appropriate `catch` block will be executed. After the exception is handled, the `finally` block will be executed, ensuring that the file is closed.

If there are not any exceptions during the `try` block, the `finally` block will still execute and the file will be closed. The `finally` block always executes, whether or not an exception has occurred.

Using throw to Create an Exception

The `throw` statement is used to create an exception. The following example demonstrates the use of `throw` (note that the throw and the handler are generally not this close together):

```
System.out.print("Now ");
try {
    System.out.print("is ");
    throw new MyFirstException();
    System.out.print("This will not execute!");
}
catch (MyFirstException m) {
    System.out.print("the ");
```

```
}
System.out.print("time.\n");
```

The preceding example will print Now is the time.

Exception handlers can be nested. If, for example, a catch block contains a throw statement, the exception will be propagated back up the nested handlers to the next level. If there is not a higher level handler, the system will handle the exception, generally by aborting the program.

Summary

Today, you learned how packages can be used to collect and categorize classes into meaningful groups. Packages are arranged in a hierarchy, which not only better organizes your programs, but allows you and the millions of Java programmers out on the Net to name and share projects uniquely with one another.

You also learned how to use packages, both your own and the many preexisting ones in the Java class library.

You then discovered how to declare and use interfaces, a powerful mechanism for extending the traditional single inheritance of Java's classes and for separating design inheritance from implementation inheritance in your programs. Interfaces are often used to call common (shared) methods when the exact class involved is not known.

Finally, exception handling was introduced. Through the use of the try...catch statement, you can add code to your Visual J++ projects to handle exception conditions, instead of relying on the built-in exception handling of the system, which generally results in aborting the program.

Q&A

Q Can you say import some.package.B* to import all the classes in that package that begin with B?

A No, the import asterisk (*) does not act like a command-line asterisk.

Q Then what exactly does import-ing with an * mean?

A Combining everything already mentioned in the chapter, the following precise definition emerges: it imports all the public classes that are directly inside the package named, and not inside one of its subpackages. (You can only import exactly this set of classes, or exactly one explicitly named class, from a given package.) By the way, Java only loads the information for a class when you actually refer to that class in your code, so the * form of import is no less efficient than naming each class individually.

Q **Why is full multiple inheritance so complex that Java abandoned it?**

A It's not so much that it is too complex, but that it makes the language overly complicated and this can cause larger systems to be less trustworthy and, therefore, less secure. For example, if you were to inherit from two different parents, each having an instance variable with the same name, you would be forced to allow the conflict. You would have to explain how the exact same references to that variable name in each of your superclasses (and you) are now different. Instead of being able to call super methods to get more abstract behavior accomplished, you would always need to worry about which of the (possibly many) identical methods you actually wished to call in which parent. Java's runtime method dispatching would have to be more complex as well. Finally, because so many people would be providing classes for reuse on the Net, the normally manageable conflicts that would arise in your own program would be confounded by millions of users mixing and matching these fully multi-inherited classes at will. In the future, if all these issues are resolved, more powerful inheritance might be added to Java, but its current capabilities are already sufficient for 99 percent of your programs.

Q **abstract classes don't have to implement all the methods in an interface themselves, but don't all their subclasses have to?**

A Actually, no. Because of inheritance, the precise rule is that an implementation must be provided by some class for each method, but it doesn't have to be your class. This is analogous to when you are the subclass of a class that implements an interface for you. Whatever the abstract class doesn't implement, the first non-abstract class below it must implement. Then, any further subclasses need do nothing further.

Q **You didn't mention callbacks. Aren't they an important use of interfaces?**

A Yes, but I didn't mention them because a good example would be too bulky in the text. Callbacks are often used in user interfaces (such as window systems) to specify which set of methods are going to be sent whenever the user does certain things (such as clicking the mouse somewhere, typing, and so forth). Because the user interface classes should not know anything about the classes using them, an interface's capability to specify a set of methods separate from the class tree is crucial in this case. Callbacks using interfaces are not as general as using, for example, the perform: method of SmallTalk because a given object can only request that a user interface object call it back using a single method name. Suppose that object wanted two user interface objects of the same class to call it back, using different names to tell them apart? It cannot do this in Java, and it is forced to use special state and tests to tell them apart. (I warned you that it was complicated!) So, although interfaces are quite valuable in this case, they are not the ideal callback facility. Facilities for callbacks are one of the more requested features in Java, and will perhaps be added to the language at a later time.

Day 19

Introduction to JavaScript

As you begin to integrate your Visual J++ applets into your HTML documents you will probably find that it would be useful if you could dynamically communicate between your applet and the other HTML components on the page. For example, you might want to have the user enter information into an HTML form and then have this information passed to your applet for processing.

This type of communication can be accomplished through scripting. There are currently two popular scripting languages available: JavaScript and VBScript. Today, you will learn the basics of JavaScript. VBScript will be introduced tomorrow, and then on the last day, you will learn how to use both scripting languages to communicate between a script, an applet, and an ActiveX component.

What Is JavaScript?

Although JavaScript is similar to Java, it is not the same. Originally called LiveScript, JavaScript was designed by Netscape to be a scripting language that can be embedded into HTML files. It is not compiled, but instead is interpreted by the browser. Unlike Java, which is first converted to easy-to-compile byte codes, JavaScript is read by the browser as source code. This makes it easy for you to learn JavaScript by example because you can see how others are using JavaScript in their pages.

This chapter will present the JavaScript programming language so that you can successfully implement JavaScript into your HTML files.

A Simple Example

We will first start with a simple example that shows you the JavaScript language and gives you an idea of some of the things that are possible. The following program will prompt the user for his or her name and then display a short message using the name that was entered. You can enter this program using a simple text editor and then view the file with a JavaScript capable Web browser, such as Internet Explorer or Netscape Navigator.

```
<HTML><HEAD>
<TITLE>A JavaScript Example</TITLE>
<SCRIPT LANGUAGE="JavaScript">
var name = window.prompt("Hello! What is your name?","");
document.write("Hello " + name + "! I hope you like JavaScript!");
</SCRIPT>
</HEAD>
<BODY>
</BODY>
</HTML>
```

Figure 19.1 shows the input prompt while Figure 19.2 shows the output to the screen after entering your name.

This example displays a prompt with the window.prompt method. The value obtained is stored in a variable called name. The variable is then combined with other strings and displayed in the browser's window using the document.write method.

Now that you have seen a brief glimpse of the functionality available through JavaScript, you will continue with a tutorial of the language itself.

Figure 19.1.

A JavaScript example before entering a name.

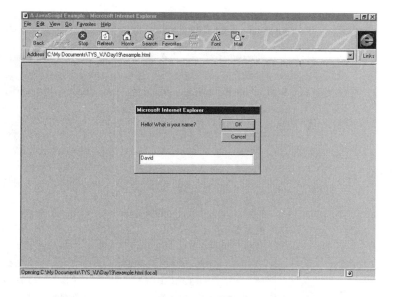

Figure 19.2.

A JavaScript example after entering a name.

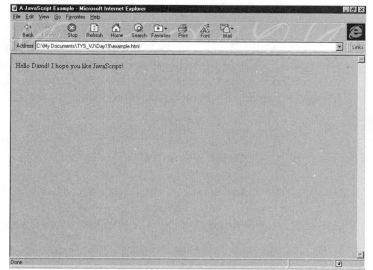

The SCRIPT Tag

The `<SCRIPT>`...`</SCRIPT>` pair of tags is what tells the browser that a script is enclosed in an HTML document. The `<SCRIPT>` tags can appear either in the `<HEAD>` or `<BODY>` section of the HTML file. The advantage of placing it in the `<HEAD>` section is that it will be loaded and ready before the rest of the document loads.

The only attribute currently defined for the `<SCRIPT>` tag is `LANGUAGE=`. This attribute is used to specify the scripting language. There are currently two values defined: JavaScript and VBScript. For your JavaScript programs you should use the following syntax:

```
<SCRIPT LANGUAGE="JavaScript">
// INSERT ALL JavaScript HERE
</SCRIPT>
```

NOTE

You might have noticed that the comment is not enclosed in normal `<--` and `-->` tags for HTML comments. This is because JavaScript supports the same style comments as C and Java. Both the single line `//` syntax and the `/*...*/` syntax for multiple lines are supported.

The difference in the syntax for comments between HTML and JavaScript allows you to hide the JavaScript code inside an HTML comment. This will hide the JavaScript from older browsers that don't support it, such as the following example:

```
<SCRIPT LANGUAGE="JavaScript">
<!-- From here the JavaScript code is hidden
// INSERT ALL JavaScript HERE
// this is where the hiding ends -->
</SCRIPT>
```

The `//` is necessary on the last line of the script so that the browser will not try to interpret the line as JavaScript code. The examples in this chapter will not include the JavaScript hiding feature; this simply helps make the code a little more readable.

Data Types

Unlike C++ or Java, JavaScript is a loosely typed language. This means that you do not have to specify a data type when a variable is declared. The data types are automatically converted to the appropriate type as necessary.

Consider the following example:

```
<HTML><HEAD>
<TITLE>A Data Type Example</TITLE>
<SCRIPT LANGUAGE="JavaScript">
var fruit = 'apples';
var numfruit = 12;
numfruit = numfruit + 20;
var temp = "There are " + numfruit + " " + fruit + ".";
document.write(temp);
</SCRIPT>
</HEAD>
<BODY>
</BODY>
</HTML>
```

JavaScript-enabled browsers will correctly handle the preceding example with the following output:

```
There are 32 apples.
```

The JavaScript interpreter will treat the numfruit variable as an integer when 20 is added and then as a string when it is combined into the temp variable.

Variables

As you have seen in the examples so far, JavaScript supports the use of variables.

NOTE A JavaScript variable must start with a letter or an underscore. A number cannot be used as the first character of a variable name, but can be used after the first character. JavaScript is case-sensitive.

There are two different scopes available for variables: global and local. A global variable can be accessed anywhere in the application (HTML file). A local variable can only be accessed in the current function. Global variables are simply declared as follows:

```
x = 0;
```

A local variable is declared inside a function with the var keyword, for example:

```
var x = 0;
```

A global variable may use the var statement as well, but it is not necessary.

Literals

Literals are values in a program that don't change; they are constant. In JavaScript there isn't a CONST type, such as in Visual Basic and C, that can be used to represent some constant value. In JavaScript, this is done by simply using a variable. JavaScript literals can be broken into four categories: integers, floating points, Booleans, and strings. Each of these will be discussed in the following sections.

Integers

Integers in JavaScript are represented as follows:

- Base 10—Integers can be represented in base 10 simply by expressing the number without a leading 0.
- Octal—Integers can be expressed in octal by prefixing with a 0.
- Hexadecimal—Integers can be expressed in hex by prefixing with a 0x.

Floating Point

A floating point literal is comprised of the following parts:

- A decimal integer
- A decimal point (.)
- A fractional integer
- An exponent

In order to be classified as a floating point literal, as opposed to an integer, there must be at least one digit followed by either a decimal point or e (or E). Examples of floating point literals are

- `9.87`
- `-0.85e4`
- `.98E-3`

Boolean

The Boolean literal is used to indicate a true or false condition. There are two values:

- `true`
- `false`

String

A string literal is represented by zero or more characters enclosed in either single or double quotes (they must match at both ends!). The following are examples of string literals:

- ☐ `"the cat ran up the tree"`
- ☐ `"the cog barked"`
- ☐ `"100"`

WARNING

> In C, C++, and Java the single quote is used to indicate a single character. This is NOT the case in JavaScript, where the single quote and double quote can be used interchangeably to represent a string of characters.

JavaScript supports several special characters that can be inside a string. These are as follows:

- ☐ `\b` indicates a backspace.
- ☐ `\f` indicates a form feed.
- ☐ `\n` indicates a new line character.
- ☐ `\r` indicates a carriage return.
- ☐ `\t` indicates a tab character.
- ☐ `\"` indicates a double quote.

Expressions

A set of literals, variables, and/or operators that evaluate to a single value is an expression. The single value can be either a string, a number, or a Boolean value. There are essentially three types of expressions in JavaScript:

- ☐ Arithmetic
- ☐ String
- ☐ Logical

Arithmetic Expressions

Arithmetic expressions evaluate to a number. For example:

(3 + 4) * (84.5 / 3) would evaluate to 197.1666666667

19

String Expressions

String expressions evaluate to a string. For example:

```
"The dog barked " + barktone + "!"
```

might evaluate to The dog barked ferociously!.

Logical Expressions

Logical expressions evaluate to a Boolean. For example:

```
temp > 32
```

might evaluate to false.

JavaScript supports a conditional expression as well. The syntax for this is

```
(condition) ? valTrue : valFalse
```

If *condition* evaluates to true, the expression evaluates to *valTrue*; if false, the expression
evaluates to *valFalse*. Consider the following example:

```
state = (temp > 32) ? "liquid" : "solid"
```

In this example, the variable state would be assigned the value of liquid if the variable temp
was greater than 32. Otherwise, the value of state would be set to solid.

Operators

Like most programming languages, JavaScript provides an array of operators for your use.
The operators available in JavaScript can be grouped into the following major categories:

- Assignment
- Comparison
- Arithmetic
- String
- Logical
- Bitwise

Assignment Operators

The assignment operator is the equal sign, =, which assigns the value of the right operand to
the left operand. In addition, JavaScript supports several shortcut operators as follows:

☐ x += y means x = x + y

☐ x -= y means x = x - y

☐ x *= y means x = x * y

☐ x /= y means x = x / y

☐ x %= y means x = x % y

There are also some shortcut bitwise operators:

☐ x <<= y means x = x << y

☐ x >>= y means x = x >> y

☐ x >>>= y means x = x >>> y

☐ x &= y means x = x & y

☐ x ^= y means x = x ^ y

☐ x ¦= y means x = x ¦ y

Comparison Operators

The purpose of a comparison operator is to compare two operands and return true or false based on the comparison. The following comparison operators are supported by JavaScript:

☐ ==   Returns true if the operands are equal

☐ !=   Returns true if the operands are not equal

☐ >   Returns true if the left operand is greater than the right operand

☐ >=   Returns true if the left operand is greater than or equal to the right operand

☐ <   Returns true if the left operand is less than the right operand

☐ <=   Returns true if the left operand is less than or equal to the right operand

19

Arithmetic Operators

In addition to the standard operators (+, -, *, /) for addition, subtraction, multiplication, and division, JavaScript supports the following additional arithmetic operators:

☐ var1 % var2   The Modulus operator returns the remainder of the integer division of var1 by var2.

☐ -   The unary negation operator simply negates its operand.

☐ var++   The increment operator will add one to var. This can also be represented by ++var.

☐ var--   The decrement operator will subtract one from var. This can also be represented by --var.

NOTE

> If you are assigning the result of an increment or decrement to another variable, such as y = x++, there are different results, depending upon whether the ++ or -- appears before or after the variable name (x in this case). If the ++ or -- is used before x (prescript) then x would be incremented or decremented before the value of x is assigned to y. If the ++ or -- is after x (postscript), the value of x is assigned to y before it is incremented or decremented.

String Operator

When used with a string, the + operator becomes the concatenation operator and will simply combine the two strings. For example,

```
"abc" + "xyz"
```

will evaluate to abcxyz.

Logical Operators

JavaScript supports the following logical operators:

- [ ] *expr1* && *expr2*   The logical AND operator will return true if both *expr1* and *expr2* are true.

- [ ] *expr1* ¦¦ *expr2*   The logical OR operator will return true if either *expr1* or *expr2* are true. Only if both are false will false be returned.

- [ ] !*expr*   The logical NOT operator negates *expr*. It causes *expr* to become false if it was true and true if it was false.

Bitwise Operators

For bitwise operations, the values are first converted to 32-bit integers and then evaluated bit by bit. The following operators are supported:

- [ ] & The bitwise AND operator compares each bit and returns a 1 if both bits are 1.

- [ ] ¦ The bitwise OR operator compares each bit and returns a 1 if either of the bits is 1.

- [ ] ^ The bitwise XOR operator compares each bit and returns a 1 if only one of the bits is 1.

There are also several bitwise shift operators available. These are also converted to 32-bits for the shift operation. They are converted to the type of the left operand when complete. The bitwise shift operators are as follows:

- □   `<<`   The left shift operator will shift the left operand the right operand number of bits to the left. For example, `4<<2` will become `16` (`100` becomes `10000`). Bits shifted off to the left are discarded and zeros appear on the right in their place.

- □   `>>`   The right shift operator will shift the left operand the right operand number of bits to the right. For example, `16>>2` will become `4` (`10000` becomes `100`). Bits shifted off to the right are discarded. The sign of the left operator is preserved.

- □   `>>>`   The zero-fill right shift operator will shift the left operand the right operand number of bits to the right. The sign bit will be shifted in from the left (unlike the >> operator). Bits shifted off to the right are discarded. For example, `8>>>2` will become `1073741822` because the sign bit becomes part of the number. Of course >>> and >> will yield the same result for positive numbers.

Statements

The statements that are available in JavaScript can be grouped into the following categories:

- □ Conditional
- □ Loop
- □ Object Manipulation

Conditional Statements

Conditional statements provide the ability for a program to make a decision and perform specific actions based on the result of that decision. JavaScript provides this support through the if...else statement.

if...else

The if...else statement allows you to check for a certain condition and execute statements based on that condition. The optional else statement allows you to specify a set of statements to execute if the condition is not true.

```
if (condition) {
   statements for true condition }
else {
   statements for false condition}
```

The following is an example:

```
if (x == 10) {
   document.write("x is equal to 10, setting x=0.");
   x = 0; }
else
   document.write("x is not equal to 10.");
```

> **NOTE**
>
> The { and } characters are used to separate blocks of code, just like in C, C++, or Java. For example, notice that the { and } were used for the true condition in the preceding example because there were two lines of statements. The false condition is only a one line statement so the { and } are not necessary.

Loop Statements

Loop statements provide a means for looping through a section of code until an expression evaluates to true. JavaScript provides two types of loop statements:

- ☐ for loop
- ☐ while loop

for...

The for loop will set an initial expression, *initExpr*, then loop through a section of JavaScript statements as long as a *condition* expression evaluates to true. Each time through the loop the expression *incrExpr* is executed.

```
for (initExpr; condition; incrExpr) {
// statements to execute while looping
}
```

The following is an example:

```
for (x=1; x<=10; x++){
y = x * 25;
document.write("x="+ x + " y=" + y + "<BR>");
}
```

The preceding example will loop through the code until x is greater than 10. The output can be seen in Figure 19.3.

Figure 19.3.

A for *loop example.*

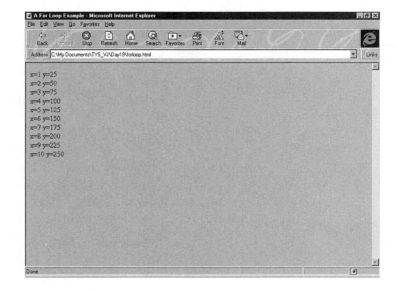

while...

The while loop will continue as long as a specified *condition* evaluates to true.

SYNTAX

```
while (condition) {
//  statement to execute while looping;
}
```

The following is an example:

```
x = 1;
while (x <= 10) {
y = x * 25;
document.write("x="+ x + " y=" + y + "<BR>");
x++;
}
```

The preceding example will produce the same result as the for loop example in Figure 19.3.

break

The break statement can be used to terminate the execution of a for or while loop. The program flow will continue at the statement following the end of the loop.

```
break;
```

The following is an example:

The following example will loop until x is greater than or equal to 100. However, if the loop is entered with a value less than 50 then the loop will terminate and execution will continue after the loop.

```
while (x < 100) {
   if (x < 50) break;
   x++;
}
```

continue

The continue statement is similar to the break statement except that execution is terminated and restarted at the beginning of the loop. For a while loop, control is returned to the *condition*. For a for loop, control is returned to the *incrExpr*.

```
continue;
```

The following is an example:

The following example will increment x from 0 to 5, skip to 8, and continue incrementing to 10.

```
x = 0;
while (x <= 10) {
   document.write("The value of x is " + x + "<BR>");
   if (x == 5) {
      x = 8;
      continue;
   }
   x++;
}
```

Object Manipulation Statements

JavaScript includes several statements that are designed to work with objects.

for...in

The for...in statement is used to loop through all the properties of an object. The variable can be any arbitrary variable name that you desire. It is simply needed to give you something to refer to as you use the property in statements inside the loop. The following example should help in understanding this statement.

NOTE

Microsoft Internet Explorer 3.0 does not properly support the for...in statement. The following example will only work in Netscape Navigator 3.0.

SYNTAX

```
for (variable in object) {
//  statements
    }
```

The following example will cycle through all of the properties of the Window object and print the name of each property. The output is shown in Figure 19.4.

```
<HTML><HEAD>
<TITLE>A For In Example</TITLE>
<SCRIPT LANGUAGE="JavaScript">
document.write("The properties of the Window object are: <BR>");
for (var x in window){
    document.write(x + "<BR>");
}
</SCRIPT>
</HEAD>
<BODY>
</BODY>
</HTML>
```

Figure 19.4.

Output from the for...in *example.*

19

new

The new variable is used to create a new instance of an object.

SYNTAX

```
objectvar = new objecttype ( param1 [, param2] … [,paramN] )
```

The following example will create an object called person that will have the properties of firstname, lastname, age, and sex. Note that the this keyword is used to refer to the object in the person function. Then, two instances of person will be created using the new statement.

```
<HTML><HEAD>
<TITLE>A New Example</TITLE>
<SCRIPT LANGUAGE="JavaScript">
function person(firstname, lastname, age, sex){
    this.firstname = firstname;
    this.lastname = lastname;
    this.age = age;
    this.sex = sex;
}
person1= new person("Logan", "Blankenbeckler", "1", "Male");
person2= new person("Kimberly", "Blankenbeckler", "27", "Female");
document.write("The first person's name is ", person1.firstname + ". <BR>");
document.write("The second person's name is ", person2.firstname + ".");
</SCRIPT>
</HEAD>
<BODY>
</BODY>
</HTML>
```

this

The this keyword is used to refer to the current object. The calling object is generally the current object in a method or function.

SYNTAX

```
this[.property]
```

See the previous example for new for a demonstration of this.

with

The with statement is used to set the default object for a series of statements. The properties can then be referred to without using the parent object.

SYNTAX

```
with(object){
    statements;
}
```

The following example shows the use of the with statement to set the default object to document so that the write method can be used without having to refer to the document object itself, such as document.write.

```
<HTML><HEAD>
<TITLE>A With Example</TITLE>
```

```
<SCRIPT LANGUAGE="JavaScript">
with (document) {
   write("This is an example of the things that can be done <BR>");
   write("with the <B>with</B> statement.<P>");
   write("This can really save some typing!");
}
</SCRIPT>
</HEAD>
<BODY>
</BODY>
</HTML>
```

Functions

JavaScript supports the use of functions. Although not necessary, a function may have one or more parameters and one return value. Because JavaScript is a loosely typed language, it is not necessary to define parameter or return types for a JavaScript function. In addition, a function may be a property of an object, in which case it will act as a method for that object.

SYNTAX

```
function fnName([param1][,param2]…[,paramN]){
   // function statements;
}
```

The following example shows how to create and use a function as a member of an object. The printStats function is created as a method of the object person.

```
<HTML><HEAD>
<TITLE>A Function Example</TITLE>
<SCRIPT LANGUAGE="JavaScript">
function person(firstname, lastname, age, sex){
   this.firstname = firstname;
   this.lastname = lastname;
   this.age = age;
   this.sex = sex;
   this.printStats = printStats;    //makes printStats a method of person
}
function printStats(){
   document.write(this.firstname + " " + this.lastname + "'s stats are:<BR>");
   document.write("Age: " + this.age + "<BR>");
   document.write("Sex: " + this.sex + "<BR>");
}
person1= new person("David", "Blankenbeckler", "27", "Male");
person2= new person("Kimberly", "Blankenbeckler", "27", "Female");
person1.printStats();
</SCRIPT>
</HEAD>
<BODY>
</BODY>
</HTML>
```

19

Built-in Functions

JavaScript contains several built-in functions. These functions are built into the language itself and are not a part of an object. The built-in functions are

☐ eval

☐ parseInt

☐ parseFloat

eval

The eval function is used to evaluate expressions or statements. Any expression, statement, or object property can be evaluated. This is useful for evaluating expressions that are entered by the user (otherwise it could be evaluated directly).

```
returnval = eval( any legal Java expressions or statements )
```

The following is an example:

```
<HTML><HEAD>
<TITLE>An Eval Example</TITLE>
<SCRIPT LANGUAGE="JavaScript">
var string = "10 + Math.sqrt(64)";
document.write(string + " = " + eval(string));
</SCRIPT>
</HEAD>
<BODY>
</BODY>
</HTML>
```

parseInt

The parseInt function takes a string value and attempts to convert it to an integer of the specified base. The base is specified by an optional second parameter. This function can be used to convert different bases back to base 10 or to ensure that character entered data is converted to integer before being used in calculations. In the case of bad input data, the parseInt function will read and convert a string until the point where it finds non-numeric characters. In addition, parseInt will truncate floating point numbers.

```
parseInt(string [, radix]);
```

The following is an example:

```
<HTML><HEAD>
<TITLE>An parseInt Example</TITLE>
<SCRIPT LANGUAGE="JavaScript">
document.write("Converting 0xC hex to base-10: " + parseInt(0xC, 10) + "<BR>");
document.write("Converting 1100 binary to base-10: " + parseInt(1100, 2));
</SCRIPT>
```

19

```
</HEAD>
<BODY>
</BODY>
</HTML>
```

parseFloat

This built-in function is similar to the parseInt function except that it returns a floating-point representation of string input.

SYNTAX

```
parseFloat(string);
```

The following example shows how parseFloat works for several different types of strings. The output is shown in Figure 19.5.

```
<HTML><HEAD>
<TITLE>An parseFloat Example</TITLE>
<SCRIPT LANGUAGE="JavaScript">
document.write("This script will show how different strings ");
document.write("are converted using parseFloat.<BR>");
document.write(parseFloat("137") + "<BR>");
document.write(parseFloat("137abc") + "<BR>");
document.write(parseFloat("abc137") + "<BR>");
document.write(parseFloat("1abc37") + "<BR>");
</SCRIPT>
</HEAD>
<BODY>
</BODY>
</HTML>
```

Figure 19.5.

Screen output from the parseFloat *example.*

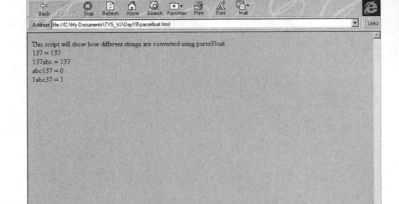

Arrays

Although there is no explicit support for arrays, Netscape published a method that allows you to create your own. This is accomplished by creating a function that initializes the array as follows:

```
function InitArray(numElements) {
   this.length = numElements;
   for (var x = 1; x <= numElements; x++) {
       this[x] = 0 }
   return this;
}
```

This will create an array of the specified size and fill it with zero. Note that the first element is the length of the array and should not be used.

To create an array, you simply do the following:

```
myArray = new InitArray(10);
```

This will create myArray[1] through myArray[10], with each element containing a zero. The array can be populated with data as follows:

```
myArray[1] = "South Carolina";
myArray[2] = "Oregon";
```

The following is a full example:

```
<HTML><HEAD>
<TITLE>An Array Example</TITLE>
<SCRIPT LANGUAGE="JavaScript">
function InitArray(numElements) {
   this.length = numElements;
   for (var x = 1; x <= numElements; x++) {
       this[x] = 0 }
   return this;
}
myArray = new InitArray(10);
myArray[1] = "South Carolina";
myArray[2] = "Oregon";
document.write(myArray[1] + "<BR>");
document.write(myArray[2] + "<BR>");
</SCRIPT>
</HEAD>
<BODY>
</BODY>
</HTML>
```

The output should appear as follows:

```
South Carolina
Oregon
```

Events

JavaScript is an event-driven language. An event-driven program can respond to certain events, such as a mouse click or the loading of a document. An event can cause a section of code to execute (known as an event handler) to allow the program to respond appropriately.

Event Handlers

The program that responds to an event is called an event handler. The event handler is specified as an attribute of an HTML tag:

```
<tagName eventHandler="JavaScript Code or Function">
```

The following example will call the `CheckAge()` function when the value of the text field is changed.

```
<INPUT TYPE=TEXT NAME="AGE" onChange="CheckAge()">
```

The `eventHandler` code does not have to be a function. It can be JavaScript statements separated by semicolons. However, for purposes of modularity and code cleanliness, it is typically a separate function.

The following list describes the event handlers available in JavaScript:

- ☐ `onBlur`—occurs when input focus is removed from form element
- ☐ `onClick`—occurs when user clicks on form element or link
- ☐ `onChange`—occurs when text, text area, or select element value is changed
- ☐ `onFocus`—occurs when form element gets the focus
- ☐ `onLoad`—occurs when the page is loaded
- ☐ `onMouseOver`—occurs when the mouse is moved over a link or anchor
- ☐ `onSelect`—occurs when the user selects a form element's input field
- ☐ `onSubmit`—occurs when the user submits a form
- ☐ `onUnload`—occurs when the user exits a page

The following example shows a simple event handler script that will validate a value entered into a text field. The user's age is entered in the field and the event handler will check to be sure that a valid age was entered. If not, a message will appear asking the user to re-enter the value. The event handler is called when the AGE field is changed and the focus is moved to another field. The screen output is shown in Figure 19.6.

```
<HTML>
<HEAD>
<TITLE>An Event Handler Example</TITLE>
```

19

```
<SCRIPT LANGUAGE="JavaScript">
function CheckAge(form) {
   if ((form.age.value < 0) || (form.age.value > 120)) {
      alert("Please enter your real age!");
      form.age.value = 0;
   }
}
</SCRIPT>
</HEAD>
<BODY>
<FORM NAME="SURVEY">
Please enter your name and age:<BR>
First<INPUT TYPE=TEXT NAME="FNAME" MAXLENGTH=15 SIZE=10>
MI<INPUT TYPE=TEXT NAME="MI" MAXLENGTH=1 SIZE=1>
Last<INPUT TYPE=TEXT NAME="LNAME" MAXLENGTH=20 SIZE=15><BR><BR>
Age<INPUT TYPE=TEXT NAME="AGE" MAXLENGTH=3 SIZE=2 onChange="CheckAge(SURVEY)">
<P>
Please select your favorite season of the year:<BR>
Spring<INPUT TYPE=RADIO NAME="SEASON" VALUE="Spring">
Summer<INPUT TYPE=RADIO NAME="SEASON" VALUE="Summer">
Fall  <INPUT TYPE=RADIO NAME="SEASON" VALUE="Fall">
Winter<INPUT TYPE=RADIO NAME="SEASON" VALUE="Winter">
<P>
Please check all of the outdoor activities that you enjoy:<BR>
Hiking<INPUT TYPE=CHECKBOX NAME="ACT" VALUE="Hiking">
Skiing<INPUT TYPE=CHECKBOX NAME="ACT" VALUE="Sking">
Water Sports<INPUT TYPE=CHECKBOX NAME="ACT" VALUE="Water">
Cycling<INPUT TYPE=CHECKBOX NAME="ACT" VALUE="Cycling">
<P>
<INPUT TYPE=SUBMIT><INPUT TYPE=RESET>
</FORM>
</BODY>
</HTML>
```

Figure 19.6.

An event handler example.

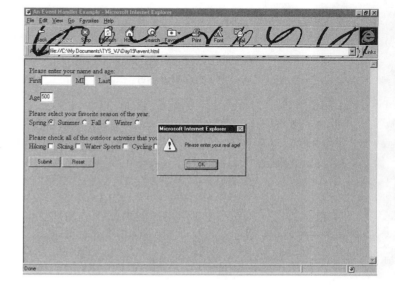

JavaScript Objects

JavaScript is an object-based language. It is not an object-oriented programming language primarily because it does not support classes or inheritance. This section will present the objects available for your JavaScript programs.

In the JavaScript object hierarchy, the descendant objects are actually properties of the parent object. Referring to the previous example for the event handler, the form, named SURVEY, would be a property of the document object; the text field, named AGE, would be a property of the form. To reference the value of AGE, you could use the following:

```
document.SURVEY.AGE.value
```

Objects in JavaScript have properties, methods, and event handlers associated with them. For example, the Document object has a title property. This property reflects the contents of the <TITLE> tag for the document. In addition, you have seen the Document.write method used in many of the examples. This method is used to output text to the document.

Objects can also have event handlers. For example, the Link object has two event handlers: onClick and onMouseOver. The onClick event handler is invoked when a link object is clicked with the mouse, while the onMouseOver is invoked when the mouse pointer passes over the link.

You will not cover all of the details of JavaScript objects today. However, each of the properties, methods, and event handlers for each JavaScript object are presented in Appendix E, "JavaScript Language Reference," for your reference.

Summary

This chapter provided a brief introduction to the JavaScript language. In addition, this chapter will serve as a useful reference during the development of your JavaScript applications.

Although this chapter, combined with Appendix E, provides a complete, concise reference to the JavaScript language, the subject is broad enough that entire books have been written about it. One useful book is *Teach Yourself JavaScript 1.1 in a Week* by Arman Danesh from Sams.net Publishing.

Because JavaScript is still a new and changing language, the reader should also refer to Netscape's Web site for the latest information concerning the language. Netscape is located at the following address:

```
http://www.netscape.com/
```

19

Tomorrow, you will learn about another choice for scripting, VBScript. On Day 21, "Integrating Applets and ActiveX Controls with Scripting," you will learn how to use both scripting languages to control both applets and ActiveX components.

Q&A

Q Why would I want to use a script when I can build all of the functionality I need into an applet?

A JavaScript provides the capability for you to easily customize your Web applications based on more generically designed applets and ActiveX controls. For example, you might design an applet to render a graphical image based on user input that is received through HTML form controls and ActiveX controls. Through the use of a scripting language, such as JavaScript or VBScript, you can communicate between these various components. Scripting is also very powerful when used simply for form validation, as in the example shown in Figure 19.6.

Q I already know Visual Basic and would rather just use VBScript. What are the advantages of using JavaScript?

A JavaScript has one major advantage over VBScript in that it is supported by a large majority of Web browsers, which primarily consists of Netscape Navigator 3.0 and Microsoft Internet Explorer 3.0. VBScript, on the other hand, is currently only supported by Microsoft's browser and does not appear to be in Netscape's plans for future versions.

Q I did not notice any mention of error handling in JavaScript. What error handling capabilities does JavaScript have?

A JavaScript does not have any built-in error handling capabilities like Visual C++ or Java. One method of preventing errors for numeric calculations might be the `parseInt` and `parseFloat` built-in functions. These functions can be used to ensure that user-entered data is valid before attempting a calculation.

Day 20

Introduction to VBScript

What Is VBScript?

Yesterday you learned how to use JavaScript in your Web pages. We also mentioned another choice for writing scripts for your HTML documents: VBScript. The VBScript language works in much the same manner as JavaScript. The code is written and saved in text format in your HTML documents. When the browser sees VBScript code, it is automatically interpreted and run.

Many programmers are familiar with Microsoft's Visual Basic programming language. This is one of the key benefits that VBScript has over JavaScript. VBScript is a subset of the Visual Basic programming language. It is fully upward compatible with Visual Basic.

VBScript is currently only supported by Microsoft Internet Explorer. This is a major drawback to VBScript because Netscape has such a large user base. Supposedly, however, other browser vendors are planning to license VBScript from Microsoft and incorporate it into their browsers soon.

Today you will learn how to successfully implement the VBScript programming language into your HTML files. This chapter should also serve as a convenient reference to the VBScript language in your future programming projects.

A Simple Example

First start with a simple example to show you the VBScript language and give you an idea of some of the things that are possible. The following program will prompt the user for his or her name and then display a short message using the name that was entered:

```
<HTML><HEAD>
<TITLE>A VBScript Example</TITLE>
<SCRIPT LANGUAGE="VBScript">
dim name
name = InputBox("Hello! What is your name?")
Document.Write "Hello " & name & "! I hope you like VBScript!"
</SCRIPT>
</HEAD>
<BODY>
</BODY>
</HTML>
```

Figure 20.1 shows the input prompt. Figure 20.2 shows the output to the screen after the name was entered.

NOTE

You might notice that a lot of the examples presented today are the same as the ones presented yesterday while you were learning JavaScript. This will help you to better compare and contrast the two languages.

The preceding example displays a prompt with the InputBox function. The value obtained is stored in a variable called name. The variable is then combined with other text and displayed in the browser's window using the Document.Write method.

Now that you have seen a little of the functionality available through VBScript, you will continue with a tutorial of the language itself.

Differences Between VBScript and Visual Basic

As mentioned, VBScript is a subset of Visual Basic. There might be readers who are very familiar with Visual Basic and simply need to know what Visual Basic features are not available in VBScript. This section will briefly discuss the major differences between the two. Readers who are unfamiliar with Visual Basic might want to skip ahead to the next section titled "The <SCRIPT> Tag."

Figure 20.1.

A simple VBScript example (before entering a name).

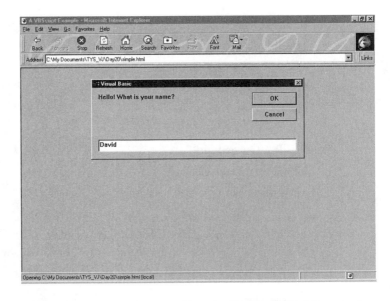

Figure 20.2.

A simple VBScript example (after entering a name).

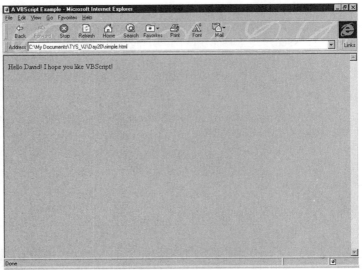

The following list identifies the most significant features of Visual Basic that are not supported by VBScript:

☐ VBScript only supports the Variant data type.

☐ The Const statement.

☐ The Like operator.

- ☐ The `On Error GoTo` statement.
- ☐ The `Resume` and `Resume Next` statements.
- ☐ The `End` and `Stop` statements.
- ☐ The `DoEvents` function.
- ☐ The `Date` and `Time` statements.
- ☐ The `Timer` function
- ☐ All file I/O capability.
- ☐ All the financial functions.
- ☐ Array lower bound other than zero.

As you might notice, most of the exclusions from VBScript were because they didn't make sense in an HTML scripting language or they violated the security features necessary for Web use. For example, the file I/O capabilities of Visual Basic would clearly cause security violations with Web applications.

The `<SCRIPT>` Tag

The `<SCRIPT>`...`</SCRIPT>` pair of tags tell the browser that a script is enclosed. The `<SCRIPT>` tags can appear either in the `<HEAD>` or `<BODY>` section of the HTML file. The advantage of placing it in the `<HEAD>` section is that it will be loaded and ready before the rest of the document loads.

The only attribute currently defined for the `<SCRIPT>` tag is `LANGUAGE=`. This attribute is used to specify the scripting language. There are currently two values defined: JavaScript and VBScript. The following syntax should be used for your VBScript applications:

```
<SCRIPT LANGUAGE="VBScript">
' INSERT ALL VBScript HERE
</SCRIPT>
```

NOTE

You might have noticed that the comment is not enclosed in normal `<--` and `-->` tags for HTML comments. This is because VBScript supports the same style comments as Visual Basic. A single apostrophe or the `Rem` statement is used to indicate a comment in VBScript (and Visual Basic).

The difference in commenting syntax between HTML and VBScript allows you to hide the VBScript code inside an HTML comment. This will hide the VBScript from older browsers that don't support it, for example:

```
<SCRIPT LANGUAGE="VBScript">
<!-- From here the VBScript code is hidden
' INSERT ALL VBScript HERE
' this is where the hiding ends
-->
</SCRIPT>
```

The examples in this chapter will not include the script hiding feature; this will help make the code a little more readable. However, you should always include this in your code so that non–VBScript-enabled browsers can be handled properly.

Data Types

Like JavaScript, VBScript is a loosely typed language. This means that you do not have to specify a data type when a variable is declared. All variables are of type `Variant`. The `Variant` is automatically converted to the following subtypes as necessary:

- ☐ `Boolean`—true or false
- ☐ `Byte`—integer from 0 to 255
- ☐ `Date`—represents a date or time from Jan. 1, 100 to Dec. 31, 9999.
- ☐ `Double`—a floating-point number from +/- 4.94065645841247E-324 to +/- 1.79769313486232E308
- ☐ `Empty`—indicates that a value has not been assigned yet
- ☐ `Error`—indicates an error number
- ☐ `Integer`—an integer from -32768 to 32767
- ☐ `Long`—an integer from -2,147,483,648 to 2,147,483,647
- ☐ `Null`—purposefully set to no valid data
- ☐ `Object`—an object
- ☐ `Single`—a floating point number from +/- 1.401298E-45 to +/- 3.402823E38.
- ☐ `String`—a string

As mentioned, VBScript automatically converts a `Variant` to the appropriate subtype as needed. Consider the following example:

```
<HTML><HEAD>
<TITLE>A Data Type Example</TITLE>
<SCRIPT LANGUAGE="VBScript">
dim fruit
dim numfruit
dim temp
fruit = "apples"
numfruit = 12
numfruit = numfruit + 20
temp = "There are " & numfruit & " " & fruit & "."
```

20

```
Document.Write temp
</SCRIPT>
</HEAD>
<BODY>
</BODY>
</HTML>
```

VBScript-enabled browsers will correctly handle the preceding example with the following output:

```
There are 32 apples.
```

The VBScript interpreter will treat the numfruit variable as an integer when 20 is added and then as a string when it is combined into the temp variable.

Variables

As you have seen in the examples so far, VBScript supports the use of variables. A VBScript variable must start with a letter. A number cannot be used as the first character of a variable name, but can be used after the first character. VBScript is not case-sensitive. A variable is declared in VBScript with the Dim statement, such as the following example:

```
Dim myvariable
```

Multiple variables can be declared together if you separate each variable name by a comma, as shown in the following example:

```
Dim myvariable, x, y, AVeryLongVariableNameWithANumberInIt8
```

NOTE

Like Visual Basic, VBScript supports the use of variables without first declaring them with Dim. However, this is generally not considered good programming practice. The Option Explicit statement will force all variables to require declaration with the Dim statement. This statement should simply be placed at the beginning of VBScript code. This will ensure that the variable names you have chosen are spelled consistently throughout your program because an error message will appear the first time you try to run the script if there are any undeclared variables being used.

There are two scopes available for variables: global and local. A global variable can be accessed anywhere in the script and lasts for as long as the script is running. A local variable is declared inside a procedure or function and can only be accessed in that procedure or function. In addition, local variables only last as long as you are executing that procedure.

Literals (Constants)

Literals are values in a program that don't change; they are constant. In VBScript, there isn't a CONST statement like in Visual Basic that can be used to represent some constant value. In VBScript, this is done by using a variable.

Expressions

A set of literals, variables, and/or operators that evaluates to a single value is an expression. The single value can be either a string, a number, or a Boolean value. There are essentially four types of expressions in VBScript:

- ☐ Arithmetic
- ☐ String
- ☐ Date
- ☐ Logical

Arithmetic

An expression that evaluates to a number is an arithmetic expression. For example,

```
( 3 + 4 ) * (84.5 / 3)
```

would evaluate to 197.1666666667.

String

An expression can also evaluate to a string. Literal strings are enclosed in double quotes. For example:

```
"The dog barked " & barktone & "!"
```

might evaluate to The dog barked ferociously!.

Date

A date can also be used in an expression. To assign a literal date to a variable, enclose the date in # characters. The variable containing the date can then be used in a date expression. For example, the following code will assign a date to a variable and then use the variable in an expression to add 5 days.

```
Dim thisDay
thisDay = #8/17/96#
Document.Write "In 5 days it will be " & (thisDay + 5)
```

20

The output from the preceding code is

```
In 5 days it will be 8/22/96
```

This capability, combined with the many date functions in VBScript, make working dates very easy. The VBScript date functions are covered in Appendix F, "VBScript Language Reference."

Logical

VBScript also supports logical expressions. These expressions evaluate to either true or false. They are then typically used with conditional statements. An example of a logical expression is

```
temp > 32
```

This expression might evaluate to true or false, depending on the value of temp.

Arrays

Unlike JavaScript, the VBScript language has direct support for arrays. This section assumes that you already have a basic understanding of arrays.

WARNING

Unlike C, C++, and Java, VBScript uses the parentheses for initializing and accessing an array. In C, C++, and Java the square brackets are used.

Declaring arrays is very similar to declaring other types of variables. To declare in array, you simply use the Dim statement and follow the array name by the upper bound in parentheses. For example, the following line would create an array of 12 elements called monthlySales:

```
Dim monthlySales(11)
```

Notice that 11 is used but there are 12 elements. This is because the first element of an array in VBScript is always zero. The feature of Visual Basic that allows you to declare arrays with a lower bound other than zero is not supported in VBScript.

To access an array element, you use the variable name followed by the element in parentheses. For example, to reference the fifth element you would use the following:

```
monthlySales(4)
```

Multiple dimension arrays are supported in VBScript. Up to 60 dimensions can be used. To declare a multidimensional array, you add an upper bound parameter for each dimension separated by commas. For example, consider the following three-dimensional array declaration:

```
ThreeDCoord(99,99,99)
```

VBScript also supports dynamic arrays with the ReDim statement. In order for an array to be declared as dynamic it must initially be declared without upper bounds, such as empty parentheses. The ReDim statement can then be used to set the upper bounds later in the script. The ReDim statement can be used as often as necessary. Unless the Preserve keyword is used, the contents of the array will be lost after each ReDim. Also, if an array is re-dimensioned to a smaller size with the Preserve keyword, the excess contents will be lost. Consider the following example:

```
Dim monthlySales()
' VBScript code can go here
' Later a ReDim statement is used
ReDim monthlySales(11)
monthlySales(7) = 20000
ReDim Preserve monthlySales(23)
' The monthlySales(7) value is preserved
' and the array is enlarged to 24 elements
ReDim montlySales(35)
' All montlySales contents are lost since Preserve was not used
```

Operators

The operators available in VBScript can be categorized as follows:

- Assignment
- Comparison
- Arithmetic
- String
- Logical
- Bitwise

20

Assignment Operator

The assignment operator is the equal sign, =, which assigns the value of the right operand to the left operand. For example, the following line assigns the value of 3 to the variable x:

```
x = 3
```

Comparison Operators

The purpose of a comparison operator is to compare two operands and return true or false based on the comparison. The following comparison operators are supported by VBScript:

- ☐ =   Returns true if the operands are equal
- ☐ <>   Returns true if the operands are not equal
- ☐ >   Returns true if the left operand is greater than the right operand
- ☐ >=   Returns true if the left operand is greater than or equal to the right operand
- ☐ <   Returns true if the left operand is less than the right operand
- ☐ <=   Returns true if the left operand is less than or equal to the right operand
- ☐ Is   Returns true if the left object is the same as the right object

Arithmetic Operators

In addition to the standard operators (+, -, *, /) for addition, subtraction, multiplication, and division, VBScript supports the following additional arithmetic operators:

num1 \ num2	The integer division operator will divide num1 by num2 and return an integer result.
var1 Mod var2	The Modulus operator returns the remainder of the integer division of var1 by var2.
-num	The unary negation operator simply negates num.
num^exp	The exponentiation operator will raise num to the power of exp.

String Operator

VBScript has a special operator that is used for concatenating (or combining) strings:

- ☐ str1 & str2   The string concatenation operator, &, will combine str1 with str2.

Logical Operators

VBScript supports the following logical operators that return a Boolean value:

- ☐ expr1 And expr2   The logical And operator will return true if both expr1 and expr2 are true.
- ☐ expr1 Or expr2   The logical Or operator will return true if either expr1 or expr2 are true. Only if both are false will false be returned.

☐ Not *expr*   The logical Not operator negates *expr*. It causes *expr* to
                            become false if it was true and true if it was false.

☐ *expr1* Xor *expr2*   The logical Xor operator will return true if either *expr1* or
                            expr2 is true, but not both. If both *expr1* and *expr2* are true,
                            false will be returned.

☐ *expr1* Eqv *expr2*   The equivalence operator will return true if either *expr1* and
                            expr2 are both true or *expr1* and *expr2* are both false.

☐ *expr1* Imp *expr2*   The implication operator will return a value based on the
                            following table:

expr1 Imp	*expr2*	=	result
False Imp	False	=	True
False Imp	True	=	True
True Imp	False	=	False
True Imp	True	=	True
Null Imp	False	=	Null
Null Imp	True	=	True
False Imp	Null	=	True
True Imp	Null	=	Null
Null Imp	Null	=	Null

Bitwise Operators

If two numeric expressions are used with the logical operators previously defined, a bitwise
comparison will be performed. The following operators are supported:

☐ *expr1* And *expr2*   The bitwise And operator compares each bit and returns a 1 if
                            both bits are 1.

☐ *expr1* Or *expr2*   The bitwise Or operator compares each bit and returns a 1 if
                            either of the bits is 1.

☐ *expr1* Xor *expr2*   The bitwise Xor operator compares each bit and returns a 1 if
                            only one of the bits is 1.

☐ Not *expr*   The bitwise Not operator will invert the value of each bit. A 0
                            will become a 1, and a 1 will become a 0.

☐ *expr1* Eqv *expr2*   The bitwise Eqv operator compares each bit and returns a 1 if
                            either both bits are 0 or both are 1.

☐ *expr1* Imp *expr2*   The implication operator will compare each bit and return a
                            value based on the following table when used with numeric
                            expressions:

20

```
expr1 Imp expr2 = result
   0    Imp  0    =    1
   0    Imp  1    =    1
   1    Imp  0    =    0
   1    Imp  1    =    1
```

Statements

The statements that are available in VBScript can be grouped into the following categories:

- ☐ Conditional
- ☐ Loop

Conditional Statements

Conditional statements provide the ability for a program to make a decision and perform specific actions based on the result of that decision. VBScript provides two types of conditional statements:

- ☐ `If...Then...Else`
- ☐ `Select Case`

If...Then...Else

The `If...Then...Else` statement allows you to check for a certain *condition* and execute statements based on that condition. The optional `else` statement allows you to specify a set of statements to execute if *condition* is not true.

SYNTAX

```
If condition Then
'    statements for true condition
Else
'    statements for false condition
End If
```

The `End If` statement is only necessary if there is more than one line of statement following the true or false condition.

The following is an example:

```
If x = 10 Then
   Document.Write "x is equal to 10, setting x = 0."
   x = 0
Else
   Document.Write "x is not equal to 10."
End If
```

Note that the End If statement is not necessary in the following simple comparison:

```
If myVar = True Then yourVar = false
```

Select Case

The Select Case statement is useful when a single condition needs to be checked and there are multiple outcomes based on the result.

```
Select Case expr
    Case n
        ' statements for this case
    Case m
        ' statements for this case
    '… additional case statements as necessary
    [Case Else]
        ' statements for the default case
End Select
```

The following example would evaluate the variable Day and print to the screen the appropriate message:

```
Select Case Day
    Case 0
        Document.Write "Today is Sunday.<BR>"
    Case 1
        Document.Write "Today is Monday.<BR>"
    Case 2
        Document.Write "Today is Tuesday.<BR>"
    Case 3
        Document.Write "Today is Wednesday.<BR>"
    Case 4
        Document.Write "Today is Thursday.<BR>"
    Case 5
        Document.Write "Today is Friday.<BR>"
    Case 6
        Document.Write "Today is Saturday.<BR>"
    Case Else
        Document.Write "ERROR: Invalid value for Day!<BR>"
End Select
```

Loop Statements

Loop statements provide a means for looping through a section of code until an expression evaluates to true. VBScript provides three different types of loop statements:

- [ ] For...Next loop
- [ ] While loop
- [ ] Do loop

For...Next

The For loop will set *var* to *init* then loop through a section of VBScript statements incrementing *var* by 1 before each loop. When *var* equals *final*, the loop executes one final time, the loop ends, and the statement following Next is executed. If *var* is incremented to a value greater than *final*, the loop will also terminate.

If Step is specified, *var* will be incremented (or decremented) by the value of *step* each loop. When *step* is negative, the value of *var* will be decremented by *step* each loop. In this case, when *var* is less than *final*, the loop will terminate.

SYNTAX

An optional Exit For statement can be used to terminate the loop at any time by simply placing one or more Exit For statements inside the loop.

```
For var = init To final [Step step]
' statements to execute while looping
  [Exit For]
Next
```

The following is an example:

```
For x=0 To 10 Step 2
    y = x * 25
    Document.Write "x=" & x & " y=" & y & "<BR>"
Next
```

The preceding example will loop through the code until x is equal to 10. The output can be seen in Figure 20.3.

Figure 20.3.

A For...Next *loop example.*

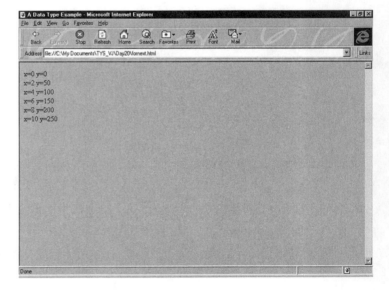

While...Wend

The While loop will continue as long as a specified *condition* evaluates to true. When *condition* no longer evaluates to true, the loop will immediately exit and the statement following Wend will be executed.

```
While condition
' statements to execute while looping
Wend
```

The following is an example:

```
x = 0
While x <= 10
  y = x * 25
  Document.Write "x="& x & " y=" & y & "<BR>"
  x = x + 2
Wend
```

The preceding code will produce the same result as the For loop example in Figure 20.3.

Do...Loop

The Do...Loop provides several different forms, with the differences being in how the loop is exited. The loop can be exited by either a While or an Until condition. In addition, an optional Exit Do can be used either as the sole means of exiting the loop or in combination with While or Until.

A Do While loop will continue to execute as long as a certain *condition* remains true.

A Do Until loop will continue to execute until a certain *condition* is true.

The Do Loop can be used with either the While condition or the Until condition. The syntax of each is shown in the following examples:

```
Do While condition
' statements to execute while looping
[Exit Do]
' statements to execute while looping
Loop
```

```
Do Until condition
' statements to execute while looping
[Exit Do]
' statements to execute while looping
Loop
```

The Until or While keyword can also be placed at the end of the loop. It is simply a matter of taste, but the same result will be obtained as shown in the following example:

```
Do
' statements to execute while looping
Loop [Until¦While]
```

20

The following two Do loop examples show the use of the Do loop using the Until condition (Listing 20.1) and the While condition (Listing 20.2):

TYPE   **Listing 20.1. A Do...Until example.**

```
<HTML><HEAD>
<TITLE>A Do...Until Example</TITLE>
<SCRIPT LANGUAGE="VBScript">
dim x
x = 0
Do
    y = x * 25
    Document.Write "x=" & x & " y=" & y & "<BR>"
    x = x + 2
Loop Until x > 10
</SCRIPT>
</HEAD>
<BODY>
</BODY>
</HTML>
```

TYPE   **Listing 20.2. A Do...While example.**

```
<HTML><HEAD>
<TITLE>A Do...While Example</TITLE>
<SCRIPT LANGUAGE="VBScript">
dim x
x = 0
Do While x <= 10
    y = x * 25
    Document.Write "x=" & x & " y=" & y & "<BR>"
    x = x + 2
Loop
</SCRIPT>
</HEAD>
<BODY>
</BODY>
</HTML>
```

The two preceding examples will produce the same result as the For...Next loop and the While...Wend loop examples in Figure 20.3.

Procedures

A procedure is a set of statements that can be called as needed from your main code or from other procedures. VBScript supports the use of two types of procedures: Sub and Function. A Sub procedure does not have a return value while a Function procedure does.

Both types of procedures can have one or more parameters passed to it. Because VBScript is a loosely typed language, it is not necessary to define parameter or return types for a VBScript procedure.

Because procedures must be defined before they are called, they should always be placed at the beginning of an HTML document in the <HEAD> section.

Sub **Procedure**

The following syntax is used to define a Sub procedure:

```
Sub SubName([param1][,param2]…[,paramN])
    ' sub procedure statements
End Sub
```

In order to call this procedure, you would use the following syntax:

```
SubName [param1][,param2]…[,paramN]
```

The following example will show the use of the Sub procedure by creating a procedure to calculate and display the area of a circle:

```
<HTML><HEAD>
<TITLE>A Sub Procedure Example</TITLE>
<SCRIPT LANGUAGE="VBScript">
Sub PrintAreaOfCircle(radius)
   Document.Write "A circle of radius " & radius & " cm has an area of "
   Document.Write 3.14159 * radius^2
   Document.Write " cm<SUP>2</SUP>.<BR>"
End Sub
' Now we will call the Sub
PrintAreaOfCircle(4)
PrintAreaOfCircle(6)
PrintAreaOfCircle(10.5)
</SCRIPT>
</HEAD>
<BODY>
</BODY>
</HTML>
```

The output from the preceding example is shown in Figure 20.4.

Function **Procedure**

The syntax for a function is very similar to that of a Sub procedure:

```
Function fnName([param1][,param2]...[,paramN])
    ' function statements
    fnName = expr
End Function
```

Figure 20.4.

An example of a Sub *procedure.*

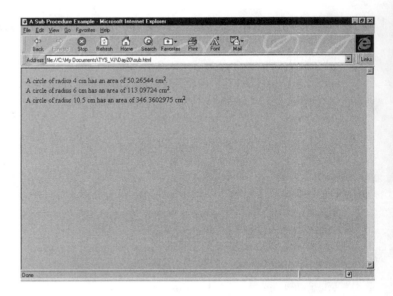

Notice that the return value for a function is given by setting the function name, *fnName*, equal to some value before the end of the function.

The syntax for calling a function is

returnVar = *fnName*([*param1*][,*param2*]…[,*paramN*])

The following example will show the use of the Function procedure by creating a procedure to calculate and display the area of a circle. The output from this example is exactly the same as the output from the Sub example in Figure 20.4.

```
<HTML><HEAD>
<TITLE>A Function Procedure Example</TITLE>
<SCRIPT LANGUAGE="VBScript">
Function AreaOfCircle(radius)
   AreaOfCircle = 3.14159 * radius^2
End Function
' Now we will call the Function three times like before
Document.Write "A circle of radius 4 cm has an area of "
Document.Write AreaOfCircle(4) & " cm<SUP>2</SUP>.<BR>"
Document.Write "A circle of radius 6 cm has an area of "
Document.Write AreaOfCircle(6) & " cm<SUP>2</SUP>.<BR>"
Document.Write "A circle of radius 10.5 cm has an area of "
Document.Write AreaOfCircle(10.5) & " cm<SUP>2</SUP>.<BR>"
</SCRIPT>
</HEAD>
<BODY>
</BODY>
</HTML>
```

Built-in Functions

VBScript contains a wide selection of built-in functions. In order to organize all of these functions, it is useful to categorize them as follows:

- Math
- Dates and time
- String manipulation
- User interface
- Data type (conversions, and so on)

A reference for all of the VBScript built-in functions is included in Appendix F, "VBScript Language Reference."

Events

VBScript is an event-driven language. An event-driven program can respond to certain events, such as a mouse click or the loading of a document. An event can cause a section of code to execute (known as an event handler), to allow the program to respond appropriately.

Event Handlers

The program that responds to an event is called an event handler. The event handler is specified as an attribute of an HTML tag:

```
<tagName eventHandler="VBScript Statement or Procedure">
```

The following example will call the CheckAge Sub when the text field is changed:

```
<INPUT TYPE=TEXT NAME="AGE" onChange="CheckAge">
```

The eventHandler code does not have to be a procedure; it can be a single VBScript statement. Because only a single statement can be used and because a separate procedure is more readable, the event handler is typically a separate procedure.

The following list describes the event handlers available in VBScript:

- onBlur   Occurs when the input focus is removed from a form element
- onClick   Occurs when the user left clicks on a form element or link
- onChange   Occurs when a text, text area, or select element value is changed
- onFocus   Occurs when a form element gets the focus

20

☐	onLoad	Occurs when the page is loaded
☐	onMouseOver	Occurs when the mouse is moved over a link or anchor
☐	onSelect	Occurs when the user selects a form element's input field
☐	onSubmit	Occurs when the user submits a form
☐	onUnload	Occurs when the user exits a page

The following example shows a simple event handler script that will validate a value entered into a text field. The user's age is entered in the field and the event handler will check to be sure that a valid age was entered. If not, a message will appear asking the user to re-enter the value. The event handler is called when the AGE field is changed and the focus is moved to another field. The screen output is shown in Figure 20.5.

```
<HTML>
<HEAD>
<TITLE>An Event Handler Example</TITLE>
<SCRIPT LANGUAGE="VBScript">
Sub CheckAge(form)
   If ((form.age.value < 0) Or (form.age.value > 120)) Then
      alert "Please enter your real age!"
      form.age.value = 0
   End If
End Sub
</SCRIPT>
</HEAD>
<BODY>
<FORM NAME="SURVEY">
Please enter your name and age:<BR>
First<INPUT TYPE=TEXT NAME="FNAME" MAXLENGTH=15 SIZE=10>
MI<INPUT TYPE=TEXT NAME="MI" MAXLENGTH=1 SIZE=1>
Last<INPUT TYPE=TEXT NAME="LNAME" MAXLENGTH=20 SIZE=15><BR><BR>
Age<INPUT TYPE=TEXT NAME="AGE" MAXLENGTH=3 SIZE=2 onChange="CheckAge(SURVEY)">
<P>
Please select your favorite season of the year:<BR>
Spring<INPUT TYPE=RADIO NAME="SEASON" VALUE="Spring">
Summer<INPUT TYPE=RADIO NAME="SEASON" VALUE="Summer">
Fall  <INPUT TYPE=RADIO NAME="SEASON" VALUE="Fall">
Winter<INPUT TYPE=RADIO NAME="SEASON" VALUE="Winter">
<P>
Please check all of the outdoor activities that you enjoy:<BR>
Hiking<INPUT TYPE=CHECKBOX NAME="ACT" VALUE="Hiking">
Skiing<INPUT TYPE=CHECKBOX NAME="ACT" VALUE="Sking">
Water Sports<INPUT TYPE=CHECKBOX NAME="ACT" VALUE="Water">
Cycling<INPUT TYPE=CHECKBOX NAME="ACT" VALUE="Cycling">
<P>
<INPUT TYPE=SUBMIT><INPUT TYPE=RESET>
</FORM>
</BODY>
</HTML>
```

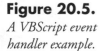

Figure 20.5.

A VBScript event handler example.

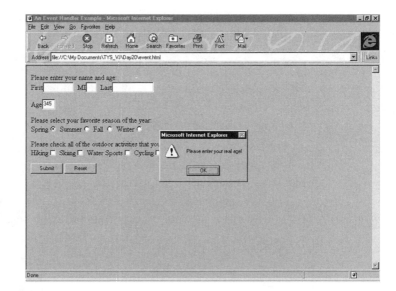

VBScript Object Model

The object hierarchy for VBScript is very similar and compatible to the JavaScript object hierarchy. The primary difference is that there is not a built-in Math, Date, or String object. Of course, these are not needed because there are built-in functions to handle these types of operations.

See Appendix E, "JavaScript Language Reference," for descriptions of each object and its associated properties, methods, and event handlers. As mentioned, each of these objects apply equally to VBScript except for the Math, String, and Date objects.

Summary

Today you were exposed to a brief introduction and reference of the VBScript language. Although this chapter is essentially a complete, concise guide to the language, VBScript could easily be the subject of an entire book. At the time of this writing, the author is not aware of any books that focus solely on VBScript programming. However, there will likely be many to choose from in the near future, probably even by the time this book is printed.

The creator of VBScript, Microsoft, maintains information on their Web site:

```
http://www.microsoft.com
```

20

A particularly useful page for Web developers is

```
http://www.microsoft.com/workshop
```

Tomorrow, you will expand your knowledge of both VBScript and JavaScript as you learn to use these scripting languages to control applets and ActiveX controls.

Q&A

Q If VBScript is only supported by Microsoft Internet Explorer, why would I want to use it instead of JavaScript?

A The lack of broad browser support for VBScript is definitely a serious disadvantage. This is especially true because it is not supported by Netscape Navigator. However, if you are developing an intranet application and you know that everyone in your company uses Internet Explorer, VBScript might be a wise choice. This is especially true if you are already familiar with Visual Basic.

Q Visual Basic has a wide range of built-in financial functions. Are these available for me to use in my VBScript programs?

A Unfortunately, the financial functions are not available to VBScript.

Q Are the file I/O functions that are in Visual Basic available in VBScript?

A As you can probably imagine, there would be serious security issues if the file I/O functions of Visual Basic were available in VBScript. If these functions were available, a Web programmer could read, write, and even delete data on the user's hard disk. Because of these reasons, VBScript, like Java applets, do not have user file access functionality.

Day 21

Integrating Applets and ActiveX Controls with Scripting

In the last two days you learned about JavaScript and VBScript. You might be wondering what all this stuff has to do with Visual J++ and Java applets. Today you will answer this question by building a document that contains an applet, an ActiveX control, an HTML form, and a script. The ability to combine all of these elements through scripting can be very powerful indeed.

You will begin by building a simple Java applet and inserting it into an HTML file. You will then briefly review how to pass parameters to the applet from within the HTML file.

The example will then be expanded to show how to use JavaScript and VBScript to access the applet's methods and variables. Finally, ActiveX controls will be introduced to the example and you will glue everything together with JavaScript and VBScript. This final example will demonstrate using scripts to communicate between both an HTML form and an ActiveX control to an applet.

The `Circle` **Applet**

The applet that you will use throughout today's lesson simply draws a circle of the color that is specified. The applet will have three parameters that are used to control the color of the circle. These parameters are r, g, and b. They are used to indicate the red, green, and blue components for the color of the circle. The valid range of values of each of the color components is 0 to 255.

You will first build the applet using Visual J++. The applet will then be integrated into HTML and the color of the circle will be set by passing parameters. The second half of the day will be spent exploring different ways to control the applet (set the color) using scripts, forms, and ActiveX controls.

The first step is to run Applet Wizard to create a new applet. If you are unfamiliar with Applet Wizard, you might wish to review Day 9, "Java Applet Basics."

Create a New Project

Refer to Figure 21.1 as you perform the following steps to create a new project:

1. Select New from the File menu.
2. Select Project Workspace and OK.
3. Select Java Applet Wizard and enter Circle for the Name of the Project Workspace.
4. Select Create.

Figure 21.1.

Creating the Circle *Project.*

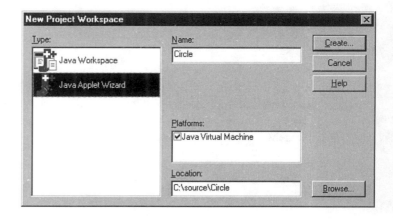

21

Step 1: Name the Applet

The applet should be named `Circle`. Refer to Figure 21.2 as you perform the following steps:

1. Enter Circle as the name of the applet class.
2. Select Next.

Figure 21.2.

Step 1 of Applet Wizard.

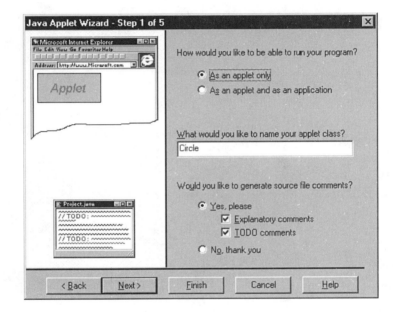

Step 2: Enter the Width and Height of the Applet

The width and height of the applet should be set to 60. Refer to Figure 21.3 as you perform the following steps:

1. Enter 60 for the width and height.
2. Select Next.

Step 3: Turn Off Animation and MultiThread Support

The `Circle` applet will not need support for animation or multithreading. To keep things simple, these two options should be disabled. Refer to Figure 21.4 as you perform the following steps:

1. Select No for multithreaded.

21

2. Select No for Animation support.

3. Select Next.

Figure 21.3.

Step 2 of Applet Wizard.

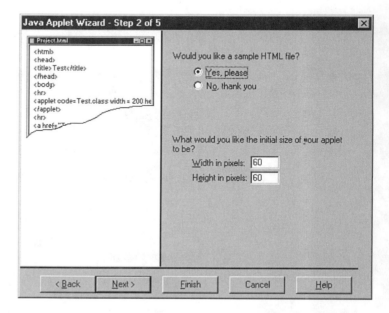

Figure 21.4.

Step 3 of Applet Wizard.

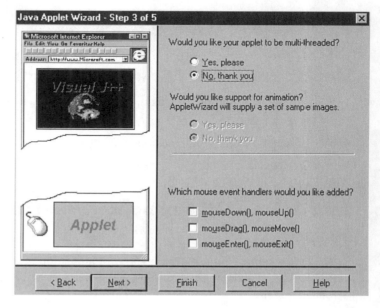

21

Step 4: Enter Three Parameters for r, g, and b

The Circle applet will need three parameters for passing red, green, and blue color values. Refer to Figure 21.5 as you perform the following steps:

1. Enter r, g, and b in the name column.

2. Select int for the type of each parameter.

3. Select Next.

Figure 21.5.

Step 4 of Applet Wizard.

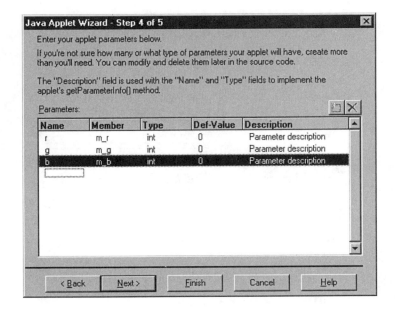

Step 5: Enter Author Information

All that is left is to enter the author information and let Applet Wizard generate the code. Refer to Figure 21.6 as you perform the following steps:

1. Enter the author information.

2. Select Finish.

The generated code is shown in Listing 21.1. A few of the comments have been removed to simplify the listing.

21

Figure 21.6.

Step 5 of Applet Wizard.

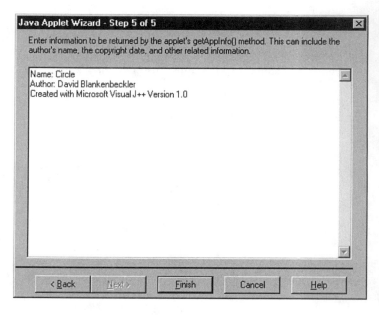

> Enter information to be returned by the applet's getAppInfo() method. This can include the author's name, the copyright date, and other related information.
>
> Name: Circle
> Author: David Blankenbeckler
> Created with Microsoft Visual J++ Version 1.0
>
> [< Back] [Next >] [Finish] [Cancel] [Help]

TYPE   **Listing 21.1. The basic `Circle` applet.**

```
//**************************************************************************
// Circle.java:    Applet
//
//**************************************************************************
import java.applet.*;
import java.awt.*;

//==========================================================================
// Main Class for applet Circle
//
//==========================================================================
public class Circle extends Applet
{
    //----------------------------------------------------------------------
    // Members for applet parameters
    // <type>        <MemberVar>    = <Default Value>
    //----------------------------------------------------------------------
    private int m_r = 0;
    private int m_g = 0;
    private int m_b = 0;

    // Parameter names.  To change a name of a parameter, you need only make
    // a single change.  Simply modify the value of the parameter string below.
    //----------------------------------------------------------------------
    private final String PARAM_r = "r";
    private final String PARAM_g = "g";
    private final String PARAM_b = "b";

    // Circle Class Constructor
    //----------------------------------------------------------------------
```

21

```
public Circle()
{
    // TODO: Add constructor code here
}

// APPLET INFO SUPPORT:
//    The getAppletInfo() method returns a string describing the applet's
// author, copyright date, or miscellaneous information.
    //--------------------------------------------------------------------

public String getAppletInfo()
{
    return "Name: Circle\r\n" +
           "Author: David Blankenbeckler\r\n" +
           "Created with Microsoft Visual J++ Version 1.0";
}

// PARAMETER SUPPORT
//    The getParameterInfo() method returns an array of strings describing
// the parameters understood by this applet.
//
    // Circle Parameter Information:
    //  { "Name", "Type", "Description" },
    //--------------------------------------------------------------------

public String[][] getParameterInfo()
{
    String[][] info =
    {
        { PARAM_r, "int", "Parameter description" },
        { PARAM_g, "int", "Parameter description" },
        { PARAM_b, "int", "Parameter description" },
    };
    return info;
}

// The init() method is called by the AWT when an applet is first loaded or
// reloaded.  Override this method to perform whatever initialization your
// applet needs, such as initializing data structures, loading images or
// fonts, creating frame windows, setting the layout manager, or adding UI
// components.
    //--------------------------------------------------------------------

public void init()
{
    // PARAMETER SUPPORT
    //    The following code retrieves the value of each parameter
    // specified with the <PARAM> tag and stores it in a member
    // variable.
    //--------------------------------------------------------------------
    String param;

    // r: Parameter description
    //--------------------------------------------------------------------
    param = getParameter(PARAM_r);
    if (param != null)
```

continues

Listing 21.1. continued

```
            m_r = Integer.parseInt(param);

        // g: Parameter description
        //-------------------------------------------------------------------
        param = getParameter(PARAM_g);
        if (param != null)
            m_g = Integer.parseInt(param);

        // b: Parameter description
        //-------------------------------------------------------------------
        param = getParameter(PARAM_b);
        if (param != null)
            m_b = Integer.parseInt(param);

//-------------------------------------------------------------------
        resize(60, 60);

        // TODO: Place additional initialization code here
    }

    // Place additional applet clean up code here.  destroy() is called when
    // when you applet is terminating and being unloaded.
    //-------------------------------------------------------------------
    public void destroy()
    {
        // TODO: Place applet cleanup code here
    }

    // Circle Paint Handler
    //-------------------------------------------------------------------
    public void paint(Graphics g)
    {
        g.drawString("Created with Microsoft Visual J++ Version 1.0", 10, 20);
    }

    //   The start() method is called when the page containing the applet
    // first appears on the screen. The AppletWizard's initial implementation
    // of this method starts execution of the applet's thread.
    //-------------------------------------------------------------------
    public void start()
    {
        // TODO: Place additional applet start code here
    }

    //   The stop() method is called when the page containing the applet is
    // no longer on the screen. The AppletWizard's initial implementation of
    // this method stops execution of the applet's thread.
    //-------------------------------------------------------------------
    public void stop()
    {
    }

    // TODO: Place additional applet code here
}
```

The Java applet is almost complete! All you have to do now is add a few lines of code to draw a circle. Java has a function in the `java.awt.Graphics` class that can be used to draw the circle. To use this class you must first import it into your source. Visual J++ has already done this with the following line at the beginning of the source:

```
import java.awt.*;
```

All that remains is to add the code to set the color and draw the circle. For more information about the `java.awt.Graphics` class, see Day 10, "Graphics, Fonts, and Color."

Before drawing the circle, you need to set the color. This can be accomplished with the `setColor()` method. After setting the color, you can draw the circle using the `fillOval()` method.

Replace the default line that the Applet Wizard placed in `Circle`'s paint method (`g.drawString(Created with...`) with the following lines:

```
public void paint(Graphics g)
{
    g.setColor(new Color(m_R, m_G, m_B));
    g.fillOval(10, 10, 40, 40);
}
```

As you can see, the `setColor()` function will use the parameters that you passed for red, green, and blue to set the color. These are the parameters that were defined in Figure 21.5.

You can now build the Java applet and view it in your Java-enabled Web browser. You can use the `Circle.html` file that was created automatically by the Applet Wizard to view the applet. The output should appear similar to Figure 21.7.

Figure 21.7.

The Circle *applet.*

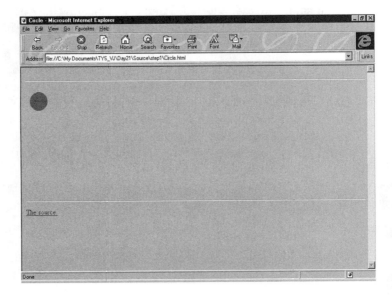

Integrating a Java Applet to HTML

The Applet Wizard automatically created an HTML file for you because you selected the option to do so. In order to learn more about the <APPLET> tag, you should review the HTML file that was created. To view the HTML file, click the FileView tab in the Project Workspace window and then double-click Circle.html. The screen should appear as in Figure 21.8.

Figure 21.8.

The Applet Wizard-generated Circle.html.

Your applet, Circle, is included in the document by the <APPLET> tag. The code= attribute is used to specify the Circle class. In addition, you can see the initial height and width of the applet is set to 60.

The ID attribute that was automatically inserted by Applet Wizard is not a standard attribute for the <APPLET> tag. Instead, the NAME attribute should be used. The ID or NAME attribute is used when referencing the applet elsewhere in the HTML file, such as in a script. Although the ID attribute will work properly for Internet Explorer 3.0, it will not work correctly with Netscape Navigator 3.0. For this reason, the ID attribute should be changed to NAME. The NAME attribute will work properly for both browsers. Change the ID attribute to NAME as follows:

```
<applet
    code=Circle.class
    name=Circle
    width=60
    height=60 >
    <param name=r value=0>
    <param name=g value=0>
    <param name=b value=0>
</applet>
```

The three parameters that you created, r, g, and b, were also automatically created in the HTML file by Applet Wizard. As you can see, all three of these were set to 0, which represents the color black.

Passing Parameters to a Java Applet

In order to change the initial color of the circle, you need to set the parameters to different values. For example, the following HTML code will create a green circle because parameter g is set to 255 and the other two are set to 0.

```
<html>
<head>
<title>Circle</title>
</head>
<body>
<hr>
<applet
    code=Circle.class
    name=Circle
    width=60
    height=60 >
    <param name=r value=0>
    <param name=g value=255>
    <param name=b value=0>
</applet>
<hr>
<a href="Circle.java">The source.</a>
</body>
</html>
```

Although this is useful for specifying the default color, it does not give you dynamic control over the color of the circle. In order to change the color of the circle dynamically, you need to use a scripting language such as VBScript or JavaScript (or build that functionality into the Java applet itself). You will now explore the use of VBScript and JavaScript in controlling a Java applet.

Controlling a Java Applet with VBScript

You will now add buttons to the form so that the user can change the color of the circle. But first, you need to add a function to your applet to provide you access to the variables m_r, m_g, and m_b. These three variables are private variables that the applet sets to the values of the passed parameters, r, g, and b.

You could simply make the m_r, m_g, and m_b variables public. However, as you learned earlier this week, this is not good object-oriented programming practice. Instead, an accessor method should be used to change the values of these variables. Instead of creating three

21

different accessor methods (one for each r, g, and b), you can simply create a single method
called `setCircleColor`.

```
public void setCircleColor(int red, int green, int blue)
{
   m_r = red;
   m_g = green;
   m_b = blue;
}
```

You also need to create a means to make the applet repaint. Simply changing the member
variables for the colors will not cause the circle to be repainted. This is easily accomplished,
however, by adding a call to the `repaint()` method in your `setCircleColor` method, such as
the following example:

```
public void setCircleColor(int red, int green, int blue)
{
m_r = red;
m_g = green;
m_b = blue;
repaint();
}
```

Because you have declared the `setCircleColor` method as public, you can access it from a
script in an HTML document. The new version of your Circle applet can now be rebuilt.

NOTE

After rebuilding your applet, you will most likely need to restart the
Web browser because the old version will still be in the cache.

With these changes, you can now access the private member variables, m_r, m_g, and m_b, from
your script using the accessor method that you created called `setCircleColor`. You will first
add three buttons to change the color to either red, green, or blue. These buttons can be added
by placing the following form definition after the applet definition in `Circle.html`:

```
<FORM>
<INPUT TYPE="BUTTON" NAME="cmdRED" VALUE="RED"><P>
<INPUT TYPE="BUTTON" NAME="cmdGREEN" VALUE="GREEN"><P>
<INPUT TYPE="BUTTON" NAME="cmdBLUE" VALUE="BLUE"><P>
</FORM>
```

The preceding form definition will create three buttons named `cmdRED`, `cmdGREEN`, and
`cmdBLUE`. You now need an event handler script for the `On_Click` event for each button. Each
of the `On_Click` event handlers will set the color variables to the appropriate values using the
`setCircleColor` method that you created. For example, to handle the clicking of the red
button you would use the following:

```
Sub cmdRED_OnClick
   call document.Circle.setCircleColor(255, 0, 0)
End Sub
```

As you can see, accessing the private variables of an applet through a public accessor method is fairly easy. Although it is similarly easy to access the variables directly by defining them as public, this is generally not good programming practice. However, if it is desired, it is simply a matter of defining the variable with the public modifier. The variable can then be defined just like the method, such as the following example:

```
' DO NOT ADD THIS TO THE SCRIPT WE ARE BUILDING
' THIS IS JUST AN EXAMPLE OF ACCESSING PUBLIC VARIABLES OF AN APPLET
Sub directVariableAccess
    document.Circle.m_r = 255
    document.Circle.m_g = 0
    document.Circle.m_b = 0
End Sub
```

Adding the event handlers for the green and blue buttons is accomplished in a similar manner: calling the setCircleColor method with the appropriate parameters. Listing 21.2 shows the modified HTML file after the addition of the buttons and their associated event handlers.

TYPE   **Listing 21.2. Controlling the `Circle` applet with VBScript.**

```
<html>
<head>
<title>Circle</title>
</head>
<body>
<hr>
<applet
    code="Circle.class"
    name=Circle
    width=60
    height=60 >
    <param name=R value=0>
    <param name=G value=0>
    <param name=B value=0>
</applet>
<SCRIPT LANGUAGE="VBScript">

Sub cmdRED_OnClick
    call document.Circle.setCircleColor(255, 0, 0)
End Sub

Sub cmdGREEN_OnClick
    call document.Circle.setCircleColor(0, 255, 0)
End Sub

Sub cmdBLUE_OnClick
    call document.Circle.setCircleColor(0, 0, 255)
End Sub
```

21

continues

Listing 21.2. continued

```
</SCRIPT>
<FORM>
<INPUT TYPE="BUTTON" NAME="cmdRED" VALUE="RED"><P>
<INPUT TYPE="BUTTON" NAME="cmdGREEN" VALUE="GREEN"><P>
<INPUT TYPE="BUTTON" NAME="cmdBLUE" VALUE="BLUE"><P>
</FORM>

<hr>
<a href="Circle.java">The source.</a>
</body>
</html>
```

You can now view the changes to `Circle.html` in your Web browser. Clicking one of the three buttons changes the color of the circle. The output should now appear similar to Figure 21.9.

Figure 21.9.

The `Circle` *applet with VBScript.*

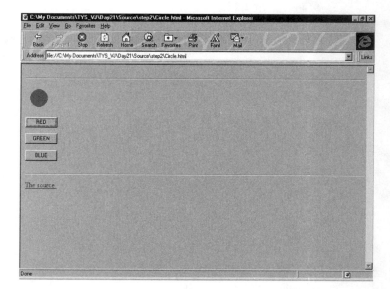

Controlling a Java Applet with JavaScript

Controlling an applet with JavaScript is very similar to using VBScript, the difference being entirely related to the syntax of the language. The form definition for JavaScript is slightly different because you specify the event handler code in the form control tag. For example, the form definition would be as follows:

```
<FORM>
<INPUT TYPE="BUTTON" NAME="cmdRED" VALUE="RED" onClick="setRED()"><P>
<INPUT TYPE="BUTTON" NAME="cmdGREEN" VALUE="GREEN" onClick="setGREEN()"><P>
<INPUT TYPE="BUTTON" NAME="cmdBLUE" VALUE="BLUE" onClick="setBLUE()"><P>
</FORM>
```

As you can see, the first button, named cmdRED, has an onClick event handler called setRED(). Similarly, there is an onClick event handler for the green and blue buttons. The event handlers would then be added as follows:

```
function setRED() {
    document.Circle.setCircleColor(255,0,0);
}
```

The setGREEN and setBLUE event handlers should be added in a similar fashion, changing the calling parameters appropriately. The complete HTML listing should now look as shown in Listing 21.3.

TYPE   **Listing 21.3. Controlling the `Circle` applet with JavaScript.**

```
<html>
<head>
<title>Circle</title>
</head>
<body>
<hr>
<applet
    code="Circle.class"
    name=Circle
    width=60
    height=60 >
    <param name=R value=0>
    <param name=G value=0>
    <param name=B value=0>
</applet>

<SCRIPT LANGUAGE="JavaScript">
function setRED() {
    document.Circle.setCircleColor(255,0,0);
}

function setGREEN() {
    document.Circle.setCircleColor(0,255,0);
}
function setBLUE() {
    document.Circle.setCircleColor(0,0,255);
}
</SCRIPT>

<FORM>
<INPUT TYPE="BUTTON" NAME="cmdRED" VALUE="RED" onClick="setRED()"><P>
<INPUT TYPE="BUTTON" NAME="cmdGREEN" VALUE="GREEN" onClick="setGREEN()"><P>
<INPUT TYPE="BUTTON" NAME="cmdBLUE" VALUE="BLUE" onClick="setBLUE()"><P>
</FORM>

<hr>
<a href="Circle.java">The source.</a>
</body>
</html>
```

21

This HTML document should now appear and work just like the VBScript file in Figure 21.9.

The <OBJECT> Tag

The <OBJECT> tag is used to insert objects into an HTML document. An object can be a Java applet, an ActiveX control, an AVI file, and so on. Because the <APPLET> tag was introduced before the <OBJECT> tag, it is still generally used for adding applets. However, the <OBJECT> tag could also be used, and actually has greater functionality.

The object definition begins with <OBJECT> and ends with </OBJECT>. The following attributes are available:

☐ ALIGN= LEFT ¦ CENTER ¦ RIGHT ¦ BASELINE ¦ MIDDLE ¦ TEXTBOTTOM ¦ TEXTMIDDLE ¦ TEXTTOP

The ALIGN attribute is used to align the object in the document. The values are defined as follows:

LEFT—The object is positioned to the left and subsequent text is flowed past the right side of the object.

CENTER—The object is centered after the current line and subsequent text begins on the line following the object.

RIGHT—The object is positioned to the right and subsequent text is flowed past the left side of the object.

BASELINE—The bottom of the object is aligned vertically with the baseline.

MIDDLE—The middle of the object is aligned vertically with the baseline.

TEXTBOTTOM—The bottom of the object is aligned vertically with the bottom of the text.

TEXTMIDDLE—The middle of the object is aligned vertically halfway between the baseline and the x-height of the text. The x-height is the top of a lowercase x in the current font.

TEXTTOP—The top of the object is aligned vertically with the top of the text.

☐ BORDER=width

When an object is defined to be a hyperlink, this attribute specifies the suggested width of the border.

☐ CLASSID=object

The URL that identifies the object implementation.

☐ CODEBASE=*objectURL*

Used to specify a base URL for the object if it is not in the same location as the calling HTML.

☐ CODETYPE=*mediaType*

Used to specify the Internet media type of the object specified by CLASSID. This might be used by some browsers to speed network access.

☐ DATA=*dataURL*

The URL that identifies the object's data, if necessary. If the object consists entirely of data, like an AVI file, the browser can determine the media type from the TYPE attribute and load the appropriate object implementation. A CLASSID is not necessary in this case.

☐ DECLARE

Indicates that the object should be declared but not instantiated. This can be used when you are referencing the object later in the document.

☐ HEIGHT=*value*

Specifies the suggested height of the object in standard units.

☐ HSPACE=*value*

Specifies the horizontal space of the object in standard units. This is the amount of space between the object and text before and after the object.

☐ ID=*idName*

Used to specify an identifier that can be used inside the current document to refer to the object.

☐ NAME=*value*

Used to provide a name for the object when it is used as part of a form.

☐ SHAPES

Used to indicate that the object has hyperlinks associated with shapes on the object.

☐ STANDBY=*message*

Used to specify a short message to display while the object is loading.

☐ TYPE=*mediaType*

Used to specify the Internet media type of the data specified by DATA.

☐ USEMAP=*mapURL*

Used to specify an image map.

21

☐ VSPACE=*value*

Specifies the vertical space of the object in standard units. This is the amount of space above and below the object.

☐ WIDTH=*value*

Specifies the suggested width of the object in standard units.

Like the applet, an object can have parameters passed to it. This is done using the same method as the applet, through the <PARAM> tag. The <PARAM> tag is used as follows:

<PARAM NAME=*paramName* VALUE=*paramValue*>

Integrating ActiveX Controls into HTML

Now that you have learned about the structure and parameters of the <OBJECT> tag, put it to use in your Circle document to add scrollbar controls for changing the three colors. Microsoft provides ActiveX controls that you can use for the scrollbars. Microsoft also provides a very useful tool to assist with inserting ActiveX controls into HTML documents called the ActiveX Control Pad. The ActiveX Control Pad is included with Microsoft Internet Explorer 3.0.

WARNING

In order for the ActiveX examples to work in Internet Explorer, you must have enabled the appropriate features for active content. These can be changed by selecting Options from the View menu. The Security tab contains the options for Active Content. The following four options should be enabled:

☐ Allow downloading of active content

☐ Enable ActiveX controls and plug-ins

☐ Run ActiveX scripts

☐ Enable Java programs

ActiveX Control Pad

The ActiveX Control Pad provides a nice user interface for inserting ActiveX controls and other objects into your HTML file. You will step through the process of inserting a scrollbar control to show how useful this powerful tool can be. Refer to Figure 21.10 for the first four steps.

1. Run the ActiveX Control Pad and open the `Circle.html` file.

2. Position the cursor before the beginning of the form and select Insert ActiveX Control from the Edit menu.

3. Select Microsoft Forms 2.0 Scrollbar from the list.

4. Select OK.

Figure 21.10.

Inserting an ActiveX control with the ActiveX Control Pad.

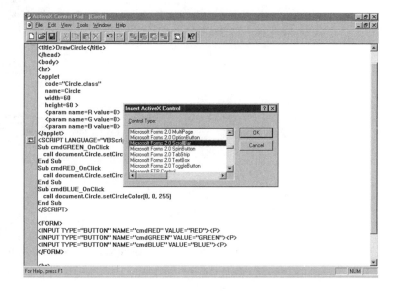

The Properties dialog box and another box showing the size and orientation of the control will now appear. The screen should appear similar to Figure 21.11. You will now modify a few of the properties using the dialog box and then change the orientation of the scrollbar in the other box.

First, change the ID attribute to a more meaningful name, sbRED. You will then change the upper and lower limits of the scrollbar to the upper and lower limits for the red setting, 0 and 255.

5. In the properties dialog, change the following properties:

```
ID = sbRED
Min = 0
Max = 255
```

The scrollbar defaults to a vertical position. This can easily be changed by using the mouse to adjust the orientation and size of the control in the other dialog box.

6. Use the mouse to turn the scrollbar to a horizontal position as shown in Figure 21.11.

21

Figure 21.11.

Modifying an ActiveX control with the ActiveX Control Pad.

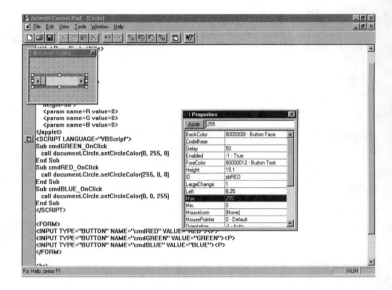

7. Close the Properties dialog box, and the `<OBJECT>` tag will be automatically added to the HTML document.

That is all it takes to add an ActiveX scrollbar control to your HTML file! All that is left is to add the event handler code to respond to the scrollbar events.

Repeat the preceding instructions to insert two more scrollbars for control of green and blue. These will have the ID `sbGREEN` and `sbBLUE`.

To clean things up a bit and provide captions for the scrollbars, add the following HTML code after each `</OBJECT>` tag:

```
   Red<P>
```

This will add two non-breaking spaces and a color identifier followed by a paragraph break. Replace Red with Green and Blue, respectively, for the other two scrollbar captions.

The resulting HTML file should now appear as in Listing 21.4.

TYPE **Listing 21.4. ActiveX objects inserted into HTML.**

```
<html>
<head>
<title>Circle</title>
</head>
<body>
<hr>
<applet
```

```
        code="Circle.class"
        name=Circle
        width=60
        height=60 >
        <param name=R value=0>
        <param name=G value=0>
        <param name=B value=0>
</applet>
<SCRIPT LANGUAGE="VBScript">

Sub cmdRED_OnClick
    call Document.Circle.setCircleColor(255,0,0)
End Sub

Sub cmdGREEN_OnClick
    call Document.Circle.setCircleColor(0,255,0)
End Sub

Sub cmdBLUE_OnClick
    call Document.Circle.setCircleColor(0,0,255)
End Sub

</SCRIPT>
<P>

<OBJECT ID="sbRED" WIDTH=104 HEIGHT=20
 CLASSID="CLSID:DFD181E0-5E2F-11CE-A449-00AA004A803D">
    <PARAM NAME="Size" VALUE="2752;529">
    <PARAM NAME="Max" VALUE="255">
</OBJECT>   Red<P>

<OBJECT ID="sbGREEN" WIDTH=104 HEIGHT=20
 CLASSID="CLSID:DFD181E0-5E2F-11CE-A449-00AA004A803D">
    <PARAM NAME="Size" VALUE="2752;529">
    <PARAM NAME="Max" VALUE="255">
</OBJECT>   Green<P>

<OBJECT ID="sbBLUE" WIDTH=104 HEIGHT=20
 CLASSID="CLSID:DFD181E0-5E2F-11CE-A449-00AA004A803D">
    <PARAM NAME="Size" VALUE="2752;529">
    <PARAM NAME="Max" VALUE="255">
</OBJECT>   Blue <P>

<FORM>
<INPUT TYPE="BUTTON" NAME="cmdRED" VALUE="RED"><P>
<INPUT TYPE="BUTTON" NAME="cmdGREEN" VALUE="GREEN"><P>
<INPUT TYPE="BUTTON" NAME="cmdBLUE" VALUE="BLUE"><P>
</FORM>

<hr>
<a href="Circle.java">The source.</a>
</body>
</html>
```

21

Controlling ActiveX with Scripting

Your final task is to provide scripting to support the ActiveX controls that you added. There are essentially two things that need to be added for each control:

☐ A Change event handler to respond to changes in the position of the scrollbar by changing the color of the circle accordingly.

☐ Modifications to the OnClick event handlers for the buttons so that they can set the scrollbars to correspond to changes caused by clicking the buttons. For example, if the scrollbars are all set midway and then the Red button is pressed, the Red scrollbar should be set to 255 and the Green and Blue scrollbars to 0.

First, you will add the three event handlers to change the color of the circle when the scrollbar is changed. These event handlers are very similar to the ones that you created for the buttons. The difference is that you reference the color values to the values of the three scrollbars. For example, the event handler for the Red scrollbar would look like the following:

```
Sub sbRED_Change
  call Document.Circle.setCircleColor(sbRED.Value, sbGREEN.Value, sbBLUE.Value)
End Sub
```

This event handler will respond to changes to sbRED, which is the red scrollbar. When a change occurs, the setCircleColor method is called with the current values of the red, green, and blue scrollbars. This will cause the m_r, m_g, and m_b variables in the Circle Java applet to be updated and the repaint() method called. The color of the circle will then change to reflect the new amount of each color specified by the scrollbars.

Add two similar functions to support the change events of the other two scrollbars: sbGREEN and sbBLUE.

Now you need to modify the event handlers for the button's OnClick events. Three statements need to be added to each handler to update the current value of each of the scrollbars. For example, the cmdRED_OnClick event handler should have the following three lines added to it:

```
sbRED.Value = 255
sbGREEN.Value = 0
sbBLUE.Value = 0
```

When the red button is clicked, the scrollbars will be updated to reflect the correct color of the circle. Similar statements should be added to the cmdGREEN_OnClick and cmdBLUE_OnClick handlers. The final code listing is shown in Listing 21.5. The final screen output is shown in Figure 21.12.

TYPE **Listing 21.5. Controlling ActiveX with VBScript.**

```
<html>
<head>
<title>Circle</title>
</head>
<body>
<hr>
<applet
    code="Circle.class"
    name=Circle
    width=60
    height=60 >
    <param name=R value=0>
    <param name=G value=0>
    <param name=B value=0>
</applet>
<SCRIPT LANGUAGE="VBScript">
Sub cmdRED_OnClick
  call Document.Circle.setCircleColor(255,0,0)
  sbRED.Value = 255
  sbGREEN.Value = 0
  sbBLUE.Value = 0
End Sub

Sub sbRED_Change
  call Document.Circle.setCircleColor(sbRED.Value, sbGREEN.Value, sbBLUE.Value)
End Sub

Sub cmdGREEN_OnClick
  call Document.Circle.setCircleColor(0,255,0)
  sbRED.Value = 0
  sbGREEN.Value = 255
  sbBLUE.Value = 0
End Sub

Sub sbGREEN_Change
  call Document.Circle.setCircleColor(sbRED.Value, sbGREEN.Value, sbBLUE.Value)
End Sub

Sub cmdBLUE_OnClick
  call Document.Circle.setCircleColor(0,0,255)
  sbRED.Value = 0
  sbGREEN.Value = 0
  sbBLUE.Value = 255
End Sub

Sub sbBLUE_Change
  call Document.Circle.setCircleColor(sbRED.Value, sbGREEN.Value, sbBLUE.Value)
End Sub

</SCRIPT>
<P>
```

21

continues

Listing 21.5. continued

```
<OBJECT ID="sbRED" WIDTH=104 HEIGHT=20
 CLASSID="CLSID:DFD181E0-5E2F-11CE-A449-00AA004A803D">
    <PARAM NAME="Size" VALUE="2752;529">
    <PARAM NAME="Max" VALUE="255">
</OBJECT>   Red<P>

<OBJECT ID="sbGREEN" WIDTH=104 HEIGHT=20
 CLASSID="CLSID:DFD181E0-5E2F-11CE-A449-00AA004A803D">
    <PARAM NAME="Size" VALUE="2752;529">
    <PARAM NAME="Max" VALUE="255">
</OBJECT>   Green<P>

<OBJECT ID="sbBLUE" WIDTH=104 HEIGHT=20
 CLASSID="CLSID:DFD181E0-5E2F-11CE-A449-00AA004A803D">
    <PARAM NAME="Size" VALUE="2752;529">
    <PARAM NAME="Max" VALUE="255">
</OBJECT>   Blue <P>

<FORM>
<INPUT TYPE="BUTTON" NAME="cmdRED" VALUE="RED"><P>
<INPUT TYPE="BUTTON" NAME="cmdGREEN" VALUE="GREEN"><P>
<INPUT TYPE="BUTTON" NAME="cmdBLUE" VALUE="BLUE"><P>
</FORM>

<hr>
<a href="Circle.java">The source.</a>
</body>
</html>
```

Figure 21.12.

The final Circle *applet with the ActiveX controls.*

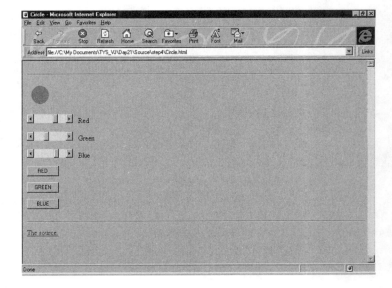

You should now be able to change the color of the circle by either pressing one of the three color buttons or changing one of the three color scrollbars. In addition, pressing the buttons should cause the scrollbars to be updated to reflect the current color of the circle.

This example could also be created using JavaScript instead of VBScript. Listing 21.6 shows this same example created with JavaScript.

Type **Listing 21.6. Controlling ActiveX with JavaScript.**

```html
<html>
<head>
<title>Circle</title>
</head>
<body>
<hr>

<applet
    code="Circle.class"
    name=Circle
    width=60
    height=60 >
    <param name=R value=0>
    <param name=G value=0>
    <param name=B value=0>
</applet>

<SCRIPT LANGUAGE="JavaScript">
function setRED(){
   Document.Circle.setCircleColor(255,0,0);
   sbRED.Value = 255;
   sbGREEN.Value = 0;
   sbBLUE.Value = 0;
}

function sbRED_Change(){
   Document.Circle.setCircleColor(sbRED.Value, sbGREEN.Value, sbBLUE.Value)
}

function setGREEN(){
   Document.Circle.setCircleColor(0,255,0);
   sbRED.Value = 0;
   sbGREEN.Value = 255;
   sbBLUE.Value = 0;
}

function sbGREEN_Change(){
   Document.Circle.setCircleColor(sbRED.Value, sbGREEN.Value, sbBLUE.Value)
}

function setBLUE(){
   Document.Circle.setCircleColor(0,0,255);
```

21

continues

Listing 21.6. continued

```
        sbRED.Value = 0;
        sbGREEN.Value = 0;
        sbBLUE.Value = 255;
}

function sbBLUE_Change(){
    Document.Circle.setCircleColor(sbRED.Value, sbGREEN.Value, sbBLUE.Value)
}

</SCRIPT>
<P>

<OBJECT ID="sbRED" WIDTH=104 HEIGHT=20
 CLASSID="CLSID:DFD181E0-5E2F-11CE-A449-00AA004A803D">
    <PARAM NAME="Size" VALUE="2752;529">
    <PARAM NAME="Max" VALUE="255">
</OBJECT>   Red<P>

<OBJECT ID="sbGREEN" WIDTH=104 HEIGHT=20
 CLASSID="CLSID:DFD181E0-5E2F-11CE-A449-00AA004A803D">
    <PARAM NAME="Size" VALUE="2752;529">
    <PARAM NAME="Max" VALUE="255">
</OBJECT>   Green<P>

<OBJECT ID="sbBLUE" WIDTH=104 HEIGHT=20
 CLASSID="CLSID:DFD181E0-5E2F-11CE-A449-00AA004A803D">
    <PARAM NAME="Size" VALUE="2752;529">
    <PARAM NAME="Max" VALUE="255">
</OBJECT>   Blue <P>

<FORM>
<INPUT TYPE="BUTTON" NAME="cmdRED" VALUE="RED" onClick="setRED()"><P>
<INPUT TYPE="BUTTON" NAME="cmdGREEN" VALUE="GREEN" onClick="setGREEN()"><P>
<INPUT TYPE="BUTTON" NAME="cmdBLUE" VALUE="BLUE" onClick="setBLUE()"><P>
</FORM>

<hr>
<a href="Circle.java">The source.</a>
</body>
</html>
```

Summary

This concludes your final week of *Teach Yourself Visual J++ in 21 Days*! Today you learned how to use both JavaScript and VBScript to control both applets and ActiveX objects. You should now have a good understanding of all the glue that bonds your Visual J++ creations together into its final form, an HTML document. Although it is true that Visual J++ can be used to create stand-alone Java applications, it will most likely be used for the creation of Java applets, at least in the near future. Through the use of HTML and the two scripting languages, applets can be generalized and modularized. This is a powerful concept because it creates the opportunity for reusable modules.

As an example, consider designing a Web document that requires graphing and database capabilities. You could approach this task in two ways. First, you could design everything into a Java applet. This would definitely work, but it doesn't create nice, clean generic modules that can be used again in future projects. A second approach would be to create generic modules and glue them together using scripts. The graphing capability could be provided by a generic graphing ActiveX control. The database might be a custom applet that you design. These two components can then communicate with each other through a scripting language such as VBScript or JavaScript. When used in this way, scripting is a powerful tool that you can use in your Visual J++ projects.

Q&A

Q **It seems like it would have been easier to just declare the `m_r`, `m_g`, and `m_b` variables as public. Couldn't I have then just set those variables to the correct values in my scripts?**

A There are two things that should be considered before taking this approach. The first is that it is generally not good object-oriented programming practice to declare member variables as public. The other consideration is that even if you did simply define the variables as public and set them in your script, you would still have to create a `public` function to cause the repaint. The best solution in this case was to create one function that set all three colors and did the repaint.

Q **I noticed that you used the `call` statement when calling the applet's `setCircleColor` method while using VBScript. Is the `call` statement necessary?**

A Use of the `call` statement is optional and a matter of preference. If you use the `call` statement, the argument list must be surrounded by parentheses. If you do not use the `call` statement, the argument list should not be enclosed in parentheses.

Q **I tried the ActiveX scrollbar example with Netscape Navigator 3.0, and it did not work. Why not?**

A Netscape Navigator 3.0 does not directly support ActiveX controls. In order to use ActiveX with Navigator, you must install an ActiveX plug-in. One such plug-in, `ControlActive`, is available from NCompass Labs at the following address:

`http://www.ncompasslabs.com/`

Although this will allow you to use ActiveX controls, the plug-in does not support scripting of ActiveX controls. In order to script ActiveX controls with Netscape Navigator, additional support is necessary. One such solution is ScriptActive, also from NCompass Labs. There are different ScriptActive offerings available to support either VBScript or JavaScript.

21

Java Language Reference

This appendix contains a summary or quick reference for the Java language, as described in this book.

TECHNICAL NOTE

This is neither a grammar, nor is it a technical overview of the language itself. It's a quick reference to be used after you already know the basics of how the language works. If you need a technical description of the language, your best bet is to visit the Java Web Site (`http://java.sun.com`) and download the actual specification, which includes a full description of the Java language.

Language keywords and symbols are shown in a monospace font. Arguments and other parts to be substituted are in italic monospace.

Optional parts are indicated by brackets (except in the array syntax section). If there are several options that are mutually exclusive, they are shown separated by pipes (¦) like this:

```
[ public ¦ private ¦ protected ] type varname
```

Reserved Words

The following words are reserved for use by the Java language itself (some of them are reserved but not currently used). You cannot use these terms to refer to classes, methods, or variable names:

abstract	double	int	static
boolean	else	interface	super
break	extends	long	switch
byte	final	native	synchronized
case	finally	new	this
catch	float	null	throw
char	for	package	throws
class	goto	private	transient
const	if	protected	try
continue	implements	public	void
default	import	return	volatile
do	instanceof	short	while

Comments

```
/*      this is a multiline comment */


//      this is a single-line comment


/**     Java documentation comment */
```

Literals

number	Type int (for example, 8)
number[l ¦ L]	Type long (for example, 4527543L)
0x*hex*	Hex integer (for example, 0x3F8)
0*octal*	Octal integer (for example, 034)
[*number*].*number*	Type double (for example, 2483.875)
number[f ¦ F]	Type float (for example, 435f)
number[d ¦ D]	Type double (for example, 435d)
[+ ¦ -] *number*	Signed (for example, -345.67)
*number*ε*number*	Exponent (for example, 234.95e6)
*number*E*number*	Exponent (for example, 234.95E6)
'*character*'	Single character
"*characters*"	String
" "	Empty string
\b	Backspace
\t	Tab
\n	Line feed
\f	Form feed
\r	Carriage return
\"	Double quote

`\'`	Single quote
`\\`	Backslash
`\uNNNN`	Unicode escape (NNNN is hex)
`true`	Boolean
`false`	Boolean

Variable Declaration

`[ byte ¦ short ¦ int ¦ long ] varname`	Integers
`[ float ¦ double ] varname`	Floats
`char varname;`	Characters
`boolean varname`	Boolean
`classname varname;`	Class types
`interfacename varname;`	Interface types
`type varname1[, varnameN];`	Multiple variables

The following options are available only for class and instance variables. Any of these options can be used with a variable declaration:

`[ static ] variableDeclaration`	Class variable
`[ final ] variableDeclaration`	Constants
`[ public ¦ private ¦ protected ] variableDeclaration`	Access control
`[ volatile ] varname`	Modified asynchronously
`[ transient ] varname`	Not persistent

Variable Assignment

`variable = value`	Assignment
`variable++`	Postfix Increment
`++variable`	Prefix Increment
`variable--`	Postfix Decrement
`--variable`	Prefix Decrement
`variable += value`	Add and assign

`variable —= value`	Subtract and assign
`variable *= value`	Multiply and assign
`variable ÷= value`	Divide and assign
`variable %= value`	Modulus and assign
`variable &= value`	AND and assign
`variable ¦= value`	OR and assign
`variable ^= value`	XOR and assign
`variable <<= value`	Left-shift and assign
`variable >>= value`	Right-shift and assign
`variable <<<= value`	Zero-fill right-shift and assign

Operators

`arg + arg`	Addition
`arg — arg`	Subtraction
`arg * arg`	Multiplication
`arg ÷ arg`	Division
`arg % arg`	Modulus
`arg < arg`	Less than
`arg > arg`	Greater than
`arg <= arg`	Less than or equal to
`arg >= arg`	Greater than or equal to
`arg == arg`	Equal
`arg != arg`	Not equal
`arg && arg`	Logical AND
`arg ¦¦ arg`	Logical OR
`! arg`	Logical NOT
`arg & arg`	AND
`arg ¦ arg`	OR
`arg ^ arg`	XOR
`arg << arg`	Left-shift
`arg >> arg`	Right-shift

`arg >>> arg`	Zero-fill right-shift
`~ arg`	Complement
`(type)thing`	Casting
`arg instanceof class`	Instance of
`test ? trueOp : falseOp`	Ternary (`if`) operator

Objects

`new class();`	Create new instance
`new class(arg1[,argN])`	New instance with parameters
`object.variable`	Instance variable
`object.classvar`	Class variable
`Class.classvar`	Class variable
`object.method()`	Instance method (no args)
`object.method(arg1[,argN])`	Instance method
`object.classmethod()`	Class method (no args)
`object.classmethod(arg1[,argN])`	Class method
`Class.classmethod()`	Class method (no args)
`Class.classmethod(arg1[,argN])`	Class method

Arrays

NOTE   The brackets in this section are parts of the array creation or access statements. They do not denote optional parts as they do in other parts of this appendix.

`type varname[]`	Array variable
`type[] varname`	Array variable
`new type[numElements]`	New array object
`array[index]`	Element access
`array.length`	Length of array

Loops and Conditionals

```
if ( test ) block                          Conditional


if ( test ) block                          Conditional with else
else block


switch ( test ) {                          switch (only with integer
    case value : block                     or char types)
    case value : block
    ...
    default : block
}


for (initializer, test, change ) block     for loop


while ( test ) block                       while loop


do block                                   do loop
while ( test )


break [ label ]                            break from loop or switch


continue [ label ]                         continue loops


label:                                     Labeled loops
```

Class Definitions

The basic class definition looks like this:

```
class classname block     Simple Class definition
```

Any of the following optional modifiers can be added to the class definition:

`[ final ] class classname block`	No subclassed
`[ abstract ] class classname block`	Cannot be instantiated
`[ public ] class classname block`	Accessible outside package
`class classname [ extends Superclass ] block`	Define superclass
`class classname [ implements interfaces ] block`	Implement one or more interfaces

Method and Constructor Definitions

The basic method looks like this, where `returnType` is a type name, a class name, or `void`.

`returnType methodName() block`	Basic method
`returnType methodName(parameter1[, parameterN]) block`	Method with parameters

Method variations can include any of the following optional keywords:

`[ abstract ] returnType methodName() block`	Abstract method
`[ static ] returnType methodName() block`	Class method
`[ native ] returnType methodName() block`	Native method
`[ final ] returnType methodName() block`	final method
`[ synchronized ] returnType methodName() block`	Thread lock before executing
`[ public ¦ private ¦ protected ] returnType methodName()`	Block access control

Constructors look like the following:

`classname() block`	Basic constructor
`classname(parameter1[, parameterN]) block`	Constructor with parameters
`[ public ¦ private ¦ protected ] classname()block`	Access control

In the method/constructor body you can use these references and methods:

`this`	Refers to current object
`super`	Refers to superclass
`super.methodName()`	Call a superclass' method

```
this(...)                 Calls class' constructor
super(...)                Calls superclass' constructor
return [ value ]          Returns a value
```

Packages, Interfaces, and Importing

```
import package.className                      Imports specific class name
import package.*                              Imports all public classes
                                             in package

package packagename                           Classes in this file belong
                                             to this package

interface interfaceName [ extends anotherInterface ] block
[ public ] interface interfaceName block
[ abstract ] interface interfaceName block
```

Exceptions and Guarding

```
synchronized ( object ) block     Waits for lock on object


try block                         Guarded statements
catch ( exception ) block         Executed if exception is thrown
[ finally block ]                 Cleanup code


try block                         Same as previous example (can
[ catch ( exception ) block ]     use optional catch or finally,
finally block                     but not both)
```

APPENDIX

B

Class Hierarchy Diagrams

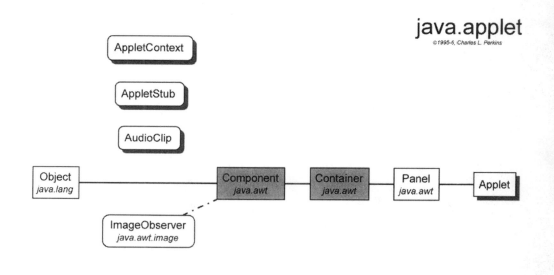

java.applet
©1995-6, Charles L. Perkins

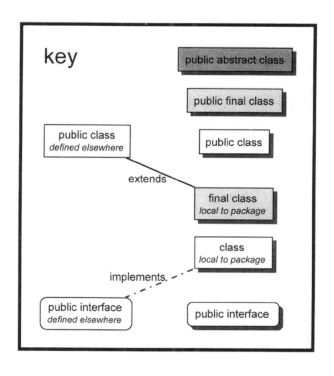

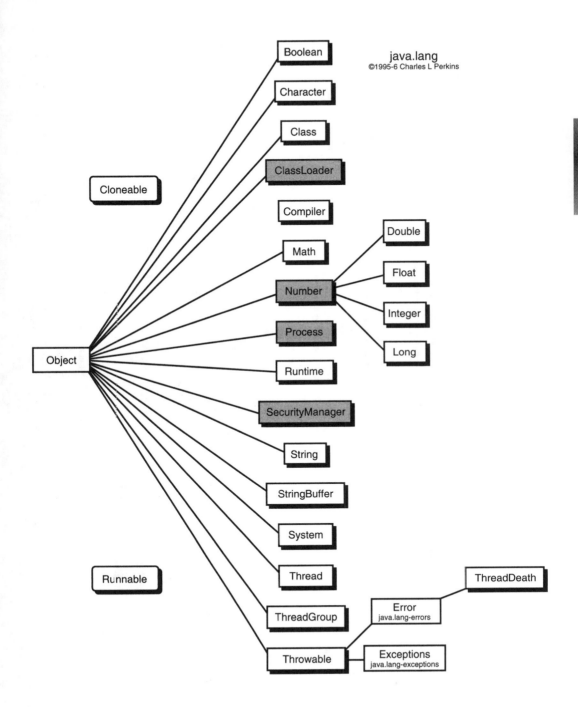

java.lang
©1995-6 Charles L Perkins

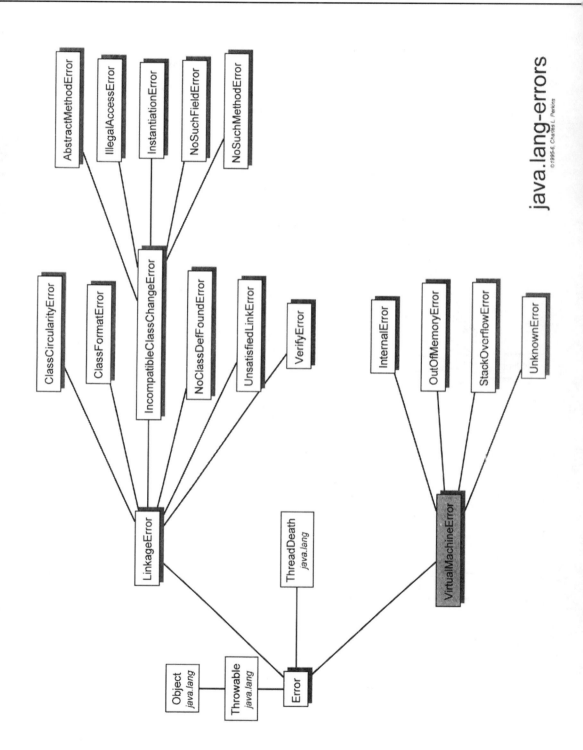

java.lang-errors

© 1995-6, Charles L. Perkins

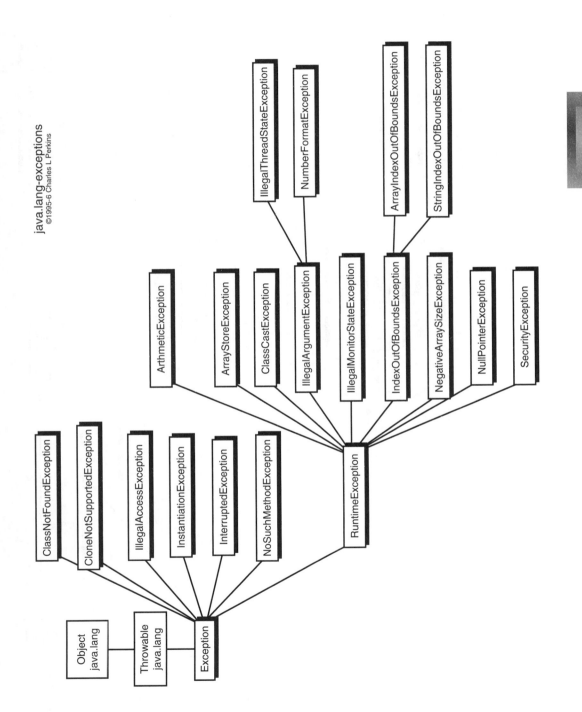

java.lang-exceptions
©1995-6 Charles L Perkins

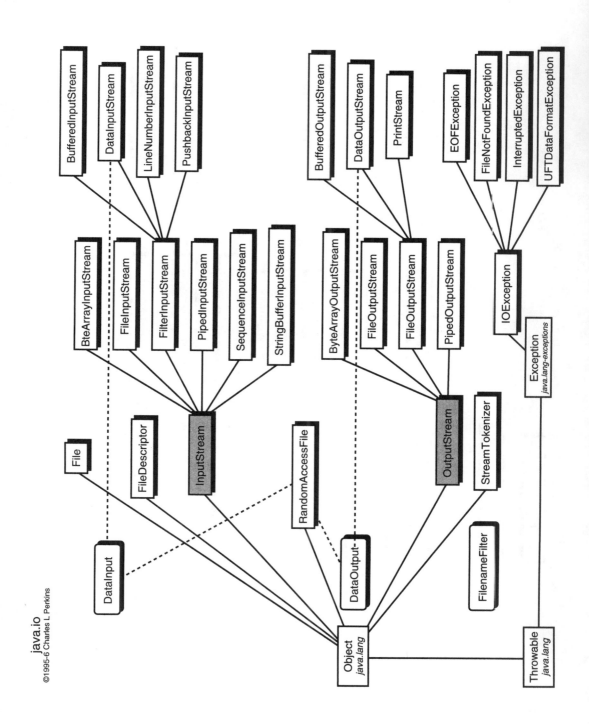

java.io
©1995-6 Charles L Perkins

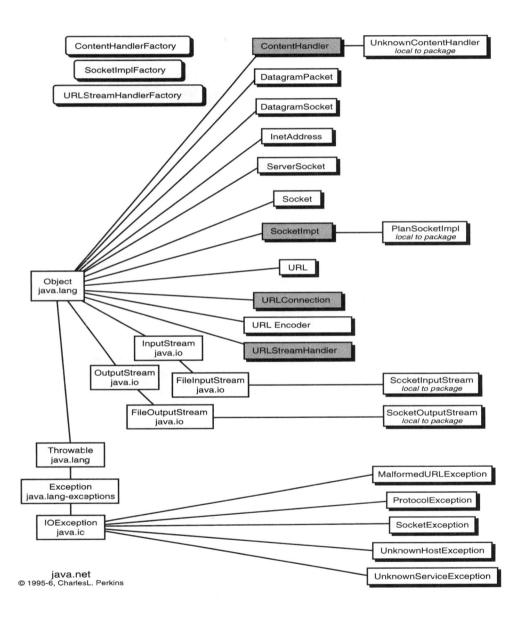

java.net
© 1995-6, Charles L. Perkins

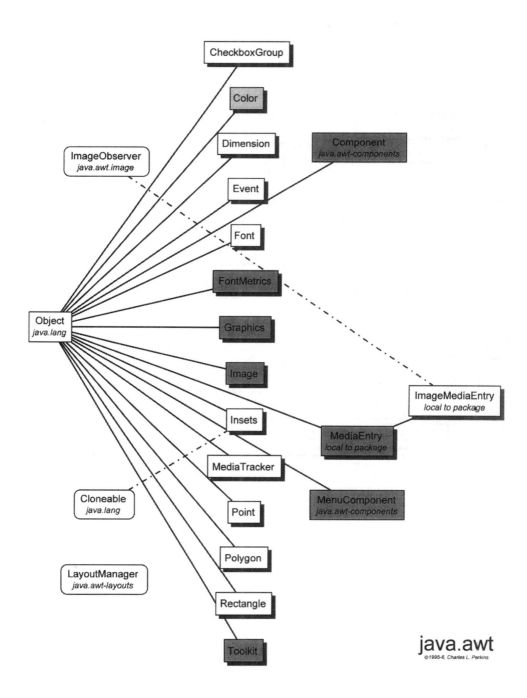

CheckboxGroup

Color

Dimension

Component
java.awt-components

ImageObserver
java.awt.image

Event

Font

FontMetrics

Object
java.lang

Graphics

Image

ImageMediaEntry
local to package

Insets

MediaEntry
local to package

MediaTracker

MenuComponent
java.awt-components

Cloneable
java.lang

Point

Polygon

LayoutManager
java.awt-layouts

Rectangle

java.awt
©1995-6, Charles L. Perkins

Toolkit

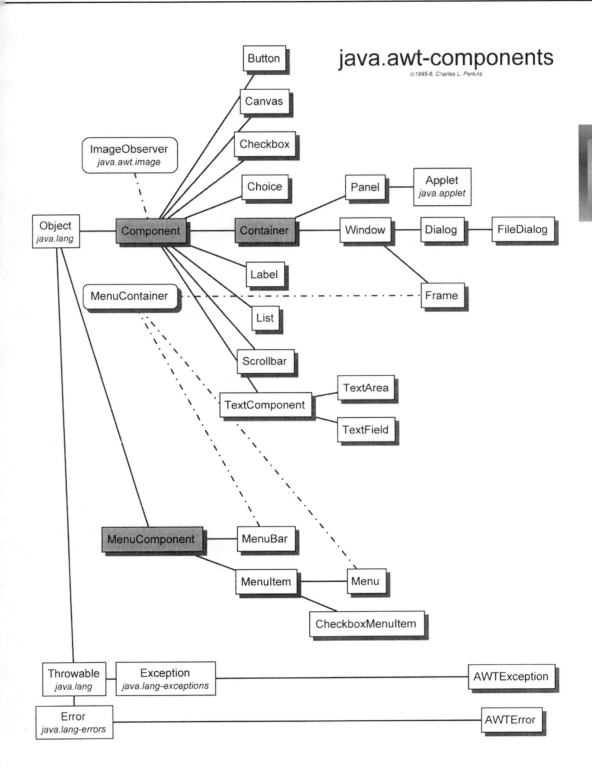

java.awt-components

©1995-6, Charles L. Perkins

java.awt-layouts

©1995-6, Charles L. Perkins

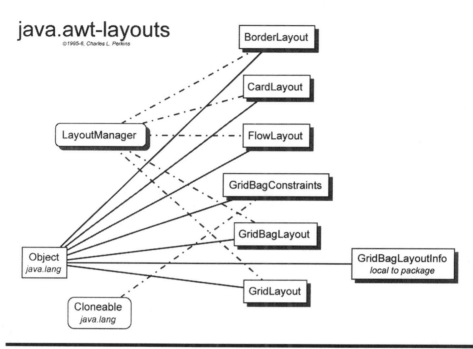

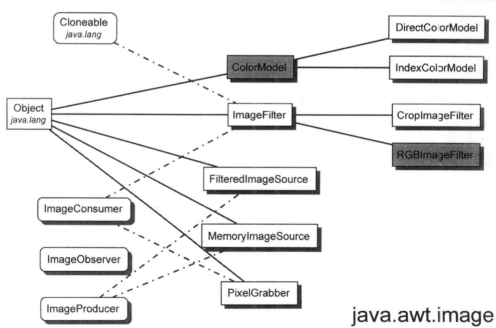

java.awt.image

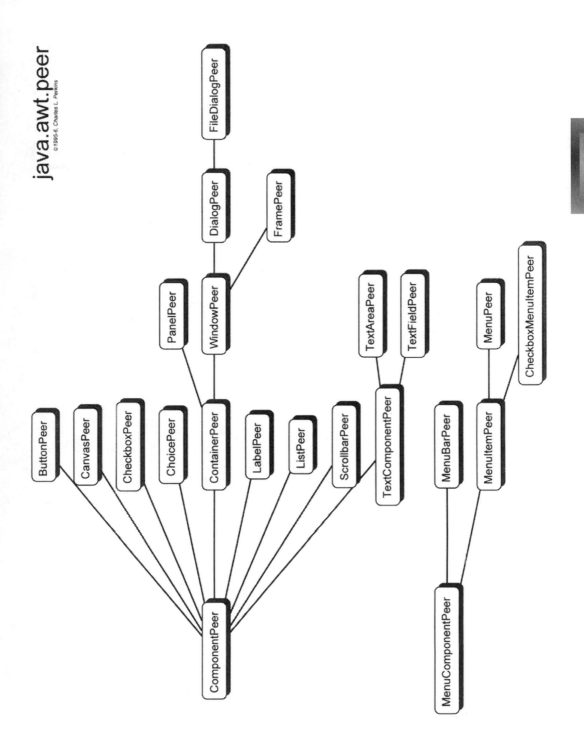

java.awt.peer
©1995-6, Charles L. Perkins

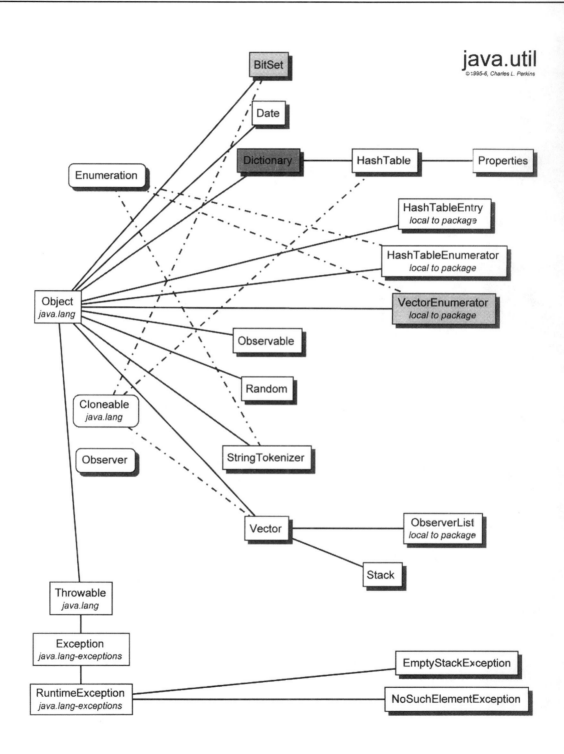

java.util
© 1995-6, Charles L. Perkins

About These Diagrams

The diagrams in this appendix are class hierarchy diagrams for the package java and for all the subpackages recursively below it in the Java 1.0 binary release.

Each page contains the class hierarchy for one package (or a subtree of a particularly large package) with all its interfaces included, and each class in this tree is shown attached to its superclasses, even if they are on another page. A detailed key is located on the first page of this appendix.

I supplemented the API documentation by looking through all the source files to find all the (missing) package classes and their relationships.

I've heard there are various programs that auto-layout hierarchies for you, but I did these the old-fashioned way (in other words, I earned it, as J.H. used to say). One nice side effect is that these diagrams should be more readable than a computer would produce, though you will have to live with my aesthetic choices. I chose, for example, to attach lines through the center of each class node, something which I think looks and feels better overall but which on occasion can be a little confusing. Follow lines through the center of the classes (not at the corners, nor along any line not passing through the center) to connect the dots mentally.

APPENDIX

C

The Java Class Library

This appendix provides a general overview of the classes available in the standard Java packages (that is, the classes that are guaranteed to be available in any Java implementation). This appendix is intended for general reference; for more specific information about class inheritance and the exceptions defined for each package, see Appendix B, "Class Hierarchy Diagrams."

java.lang

The java.lang package contains the classes and interfaces that make up the core Java language.

Interfaces

Cloneable	Interface indicating that an object may be copied or cloned.
Runnable	Methods for classes that want to run as threads.

Classes

Boolean	Object wrapper for boolean values.
Character	Object wrapper for char values.
Class	Runtime representations of classes.
ClassLoader	Abstract behavior for handling class loading.
Compiler	System class that gives access to the Java compiler.
Double	Object wrapper for double values.
Float	Object wrapper for float values.
Integer	Object wrapper for int values.
Long	Object wrapper for long values.
Math	Utility class for math operations.
Number	Abstract superclass of all number classes (Integer, Float, and so on).
Object	Generic object class at the top of the inheritance hierarchy.
Process	Abstract behavior for processes such as those spawned using methods in the System class.
Runtime	Access to the Java runtime environment.
SecurityManager	Abstract behavior for implementing security policies.

String	Character strings.
StringBuffer	Mutable strings.
System	Access to Java's system-level behavior, provided in a platform-independent way.
Thread	Methods for managing threads and classes that run in threads.
ThreadGroup	A group of threads.
Throwable	Generic exception class; all objects thrown must be a Throwable.

java.util

The java.util package contains various utility classes and interfaces, including random numbers, system properties, and other useful utility classes.

C

Interfaces

Enumeration	Methods for enumerating sets of values.
Observer	Methods for allowing classes to observe Observable objects.

Classes

BitSet	A set of bits.
Date	The current system date, as well as methods for generating and parsing dates.
Dictionary	An abstract class that maps between keys and values (superclass of Hashtable).
Hashtable	A hash table.
Observable	An abstract class for observable objects.
Properties	A hash table that contains behavior for setting and retrieving persistent properties of the system or of a class.
Random	Utilities for generating random numbers.
Stack	A stack (a last-in-first-out queue).
StringTokenizer	Utilities for splitting strings into a sequence of individual "tokens."
Vector	A resizable array of objects.

java.io

The `java.io` package provides input and output classes and interfaces for streams and files.

Interfaces

`DataInput`	Methods for reading machine-independent typed input streams.
`DataOutput`	Methods for writing machine-independent typed output streams.
`FilenameFilter`	Methods for filtering file names.

Classes

`BufferedInputStream`	A buffered input stream.
`BufferedOutputStream`	A buffered output stream.
`ByteArrayInputStream`	An input stream from a byte array.
`ByteArrayOutputStream`	An output stream to a byte array.
`DataInputStream`	Enables you to read primitive Java types (`ints`, `chars`, `booleans`, and so on) from a stream in a machine-independent way.
`DataOutputStream`	Enables you to write primitive Java data types (`ints`, `chars`, `booleans`, and so on) to a stream in a machine-independent way.
`File`	Represents a file on the host's file system.
`FileDescriptor`	Holds onto the UNIX-like file descriptor of a file or socket.
`FileInputStream`	An input stream from a file, constructed using a filename or descriptor.
`FileOutputStream`	An output stream to a file, constructed using a filename or descriptor.
`FilterInputStream`	Abstract class that provides a filter for input streams (and for adding stream functionality such as buffering).
`FilterOutputStream`	Abstract class that provides a filter for output streams (and for adding stream functionality such as buffering).

InputStream	An abstract class representing an input stream of bytes; the parent of all input streams in this package.
LineNumberInputStream	An input stream that keeps track of line numbers.
OutputStream	An abstract class representing an output stream of bytes; the parent of all output streams in this package.
PipedInputStream	A piped input stream, which should be connected to a PipedOutputStream to be useful.
PipedOutputStream	A piped output stream, which should be connected to a PipedInputStream to be useful (together they provide safe communication between threads).
PrintStream	An output stream for printing (used by System.out.println(…)).
PushbackInputStream	An input stream with a one-byte push-back buffer.
RandomAccessFile	Provides random-access to a file, constructed from filenames, descriptors, or objects.
SequenceInputStream	Converts a sequence of input streams into a single input stream.
StreamTokenizer	Converts an input stream into a sequence of individual tokens.
StringBufferInputStream	An input stream from a String object.

java.net

The java.net package contains classes and interfaces for performing network operations, such as sockets and URLs.

Interfaces

ContentHandlerFactory	Methods for creating ContentHandler objects.
SocketImplFactory	Methods for creating socket implementations (instance of the SocketImpl class).
URLStreamHandlerFactory	Methods for creating URLStreamHandler objects.

Classes

ContentHandler	Abstract behavior for reading data from a URL connection and constructing the appropriate local object, based on MIME types.
DatagramPacket	A datagram packet (UDP).
DatagramSocket	A datagram socket.
InetAddress	An object representation of an Internet host (host name, IP address).
ServerSocket	A server-side socket.
Socket	A socket.
SocketImpl	An abstract class for specific socket implementations.
URL	An object representation of a URL.
URLConnection	Abstract behavior for a socket that can handle various Web-based protocols (http, ftp, and so on).
URLEncoder	Turns strings into *x-www-form-urlencoded* format.
URLStreamHandler	Abstract class for managing streams to objects referenced by URLs.

java.awt

The java.awt package contains the classes and interfaces that make up the Abstract Windowing Toolkit.

Interfaces

LayoutManager	Methods for laying out containers.
MenuContainer	Methods for menu-related containers.

Classes

BorderLayout	A layout manager for arranging items in border formation.
Button	A user interface (UI) pushbutton.
Canvas	A canvas for drawing and performing other graphics operations.
CardLayout	A layout manager for HyperCard-like metaphors.

Checkbox	A checkbox.
CheckboxGroup	A group of exclusive checkboxes (radio buttons).
CheckboxMenuItem	A toggle menu item.
Choice	A pop-up menu of choices.
Color	An abstract representation of a color.
Component	The abstract generic class for all UI components.
Container	Abstract behavior for a component that can hold other components or containers.
Dialog	A window for brief interactions with users.
Dimension	An object representing width and height.
Event	An object representing events caused by the system or based on user input.
FileDialog	A dialog for getting file names from the local file system.
FlowLayout	A layout manager that lays out objects from left to right in rows.
Font	An abstract representation of a font.
FontMetrics	Abstract class for holding information about a specific font's character shapes and height and width information.
Frame	A top-level window with a title.
Graphics	Abstract behavior for representing a graphics context and for drawing and painting shapes and objects.
GridBagConstraints	Constraints for components laid out using GridBagLayout.
GridBagLayout	A layout manager that aligns components horizontally and vertically based on their values from GridBagConstraints.
GridLayout	A layout manager with rows and columns; elements are added to each cell in the grid.
Image	An abstract representation of a bitmap image.
Insets	Distances from the outer border of the window; used to lay out components.
Label	A text label for UI components.
List	A scrolling list.
MediaTracker	A way to keep track of the status of media objects being loaded over the Net.

C

Menu	A menu is a container on a menu bar and can contain menu items.
MenuBar	A menu bar (container for menus).
MenuComponent	The abstract superclass of all menu elements.
MenuItem	An individual menu item.
Panel	A container that is displayed.
Point	An object representing a point (x and y coordinates).
Polygon	An object representing a set of points.
Rectangle	An object representing a rectangle (x and y coordinates for the top corner, plus width and height).
Scrollbar	A UI scrollbar object.
TextArea	A multiline, scrollable, editable text field.
TextComponent	The superclass of all editable text components.
TextField	A fixed-size editable text field.
Toolkit	Abstract behavior for binding the abstract AWT classes to a platform-specific toolkit implementation.
Window	A top-level window and the superclass of the Frame and Dialog classes.

java.awt.image

The java.awt.image package is a subpackage of the AWT that provides classes for managing bitmap images.

Interfaces

ImageConsumer	Methods for receiving image data created by an ImageProducer.
ImageObserver	Methods to track the loading and construction of an image.
ImageProducer	Methods for producing image data to be received by an ImageConsumer.

Classes

ColorModel	An abstract class for managing color information for images.
CropImageFilter	A filter for cropping images to a particular size.
DirectColorModel	A specific color model for managing and translating pixel color values.
FilteredImageSource	An ImageProducer that takes an image and an ImageFilter object and produces an image for an ImageConsumer.
ImageFilter	A filter that takes image data from an ImageProducer, modifies it in some way, and hands it off to an ImageConsumer.
IndexColorModel	A specific color model for managing and translating color values in a fixed-color map.
MemoryImageSource	An ImageProducer that gets its image from memory; used after constructing the image by hand.
PixelGrabber	An ImageConsumer that retrieves a subset of the pixels in an image.
RGBImageFilter	Abstract behavior for a filter that modifies the RGB values of pixels in RGB images.

java.awt.peer

The java.awt.peer package is a subpackage of AWT that provides the (hidden) platform-specific AWT classes (for example, for Motif, Macintosh, or Windows 95) with platform-independent interfaces to implement. Callers using these interfaces need not know which platform's window system these hidden AWT classes are currently implementing.

Each class in the AWT that inherits from either Component or MenuComponent has a corresponding peer class. Each of those classes is the name of the component with the word Peer added (for example, ButtonPeer, DialogPeer, and WindowPeer). Because each one provides similar behavior, they are not enumerated here.

`java.applet`

The `java.applet` package provides applet-specific behavior.

Interfaces

`AppletContext`	Methods to refer to the applet's context.
`AppletStub`	Methods for implementing applet viewers.
`AudioClip`	Methods for playing audio files.

Classes

`Applet`	The base applet class.

APPENDIX

D

How Java Differs
from C and C++

This appendix contains a description of most of the major differences between C, C++, and the Java language. If you are a programmer familiar with either C or C++, you might want to review this appendix to catch some of the common mistakes and assumptions programmers make when using Java.

Pointers

Java does not have an explicit pointer type. Instead of pointers, all references to objects—including variable assignments, arguments passed into methods, and array elements—are accomplished by using implicit references. References and pointers are essentially the same thing except that you can't do pointer arithmetic on references (nor do you need to).

References also allow you to easily create structures in Java such as linked lists without explicit pointers; merely create a linked list node with variables that point to the next and the previous node. Then, to insert items in the list, assign those variables to other node objects.

Arrays

Arrays in Java are first class objects, and references to arrays and their contents are accomplished through explicit references rather than pointer arithmetic. Array boundaries are strictly enforced; attempting to read past the ends of an array produces a compile or runtime error. As with other objects, passing an array to a method passes the original reference to that array, so changing the contents of that array reference changes the original array object.

Arrays of objects are arrays of references that are not automatically initialized to contain actual objects. Using the following Java code produces an array of type MyObject with ten elements, but that array initially contains only nulls:

```
MyObject arrayofobjs[] = new MyObject[10];
```

You must add actual MyObject objects to that array:

```
for (int i; i< arrayofobjs.length. i++) {
 arrayofobjs[i] = new MyObject();
```

Java does not support multidimensional arrays as does C and C++. In Java, you must create arrays that contain other arrays.

Strings

Strings in C and C++ are arrays of characters, terminated by a null character (\0). To operate on and manage strings, you treat them as you would any other arrays, with all the inherent difficulties of keeping track of pointer arithmetic and taking care not to stray off the end of the array.

Strings in Java are objects, and all methods that operate on strings can treat the string as a complete entity. Strings are not terminated by a null, nor can you accidentally overstep the end of a string. (As with arrays, string boundaries are strictly enforced.)

Memory Management

All memory management in Java is automatic; memory is allocated automatically when an object is created, and a runtime garbage collector (the "gc") frees that memory when the object is no longer in use. C's malloc and free functions do not exist in Java.

To "force" an object to be freed, remove all references to that object (assign all variables and array elements holding it to null). The next time the Java gc runs, that object is reclaimed.

Data Types

All Java primitive data types (char, int, long, and so on) have consistent sizes and behavior across platforms and operating systems. Java has no unsigned data types as does C and C++ (except for char, which is a 16-bit unsigned integer).

The Boolean primitive data type can have two values: true or false. Boolean is not an integer, nor can it be treated as one, although you can cast 0 or 1 (integers) to Boolean types in Java.

Composite data types are accomplished in Java exclusively through the use of class definitions. The struct, union, and typedef keywords have all been removed in favor of classes.

Casting between data types is much more controlled in Java; automatic casting occurs only when there is no loss of information. All other casts must be explicit. The primitive data types (int, float, long, char, boolean, and so on) cannot be cast to objects or vice versa; methods and special "wrapper" classes convert values between objects and primitive types.

Operators

Operator precedence and association behaves as it does in C. Note, however, that the new keyword (for creating a new object) binds tighter than dot notation (.), which is different behavior from C++. In particular, note the following expression:

```
new foo().bar;
```

This expression operates as if it were written like this:

```
(new foo()).bar;
```

You cannot overload operators in Java as you can in C++ . The , operator of C has been deleted.

The >>> operator produces an unsigned logical right shift. (Remember, there are no unsigned data types.)

You can use the + operator to concatenate strings.

Control Flow

Although the if, while, for, and do statements in Java are syntactically the same as they are in C and C++, there is one significant difference. The test expression for each control flow construct must return an actual Boolean value (true or false). In C and C++, the expression can return an integer.

The goto keyword does not exist in Java (it's a reserved word but currently unimplemented). You can, however, use labeled breaks and continues to break out of and continue executing complex switch or loop constructs.

Arguments

Java does not support mechanisms for variable-length argument lists to functions as does C and C++. All method definitions must have a specific number of arguments. In addition, you cannot use void in an empty argument list.

Command-line arguments in Java behave differently from those in C and C++. The first element in the argument vector (argv[0]) in C and C++ is the name of the program itself; in Java, that first argument is the first of the additional arguments. In other words, in Java, argv[0] is argv[1] in C and C++; there is no way to get hold of the actual name of the Java program.

Other Differences

The following other minor differences from C and C++ exist in Java:

- [ ] Java does not have a preprocessor, and as such, does not have #defines or macros. You can create constants by using the final keyword when declaring class and instance variables.

- [ ] Java does not have template classes as does C++.

- [ ] Java does not include C's const keyword or the ability to pass by const reference explicitly.

- [ ] Java is singly inherited with multiple-inheritance features provided through interfaces.

- [ ] All functions must be methods, and there are no functions that are not tied to classes.

D

APPENDIX

E

JavaScript Language Reference

This appendix contains a summary or quick reference for the JavaScript language.

Language keywords and symbols are shown in a monospace font. Arguments and other parts to be substituted are in italic monospace.

Optional parts are indicated by brackets (except in the array syntax section). If several options are mutually exclusive, they are shown separated by pipes (¦) like this:

```
[ public ¦ private ¦ protected ] type varname
```

Reserved Words

The following words are defined as part of the JavaScript language and cannot be used as variable names:

abstract	extends	interface	synchronized
boolean	false	long	this
break	final	native	throw
byte	finally	new	throws
case	float	null	transient
catch	for	package	true
char	function	private	try
class	goto	protected	var
const	if	public	void
continue	implements	return	while
default	import	short	with
do	in	static	
double	instanceof	super	
else	int	switch	

Literals

number	Base 10 Integer (for example, 8)
0number	Octal Integer (for example, 034)
0xnumber	Hex Integer (for example, 0x3F8)
num1.num2	Floating point (for example, 453.2454)
num1Enum2	Exponential floating point (for example, 24.9E6)
'characters'	String
"characters"	String

\b	Backspace
\f	Form feed
\n	New line
\r	Carriage return
\t	Tab
\"	Double quote
true	Boolean
false	Boolean

Operators

The JavaScript operators are grouped into the following categories: assignment, comparison, arithmetic, string, logical, and bitwise.

Assignment

variable = value	Assignment of value to variable
variable += expression	variable = variable + expression
variable -= expression	variable = variable - expression
variable *= expression	variable = variable * expression
variable /= expression	variable = variable / expression
variable %= expression	variable = variable % expression
variable <<= expression	variable = variable << expression
variable >>= expression	variable = variable >> expression
variable >>>= expression	variable = variable >>> expression
variable &= expression	variable = variable & expression
variable ^= expression	variable = variable ^ expression
variable ¦= expression	variable = variable ¦ expression

Comparison

==	Equal
!=	Not equal
>	Greater than
>=	Greater than or equal to
<	Less than
<=	Less than or equal to

Arithmetic

var1 + *var2*	Addition
var1 - *var2*	Subtraction
var1 * *var2*	Multiplication
var1 / *var2*	Division
var1 & *var2*	Modulus
-	Negation
var++	Postfix increment
++*var*	Prefix increment
var--	Postfix decrement
--*var*	Prefix decrement

String

string1 + *string2*	String concatenation

Logical

expr1 && *expr2*	Logical AND
expr1 ¦¦ *expr2*	Logical OR
!*expr*	Logical NOT

Bitwise

arg1 & *arg2*	Bitwise AND
arg1 ¦ *arg2*	Bitwise OR
arg1 ^ *arg2*	Bitwise XOR
arg1 << *arg2*	Left shift
arg1 >> *arg2*	Right shift
arg1 >>> *arg2*	Zero-fill right shift

Statements

JavaScript provides the traditional `conditional` and `loop` statements as well as a set of object manipulation statements.

Conditionals

```
if (condition) {
    // statements for true condition
}
else {
    // statements for false condition
}
```

Loops

```
for (initExpr; condition; incrExpr) {
    // statements to execute while looping
    [break;]
    [continue;]
}
```

```
while (condition) {
    // statements to execute while looping
    [break;]
    [continue;]
}
```

Object Manipulation

```
for (variable in object) {
    // statements
    }
```

```
objectvar = new objecttype ( param1 [, param2] ... [,paramN] );
```

```
with(object){
    // statements
}
```

```
this[.property]
```

E

JavaScript Object Hierarchy

Navigator Object

The navigator object is used to obtain information about the browser, such as the version number. The navigator object does not have any methods or event handlers associated with it.

Properties

appCodeName specifies the internal code name of the browser—for example, Atlas.

appName specifies the name of the browser.

appVersion specifies version and host operating system information for the browser.

userAgent specifies the user-agent header.

The following example displays each property of the Navigator object:

```
<HTML><HEAD>
<TITLE>A Navigator Object Example</TITLE>
<SCRIPT LANGUAGE="JavaScript">
document.write("appCodeName = " + navigator.appCodeName+ "<BR>");
document.write("appName = " + navigator.appName + "<BR>");
document.write("appVersion = " + navigator.appVersion + "<BR>");
document.write("userAgent = " + navigator.userAgent + "<BR>");
</SCRIPT>
</HEAD>
<BODY>
</BODY>
</HTML>
```

Window Object

The window object is a top-level object. The document, frame, and location objects are all properties of the window object.

Properties

defaultStatus is the default message that displays in the window's status bar.

frames is an array that reflects all the frames in a window.

length is the number of frames in a parent window.

name is the name of the current window.

parent refers to the parent window object.

`self` refers to the current window.

`status` holds a temporary status message for the window's status bar. This property gets or sets the status message and overrides `defaultStatus`.

`top` refers to the topmost window.

`window` refers to the current window.

Methods

`alert("message")`

Displays a dialog box with the string `message` and an OK button.

`clearTimeout(timeoutID)`

Clears a timeout set by `SetTimeout`. `SetTimeout` returns `timeoutID`.

`windowReference.close`

Closes the window referred to by `windowReference`.

`confirm("message")`

Displays a dialog box with the string `message`, an OK button, and a Cancel button. Returns `True` for OK and `False` for Cancel.

`[windowVar = ][window].open("URL", "windowName", ["windowFeatures"])`

Opens a new window.

`prompt("message" [,"defaultInput"])`

Opens a dialog box with a text field for input.

`TimeoutID = setTimeout(expression, msec)`

Evaluates `expression` after `msec` has elapsed.

Event Handlers

`onLoad` occurs when a window finishes loading.

`onUnload` occurs when a window is unloaded.

Location Object

The location object contains properties with information about the URL of the current document. This object does not have any methods or event handlers. Refer to the following sample URL in the property descriptions that follow:

```
http://www.abc.com/chap1/page2.html#topic3
```

Properties

hash is the current location's anchor name, such as topic3.

host is the hostname:port portion of the URL, such as www.abc.com. (Note that the port is typically the default port and not shown in the preceding example.)

hostname is the host and domain name, such as www.abc.com.

href is the entire URL for the current document.

pathname is the path portion of the URL, such as /chap1/page2.html.

port is the communications port used on the host computer (typically the default port).

protocol is the protocol being used (with the colon), such as http:.

search is a search query that may be at the end of an URL for a CGI script.

Frame Object

A window can have several frames. The frames can scroll independently, and each can have a unique URL. A frame has no event handlers. The onLoad and onUnload events are for the window object.

Properties

frames is an array of all the frames in a window.

name is the <FRAME> tag's NAME attribute.

length is the number of child frames within a frame.

parent is the window or frame containing the current frameset.

self is the current frame.

window is the current frame.

Methods

clearTimeout(*timeoutID*)

Clears a timeout set by SetTimeout. SetTimeout returns *timeoutID*.

TimeoutID = **setTimeout**(*expression*, *msec*)

Evaluates *expression* after *msec* has elapsed.

Document Object

The document object contains information about the current document and provides methods for writing information to the screen. The document object is created by the <BODY></BODY> tag pair. Several of the properties reflect attributes associated with the <BODY> tag.

The anchor, form, history, and link objects are properties of the document object.

Properties

alinkColor is the same as the ALINK attribute.

anchors is an array of all the anchors in a document.

bgColor is the same as the BGCOLOR attribute.

cookie specifies a cookie.

fgColor is the same as the TEXT attribute.

forms is an array of all the forms in a document.

lastModified is the date a document was last modified.

linkColor is the same as the LINK attribute.

links is an array of all the links in a document.

location is the complete URL of a document.

referrer is the URL of the calling document.

title is the contents of the <TITLE> tag.

vlinkColor is the VLINK attribute.

Methods

document.**clear**

Clears the current document.

document.**close**

Closes an output stream and forces data sent to layout to display.

document.**open**(["*mimeType*"])

Opens a stream to collect the output of the write or writeln methods.

document.**write**(*expression1* [,*expression2*], ...[,*expressionN*])

Writes HTML expressions to a document in the specified window.

```
document.writeln(expression1 [,expression2], ...[,expressionN])
```

Writes HTML expressions to a document in the specified window and follows them with a newline.

Anchor Object

An anchor is text in a document that can be the target of a hyperlink. The anchor is defined with the <A></A> tag pair. The anchor object has no properties, methods, or event handlers. The anchors array references each named anchor in a document. Anchors are referenced as follows:

```
document.anchors[index]
```

The anchors array has a single property, length, which stores the number of named anchors in the document. You can refer to this property as follows:

```
document.anchors.length
```

Form Object

Forms are created with the <FORM></FORM> tag pair. Most of the form object's properties reflect attributes of the <FORM> tag. The form object also has several objects as properties:

- [ ] button
- [ ] checkbox
- [ ] hidden
- [ ] password
- [ ] radio
- [ ] reset
- [ ] select
- [ ] submit
- [ ] text
- [ ] textarea

If a document contains several forms, you can reference them with the forms array. You find the number of forms with the following:

```
document.forms.length
```

Each form can be referenced as follows:

```
document.forms[index]
```

Properties

action is the ACTION attribute.

elements is an array reflecting all the elements in a form.

encoding is the ENCTYPE attribute.

length reflects the number of elements on a form.

method is the METHOD attribute.

target is the TARGET attribute.

Methods

formName.**submit**()

Submits the form named *formName*.

Event Handlers

onSubmit occurs when a form is submitted.

History Object

The history object stores information about the previous URLs visited by the user. The list of URLs is stored in chronological order. The history object has no event handlers.

Properties

length is the number of entries in the history object.

Methods

history.**back**()

Used to reference the previous URL visited (the previous URL in the history list).

history.**forward**()

Used to reference the next URL in the history list. Until either the user or a script moves backwards on the history list, this has no effect.

history.**go**(*delta* ¦ "*location*")

Used to either move forward or backward *delta* number of entries on the history list or to go to a specific URL on the history list referred to by *location*. If *delta* is used, the reference is backward if negative and forward if positive. If *location* is used, the closest URL containing *location* as a substring is called.

Link Object

A link object is text or a picture that is specified as a hyperlink. The properties of the link object deal primarily with the URL of the hyperlink. The link object does not have any methods.

The links array contains a list of all the links in a document. You can find the number of links with the following line:

```
document.links.length()
```

A specific link can be referenced by the following array:

```
document.links[index]
```

Refer to the following sample URL for the link object's properties descriptions:

```
http://www.abc.com/chap1/page2.html#topic3
```

Properties

hash is the anchor name of the link, such as topic3.

host is the *hostname:port* portion of the URL, such as www.abc.com. (Note that the port is typically the default port and is not shown in the preceding example.)

hostname is the host and domain name, such as www.abc.com.

href is the entire URL for the link.

pathname is the path portion of the URL, such as /chap1/page2.html.

port is the communications port used on the host computer (typically the default port).

protocol is the protocol with the colon, such as http:.

search is a search query that may be at the end of an URL for a CGI script.

target is the same as the TARGET attribute of <LINK>.

Event Handlers

onClick occurs when user clicks the link.

onMouseOver occurs when the mouse moves over the link.

Math Object

The math object is built in to JavaScript. This object's properties contain many common mathematical constants. The math methods provide a wide array of trigonometric and other mathematical functions. The math object has no event handlers.

The reference to *number* in the methods can be either a number or an expression that evaluates to a valid number.

Properties

E is Euler's constant, approximately 2.718.

LN2 is the natural logarithm of two, approximately 0.693.

LN10 is the natural logarithm of ten, approximately 2.302.

LOG2E is the base 2 logarithm of e, approximately 1.442.

LOG10E is the base 10 logarithm of e, approximately 0.434.

PI is the value of π, approximately 3.14159.

SQRT1_2 the square root of one half, approximately 0.707.

SQRT2 the square root of 2, approximately 1.414.

Methods

Math.**abs**(number)

Returns the absolute value of *number*.

Math.**acos**(number)

Returns the arc cosine (in radians) of *number*. The value *number* must be between -1 and 1.

Math.**asin**(number)

Returns the arc sine (in radians) of *number*. The value *number* must be between -1 and 1.

Math.**atan**(number)

Returns the arc tan (in radians) of *number*.

Math.**ceil**(number)

Returns the lowest integer equal to or greater than *number*.

Math.**cos**(*number*)

Returns the cosine of *number*.

Math.**exp**(*number*)

Returns e^{number} where e is Euler's constant.

```
Math.floor(number)
```

Returns the highest integer equal to or less than *number*.

```
Math.log(number)
```

Returns the natural log of *number*.

```
Math.max(num1, num2)
```

Returns the greater of *num1* and *num2*.

```
Math.min(num1, num2)
```

Returns the lesser of *num1* and *num2*.

```
Math.pow(base, exponent)
```

Returns the value of *base* to the *exponent* power.

```
Math.random()
```

Returns a random number between 0 and 1. Note that this method works only on UNIX platforms.

```
Math.round(number)
```

Returns the value of *number* rounded to the nearest integer.

```
Math.sin(number)
```

Returns the sine of *number*.

```
Math.sqrt(number)
```

Returns the square root of *number*.

```
Math.tan(number)
```

Returns the tangent of *number*.

Date Object

The date object is built in to JavaScript. This object provides many useful methods for getting and dealing with the time and date. The date object has no properties or event handlers associated with it.

Most of the date methods have a date object associated with it. The following method definitions use a date object named dateVar. The examples for many of the methods use the value stored in dateVar as follows:

```
dateVar = new Date("August 16, 1996 20:45:04");
```

Methods

dateVar.**getDate**()

> Returns the day of the month (1-31) for *dateVar*, such as 16.

dateVar.**getDay**()

> Returns the day of the week (0 for Sunday through 6 for Saturday) for *dateVar*, such as 5.

dateVar.**getHours**()

> Returns the hour (0-23) for *dateVar*, such as 20.

dateVar.**getMinutes**()

> Returns the minutes (0-59) for *dateVar*, such as 45.

dateVar.**getMonth**()

> Returns the month (0-11) for *dateVar*, such as 7.

dateVar.**getSeconds**()

> Returns the seconds (0-59) for *dateVar*, such as 4.

dateVar.**getTime**()

> Returns the number of milliseconds since Jan. 1, 1970, 00:00:00.

dateVar.**getTimezoneOffset**()

> Returns the offset in minutes of the current local time to GMT.

dateVar.**getYear**()

> Returns the year for *dateVar*, such as 96.

Date.**parse**(*dateStr*)

> Parses the string *datestr* and returns the number of milliseconds since Jan. 1, 1970, 00:00:00.

dateVar.**setDate**(*day*)

> Sets the day of the month to *day* for *dateVar*.

dateVar.**setHours**(*hours*)

> Sets the hours to *hours* for *dateVar*.

dateVar.**setMinutes**(*minutes*)

> Sets the minutes to *minutes* for *dateVar*.

E

dateVar.**setMonth**(*month*)

> Sets the month to *month* for *dateVar*.

dateVar.**setSeconds**(*seconds*)

> Sets the seconds to *seconds* for *dateVar*.

dateVar.**setTime**(*value*)

> Sets the time to *value*, which represents the number of milliseconds since Jan. 1, 1970, 00:00:00.

dateVar.**setYear**(*year*)

> Sets the year to *year* for *dateVar*.

dateVar.**toGMTString**()

> Returns a string representing *dateVar* as GMT.

dateVar.**toLocaleString**()

> Returns a string representing *dateVar* in the current time zone.

Date.**UTC**(*year, month, day* [,*hours*] [,*minutes*] [,*seconds*])

> Returns the number of milliseconds since Jan. 1, 1970, 00:00:00 GMT.

String Object

The string object is built in to JavaScript. This object provides many string-manipulation methods. The only property for the string object is the length.

The string object has no event handlers.

Properties

> length is the length of the string.

Methods

str.**anchor**(*name*)

> Used to dynamically create an <A> tag. The *name* parameter is the NAME attribute of the tag.

str.**big**()

> Creates the same effect as the <BIG> tag on the string *str*.

str.**blink**()

> Creates the same effect as the <BLINK> tag on the string *str*.

str.**bold**()

> Creates the same effect as the <BOLD> tag on the string *str*.

str.**charAt**(*a*)

> Returns the ath character from *str*.

str.**fixed**()

> Creates the same effect as the <TT> tag on the string *str*.

str.**fontcolor**(*color*)

> Creates the same effect as the <FONT COLOR=*color*> tag.

str.**fontsize**(*size*)

> Creates the same effect as the <FONT SIZE=*size*> tag.

str.**indexOf**(*srchStr* [,*index*])

> Returns the offset into *str* of the first appearance of *srchStr*. The string is searched from left to right. The *index* parameter can be used to start the search somewhere other than the beginning of the string.

str.**italics**()

> Creates the same effect as the <I> tag on the string *str*.

str.**lastIndexOf**(*srchStr* [, *index*])

> Returns the offset into *str* of the last occurrence of *srchStr*. The string is searched from right to left. The *index* parameter can be used to start the search somewhere other than the end of the string.

str.**link**(*href*)

> Used to create an HTML link dynamically for the string *str*. The *href* parameter is the destination URL for the link.

str.**small**()

> Creates the same effect as the <SMALL> tag on the string *str*.

str.**strike**()

> Creates the same effect as the <STRIKE> tag on the string *str*.

E

str.**sub()**

Creates a subscript for string *str*, just like the <SUB> tag.

str.**substring**(*a*, *b*)

Returns the substring of *str* indicated by the characters between the ath and b^{th} character. The character count is from left to right starting at 0.

str.**sup()**

Creates a superscript for string *str*, just like the <SUP> tag.

str.**toLowerCase**()

Converts *str* to lowercase.

str.**toUpperCase**()

Converts *str* to uppercase.

APPENDIX

F

VBScript Language Reference

This appendix contains a summary or quick reference for the VBScript language.

Language keywords and symbols are shown in a monospaced font. Arguments and other parts to be substituted are in italic monospace.

Optional parts are indicated by brackets (except in the array syntax section). If there are several options that are mutually exclusive, they are shown separated by pipes (¦) like this:

```
[ public ¦ private ¦ protected ] type varname
```

Summary of Reserved Words

The following words are defined as part of the VBScript language and cannot be used as variable names:

Abs	Erase	Len	Set
And	Err	Log	Sgn
Asc	Error	Loop	Sin
Atn	Exit	Ltrim	Sqr
Call	Exp	Mid	Step
Case	Fix	Minute	Str
Cbool	For	Mod	StrComp
Cbyte	Function	Month	String
Cdate	Hex	MsgBox	Sub
CDbl	Hour	Next	Tan
Chr	If	Not	Then
Cint	Imp	Now	Time
Clear	InputBox	Oct	TimeSerial
CLng	InStr	On	TimeValue
Cos	Int	Or	Trim
CSng	Is	Preserve	UBound
CStr	IsArray	Raise	UCase
Date	IsDate	Randomize	Until
DateSerial	IsEmpty	ReDim	Val

DateValue	IsNull	Rem	VarType
Day	IsNumeric	Right	Weekday
Dim	IsObject	Rnd	Wend
Do	Lbound	RTrim	While
Else	Lcase	Second	Xor
Eqv	Left	Select	Year

Operators

VBScript operators can be characterized as follows:

- ☐ Assignment
- ☐ Comparison
- ☐ Arithmetic
- ☐ String
- ☐ Logical
- ☐ Bitwise

Assignment

`variable = value`   Assignment of value to variable

Comparison

=	Equal
<>	Not equal
>	Greater than
>=	Greater than or equal to
<	Less than
<=	Less than or equal to
Is	Equal (objects)

Arithmetic

var1 + *var2*	Addition
var1 - *var2*	Subtraction
var1 * *var2*	Multiplication
var1 / *var2*	Division
var1 & *var2*	Modulus
var1 \ *var2*	Integer Division
-	Negation
var1^*exp*	Exponentiation

String

string1 & *string2*	String Concatenation

Logical

expr1 And *expr2*	Logical AND
expr1 Or *expr2*	Logical OR
Not *expr*	Logical NOT
expr1 Xor *expr2*	Logical Exclusive OR
expr1 Eqv *expr2*	Equivalence
expr1 Imp *expr2*	Implication

Bitwise

arg1 And *arg2*	Bitwise AND
arg1 Or *arg2*	Bitwise OR
arg1 Xor *arg2*	Bitwise XOR
Not *arg1*	Bitwise NOT
expr1 Eqv *expr2*	Bitwise Equivalence
expr1 Imp *expr2*	Bitwise Implication

Conditional Statements

VBScript supports the following conditional structures:

```
If condition Then
'    statements for true condition
[Else]
'    statements for false condition
End If
Select Case expr
    Case n
        ' statements for this case
    Case m
        ' statements for this case
    '… additional case statements as necessary
    [Case Else]
        ' statements for the default case
End Select
```

Loop Statements

VBScript supports the following loop structures:

```
For var = init To final [Step step]
' statements to execute while looping
Next

While condition
' statements to execute while looping
Wend

Do While condition
' statements to execute while looping
[Exit Do]
' statements to execute while looping
Loop

Do Until condition
' statements to execute while looping
[Exit Do]
' statements to execute while looping
Loop

Do
' statements to execute while looping
Loop [Until¦While]
```

Procedures

VBScript supports two types of procedures, `Sub` and `Function`:

```
Sub SubName([param1][,param2]...[,paramN])
   ' sub procedure statements
End Sub

Function fnName([param1][,param2]...[,paramN])
   ' function statements;
   fnName = expr
End Function
```

Built-in Functions

VBScript contains a number of built-in functions. The VBScript functions can be characterized as follows:

☐ Math

☐ Dates and Time

☐ String Manipulation

☐ User Interface

☐ Data Type

Math

VBScript provides a wide range of mathematical functions for use in your scripts. In the following function declarations, *numExpr* can be either a number or an expression that evaluates to a number. The return values of the trigonometric functions are in radians.

`Abs(numExpr)`

returns the absolute value of *numExpr*.

`Atn(numExpr)`

returns the arc tangent of *numExpr*.

`Cos(numExpr)`

returns the cosine of *numExpr*.

`Exp(numExpr)`

returns e*numExpr*where e is Euler's constant.

`Fix(`*numExpr*`)`

returns the integer portion of *numExpr*. If the number is negative, the next greater integer will be returned.

`Int(`*numExpr*`)`

returns the integer portion of *numExpr*. If the number is negative, the next lower integer will be returned.

`Log(`*numExpr*`)`

returns the natural log of *numExpr*.

`Rnd([`*numExpr*`])`

returns a pseudo-random number. The number is not really random since the same seed will always produce the same result. If *numExpr* is used, the result will be as follows:

If *numExpr* = 0, `Rnd` returns the last random number generated.

If *numExpr* > 0, `Rnd` returns the next random number in the sequence.

If *numExpr* < 0, `Rnd` returns a random number based on the seed, *numExpr*. The same seed will always return the same number.

The `Randomize` statement will generate a seed for the `Rnd` function based on the system clock. This will provide for a much better illusion of randomness, as shown in the following example:

```
Randomize
x = Rnd()
```

`Sgn(`*numExpr*`)`

returns 1 if *numExpr* is greater than 0, -1 if *numExpr* is less than 0, and 0 if *numExpr* is equal to 0.

`Sin(`*numExpr*`)`

returns the sine of *numExpr*.

`Sqr(`*numExpr*`)`

returns the square root of *numExpr*.

`Tan(`*numExpr*`)`

returns the tangent of *numExpr*.

F

Dates and Time

`Date`

returns the current date from the system clock.

`DateSerial(`*year*`, `*month*`, `*day*`)`

returns a value of subtype `Date` to represent the *year*, *month*, and *day* that were passed.

`Day(`*date*`)`

returns an integer between 1 and 31 to represent the day for the *date* that was passed.

`Hour(`*time*`)`

returns an integer between 0 and 23 to represent the hour for the *time* that was passed.

`Minute(`*time*`)`

returns an integer between 0 and 59 to represent the minute for the *time* that was passed.

`Month(`*date*`)`

returns an integer between 1 and 12 to represent the month for the *date* that was passed.

`Now`

returns the current date and time based on the system clock.

`Second(`*time*`)`

returns an integer between 0 and 59 to represent the second for the *time* that was passed.

`Time`

returns the current time from the system clock.

`TimeSerial(`*hour*`,`*minute*`,`*second*`)`

returns a value of subtype `Date` to represent the *hour*, *minute*, and *second* that were passed.

`Weekday(`*date* `[, `*firstday*`])`

returns an integer between 1 and 7 that represents the current day of the week for *date*. By default, Sunday is represented by 1, Monday 2, and so on. If a *firstday* parameter is passed, then another day can be set to be represented by 1. For example, if 2 is passed as the *firstday* parameter, then Monday would be represented by 1.

`Year(`*date*`)`

returns an integer that represents the year in *date*, such as 1996.

String Manipulation

VBScript has a wide array of built-in functions to assist you in dealing with strings. In the function declarations below, *strExpr* can be either a string or an expression that evaluates to a string.

Asc(*strExpr*)

returns an integer representing the ANSI code for the first character of strExpr.

Chr(*ANSICode*)

returns the character represented by ANSICode.

Hex(*number*)

returns a string that represents *number* in hexadecimal.

InStr([*startPos*,] *string*, *srchstr* [, *compType*])

returns the position of the first occurrence of *srchstr* in string. If *startPos* is specified, the search will begin at that position. The *compType* parameter can be either 0 or 1. The default value of 0 is case-sensitive. A compType of 1 indicates that the search should be case-insensitive.

LCase(*strExpr*)

converts *strExpr* to lowercase and returns it as a string.

Left(*strExpr*, *numChars*)

returns a substring of *strExpr* that begins at the first position (on the left) and is *numChars* in length.

Len(*strExpr* ¦ *varName*)

If a string expression is passed, Len returns the length of that string. If a variable name (*varName*) is passed, Len returns the number of bytes required to store that variable.

LTrim(*strExpr*)

removes all leading spaces from *strExpr* and returns it as a string.

Mid(*strExpr*, *startPos*, *numChars*)

returns a substring of *strExpr* that begins at *startPos* and is *numChars* in length.

Oct(*number*)

returns a string that represents *number* in octal.

F

```
Right(strExpr, numChars)
```

returns a substring of *strExpr* that begins at the last position (on the right) and is *numChars* in length.

```
RTrim(strExpr)
```

removes all trailing spaces from *strExpr* and returns it as a string.

```
StrComp(strExpr1, strExpr2 [,compType])
```

compares *strExpr1* and *strExpr2*. If they are equal, a 0 is returned. A -1 is returned if *strExpr1* is less than *strExpr2*. A 1 is returned if *strExpr1* is greater than *strExpr2*. If either string is Null, Null is returned.

The *compType* parameter can be either 0 or 1. The default value of 0 is case-sensitive. A *compType* of 1 indicates that the search should be case-insensitive.

```
String(length, character)
```

returns a string of repeating *character* that is *length* in length.

```
Trim(strExpr)
```

removes all leading and trailing spaces from *strExpr* and returns it as a string.

```
UCase(strExpr)
```

converts *strExpr* to uppercase and returns it as a string.

User Interface

```
InputBox(prompt [, title][, default][, xPos][, yPos][, helpFile, context])
```

This function will display a dialog box with a text field. The contents of the text field will be returned. The parameters are defined as follows:

prompt	The prompt that is displayed in the dialog box.
title	The text that is displayed on the title bar of the dialog box.
default	The default contents of the text field.
xPos	The distance (in twips) of the dialog box from the left edge of the screen.
yPos	The distance (in twips) of the dialog box from the top of the screen.
helpFile	The filename of the help file that should be used for context-sensitive help.
context	The context number for the appropriate help topic in *helpFile*.

```
MsgBox(prompt[, buttons][, title][, helpfile, context])
```

The MsgBox function will display a dialog box with one or more buttons, as configured by the *buttons* parameter. The parameters are defined as follows:

prompt   The prompt that is displayed in the dialog box.

buttons   A number that specifies the number and type of buttons to display in the dialog box. The number is arrived at by adding together 4 numbers to specify the number and type of buttons, the icon style, the default button, and the modality of the dialog box. The *buttons* configurations are as follows:

Number/Type Buttons	Effect
0	An OK button
1	OK and Cancel buttons
2	Abort, Retry, and Ignore buttons
3	Yes, No, and Cancel buttons
4	Yes and No buttons
5	Retry and Cancel buttons

Icon	Style
0	No icon
16	Critical Message icon
32	Warning Query icon
48	Warning Message icon
64	Information Message icon

Default	Button
0	First button
256	Second button
512	Third button
768	Fourth button

Modality	Type
0	Application Modal
4096	System Modal

Topic	Description
title	The text that is displayed on the title bar of the dialog box
helpFile	The filename of the help file that should be used for context-sensitive help
context	The context number for the appropriate help topic in helpFile

The return value provides the button that was selected.

Return Value	Button Selected
1	OK
2	Cancel
3	Abort
4	Retry
5	Ignore
6	Yes
7	No

Datatype

VBScript provides many functions to help in dealing with datatypes. The functions below that are prefixed with C are used to convert a value to a variant of a specific subtype. The functions prefixed with Is can be used to determine if an expression can be converted to a specific subtype.

CBool(*expr*)

returns *expr* converted to subtype Boolean. If *expr* is 0, False will be returned. True will be returned if *expr* is unequal to 0. A type mismatch runtime error will occur if *expr* does not represent a numeric value.

CByte(*expr*)

returns *expr* converted to subtype Byte. If *expr* can not be converted to subtype Byte, a type mismatch runtime error will occur.

CDate(*expr*)

returns *expr* converted to subtype Date. If *expr* cannot be converted to subtype Date a type mismatch runtime error will occur.

CDbl(*expr*)

returns *expr* converted to subtype Double. If *expr* can not be converted to subtype Double, a type mismatch or overflow runtime error will occur.

`CInt(expr)`

returns *expr* converted to subtype `Integer`. If *expr* can not be converted to subtype `Integer`, a type mismatch or overflow runtime error will occur.

`CLng(expr)`

returns *expr* converted to subtype `Long`. If *expr* can not be converted to subtype `Long`, a type mismatch or overflow runtime error will occur.

`CSng(expr)`

returns *expr* converted to subtype `Single`. If *expr* can not be converted to subtype `Single`, a type mismatch or overflow runtime error will occur.

`CStr(expr)`

returns *expr* converted to subtype `String`.

If *expr* is `Boolean`, either `True` or `False` is returned.

If *expr* is a `Date`, a string will be returned in the short date format for the particular system.

If *expr* is subtype `Error`, a string containing the word `Error` and the error number will be returned.

If *expr* is `Null`, a runtime error occurs.

`DateValue(string)`

returns a Variant of subtype `Date` to represent the date in *string*.

`IsArray(expr)`

returns a Boolean indicating whether or not *expr* is an array.

`IsDate(expr)`

returns a Boolean indicating whether or not *expr* can be converted to a `Date`.

`IsEmpty(expr)`

returns a Boolean indicating whether or not *expr* is empty. The intent of this function is to pass a variable name as *expr* to determine if it has been initialized.

`IsNull(expr)`

returns a Boolean indicating whether or not *expr* contains `Null`.

`IsNumeric(expr)`

F

returns a Boolean indicating whether or not *expr* can be evaluated to a numeric value.

`IsObject(`*expr*`)`

returns a Boolean indicating whether or not *expr* references a valid object.

`LBound(`*arrayName*`[, `*dimension*`])`

returns the lower bound of *arrayName* for the dimension indicated. Since VBScript does not support lower bounds other than zero, this function is not very useful.

`TimeValue(`*string*`)`

returns a variant of subtype `Date` to represent the time in *string*.

`UBound(`*arrayName*`[, `*dimension*`])`

returns the upper bound of *arrayName* for the dimension indicated.

`Val(`*strExpr*`)`

returns the first numeric value found in *strExpr*. The numeric value must be at the beginning of *strExpr*. Spaces, tabs, and linefeeds will be removed and periods converted to decimal points. The prefixes &O and &H in *strExpr* can be used to specify octal or hexadecimal values.

`VarType(`*varName*`)`

returns a number that indicates the Variant subtype of *varName* according to the following table:

Returned Value	Subtype
0	Empty
1	Null
2	Integer
3	Long
4	Single
5	Double
7	Date
8	String
9	Automation object
10	Error
11	Boolean
12	Variant
13	Non-automation object
17	Byte
8192	Array

INDEX

Laura Lemay's Web Workshop: JavaScript

— *Laura Lemay*

Readers will explore various aspects of Web publishing—whether CGI scripting and interactivity, graphics design, or Netscape Gold—in greater depth than the *Teach Yourself* books.

CD-ROM includes the complete book in HTML format, publishing tools, templates, graphics, backgrounds, and more.

Provides a clear, hands-on guide to creating sophisticated Web pages.

Covers CGI

Price: $39.99 USA/$56.95 CDN
ISBN: 1-57521-141-6
Publication Date: 9/1/96
Communications/Online–Internet

User Level: Casual–Accomplished
400 pages
Size: 7 3/8 × 9 1/8

JavaScript Unleashed

— *Richard Wagner, et al.*

Programming JavaScript is much simpler than programming for Java because JavaScript code can be embedded directly into an HTML document. *JavaScript Unleashed* unveils the mysteries of this new code, allowing programmers to exploit its full potential in their Web applications.

Covers Netscape LiveWire server system, Netscape Navigator Gold, and more.

Readers learn to use JavaScript for dynamic Web page creation.

CD-ROM includes source code from the book, sample applications, and third-party utilities.

Price: $49.99 USA/$70.95 CDN
ISBN: 1-57521-118-1
Publication Date: 10/1/96
Internet/Programming

User Level: Casual–Accomplished–Expert
900 pages
Size: 7 3/8 × 9 1/8

JavaScript Developer's Guide

— *Wes Tatters*

The *JavaScript Developer's Guide* is the professional reference for enhancing commercial-grade Web sites with JavaScript. Packed with real-world JavaScript examples, the book shows the developer how to use JavaScript to glue together Java applets, multimedia programs, plug-ins, and more on a Web site.

CD-ROM includes source code and powerful utilities. Readers discover ways to add interactivity and Java applets to Web pages.

Covers JavaScript

Price: $49.99 USA/$70.95 CDN
ISBN: 1-57521-084-3
Publication Date: 11/1/96
Internet/Programming

User Level: Casual–Accomplished–Expert
600 pages
Size: 7 3/8 × 9 1/8

Teach Yourself JavaScript in a Week, Second Edition

— *Arman Danesh*

Teach Yourself JavaScript in a Week, Second Edition, is a new edition of the bestselling JavaScript tutorial. It has been revised and updated for the latest version of JavaScript from Netscape, and includes detailed coverage of new features such as how to work with Java applets with LiveConnect, writing JavaScript for Microsoft's Internet Explorer, and more!

CD-ROM includes full version of Netscape Navigator Gold, additional tools, and ready-to-use sample scripts.

Includes in-depth instructions on how to use Netscape Navigator Gold.

Learn the new and advanced features of JavaScript.

Covers JavaScript

Price: $39.99 USA/$56.95 CDN
ISBN: 1-57521-195-5
Publication Date: 11/1/96
Internet/Programming

User Level: Beginning–Intermediate
600 pages
Size: 7 3/8 × 9 1/8

Presenting ActiveX

— Warren Ernst and John J. Kottler

This book provides a hands-on glimpse of Microsoft's new ActiveX technologies and describes the roles existing Microsoft technologies play in this new architecture.

CD-ROM contains source code from the book and powerful ActiveX utilities.

Teaches how ActiveX will let Web publishers and developers add "active" elements to their Web pages and Web applications.

Teaches how to use existing technologies to start creating ActiveX–powered Web pages today.

Covers ActiveX

Price: $29.99 USA/$42.95 CDN
ISBN: 1-57521-156-4
Publication Date: 7/1/96
Internet/Programming

User Level: Casual–Accomplished
336 pages
Size: 7 3/8 × 9 1/8

Teach Yourself ActiveX Programming in 21 Days

— Kaufman & Perkins

This 21-day tutorial teaches readers the fundamentals of Microsoft's new Internet technologies, code named "ActiveX." Coverage includes everything from Active Movie and Active VRML to Active Documents and Network services. After reading this book, programmers will be able to add activity to their applications, Web pages, and documents.

Discusses ActiveX controls that help increase functionality on the Internet.

Teaches how to use the controls included with the Internet Control Pack, and how to create new controls.

CD-ROM includes the Microsoft ActiveX Development Kit and source code from the book.

Covers ActiveX

Price: $39.99 USA/$56.95 CDN
ISBN: 1-57521-163-7
Publication Date: 11/1/96
Internet/Programming

User Level: New–Casual–Accomplished
800 pages
Size: 7 3/8 × 9 1/8

Teach Yourself VBScript in 21 Days

— Keith Brophy & Tim Koets

Readers learn how to use VBScript to create living, interactive Web pages. This unique scripting language from Microsoft is taught with clarity and precision, providing the reader with the best and latest information on this popular language.

CD-ROM contains all the source code from the book and examples of third-party software.

Teaches advanced OLE object techniques.

Explores VBScript's animation, interaction, and mathematical abilities.

Covers VBScript

Price: $39.99 USA/$56.95 CDN
ISBN: 1-57521-120-3
Publication Date: 7/1/96
Internet/Programming

User Level: New–Casual
720 pages
Size: 7 ³/₈ × 9 ¹/₈

Web Programming with Visual Basic

— Craig Eddy & Brad Haasch

This book is a reference that quickly and efficiently shows the experienced developer how to develop Web applications using the 32-bit power of Visual Basic 4. It includes an introduction and overview of Web programming, quickly delves into the specifics, and teaches readers how to incorporate animation, sound, and more to their Web applications. CD-ROM contains all the examples from the book, plus additional Visual Basic programs.

Includes coverage of Netscape Navigator and how to create CGI applications with Visual Basic.

Discusses spiders, agents, crawlers, and other Internet aids.

Covers Visual Basic

Price: $39.99 USA/$56.95 CDN
ISBN: 1-57521-106-8
Publication Date: 8/1/96
Internet/Programming

User Level: Accomplished–Expert
400 pages
Size: 7 ³/₈ × 9 ¹/₈

Add to Your Sams.net Library Today
with the Best Books for Internet Technologies

ISBN	Quantity	Description of Item	Unit Cost	Total Cost
1-57521-141-6		Laura Lemay's Web Workshop: JavaScript (Book/CD-ROM)	$39.99	
1-57521-118-1		JavaScript Unleashed (Book/CD-ROM)	$49.99	
1-57521-084-3		JavaScript Developer's Guide (Book/CD-ROM)	$49.99	
1-57521-195-5		Teach Yourself JavaScript in a Week, Second Edition (Book/CD-ROM)	$39.99	
1-57521-156-4		Presenting ActiveX (Book/CD-ROM)	$29.99	
1-57521-163-7		Teach Yourself ActiveX Programming in 21 Days (Book/CD-ROM)	$39.99	
1-57521-120-3		Teach Yourself VBScript in 21 Days (Book/CD-ROM)	$39.99	
1-57521-106-8		Web Programming with Visual Basic (Book/CD-ROM)	$39.99	
		Shipping and Handling: See information below.		
		TOTAL		

Shipping and Handling: $4.00 for the first book, and $1.75 for each additional book. If you need to have it NOW, we can ship product to you in 24 hours for an additional charge of approximately $18.00, and you will receive your item overnight or in two days. Overseas shipping and handling adds $2.00. Prices subject to change. Call between 9:00 a.m. and 5:00 p.m. EST for availability and pricing information on latest editions.

201 W. 103rd Street, Indianapolis, Indiana 46290

1-800-428-5331 — Orders   1-800-835-3202 — FAX   1-800-858-7674 — Customer Service

Book ISBN 1-57521-158-0

What's on the Disc

The companion CD-ROM contains software developed by the authors, plus an assortment of third-party tools and product demos. The disc is designed to be explored using a CD-ROM Menu program. Using the Menu program, you can view information concerning products and companies, and install programs with a single click of the mouse. To run the Menu program, follow these steps below.

Windows 3.1 and Windows NT Installation Instructions:

1. Insert the CD-ROM disc into your CD-ROM drive.
2. From File Manager or Program Manager, choose Run from the File menu.
3. Type *drive*\setup and press Enter, where *drive* corresponds to the drive letter of your CD-ROM. For example, if your CD-ROM is drive D:, type D:\SETUP and press Enter.

Windows 95 Installation Instructions

1. Insert the CD-ROM disc into your CD-ROM drive.
2. If Windows 95 is installed on your computer, and you have the AutoPlay feature enabled, the Menu program starts automatically whenever you insert the disc into your CD-ROM drive.
3. If Autoplay is not enabled, using Explorer, choose Setup from the CD drive.

NOTE

For best results, set your monitor to display between 256 and 64,000 colors. A screen resolution of 640×480 pixels is also recommended. If necessary, adjust your monitor settings before using the CD-ROM.